ELIZABETH I
AND HER PARLIAMENTS
1584-1601

SIR CHRISTOPHER HATTON

ELIZABETH I
AND HER PARLIAMENTS
1584-1601

by

J. E. NEALE

ST. MARTIN'S PRESS · NEW YORK

1958

PRINTED IN THE UNITED STATES OF AMERICA

CONTENTS

PART FOUR

THE PARLIAMENT OF 1593

PART FIVE

THE PARLIAMENT OF 1597-98

PART SIX

THE PARLIAMENT OF 1601

ILLUSTRATIONS

PREFACE

As in the previous volume, I have focused my narrative on the relations between the Crown and Parliament, though with the necessary latitude to give a general picture of the activities and personalities of the House of Commons. Since oratory is of the essence of Parliament, I have quoted liberally from the speeches as they have come down to us. I hope that they will also prove of interest and value as an unconventional corpus of Elizabethan prose. Once more an exception is made of Queen Elizabeth's speeches, which are quoted in full. They are not easy reading, but they were her own handiwork and were always distinctive. I am glad that readers of my previous volume approved of the decision not to cut or paraphrase them.

I have now completed a task that was planned when I was young and that has occupied most of my leisure, chiefly in the search for material. I find pleasure in the thought that it has been finished — though I shall miss the deadline in publication — while I still hold the Astor Chair of English History at University College, London. In my mind it is an offering — the discharge of my stewardship — to a College that I have delighted to serve for so many years.

Naturally, thoughts of the people and institutions to whom I am indebted crowd my memory at this moment. They are so many that I must again tender my thanks in general, though nonetheless sincere, terms. But there are two documentary windfalls in this volume to which I would like to refer. The one is the diary of William Fitzwilliam, belonging to the Parliament of 1584-85, for knowledge of which I must express my thanks to the alert and kindly officials of the Northamptonshire Record Society. The other 'find' consists of the three speeches of Job Throckmorton in 1586-87, which reposed, unnoticed and anonymous, in the Pierpont Morgan Library, New York. I am most grateful to the Librarian for allowing me to use these manuscripts and for the thrill I experienced in discovering their author and their quality.

Once more I offer my thanks, which are mingled with pride, to past and present members of my research seminar, who know, as I do, my debt to our co-operative and joyful work. To Miss Helen Miller and Mr. P. Collinson I am particularly indebted for the assistance they have given in preparing the diaries and speeches of these Parliaments. I also owe a special debt to my colleague, Mr. J. Hurstfield, who read the typescript of the volume and helped me with his judgment and knowledge. Mr. David Piper of the National Portrait Gallery and Mr. F. G. Emmison, the Essex County Archivist — both of them invaluable friends to historians — have very kindly assisted me over the illustrations.

I treasure my American friends: Wallace Notestein, Conyers Read, W. K. Jordan, Louis B. Wright, Leslie Hotson, Elkin C. Wilson, and many others, young and old. Elizabethan studies are an Anglo-American vocation, intimately linked with the American academic world, and my own life has been enriched by an extensive friendship with scholars from that country. Jonathan Cape and his partner, Wren Howard, have been my friends as well as my publishers for a quarter of a century. I owe much to them in both capacities. My wife remains, as always, the helpmate *par excellence*.

J. E. NEALE

ELIZABETH I
AND HER PARLIAMENTS
1584-1601

PART ONE
THE PARLIAMENT OF 1584-85

CHAPTER I

INTRODUCTORY

As the 1580s unfolded, the reign of Elizabeth I moved with gathering momentum towards its supreme crisis. To statesmen, obsessed by the cold war of Catholicism against Protestantism, there was an inexorable certainty about events. They poured out their lamentations over a Queen who remained stubbornly unfanatical, one whose instincts were, in their opinion, much too tolerant. On September 5th, 1582, the Earl of Leicester opened his heart to Sir Francis Walsingham: 'Nothing in the world', he complained, 'grieveth me more than to see her Majesty believes that this increase of Papists in her realm can be no danger to her. The Lord of His mercy can open her eyes to suffer the depths of her wisdom to look into the matter. If she suffer this increase but one year more, as she hath done these two or three past, it will be too late to give or take counsel to help it.'[1]

The Queen's enemies abroad were busy with that ambitious Catholic scheme, known as the Enterprise, which had as its purpose the overthrow of Protestantism in England. In 1581-82 their hopes were centred on Scotland, where Esmé Stuart, an emissary of the French Guise party, had captivated the susceptible young King, James VI, and routed the Anglophile party. To invade Scotland with a powerful continental army, organized by the Duke of Guise and supported by the Pope and Philip of Spain; convert country and King to Catholicism; then invade England, relying on the Catholics there as a fifth column to rise in their support; release Mary Queen of Scots and destroy Elizabeth and Protestantism: such was the stuff of their dreams. When Esmé Stuart fell from power in the autumn of 1583 they recast the Enterprise as a direct invasion of England under Guise

[1] S.P. Dom. Eliz. 155/42.

leadership, still confident of substantial support from Elizabeth's Catholic subjects. Mary Queen of Scots was deep in the plot, along with the Spanish ambassador in England; Jesuits — among them Creighton and Holt, who had been to Scotland to arrange the details, and Parsons, who had returned to the continent after the collapse of his English mission — were busy agents; and Dr. Allen, head of the Catholic seminary at Rheims and sponsor of so many of the seminary priests then at work in the English mission, was also involved.[1]

Is it any wonder that the holy and peaceable endeavours of Catholic missionaries in England appeared in another light to Elizabethan statesmen? Holy and peaceable these men doubtless were, for the most part. None the less their activities must be reckoned a stratagem of ideological warfare. The more Englishmen they converted, the better the prospect for the Enterprise: or so its planners thought.

Of the fate in store for the Queen herself there could be no doubt. In 1580 the Papal nuncio at Madrid had been approached by an Englishman — later to become a priest — professing to act on behalf of certain English gentlemen and the English Jesuits. The gentlemen — reported the nuncio — had entered into an agreement to murder Elizabeth, but as the deed might cost them their lives they wanted an assurance from the Pope that they would not thereby incur sin. He himself had not hesitated: he had urged them to get on with the deed. But, as requested, he referred the question to Rome. Back came the answer from the Papal Secretary of State: 'Since that guilty woman of England rules over two such noble kingdoms of Christendom and is the cause of so much injury to the Catholic faith and loss of so many million souls, there is no doubt that whosoever sends her out of the world with the pious intention of doing God service, not only does not sin but gains merit, especially having regard to the sentence [in the Bull of 1570] pronounced against her by Pius V of holy memory. And so, if those English gentlemen decide actually to undertake so glorious a work, your Lordship can assure them that they do not commit any sin. We trust in God also that they will escape danger.'[2]

[1] Cf. J. D. LEADER, *Mary Queen of Scots in Captivity*, pp. 496-7; E. L. TAUNTON, *History of the Jesuits in England*, p. 96; CONYERS READ, *Sir Francis Walsingham*, ii. 374.
[2] A. O. MEYER, *England & the Catholic Church under Elizabeth*, pp. 269-71, 489-91. I have substituted 'gentlemen' for Meyer's translation 'nobles'.

In the years 1582-84 the perils of the time — which it would be foolish to question simply because Elizabeth escaped them — revealed themselves to Englishmen in shock after shock. In March 1582 William of Orange, who had been put to the ban by King Philip and a price set on his head, was shot by a fanatic and narrowly escaped death. In the spring of 1583, as we know, the Duke of Guise was counting on a plan to murder Elizabeth; and in the autumn of that year a young Warwickshire squire, a Catholic, who was probably a little mad, set out for London 'to shoot the Queen with a dag', hoping 'to see her head set upon a pole, for she was a serpent and a viper'. He blabbed and was caught. A few weeks later Sir Francis Walsingham, after trying through his spy-system for well over a year to discover the nature of the conspiracy that he knew to be afoot, arrested one of its active agents, the Catholic Francis Throckmorton, and by means of the rack extorted from him particulars of the Enterprise. The Spanish ambassador's part in what became known as the Throckmorton Plot was uncovered and he was ignominiously expelled from England, vowing war. Diplomatic relations with Spain were thus severed; the horizon darkened with gathering clouds. In June 1584, shortly before Throckmorton's execution, the government published an account of his treasons for circulation in England and abroad; and in the following month, while the alarming story was still fresh in people's minds, a second fanatic shot at William of Orange, this time killing him. [1]

To English Protestants, whose sole shield was the life of their Queen, the assassination of William the Silent administered the severest shock they had yet received. The powers of darkness appeared to be concentrating against them: villainy without limit or scruple. And as though to emphasize the alarm and horror, a few weeks later, when the Jesuit Creighton was seized aboard a ship bound for Scotland, further details came to light of the wide-flung Catholic conspiracy.

The crisis called for new legislation. But as statesmen reflected on the situation, they decided that delay was dangerous. Something must be done at once. The outlook was indeed preposterous. If the Queen were slain before Parliament met, there would be a constitutional vacuum in the land. Royal officials would immedi-

---

[1] *Spanish Cal. Eliz.* iii. 464, 479; READ, *Walsingham*, ii. 381; NEWDIGATE, *Michael Drayton and his Circle*, p. 30.

ately lose their positions and all authority derived from the Queen's commission would lapse. There would be no Privy Council, no judges, no Lords Lieutenant, no justices. With government in eclipse, the way would be open for the organized forces of conspiracy, centred on the Catholic Mary Queen of Scots. It was an invitation to speedy murder.

To meet the threat, the Privy Council devised the notorious Bond of Association: a document to be circulated throughout the country, organizing its signatories into a sworn brotherhood of avengers. Walsingham, with Burghley in a revising role, seems to have been responsible for the wording. Introduced by an appropriate and impressive preamble, the first of its two main clauses was general in scope and requires no comment. It bound members of the Association to obey the Queen against all earthly powers and, with their joint forces, to withstand and pursue all persons and their abettors who should attempt anything to her harm, not desisting short of exterminating them.

The second and more specific clause has a significant history. It was directed against anyone, pretending title to the crown, who should procure an attempt against the life of Elizabeth; and, though phrased impersonally, there could be no doubt that the potential enemy was Mary Queen of Scots. As first drafted, it was unexceptionable in character. Members of the Association bound themselves never to allow or favour any such wicked person, or anyone — to wit, Mary's son, James — deriving claim from the offender; but to detest and refuse to live under their government, as unworthy before God and man to aspire to the English crown by such devilish and unlawful means. The sentiment was admirable, but the threat impotent. In the event of Elizabeth's murder, what could be more futile than the role of conscientious objector against a live Mary, to whose side all Catholics would flock, and many others, prompted by ambition, prudence or timidity?

As Councillors reflected on the wording, they must have realized that the clause was quite inadequate to meet the violent and lawless emergency contemplated. Walsingham redrafted it: the 'new clause' he now termed it. Imitating the enemy, he introduced lynch law. One fatal weakness, however, still remained. The Bond, as now worded, would only operate against Mary if she were an actual party to Elizabeth's murder. In the atmosphere of conspiracy how was this to be determined? Giving the clause further consideration, Burghley and Walsingham evidently perceived its inevitable consequence: uncertainty, confusion, defeat. And so, at last, discarding all scruples, they descended to the utter ruthlessness of their enemies.

In its final wording, the document bound members of the Association — by their corporal oath and 'in the presence of the eternal and ever-living God' — never to accept 'any such pretended successor by whom *or for whom*[1] any such detestable act shall be attempted or committed, or any that may any way claim by or from' that individual. They were 'to prosecute such person or persons to the death . . . and to take the uttermost revenge on them . . . by any possible means . . . for their utter overthrow and extirpation'.[2] Put bluntly, this meant that should an attempt be made on Elizabeth's life, Mary Queen of Scots was to be destroyed, whether a party to the action or not. And not only Mary: though the wording may seem ambiguous, it was held to involve the destruction also of her son, certainly if he claimed the throne. The inclusion of James is sufficiently explained by his place in the schemes of the conspirators and by the distrust his actions bred in England.

In October to November 1584, while elections were in progress for a new Parliament, copies of the Bond were circulating throughout the realm, in country and town, stirring the passions of the people and acquiring thousands of signatures and seals. Later on, in 1586, Elizabeth declared that she knew nothing about the document until copies were shown her, with their seals attached.[3] It is hard to believe that Councillors could either hope or dare to be as secretive as all that. She must surely have known about the scheme; and one suspects that her mind, rather than her Councillors', was reflected in the first draft, with its respect for decency at the expense of efficiency. On the other hand, we can well believe that she neither saw nor approved of the final or penultimate form. The odds are that she knew about the Bond, yet kept aloof, not unwilling to accept so dramatic a tribute to her popu-

---

[1] My italics.
[2] The stages in drafting the Bond can be traced in S.P. Dom. Eliz. 173/81 is the first draft, corrected by Walsingham. Then follow, in order, 173/83, 82; 176/23, corrected by Burghley (wrongly described and placed in the *Calendar*). Many copies of the final document, signed and sealed, are in vol. 174.
[3] See below, p. 120.

larity nor unappreciative of its propaganda value, but sceptical of the policy and desirous for many reasons to evade responsibility for it.

Catholicism, with all its ramifications, does not monopolize the background of our story. Trouble came to the government from the left, as well as the right. As every previous Parliament had shown, there existed a vociferous body of Protestants who remained dissatisfied with the conservative Religious Settlement of 1559; and the reforming zeal of these earnest, patriotic men was not likely to falter while the Catholic Counter-Reformation threatened England. Their common aim was to purge the Church of Popish remnants: of symbols and practices that emphasized its Romish paternity. They were all agreed in wanting to simplify the Prayer Book, modify vestments, and eradicate abuses and laxity in the administration of the Church. But since 1572 their clerical left-wing, backed by lay patrons and friends, had adopted a Calvinistic or Presbyterian programme, in imitation of the Genevan, Huguenot, Dutch and Scottish reformed churches.

Destructive of the existing ecclesiastical polity, this programme involved a revolutionary break with the Catholic past: in itself a commendation to those who abhorred Papistry. In place of a hierarchy of archbishops, bishops, deans, archdeacons, and so on, Calvinism knew only ministers, elders and deacons; and there was equality among ministers. Its discipline was exercised through governing bodies, arranged in pyramid structure. As English Puritans framed their Directory of Church Government in the 1580s, it provided for a consistory of ministers and elders for each individual church; above that a conference or *classis*, meeting at least once in six weeks and composed of the ministers and elders from a group of about twelve neighbouring churches; above the *classis* a provincial synod or conference, ideally representing twenty-four *classes* and meeting every half year, with two ministers and two elders from each *classis*; and finally the national synod, composed of three ministers and three elders from each province.[1]

As the history of the Huguenot church in France testifies, this was an ideal organization for a revolutionary minority movement. The *classis* countered any sense of isolation; the more general conferences ensured the maximum unity and pressure. More-

[1] *A Directory of Church Government* (1644, reprinted 1872).

over, at these meetings the Discipline imposed two typical practices: an expository Biblical exercise, undertaken in turn by one of the ministers and followed by criticism from the brethren present; and brotherly censures of one another's way of life. They were calculated to ensure uniformity of doctrine among the officers of the church and the appropriate party behaviour and enthusiasm. As for parishioners — the rank and file of the movement — they were to be controlled by the rigorous supervision of the consistory, involving domiciliary visits from the elders.

At any time and in any country such an organization would be formidable. In Elizabethan England it was a menace to the established order of Church and State: in some respects a greater, or at least a more insidious menace than Catholicism, which lacked its structural strength and was feared and hated by the majority of Englishmen.

Alive to the danger of Puritanism, the Queen in 1577 had ordered her bishops to suppress all Exercises or Prophesyings and enforce conformity on the clergy. In spite of her efforts these activities continued, and, aided by the skilful secretarial work of John Field in London, the presbyterian movement grew instead of diminishing in strength. Then in 1582 came a fateful decision to commence reforming the Church from within, quietly grafting Presbyterianism on Anglicanism and setting up 'a discipline in a discipline, presbytery in episcopacy'. In May of that year, at Cockfield in Suffolk, sixty ministers, delegates from the counties of Essex, Cambridge and Norfolk, met to confer about the Prayer Book and the limits of conformity; and in July the first General Conference or National Synod of the party was held at Cambridge, at the Commencement or annual Degree-Day. One is reminded of the first National Synod of the Huguenot Church, held in secret in Paris in 1559.[1]

Presumably it was at Cambridge that they resolved to set up their presbyterian organization. It spread into many counties. Evidence about it is unfortunately, though understandably, scanty. By good fortune, however, the minute-book or register of one *classis* — that of Dedham in Essex — has survived. Its first entry refers to the inaugural conference, held on October 22nd, 1582.[2]

[1] BANCROFT, *Dangerous Positions* (1640 reprint), pp. 44, 45.
[2] Edited by R. G. Usher in *The Presbyterian Movement, 1582-1589* (Camden Soc.).

The *classis* was the salient element in this new phase of Puritanism: hence the name, the Puritan Classical Movement. In the formative years, the superior and more general conferences do not seem to have functioned as planned, and probably no sharp distinction was drawn between Provincial and National synods. But quite early the leaders appear to have arranged to hold General Conferences, at Cambridge at the time of Commencement and of Stourbridge Fair, at Oxford at the Act or degree-time, and at London during St. Bartholomew's Fair and Parliament: all of them occasions when a large company could assemble without attracting attention. According to theory, laymen ought to have attended all these meetings, in the role of elders. In certain individual churches, it seems that the churchwardens were virtually turned into elders and little Genevas established. But the organization was secret and subversive, and consequently in danger from the law. To have established the eldership in a general way or drawn laymen into the *classes* and conferences would have courted detection and destroyed any hope of escaping the serious charge of conspiracy. Meetings were therefore confined to ministers. The Puritan Classical Movement was a clerical affair. It would be wrong to belittle its significance for that reason. Its members received widespread support among the country gentlemen and were strongly backed at Court. There must have been many of their lay sympathizers who were fully aware both of their activities and their intentions.

'You have begun this course too, too late', wrote a Puritan brother from Antwerp to John Field in June 1583. As it turned out, they had got their party organized and members subject to its discipline in the nick of time, for in September 1583, on the death of Archbishop Grindall, the Queen appointed as his successor in the see of Canterbury, John Whitgift, already notorious as the arch-critic of Thomas Cartwright, the leading expositor of English Presbyterianism. The appointment was one of the decisive events of the reign. After two over-sensitive primates — the patient Matthew Parker, whose heart was never in the business of coercing good and zealous Protestants, and the former *émigré*, Edmund Grindall, whose conscience restrained him — Elizabeth had at last acquired a disciplinarian as inflexible as herself. It was none too soon.[1]

---

[1] USHER, op. cit. p. 8.

Whitgift lost no time. With the full approbation and authority of the Queen he at once issued a series of orders to the bishops. Though some aimed at removing abuses of which the Puritans were always complaining, there was no mistaking the main object, which was to discipline the radicals. The central feature was a test to be imposed on all clergy. They were to be compelled to subscribe to three articles, on pain of suspension or deprivation. The first concerned the royal supremacy and created no difficulty. The third demanded subscription to *all* the Articles of Religion, thus brazenly ignoring the Puritan-inspired statute passed in the Parliament of 1571, which limited subscription to the doctrinal Articles. This was a stumbling block. Puritans were prepared to obey the statute, but not to go further. The flagrant, the wholly unacceptable article, however, was the second. It imposed a declaration that the Book of Common Prayer contained nothing contrary to the word of God — the antithesis of Puritan belief; and demanded a promise to use none other.[1]

Matthew Parker had devised a somewhat similar but milder test in the 1570s, and caused a furore. Whitgift now came up against opposition strengthened by the remarkable secret organization of the Puritans. 'The peace of the Church' — wrote John Field to his 'reverend brother in Christ, Dr. Chapman, teacher of God's word at Dedham', the principal member of that *classis* — 'is at an end if he be not curbed. You are wise to consider by advice and by joining together how to strengthen your hands in this work. The Lord direct both you and us that we may fight a good fight and finish with joy. Amen.' The question of subscription was an item of business at the Dedham *classis* on March 2nd, 1584; and the need for a common front and a common policy, stimulating, as it did, correspondence between the *classes* and calling for general conferences, hastened the development of the Presbyterian conspiracy.[2]

Court and country were stirred as Whitgift proceeded with his great inquisition. The *classes* discussed tactics and co-ordinated policy. They consulted lawyers; they got their lay friends to petition and protest when any of their members were suspended or deprived; they roused their supporters in the Privy Council; they plagued Burghley — as they plagued Whitgift — with their complaints.

---

[1] Strype, *Whitgift*, i. 229-32.   [2] Usher, op. cit. pp. 96, 34.

Most of the Privy Council were alarmed at the spectacle of England's first line of defence against Catholicism being harried and decimated at the very time that the future seemed so dark for Protestantism. Some did not hesitate to engage in active resistance. On September 20th, 1584, when the Bond of Association was probably taking shape in their minds, eight Councillors — conservatives among them — signed a strong letter of protest to Whitgift and the Bishop of London, relating particularly to the treatment of ministers in Essex. Contrasting the immunity of 'lewd, evil, unprofitable and corrupt' clergymen with the uncharitable proceedings against Puritans, they 'most earnestly' asked 'that the people of the realm might not be deprived of their pastors: being diligent, learned and zealous, though in some points of ceremonial they might seem doubtful, only in conscience and not of wilfulness'. The letter was one sign, among many, of how effective the propaganda of the *classes* could be.[1]

Burghley was among the signatories. He probably knew that such criticism touched the throne. Also he was a friend of Whitgift's. Deeply disturbed, he wrote letter after letter to the Archbishop, qualified as a rule by that mediatory tone of his which made him so prudent a statesman. But in one he gave rein to his anger over the *ex officio* oath employed by the Court of High Commission, the chief instrument of episcopal discipline. Under this procedure the court could summon any clergyman before it — even if he merely lay under suspicion — compel him to promise an answer to a series of undivulged questions, and then confront him with the questions seriatim, thus inveigling him into providing evidence against himself. Alternatively, if he refused the oath, he could be punished for contempt. The procedure, though in accordance with Canon Law and superficially like that employed in the Star Chamber and elsewhere, was utterly repugnant to the English Common Law. We shall hear much about it as our story unfolds. 'But now, my good Lord', wrote Burghley in this justly famous letter, 'by chance I am come to the sight of an instrument of twenty-four articles of great length and curiosity, found in a Romish style, to examine all manner of ministers . . . This kind of proceeding is too much savouring of the Romish Inquisition, and is rather a device to seek for offenders than to reform any.' He told Whitgift that he had instructed two ministers, whose case

[1] STRYPE, *Whitgift*, i. 328-30.

had led him to peruse these twenty-four articles or questions, to refuse to answer them.[1]

Anyone but Whitgift might have quailed under the tremendous attack loosed on him from many quarters. 'Tyrant, Pope, Papist, knave' were some of the epithets flung at him. Though wounded and tormented, in his self-righteous, humourless obstinacy he persisted in his policy. He was a dour man, with a streak of donnish arrogance, repeatedly scorning his opponents as young, ignorant and few. Probably only Archbishop Laud bears equal responsibility for the bitter hatred that remained so long attached to the name of bishop in the heart of Puritan England.[2]

But even Whitgift could not have withstood the storm had the Queen herself not been behind him. He was conscious of her support and repeatedly invoked it. We may be stretching the evidence a little far, but it certainly seems as if this was another of the many occasions when Elizabeth and her Privy Councillors disagreed about policy, and she pursued her own way in face of their disapproval. She was not so inclined to panic over the Catholic threat as they were, being less doctrinaire in her attitude to it. On the other hand, she had fought her radicals unceasingly since the Parliament of 1559 and possibly felt more repugnance for Geneva, with its popular, egalitarian theories, than she did for Rome, which was aristocratic, if alien. At any rate, having now got a metropolitan with congenial views and courage equal to the crisis, she did not abandon him to his enemies.

Clearly, the new Parliament summoned to meet on November 23rd, 1584, would have occasion to show its mettle. Twelve and a half years had elapsed since the last general election. Many Members had died, others had had their fill of parliamentary sessions, while the novelty of the occasion was probably also a factor in bringing forward an unusual number of new candidates. At any rate, no other Elizabethan Parliament saw so great a change in membership. Of the 460 Members of the House of Commons, only 97 had sat in the previous Parliament, and 322 were total strangers.[3] Of the notables elected in 1572 Bainbridge, Bell, Carleton, Cope, Monson, Norton, Pistor, Robin Snagge, the Wentworths and Yelverton were missing: some dead, some with-

---

[1] Ibid. iii. 104-7.   [2] Ibid. i. 315.
[3] HAZEL MATTHEWS, 'Personnel of the Parliament of 1584-85' (London Univ. M.A. thesis).

drawn permanently, some temporarily absent. William Fleetwood, Recorder of London, was back again, more at ease, more
loquacious, more prone than ever to offer his stories and precedents
to a tolerant House: surely their outstanding 'character'. Francis
Alford returned, an unrepentant conservative, still out of tune
with prevailing sentiment, yet a persistent speaker. Thomas
Digges the mathematician was there again, writing memoranda
as well as speaking often. A witty and all-too-brief anonymous
journal — a collection of parliamentary jottings — is largely
devoted to the remarks of these three Members.[1] William Strickland, the Puritan, was back after a lapse since his courageous
campaign of 1571. Surely he was active, but alas, he is almost lost
in the anonymous crowd. James Dalton was sitting again, and
so was our diarist Thomas Cromwell, who kept a journal but did
not report speeches.[2] Dalton, with advancing age and prosperity,
had shed the radical sympathies of his youth: a fact with which he
was reproached when in 1590 he acted as prosecuting counsel
against the Puritan John Udall.[3] There was also William Fitzwilliam who had sat before in 1571: a Northamptonshire gentleman, eldest son of a distinguished father, with a Sidney for
mother, and himself married to a daughter of Sir Walter Mildmay.
Like his father-in-law he was a Puritan; and we need have little
hesitation in ascribing to him a remarkable account of this Parliament, which has survived among his papers at the family seat of
Milton.[4]

There were famous names among the newcomers: Francis
Bacon, Robert Cecil, Sir Francis Drake, Walter Raleigh, Thomas
Bodley — Bodley's founder — and Fulk Greville, 'servant to Queen
Elizabeth, councillor to King James, and friend to Sir Philip
Sidney', as he described himself in his epitaph. Greville had sat in
the previous Parliament, through a by-election, but had been dis-
qualified. There were also conspicuous Puritans: Sir Richard
Knightley, whose Northamptonshire seat, Fawsley, was later on to
house the secret Marprelate press; James Morice, an official of the
Court of Wards, whose hatred of the oath *ex officio* was to land him
in serious trouble in 1593; and Dr. Peter Turner, probably the

[1] B.M. Lansdowne MS. 43, fols. 164-75.
[2] Trinity Coll. Dublin MS. N.2.12.
[3] B.M. Additional MS. 48064 (Yelverton 70), fol. 118.
[4] Northants Record Soc. Fitzwilliam of Milton Papers 2. I am indebted to the
Society's officials for bringing this important document to my notice.

Earl of Bedford's nominee at Bridport — a physician, son of William Turner, physician and botanist, who had been a Marian exile, and, though Dean of Wells, a turbulent radical and bishop-baiter. These Members joined others who wrote their names in the new phase of Puritan history; such as Robert Beale, Clerk of the Privy Council, related to Walsingham by marriage, and one of Whitgift's most implacable and troublesome critics, Sir John Higham, an eminent gentleman of Suffolk, and Edward Lewkenor, also of Suffolk. As we shall see, this Parliament, though lacking most of the truculent brethren of the past, kept its sympathies unchanged. The Knollys family (Sir Francis and four sons), Sir Walter Mildmay, and Sir Francis Walsingham, who had two Puritan secretaries with him, assured, as it were, a congenial front bench, even if Dr. Thomas Wilson was dead and gone.

An unusually young House, an unusually new House; and, as the Clerk remarked in his rough notes, there was a very large turn-out for the opening ceremonies, 'appearing upon the view not to be much less than the whole'. Recorder Fleetwood sent Lord Burghley an amusing 'diary' of the initial days: 'First there appeared in the Parliament House the knights and burgesses, out of all order, in troops standing upon the floor, making strange noises, there being not past seven or eight of the old Parliament. After this we were all called into the White Hall and there called by name before my Lord Steward and the rest of the Council; and after that we were sworn, whereby we lost the oration made by my Lord Chancellor. And after that, Mr. Treasurer moved the House to make an election of a Speaker, whereupon he himself named my brother Puckering who sat next me; and there was not one word spoken. And then I said to my companions about me, "Cry Puckering!"; and then, they and I beginning, the rest did the same. And then Mr. Speaker made his excuse, standing still in his place; and that done, Mr. Treasurer and Mr. Comptroller, being by me called upon, sitting near, they rose and set him in his place, where indeed they should have set him either before his speech or else at the beginning, and his speech should have been before the chair. And that done, we all departed until Thursday that the Speaker was presented.'[1]

Lord Chancellor Bromley's opening speech on this Monday,

---

[1] D'EWES, *Journals of the Parliaments of Elizabeth* (hereafter referred to as D'Ewes), p. 333; Lansdowne MS. 41, fol. 45.

November 23rd, may have been lost to Fleetwood and others but not to all. The speech, notes the Clerk of the Upper House, was a 'brief — for so it was commanded — but well-turned oration'. As for the person afterwards elected Speaker, he was John Puckering, Member for Bedford, a Serjeant-at-law, aged forty; and it was in keeping with this relatively inexperienced Parliament that he was one of the newcomers. He was to be made Speaker again in the following Parliament, and later became Lord Keeper of the Great Seal.[1]

Puckering was presented to the Queen on the Thursday afternoon. In his main oration he rehearsed the great benefits redounding to the Commonwealth by the most wise government of her royal Majesty and 'declared her singular virtues, her very natural and motherly care over her subjects', shown especially in summoning this Parliament to consult about the weighty affairs of the country. He earnestly admonished the bishops to provide for Church matters, and the nobility and the rest to be careful of the profit and welfare of the Commonwealth: a distinction, which if really stated so clearly must have pleased the Queen. Perhaps in his inexperience he had been coached by Burghley: at any rate, at the close of the Parliament Burghley drafted an oration for him, though he preferred to use his own.[2]

At the end of his oration Puckering made the customary petition for privileges, including freedom of speech. The Lord Chancellor — notes Fitzwilliam in his diary[3] — answered 'that her Highness willingly condescended thereunto, only she restrained the cause of religion to be spoken of among them'. As we know, there was nothing unconstitutional or even new in that. Since 1571 such a restriction had become common form in the Queen's reply, and in every session she had repeatedly insisted on it. But if the restriction was not new, the reaction of Members was both novel and striking.

'It was thought very strange', Fitzwilliam tells us, 'that the Nether House should be restrained in any matter', but especially in the cause of religion, which heretofore had very often had its beginning in that House. 'By searching of the records it appeareth that from 21 Henry VIII and a year or two after, when the Pope first began to stagger in England, very many of the Church matters

---

[1] *Lords Journals* (hereafter cited as *L.J.*), ii. 61.
[2] MILL, *Catalogue of Honour* (1610), p. 68; Lansdowne MS. 104, fols. 150-4.
[3] I call it a 'diary' merely for convenience.

took their beginning from the Nether House.' Fitzwilliam follows up this comment with a long list of such acts, from 1523 to 1581 — *pièces justificatives* for his thesis — showing in which House they originated, and ending with the medieval Statutes of Provisors and Praemunire, which he attributes to the Commons. He notes that the information was 'gathered out of the Parliament Rolls': antiquarian research harnessed to radicalism.

No doubt the novelty of the reaction owed something to the large number of inexperienced Members in this Parliament. But let us not forget the Puritan *classes*, which had been at work with their propaganda. They had, in fact, timed a national synod to meet in London during the Parliament; and it was their intentions and their agents in the House of Commons that the Queen's prohibition threatened.

CHAPTER II

THE QUEEN'S SAFETY

THE main business of the session was to provide for the Queen's safety, in the light of recent events. Two government speakers, Sir Walter Mildmay and Sir Christopher Hatton, opened the subject on Saturday morning, November 28th, in speeches that made a deep impression. 'Before this time', wrote the experienced Fleetwood to Burghley, 'I never heard in Parliament the like matters uttered, and especially the things contained in the latter speech. They were *magnalia regni*.'[1]

Mildmay's speech, according to Fleetwood, lasted 'the space of one hour and more'. We possess the text: a carefully constructed oration, suffused with eloquent pride in country, religion and Queen. 'You see', declared Mildmay, 'that we enjoy freely the preaching of the Gospel, delivered from the superstitions and tyranny of Rome — a benefit without comparison, far beyond all other, and poured upon us by the mighty and merciful hand of God. You see also that it hath pleased Him to set over us a most gracious Queen, by whose ministry this pure religion of God is restored unto us ... She is known, not only to us but to all the world, to be a princess of virtue, of wisdom, provident in government, in word and deed constant; in all actions just and true, loving to her subjects and beloved of them; tempering mercy with justice to the comfort of all those that live under her.

'Moreover, through the goodness of Almighty God by the ministry of this our gracious Queen we have enjoyed peace now full twenty-six years, the like whereof, so long together, hath not been seen in any age; the commodities whereof may appear sufficiently by comparing the blessedness of this our happy peace with the miserable state of our neighbours, long afflicted with cruel wars. We possess in all freedom and liberty our religion, which is the chief; our lands, lives and goods, our wives and children. They on the other side, through civil and intestine troubles, are bereaved of all those good things that we enjoy, in danger to fall at the length into the grievous yoke of perpetual servitude.'

[1] B.M. Lansdowne MS. 41, fol. 45.

Referring to the Queen's maintenance of amity with other nations, he particularly stressed Scotland, to which country she had brought peace, and whose young king she had preserved from his cradle 'more carefully than any mother doth her own child': it would be 'a note of perpetual infamy if ever they should be unthankful or breed this realm trouble'. England had been blessed with great plenty and wealth through peace; her justice was indifferently ministered to all the people.

Their 'most mortal and capital enemy' was the Pope: witness his 'impudent and most blasphemous Bull', 'dreaming that he is the monarch of the whole world and that the kingdoms of the earth are in his disposition, to be given and translated at his will'; witness also his intervention in Ireland; likewise the Catholic League devised at the Council of Trent, 'knitting together all Popish princes and states to the overthrow of the Gospel in all places, but especially in this kingdom', which, 'of all the monarchies in the world doth most abase the dignity of his chair'. In him was *odium implacabile*: 'we can never make our peace with him'.

'Divers other malicious and secret practisers' were dependent upon the Pope; 'the most pernicious those that are called Jesuits and seminary priests, a rabble of vagrant runagates that creep . . . into sundry parts of the realm and are occupied to stir sedition . . . under pretence of reforming men's consciences'. As for the public trials of the Jesuit, Campion, and his fellows, these men, said Mildmay, were prosecuted, 'not for the superstitious ceremonies of Rome but for most high and capital offences and conspiracies' — 'the deposing of our most gracious Queen, advancing of another in her place, alteration and subversion of this whole state and government'. 'Being asked openly whether the Pope had authority to depose the Queen and whether her Majesty was a lawful and rightful Queen, notwithstanding anything that the Pope hath or might do', they had answered, 'It is a question of divinity: we pray you demand no such thing of us'.

Two recent pamphlets — he remarked — deserved attention: Allen's *Defence of English Catholics*, which, by historical examples, maintained the Pope's right to depose princes, and Parson's *De Persecutione Anglicana*, which amplified the persecution of Catholics 'with a number of false and impudent lies, as though we lived here in England under Nero, Domitian, Caligula, and such other tyrants, and not under a most gracious and merciful Queen;

forgetting in the meantime the great favour and clemency showed to all Papists, even to those that be most obstinate, and forgetting also the cruel persecutions used in the days of Queen Mary'; 'passing over in silence those most horrible massacres and murders of many innocents that for the profession of the Gospel have lost their lives in other countries'.

The tale of Papal dependants continued. There were the Catholic seminary schools at Rome and Rheims, 'where among others are maintained Allen and Parsons, two notable and false traitors to their country'; there were 'home Papists, their scholars', who stubbornly refuse to come to church, secretly harbour Jesuits and priests, educate their own children and kinsmen in Popery, and utter violent threats against the régime; there were also rebels and fugitives that busy themselves to work all the harm they can on us; and, finally, ambitious foreign princes, 'devoted to Rome and ready at the Pope's beck to trouble the State, of whose might and force our adversaries make great vaunts'.

'I beseech you consider what a change there would be if, in the place of the present rulers, those priests, rebels, fugitives and Papists, known to be cruel and dissolute and vain, were set at the helm of the Church and Commonwealth. And if any doubt what a miserable change this would be, let him but remember the late days of Queen Mary, when . . . the Pope's authority was wholly restored, and for continuance thereof a strange nation [Spain], proud and insolent, brought into this land to be lords over us: which no doubt would have followed if God in His mercy had not delivered us and preserved as the apple of His eye this precious jewel, our most gracious Queen. Look, I beseech you, a little back into that time and see what terrible fear all the subjects of this realm — yea, the most forward in Popery — were overwhelmed with, both for the doubt they had to live under the yoke of strangers and for the fear they had to lose their Abbey-lands.' The Pope does not regard himself as bound by any Acts of our Parliament, 'for his power is so large and high above all kingdoms of the world — as Story, a devout servant of his said once in this House — that for us here to bind the Pope was as much as if London would make an Act to bind all England'. Nor do they keep faith with those they call heretics. As Throckmorton's confession shows, they plan invasion; and thereof would follow 'devastation of whole countries, sacking, spoiling and burning of

cities and towns and villages, murdering of all kind of people
without respect of person, age or sex, and so the ruin, subversion
and conquest of this noble realm, the utter rooting out of the whole
nobility and people . . . and the placing in of strangers'.

Having sounded this terrifying tocsin, Mildmay turned to
measures of defence; and first, defence of the Queen. As in a
natural body all the members are ready to adventure any danger
to preserve the head, so all subjects of a realm 'ought to shun no
hazard to preserve the prince their head, without whom all they
must needs perish'. By the strongest laws we must provide a
sufficient surety for the Queen's person against all malicious
enemies, 'adding thereunto strait laws also against troublers of this
State under pretence of titles, either present or future, thereby to
cut off their expectation if they or any of them dare to lift up
their hands or hearts to endanger the person or state of our gracious
Queen'. Here the speech was couched in terms of the Bond of
Association and of an Act for the Queen's Safety, the principal
measure planned for this Parliament.

An Act against Jesuits and seminary priests was to be the
second great measure this session. Mildmay now turned to that
project. 'Like as raging waters would destroy whole countries
except they were kept in with strong banks, even so, lest these
malicious, raging runagates, these Jesuits and priests, should over-
flow and overrun all the corners of this realm to the destruction
of us all, let us provide strong and strait laws to keep them
under . . . letting them find how dangerous it shall be for them
to come here or once to put their foot on land within any her
Majesty's dominions.'

A short peroration on the blessedness of their present state
brought the oration to its close.[1]

Sir Christopher Hatton's speech followed, lasting — Fleetwood
tells us — 'above two hours'. We possess only a résumé of one
section. 'Among other matters', says our reporter, he 'delivered
these points concerning the King of Spain's dishonourable dealing
with her Majesty, her Majesty most sincerely seeking amity and
peace with him'. The 'points' constituted a history of Anglo-
Spanish relations, beginning with the early months of Elizabeth's
reign and continued through the 'injurious' treatment of Dr. John

---

[1] My text is from Fitzwilliam's diary, but the speech is also in B.M. Sloane MS.
326, fols. 71 seqq.

Man — sent to Spain as England's ambassador in 1566 — down to the recent expulsion of the Spanish ambassador for his part in the Throckmorton Plot. In the nature of things, it was a one-sided tale, distorted by recent events.[1]

The speech ended, a great committee was appointed to meet that afternoon in the Exchequer Chamber; but before the House rose, there occurred an incident, vividly revealing the emotional strain produced by the speeches of Mildmay and Hatton. A stranger — a skinner named Richard Robinson, dwelling at the Hart's Horns in Gracechurch Street — had sat there 'the whole day and heard what was said'. Being discovered, his pockets were searched, he was stripped to the shirt and committed to custody for further examination. On the Monday, when passions had calmed, he was censured, made to take the oath of supremacy, sworn to secrecy, and imprisoned in the Serjeant's ward for a week.[2]

The great committee met, as ordered, on Saturday afternoon, and Sir Walter Mildmay opened the proceedings, defining their task in summary form as that of providing the highest penalty to avert three types of danger: invasion, rebellion, and violence to the Queen.[3]

So far nothing had been said about Mary Queen of Scots. We can only conclude that Mildmay and Hatton had deliberately kept her out of their story. Now, however, Members broke the silence. They insisted on mentioning the nameless one. 'No way', they contended, 'could be invented so perfect for her Majesty's safety as to take away that person in respect of whom all the mischiefs had been heretofore wrought.' Their proceedings would be vain unless they ensured that no mischief could proceed from her, the fountain of all mischief. In other words, independent Members wanted to convert the session into an echo of the Parliament of 1572. They were stopped. No particular person was to be named, they were told. The Queen, in fact, was at that very time negotiating for Mary's return to Scotland, there, under careful safeguards, to share the throne with her son. It was a last — a vain — effort to solve this desperate problem without the abhorrent stroke of the axe.

The demand for Mary's death having been silenced by a com-

---

[1] Fitzwilliam's diary.   [2] D'Ewes, p. 334; Lansdowne MS. 41, fol. 45.
[3] The following account of the committee's proceedings is from Fitzwilliam's diary.

bination of argument and veto, five of the committee — an official group — were appointed to draft a bill. As we happen to know, the Attorney General had already drawn the lines of the measure wanted by the government.[1]

On December 1st, when the committee next met, the bill for the Queen's safety was ready. Though inspired by the Bond of Association, it was more directly focused on the succession to the throne. Its first provision envisaged a claimant directly involved in an unsuccessful invasion, rebellion or plot against the Queen. In that event a commission, consisting of Councillors, Lords Spiritual and Temporal, and judges, was to investigate the facts and proclaim its judgment. If found guilty, not only the claimant, but his heirs also were to lose title to the Crown.

'Upon this clause', Fitzwilliam tells us, 'grew some speech that the law would seem unjust', since 'in all criminal causes there ought to be an accuser, the party accused, and the judge'. The committee accepted this criticism and added a proviso enabling the accused to defend himself before the commission. Unfortunately, Fitzwilliam does not name his speakers. The scruple was of a kind we should rather have expected from the Queen herself than her Commons; but this committee was evidently a sober body, more amenable to official leadership than in the past.

The following provisions of the bill dealt specifically with attempts on the Queen's life made for the purpose of advancing a claimant to the throne. As in the Bond of Association, both the claimant and his heirs were involved, whether parties to the attempt or not. They were disabled from any claim to the throne, and to support their title was declared treason. A further clause authorized anyone to pursue both culprits and claimant to the death, thus reproducing the lynch-law feature of the Bond of Association. Here, however, there was a difference. The claimant's heirs were not included; and a proviso emphasized this significant modification by permitting the Queen to restore the title of an heir, endangered by the earlier provision of the bill. In other words, the full rigour of the Bond of Association was preserved for Mary Queen of Scots, while James VI was partly, and could be wholly exempt from it.

These sections provoked much debate. Critics fastened upon a flaw that we have already met and shall meet again. If the

[1] S.P. Dom. Eliz. 176/34.

Queen were killed and all authority lapsed, how could effective action be taken? Some prophesied that friends of a claimant, in the manner of Machiavelli's Caesar Borgia, would put up a lewd person to kill the Queen, and then, slaying the assassin themselves, would proclaim their patron's innocence. Others anticipated that the factions of rival claimants would compete to lay the blame on each other, whence would follow an orgy of mutual slaughter. To counter this danger they wanted statutory provision for an inter-regnum. But, as Fitzwilliam tells us, 'this was rejected as a thing that very hardly might be done': that is to say, the Councillors present, knowing their mistress's opposition, vetoed it.

'Great argument' arose over the favourable proviso for James VI. The Oath of Association bound those who had taken it to pursue him to the death if he claimed the throne after an attempt on Elizabeth's life. Could they in conscience — it was asked — yield the Queen this concession? How could she dispense them from their oath? The answer given by Councillors amounted to a condemnation of their own handiwork, the Bond of Association. They stressed the intent, against the letter of the oath. They talked of equity and justice. The fact was that the situation in Scotland had changed and relations with that country now demanded a modification of the Bond and some such escape for James as the proviso envisaged. It would operate as a strong inducement to him to behave himself; a salutary threat if he did not.

'The day after this long argument and small satisfaction' — to use Fitzwilliam's words — a member came forward with a proviso, sounding the authentic radical note of the past: 'That if any successor should combine himself in league with the Pope, allowing and receiving his religion, [he] should for that fact be disabled for ever to claim the Crown'. Its effect would have been to remove Mary Queen of Scots from the succession immediately.

'This proviso', says Fitzwilliam, 'could in no sort be allowed.' The reasons, he tells us, were three; and very interesting they are. First, 'it meddled with succession and in effect limited it in the way it should go: a thing most disliking to her Majesty and utterly forbidden us to deal with'. Secondly, 'it pointed at a special successor' — Mary Stuart — disabling her at once, 'whereby might follow present war'. The third reason was its probable effect on the general cause of religion. The Pope and the Duke of Guise would doubtless prevail on the King of France to retort by disabling the Huguenot, Henry of Navarre, upon whose succession to the throne of that kingdom, 'so far as worldly wit can stretch, the eye of the whole Church is at this day fixed'. Moreover, comparing the recent past, 'what great mischief had fallen upon ourselves had this been put in practice by our predecessors? For had Queen Mary done the like, what had become of our Sovereign, by whom we now at this day enjoy the Gospel?' It is difficult to believe that this last bit of sophistry carried any conviction. But the triple argument, with the royal veto, did: the proviso was handed back to its zealous author, 'and no more speech had of it'.

Having run its course in committee, the bill was brought into the House of Commons for a first reading on December 14th, in the afternoon, and was read a second time next morning.[1] There was little debate. Either this young and inexperienced House suffered from lack of leaders of the quality of Thomas Norton and the more daring independents of 1572, or the government had succeeded in its policy of getting discussion over in committee, instead of in the House. Members, however, were not happy; nor were they of one mind. 'It was read and heard in sad silence and little said to it', records Thomas Digges. Many were disturbed by its conflict with the Bond of Association, and perhaps a majority, for one reason or another, disliked the proviso which permitted Elizabeth to restore the title of a claimant's heir. Also, there had been courageous people — godly men, of the type of Peter Wentworth, among them — who had refused to be stampeded into taking the Oath of Association, objecting to its more unjust provisions, especially to killing the heir of a claimant, who might well be wholly innocent. Reluctant to oppose the government's wishes or meddle with its committee's work, the House sent the bill to be ingrossed.[2]

At this point the Queen intervened. She had evidently been biding her time, awaiting an opportunity to assert her more moderate views; and the conflict of opinion in the House gave her the opening. On December 18th Sir Christopher Hatton rose to inform Members that her Majesty had desired to understand the points of the bill which they had in hand for her safety. She very thankfully accepted their care for her; which, 'her Majesty said

---

[1] D'EWES, pp. 339-40; Cromwell's diary. The paper bill, endorsed with its two readings, is in the House of Lords Papers, 1582-85, at Westminster.
[2] Lansdowne MS. 98, fols. 14-18; PETER WENTWORTH, *Pithie Exhortation* (1598), the 'Treatise' appended to this tract, p. 22.

(but he might not say), was more than her merit'. She expressed approval of the bill, but added that her confidence 'was in God only for her safety'. She 'would not consent that anyone should be punished for the fault of another . . . , nor that anything should pass in that Act that should be repugnant to the Law of God or the Law of Nature, or grievous to the conscience of any of her good subjects, or that should not abide the view of the world, as well enemies as friends . . . in foreign nations as at home'. Finding that the proviso — for James VI — had bred such argument and made such division, she 'would have it clean dashed out'; but she wanted all persons barred or disabled by the Act to be first called to answer and their excuse heard, and particularly she did not wish the penalties to extend 'to the issue of the offender' — to James VI — 'except the issue was also found faulty'.[1]

The message, we are told, brought 'unspeakable joy and comfort' to the whole House, and on Hatton's motion the bill, by now ingrossed, was referred back to the committee, to whose number Mr. George Ireland was added, perhaps for the views he had expressed. In 1572 Ireland had shown himself a blunt and fervent enemy of the Scottish Queen.

The committee met that afternoon and, having struck out the proviso and finally revised the bill, suddenly encountered fundamental opposition. One of the members — Ireland, perhaps — declared that he could in no wise give his consent to it as then penned. His reasons were two: his duty towards God and his credit in the world. As to the first, the Oath of Association bound him to do more than the bill would warrant by law: it included the heirs of a claimant, whereas the bill was limited to the claimant. His credit was affected because 'the world might justly condemn him and all others of great want in judgment, who so rashly would enter into the Oath of Association for doing of a thing which afterwards, upon better advisement, they could not warrant themselves to do by law'. He was answered, apparently at considerable length; but whether the specious arguments of embarrassed Councillors, who talked about identity of purpose and the equity of the Oath, convinced him and those who thought like him, may be doubted.

In any case, a temporary halt was imposed upon the measure

---

[1] Reports of the message are in D'EWES, p. 341; Cromwell's diary; Lansdowne MS. 98, fols. 14-18; Fitzwilliam's diary. Mine is a composite epitome.

from on high: for Queen Elizabeth was evidently still a prey to misgivings, and her maxim when in doubt was delay. She commanded her Councillors to proceed no further. The bill was put aside for the Christmas recess.

The committee had also been working on the second great bill, which, in the words of our diarist Fitzwilliam, was 'to bar the coming in of Jesuits and seminary priests, the only disturbers of the peace of the realm and the very instruments to work her Majesty's destruction'.

By the main provision of this bill all Jesuits, seminary priests, and others who had entered the Catholic priesthood since 1559 were to leave the realm within forty days: the government is said to have taken 120 of them from the prisons and sent them into banishment.[1] To remain in or enter the Queen's dominions afterwards would be treason. Fitzwilliam tells us that some Member — evidently musing on a lamentable necessity — commented 'that it might seem a very hard case to make it treason for a man to come into the realm without doing of any other thing'. That might also be our reflection about an Act which has often been misrepresented and unwarrantably maligned. In fact it was a humane and reasonable attempt to resolve the dilemma of a state, exposed by ideological warfare to insidious and deadly peril. If a society has the right to defend its existence, the individual can hardly claim a conflicting right to remain within the community while acknowledging an external allegiance that threatens to destroy it. English Catholic priests were at liberty to retain their religion, provided they lived abroad. The sanction behind banishment was the penalty of treason. It proved — such is man's unconquerable mind — inadequate. This may evoke our admiration, as the courage of the secret agent does in wartime; but we can hardly argue that the penalty was too severe. In the ideological state treasons multiply: they are no less treason because of that.

During the debate in committee the government demonstrated its anxiety to keep clear its principle. 'It was moved', says Fitzwilliam — though alas, no name is attached to the motion — 'that whosoever should teach the Romish religion should be as a traitor, because between the Queen and the Pope there can be no communion'. This motion, we are told, was rejected because it

---

[1] HOLINSHED, *Chronicles* (1587), iii. 1379a.

confounded treason and heresy and would be of great advantage
to the adversary, enabling him to say that as Protestants could not
refute Catholic doctrine by their doctrine, they sought to quench
it by making it treason. Consequently, unless a clear distinction
was drawn between treason and heresy, it was not wise to have
them thus coupled together. Some members wanted to extend the
bill to include Catholic priests of any nation; but this, they were
told, 'would be construed as a dishonourable law'. Moreover,
it was 'our home Jesuits who did all the hurt among us'; 'Englishmen would not be led with strange priests'.

By the bill's second provision it became treason for anyone
wittingly to receive or aid Jesuits or priests. Some critics, conscious
no doubt of the ease — the surprising ease — with which disguised
missionaries moved about from one country house to another in
those days of ready and almost indiscriminate hospitality, and of the
danger to which inoffensive hosts might consequently be exposed,
wanted to add a proviso making any accusation depend on two
witnesses, as was required by the Civil Law 'throughout all places
of the world'. The proposal was rejected. 'We that be Englishmen' — ran the answer — 'have nothing to do with' the Civil Law,
'but must look to our own law . . . In all the laws that ever were
made against traitors no proviso was used, and therefore in this
case not to be allowed.' The clause, be it added, duly passed the
Commons, but in the Lords its penalty was scaled down to felony:
whether on instructions from the Court or not, we do not know.[1]
In any case, the provision was not rigorously enforced. Many,
indeed, suffered death under the principal clause of the Act, but
even for priests the law was often merely held *in terrorem*.

The bill had other clauses. One of them ordered the return
within a time limit of English scholars at Catholic seminaries
abroad, the penalty being treason if found within the realm otherwise. Another clause imposed the penalties of praemunire on
anyone sending relief to priests or to their seminaries abroad.
The zealots at this point wanted to make a second offence treason;
but they were resisted, on the ground that the penalty should not
exceed the offence. A further section, forbidding the sending of
children abroad, except by special licence, met with some criticism,
was slightly modified, and was restricted in duration to the Queen's

---

[1] The original Act at Westminster (27 Eliz. cap. 2) has two papers attached,
showing the Lords' amendments and subsequent amendments by the Commons.

THE QUEEN'S SAFETY: I

lifetime. Altogether, it is an Act on which we in our day might well reflect.[1]

The bill was brought into the House of Commons for a first reading on December 12th, and, along with the bill for the Queen's safety, was given its main, second reading three days later. There seems to have been little or no debate: the House was apparently content with the discussion that had taken place in committee.

However, when the bill came up for its third reading on December 17th, the unexpected happened. A Member, Dr. William Parry, whose name a few weeks later was to send a shudder through Protestant England, rose, and, while affirming that 'he favoured not the Jesuits or seminaries but was to speak for English subjects', 'in very violent terms' — 'not in any orderly sort, considering the parts by themselves' — 'spake directly against the whole bill'. He denounced it as savouring of treasons; 'full of blood, danger, despair and terror to the English subjects of this realm'; full also 'of confiscations — but unto whom?' he asked. 'Not, said he to her Majesty (which he wished they were)', but to others. He did not doubt that zeal would carry the bill through both Houses, 'but yet he hoped, when it should come into her Highness's most merciful hands, that it would stay and rest there; until which time (he said) he would reserve his reasons of his negative voice against the bill, then to be discovered by him only unto her Majesty'.[2]

Amazed and indignant, the House once more found itself considering the limitations on freedom of speech — not as imposed by the Crown, but as prompted by their own passion and prejudice. They were greatly grieved, Fitzwilliam tells us, in two respects: first, that one Member 'should charge the whole body of that grave assembly with so horrible matters as the seeking of blood, danger, terror, despair and confiscation . . . , not so much for the Queen's safety . . . as for the satisfying of their own greedy desires'; and secondly, because he would give no reason for using those words — 'a thing contrary to the orders of the House' and in contempt of the whole Council.

It was moved that Parry be immediately taken out of the

---

[1] The foregoing account is from Fitzwilliam's diary.
[2] My account of Parry is a composite one from D'EWES, pp. 340 seqq. and the diaries of Fitzwilliam and Cromwell.

House in the Serjeant's custody, 'according to the ancient custom', so that he should neither see his critics nor hear their invectives. This was done, though not without opposition from one Member, who 'thought it not agreeable to the liberties and freedom of the House that any Member thereof, for showing his opinion in a bill read among themselves, should be taken from his seat and sequestered from the society'. It would touch the majesty of the House and be most perilous. 'The only way to have matters perfectly understood and rightly digested was to suffer men freely to utter their conceits of both sides.' Moreover — added he — being all equal, they had no authority over each other. This last was a curious, sterile doctrine. If only we knew who made the speech, we might be able to assess its value and significance: perhaps he was a newcomer, as Parry so obviously was.

In the offender's absence discussion continued. 'The liberty and freedom of the House', said one speaker, 'suffered every man freely to deliver his opinion of the bill read . . . ; but if any man would speak impertinently to the cause', abruptly uttering 'a speech to the offence of the whole company . . . , that was by ancient precedents severely to be punished'. Two precedents were cited from Edward VI's and Mary's reigns, and two from the current reign — those of Peter Wentworth, 'a good Member of the House', and of Arthur Hall.

Parry was then brought back and, kneeling at the bar, was invited by the Speaker to state the reasons for his speech or otherwise excuse his contempt. He answered that he had meant no offence either to the Queen or the House; but he proceeded to repeat his former words, talked about his good services done to her Majesty and his reputation with persons of good sort, and concluded by saying that he would still reserve his reasons for the Queen, and hoped to be delivered.

Parry — a Doctor of Laws — is a puzzling person to the historian. He described himself as a 'servant' of the Queen. He had led a disreputable life and was fairly recently returned from the continent where he had moved in Catholic circles, acting as a spy for Burghley while also undertaking with his Catholic friends or dupes to accomplish the assassination of Queen Elizabeth, for which project — or so it seems — he received Papal absolution through the Cardinal of Como, the Papal Secretary. Whether he was an *agent provocateur*, or was double-crossing Elizabeth and

Burghley, or was just drifting about in perilous seas, irresolute, exalted by conceit, a little mad: these are questions that later events pose. At the moment he was in favour at Court, with his revelations about Catholic plots, and probably it was through Court influence that he had obtained a seat in Parliament for Queenborough. We may presumably describe him as a Catholic, in faith or sympathy, though this had not prevented him from taking the Oath of Supremacy as a Member of Parliament. He evidently was genuine in desiring lenient treatment for Catholics. Perhaps — such was his crazy vanity — he hoped that he might influence the Queen by his protest in Parliament, and thus ease his conscience of the undertaking to kill her. He knew her merciful disposition. In his later confession he said that she had remarked to him, early in 1584, 'that never a Catholic should be troubled for religion or supremacy, so long as they lived like good subjects'.[1]

After his unsatisfactory answer to the Speaker, Parry was remitted to the Serjeant's custody, the day being 'very far spent'. At Court Elizabeth and Burghley seem to have found themselves embarrassed by the predicament of their 'spy' and the possibility of awkward revelations that might follow. Before the House met again the Queen had him examined by her Councillors, and then sent a message to the Commons through Sir Christopher Hatton, commending their grave discretion in forbearing, for the time, to inflict any sharp correction, seeing that Parry had reserved his explanations for herself. These she had now heard and was partly satisfied. He had given just cause of offence to the House, but she thought that on his humble submission he might be pardoned.

Thereupon Parry was brought to the bar, proved appropriately contrite, and pleaded ignorance as a newcomer. He was withdrawn and some discussion took place; but, being brought back and repeating his unqualified confession of guilt, 'protesting further that if ever after he should give any just cause of offence again to the House or any Member thereof, he would never after crave any more favour of them', he was discharged. Little did any of those present guess how soon and how violently the name of Parry would once more disturb them.

In a letter, written in October, Sir Francis Walsingham had told a correspondent that the duration of the forthcoming Parlia-

[1] D. JARDINE, *Criminal Trials*, i. 258.

ment was not intended to be 'much above twenty days'. By now that time had elapsed, the principal business had made wretched progress, Christmas was approaching, and there was nothing for it but to prolong the session. On Saturday, December 19th, the Queen sent a message through Hatton to announce that she intended on the Monday to adjourn the Parliament over Christmas, enabling Members to return home 'for their better ease and recreation'. Stirred by the gracious wording of the message, the Speaker, backed by others, proposed that their Councillor-Members should in return express their most humble, loyal and dutiful thanks for her good opinion of them.[1]

Here was an opportunity, such as Queen Elizabeth rarely missed, of engendering still deeper rapture. On the Monday, Sir Christopher Hatton, 'standing up, did very eloquently and very earnestly set forth her Majesty's most princely, gracious and kind acceptation' of their thanks,which gave her 'right great and high satisfaction, joy and comfort', though she would not confess to have deserved them. In return she rendered 'most hearty and loving thanks unto this whole House, yea and that in redoubling to them their thanks ten-thousand-thousand fold'. A politic romance! On the one side, the affection of the whole House, 'very excellently, amply and aptly' set forth by Hatton; on the other, 'her Highness's incomparable princely accompt and regard of all such loyal, loving and faithful subjects'. The Queen's pleasure, continued Hatton, was 'that this House should well know that in the consideration of the free course of the Gospel of Jesus Christ amongst us, our long-continued peace and plenty of God's good blessings and benefits bestowed upon us under the ministry of her Highness, her Majesty doth most sincerely ascribe all the same only and wholly to the great goodness and mercy of Almighty God, attributing the cause of these good effects (next under God's providence) to the good demerits[2] of so religious, godly and obedient subjects, of whom, how well and kindly her Majesty doth think and conceive, her Highness had much rather have told them in her own most royal person than have signified it unto them by any other.' The message ended with some injunctions about business when they returned after the recess.[3]

---

[1] S.P. Scotland (Mary Q. of Scots), 14/10.
[2] In the now obsolete meaning of 'merits'.
[3] D'EWES, pp. 343-4; Cromwell's diary.

Later that morning, the Lord Chief Justice and other judges came down from the Lords to announce that the Queen had by commission adjourned Parliament till February 4th, that this adjournment had been pronounced in the Lords and they now notified it to the Commons. 'This', comments Fitzwilliam, 'was thought strange.' Hitherto, the two Houses, by consent, had adjourned the Parliament for a week at Christmas or Shrovetide. It was 'never seen that so long a vacation as six weeks was had without the presence of the Prince's person'. After the Speaker had reported the Lords' message to the House, Sir Christopher Hatton rose and, reminding them of the loving exchange between them and their Queen, moved that they should join in prayer to God 'for the long continuance of the most prosperous preservation of her Majesty, with most due and thankful acknowledgement of His infinite benefits and blessings poured upon this whole Realm through the mediation of her Highness's ministry under Him'. He had with him — he said — a prayer, 'devised and set down by an honest, godly and learned man', which, though the calligraphy was poor, he offered to read, if Members would repeat it after him. And so, 'most willingly . . . everyone kneeling upon his knees', the whole House echoed him in prayer.

This done, and with the Queen's bewitching words and the emotional response to Hatton's prayer in their minds, our Members wended their ways home to celebrate the Christmas season according to their gay or sober inclinations.

CHAPTER III

THE QUEEN'S SAFETY

(CONTINUED)

DURING the Christmas recess, Burghley and others devoted themselves to the task of transforming the bill for the Queen's safety into an effective and acceptable measure. The essence of the problem — especially now that negotiations with James VI to send his mother back to Scotland had failed — was to ensure that, in the event of Elizabeth being murdered, Mary Queen of Scots would not obtain the throne nor Catholicism triumph. The less likely this appeared, the more effective the deterrent to plot and invasion.

The crucial need was to prevent anarchy at Elizabeth's death. In the committee's debates Members had wanted to provide for an interregnum, but had been silenced by knowledge that the Queen objected. In all likelihood, our mathematical Member for Southampton, Thomas Digges, had been prominent in that discussion. At any rate he came forward now. In January he wrote a Discourse, analysing the defects of the Oath of Association and of the draft bill for the Queen's safety. He also condemned the bill against Jesuits, thinking it hastily passed and dangerous. It was too lenient in his opinion. 'These hellhounds', he wrote, 'cladding themselves with the glorious name of Jesus, and such wretched souls as they bewitch with their wicked doctrine, are indeed the only dangerous persons to her Majesty . . . They are fully persuaded her Majesty's life is the only stay why their Roman kingdom is not again established here. They also teach their disciples that it is not only lawful in this case to lay hands on God's anointed and to murder schismatic and excommunicate princes, but meritorious also: yea, they assure them Heaven for it . . . This persuasion of conscience was it that gave boldness and ability to two murderous Popish wretches to take the life of that worthy Prince of Orange.' Though the first had been cut in pieces, and the people offended that he had not been reserved for most exquisite torments, nevertheless, in spite of the warning, the second did the exploit, 'and in the midst of horrible torments triumphed as if that act had assuredly purchased him the eternal joys of Paradise . . . Against persons so persuaded, no peril of death, no horror of punishment or torments can prevail. They desire the one, they triumph in the other.'[1]

All his arguments led to one conclusion: take away Catholic hopes by providing for an interregnum, organized politically and militarily to cope with the situation. Digges also wrote another short treatise to explain how at no cost to the Queen a force of forty thousand well-armed, trained soldiers could be created, ready for the crisis, making the realm terrible to foreign enemies.[2]

To Burghley and other Councillors the device of an interregnum was not new. It had been suggested — and rejected — as long ago as 1563.[3] They were now resolved to make another attempt to wrest from their sceptical, obstinate mistress her consent to legislate along these lines. Perhaps Burghley and Leicester decided to invoke the aid of Digges, who was a client of Leicester's. At any rate, this gentleman's Discourse came into Burghley's hands and was followed by another — entitled 'Brief', though even the title was long — addressed to the Queen herself, setting forth the general argument for an interregnum. Presumably this 'Brief Discourse' reached the Queen.[4]

At much the same time Burghley was at work, starting — as he often did — with short notes forming a chain of logical argument, proceeding thence to points and afterwards to 'articles' for a bill, and finally to the full draft of a bill to be added to the existing one.[5] Though it came to nothing, this draft bill is an arresting document, more congenial to the Commonwealth period of the next century than to the Tudor constitution. It provided, in the event of Elizabeth being murdered, for all officials to continue in office 'in the name of the Crown of England', and for an executive body to be set up, called a 'Grand Council', consisting of 'the great officers of the Realm' and all Privy Councillors, who were to be served by the Royal Household. This Council was temporarily to have the same authority to govern the Realm as the

---

[1] B.M. Lansdowne MS. 98, fols. 14-18, endorsed by Burghley, 'January 1584, Mr. Digges discourse upon the Association'. Copy in B.M. Additional MS. 38823, fols. 14 seqq.

[2] Lansdowne MS. 119, fols. 123-32.

[3] Cf. my Elizabeth I and her Parliaments, 1559-81, pp. 112-13.

[4] S.P. Dom. Eliz. 176/32.

[5] The documents, in sequence of composition, are S.P. Dom. Eliz. 176/28, 29, 30, 22, the last being the draft bill.

Queen and her Privy Council possessed, including the conduct of diplomacy, control of naval and military affairs, and charge of the national treasure and expenditure. Its immediate task was to search for the malefactors concerned in the Queen's death, and to have them indicted, tried, and executed 'in some notable manner for example to the world to behold the zeal of devoted, true and loving servants and subjects to the person of their blessed Queen'.

The Council was speedily to summon the same Parliament as had last sat in the Queen's reign; and 'the Three Estates' were then to become the sovereign body of the country. 'The continuance, cessation or alteration' of the Council's authority or of 'their numbers and the ratification of their acts' were to be submitted to the judgment of Parliament, which was also to take over control of the national finances, operating through a committee of twenty, named by both Houses and chosen half from each. If the Council had not already dealt with those involved in the Queen's murder, Parliament's first task was quickly to complete the work. This done, it was to hear and determine all claims to the succession to the Crown, choosing the person who appeared 'to have best right . . . in blood by the royal laws of the Realm'; and its decision was to be announced by proclamation under the Great Seal, in the form of an Act of Parliament. All other claims were then to cease under pain of treason, and the interregnum was to end.

Burghley's scheme never came before the House of Commons or even its committee. It was born and died during the Christmas recess, leaving a mere relic in the ultimate statute. Its author had inserted into its enacting phrase, in his own hand, the words, *upon sure hope of the* assent of our Sovereign Lady'. The hope was misplaced. The Queen must have rejected Digges's arguments and placed her ban on Burghley's bill, though in doing so she was clearly setting her reason and instinct against the earnest advice and utmost pressure of her principal Councillors.

Elizabeth has left no defence of her action. It therefore falls to us to ask, who was the shrewder judge of the situation? Had Elizabeth been killed during Mary Queen of Scots' lifetime — a calamity that Councillors, Parliament and people thought all too likely — then, short of a miracle, the gloomy prognostications of Digges and others would have come to pass. For a Queen to reject her statesmen's advice, calculated to minimize both the risk of assassination and of consequent anarchy, was surely an astounding act of moral courage or wilfulness. That she was courageous in face of the danger to herself we need not doubt. She seems also to have been further from panic than those about her. She spoke often of God's providence; and why not accept her words as an expression of genuine faith? But there was more behind her decision. She evidently did not believe that Burghley's interregnum would achieve its purpose. She had seen — so, for that matter, had Burghley — the Duke of Northumberland's Council and governmental machine break up and collapse before the attraction of her sister Mary's claim to the throne in 1553. In November 1558 she herself had been organized to fight for her throne, ready to defy any official or unofficial opposition.[1] Experience, scepticism, realism may have led her to believe that any interregnum was bound to disintegrate and resolve itself into one of the factions contending for a vacant throne; that nothing could prevent civil strife if she were killed; and that the only sound policy was to accept the risks, trust in providence, and gamble on surviving the crisis. 'Time!' Elizabeth had exclaimed on seeing a figure of Father Time in her Coronation procession through the City, 'Time hath brought me hither.' Time had so often mocked prophets that she would not be stampeded into doubtful courses. Take, for instance, the bill's provision for Parliament to adjudicate among the claimants to the throne: in 1566 she had poured scorn on the proposal. To meet the practical difficulties attending open debate on the subject, Digges had suggested that Members might write out their speeches, place them in a ballot-box, and have them read by the Clerk anonymously, thus promoting courage and honesty. It is a pity we do not possess the Queen's comments on so fatuous a notion.

There was both mind and instinct in Elizabeth's decision: prejudice, also, no doubt. Surely her regal pride was shocked by Burghley's bill. To put the Crown of England into commission, even temporarily, by creating a Grand Council was barely digestible. But to envisage a sovereign Parliament! that was revolution. Digges described it as 'a cause to immortalize your Majesty's fame and renown with all posterity, being the first

---

[1] Cf. my article 'The Accession of Queen Elizabeth I' in *History Today*, iii. 293-300. Letters have since come to light among the Thynne Papers at Longleat, reinforcing my thesis.

estate royal that ever in England established so rare a provision'. It was not the sort of immortality Elizabeth coveted: to undermine monarchy and be the agent of 'popularity'. The interregnum would probably have lasted some time. After penetrating the mystery of executive power — the Holy of Holies — how would Parliament have emerged from such experience? Surely, personal monarchy as Elizabeth and her dynasty had known it would have been at an end. That such proposals could even be framed is of deep significance to the historian. Stuart days were not far distant.

Elizabeth's gamble on survival succeeded. We must not let that blind us to the fact that in making it she risked — and surely knew she risked — leaving a name of infamy in English history. Perhaps there is an indication of the concern the decision caused her in a letter from Hatton to Burghley, written on January 26th, telling him that the Queen wished him and the Lord Chancellor and Leicester to be at Court on the 27th, 'at night', 'about the matter of Parliament, wherewith I find her Majesty somewhat troubled'. On January 30th there was a rumour flying about that Parliament was to be further adjourned. It looks as if the final struggle between the Queen and her ministers took place during these days.[1]

Shortly after Parliament reassembled, the awful peril that threatened the country was brought dramatically home to Members. They had been acutely conscious of the similarity between the position of their Queen and that of the murdered William of Orange. Somerville's plot to assassinate Elizabeth had seemed a close parallel to the first, abortive attempt to kill the Prince of Orange. Now came the news of another plot; and the would-be assassin was the egregious Dr. William Parry, whose passionate Catholic outburst in the House of Commons had so recently enraged them.

The previous summer Parry had been discussing his undertaking to kill the Queen with one, Edmund Neville, a malcontent whom he tried to persuade to partner him in the deed, explaining that his ready access to the Court made the venture simple. After his rebuff in Parliament, which may have revived his resolution, he was again in touch with Neville, but this dubious person betrayed the plot to the authorities in the second week of February. Parry

---

[1] NICOLAS, *Sir Christopher Hatton*, p. 411; Seymour Papers (Longleat), v. fol. 162 (a reference I owe to Mrs. S. T. Bindoff).

was given his chance to explain matters: a chance he should have
taken, if his offence had been simply that of acting as an un-
authorized *agent provocateur*. His initial assertion of ignorance
inevitably turned the law against him. He was tried and condemned to a traitor's death.

News of Parry's plot was known to Members of the House of
Commons by Monday, February 15th, in the afternoon of which
day the great committee was to renew its discussion of the bill for
the Queen's safety; and that morning the zealous Puritan, Edward
Lewkenor, moved that some be appointed 'to draw a form of
prayer and thanksgiving to be used in this House for the great
benefits and blessings of God bestowed upon this whole realm in
her Majesty, and for the long continuance of the same'. Prayers
of thanksgiving for the wonderful preservation from manifold
perils of God's servant, Queen Elizabeth, were not confined to
Parliament. They were said, with an appropriate sermon on the
authority and majesty of princes, accompanied by details of
Parry's plot, in the churches of the land, and were reinforced by a
lengthy government tract on the subject.[1]

On February 18th, possibly before all the details were known in
the House, Thomas Digges moved that Parry be 'disburgessed',
or, as we should say, unseated. 'It is your pleasure he shall be disburgessed?' asked the Speaker. 'Yea, yea, yea', answered the
House: and a warrant was drawn up for the issue of a new writ.
Though the trial did not take place until February 25th, the
shocking nature of the offence was fully known by the 23rd. On
that day Sir Thomas Lucy and Sir William More — two elderly,
staid and substantial country gentlemen — moved that as Parry
had plotted while a Member of that House, many of whom
belonged to the Bond of Association, suit be made to the Queen for
permission to devise a law for his execution (after conviction) in a
manner fitting 'his so extraordinary and most horrible kind of
treason'. They wanted tortures more terrible than those of a
traitor's death. Knollys and Hatton were commissioned to convey
this request to the Queen.[2]

The next day Hatton brought Elizabeth's reply. She took their
suit 'very thankfully', but 'would not agree to other dealing' than
'the ordinary course of law'. Hatton then went on, 'for some satis-

---

[1] D'EWES, p. 349; STRYPE, *Annals*, III. i. 376-80, III. ii. 330-7.
[2] D'EWES, pp. 352, 355; Lansdowne MS. 43, fol. 169.

faction to the House', to give a detailed account of the life and treasons of Parry, after the manner of the narrative that the government subsequently published. Our diarist, Thomas Cromwell, nowadays reticent about speeches, was stirred to report it at great length, while the anonymous diarist — in an entry probably belonging to this occasion — jotted down an emotional outburst by George Ireland, expressing the romantic attachment of these ardent Englishmen to their Queen: 'It makes my heart leap for joy to think we have such a jewel. It makes all my joints to tremble for fear when I consider the loss of such a jewel'. 'Her Majesty', replied Hatton, 'takes it in most gracious and kind part your great care for her: that you esteem her to be such a jewel. She saith herself — though I may not, nor will not say it — that your care is far above her worthiness.'[1]

On this or some recent day a proposal was made, which Elizabeth related in a letter to Mary Queen of Scots on March 22nd. Since the Parry Plot, she told Mary, 'in open Parliament motion has been made, with a general applause of the whole House, to revive the former judicial proceedings against you, propounded thirteen years past in Parliament [i.e. in 1572]: which, as you know, being assented to by both the nobility and Commons, was only stayed at that time by us, as it was also at this present on the same motion; and not without the great misliking and discontentment of our best devoted subjects'. That the Commons would gladly have proceeded at once to extremities against Mary, who can doubt?[2]

It was with the Parry plot for background that work was resumed on the bill for the Queen's safety. The committee met on February 15th, Mildmay opening the proceedings as government spokesman. It seems as if he did not know what to do: try to amend the old bill, suspended by the Queen's command in December, or frame a new one in the light of the Parry plot. The initiative of statesmen had evidently been paralysed by the ban on Burghley's scheme for an interregnum. In the normal way of human affairs, one might have expected the new crisis to prove a godsend to Councillors, enabling them to scare and coerce their mistress into acquiescence in their plans. But no: the adamantine quality of her will was proof against that.

[1] Cromwell's diary; Lansdowne MS. 43, fol. 168; D'EWES, p. 356.
[2] *Scottish Cal.* vii. 597.

After Mildmay had spoken, someone reverted to the old difficulty about the Oath of Association not agreeing with the bill, and proposed to insert an explanation of the Oath acceptable to everybody. This, Fitzwilliam tells us — and, in view of the ultimate wording of the Act, the decision is worth noting — was not allowed because oaths were sacrosanct. Either the Oath should be made law or it should be annexed to the law and those executing it freed from the danger of losing land, life or goods. In order to deter a would-be assassin, the committee — or some of them — would have liked to add a clause debarring the Queen or her successor from pardoning anyone guilty of so horrible an offence: an indication, maybe, that they feared Elizabeth might pardon Parry, certainly that they thought her too merciful. However, it was pointed out: first, that a successor could not be bound by the law since he was not present to consent to it; and secondly, that it would limit the prerogative, which was something that could not be achieved. Having talked themselves into a deadlock, they decided that 'the best course' was 'to make her Majesty privy' to their proceedings 'and to ask her advice' as to what they should now do. One marvels at the situation. The Queen's wilfulness, coupled with the inherent difficulties of the problem, had left them leaderless and helpless.[1]

At this point in the story our evidence fails us; but it would seem that twelve days elapsed while someone — Burghley no doubt — drafted a new bill in consultation with the Queen. The committee met again on February 27th, and on March 3rd Sir Christopher Hatton introduced the bill into the House of Commons for a first reading.

Its text was based on the earlier bill, but there were changes which took account both of Elizabeth's wishes and of the many debates in committee. In case of invasion, rebellion, or plot against the Queen, by or for any claimant to the throne, commissioners — as in the earlier bill — were to investigate the facts and pronounce judgment. Thereafter, all subjects — in the words of the Act — 'shall and may lawfully, by virtue of this Act and her Majesty's direction', pursue to the death anyone pronounced by the commission to be concerned with or privy to the offence. This provision fully recognized Elizabeth's principle that only the guilty should suffer: a principle in conflict with the Oath of Association.

[1] Fitzwilliam's diary.

The next provision — contemplating a successful attempt on the Queen's life — was a compromise between conflicting views. Councillors and Commons got their way in ensuring that Mary Queen of Scots — the nameless claimant — should be excluded from the throne: from Elizabeth's point of view it can have been merely a minor defeat, for she surely no longer contemplated Mary's succession with equanimity. But the Queen's will prevailed in exempting the heir — James VI — from this penalty, unless he were 'assenting and privy' to the offence. Her principle triumphed completely in the lynch-law provision, for only those 'by whom or by whose means' the assassination had been effected were to be pursued to the death; and their children — i.e. James VI — were included only if 'assenting and privy'.

Unless accompanied by other provisions, the concessions to Elizabeth's scruples threatened, in the event of assassination, to create utter uncertainty and anarchy. Burghley's solution of the problem, as we have seen, had been an interregnum. The provision in this bill was a statutory commission of Privy Councillors and others, whose sole function was to destroy the guilty. It differed profoundly from Burghley's scheme. The commission was not a Grand Council; there was to be no sovereign Parliament; there was no provision for determining the succession. Here, indeed, was a reflection of Elizabeth's mind: and, so far as we know, of no one else's. She was still gambling on surviving the crisis. Even more significant, she was defending James VI's title to the succession, probably regarding it as legally and morally right and bound therefore to prevail. On this point, few of her Councillors, certainly few Members of Parliament, in the raging passions of the moment, would have agreed with her.

As the course of debate had shown, it was essential to reconcile the terms of the Oath of Association with those of the bill. In January, Burghley had drafted a long-winded clause to this effect. An admirable epitomist reduced it to a brief declaration that the obligations of the Association were to be expounded according to the true intent of this Act.[1]

What, in conclusion, are we to say about this striking victory of the Queen over her statesmen and Parliament? Perhaps the best tribute to the shrewdness and sanity of her amendments is that

[1] D'EWES, pp. 361-2; *Statutes of the Realm*, IV. i. 704-5 (27 Eliz. cap. 1); S.P. Dom. Eliz. 176/11.

the Act, framed in the excitement of plots against her life, did not subsequently have to be amended and was only repealed in the reign of Queen Victoria. It served in 1586 for the trial of Mary Queen of Scots by respectable judicial process. It neither blocked nor hampered James VI's accession to the throne of England. In the latter respect alone, it proved an invaluable diplomatic asset when in 1586 James made threatening *démarches* to save his mother's life. Had his title to the succession then been affected by his mother's guilt — as the original bill provided — there is no knowing what Scotland would have done, nor what additional danger would have confronted Elizabethan England.

Though committed and amended, the bill was not materially altered when it came before the House of Commons.[1] To most Members it cannot have been palatable. Our Puritan, Edward Lewkenor, evidently accepted it in a spirit of resignation. 'I mean not to speak against the bill', he said. 'But if it might prolong her Majesty's life but for one year, I protest I would be content to suffer death with the most exquisite torments that might be devised.' He mentioned that Papists had taken the Oath of Association: their intention was not honest. A Mr. Harris — perhaps the lawyer — harped again on the divergences between the Oath and the Act: 'we may be in a dangerous dilemma by this statute'. Mr. Craddock, Recorder of Stafford — odd man out — offered a proviso permitting the Queen, by proclamation, to repeal the Act in part or whole at her discretion. It was promptly rejected as 'a dangerous precedent'. In the Lords the bill had ready passage and by March 13th it was ready for the royal assent.[2]

The second great measure of the session — the bill against Jesuits and Catholic priests — had passed the Commons in mid-December. The Lords got down to it after the Christmas recess, committed it, and made a considerable number of amendments, the chief of which — as we have already noticed — reduced the offence of receiving or aiding priests from treason to felony. There were 'some speeches and arguments' when these amendments were considered by the Commons. Digges, who had roundly condemned the measure in one of his January Discourses, spoke.

---

[1] The paper bill, showing amendments, is in House of Lords Papers, 1582-85, at Westminster.

[2] D'EWES, pp. 363-4, 367; *L.J.* ii. 95-7; Lansdowne MS. 43, fol. 173.

'I am against the body of the bill', he declared. 'You speak too late,' he was told: 'it is passed already.' 'Then I speak to the additions by the Lords', retorted Digges. 'They would make it felony where we have made it treason. The punishment is too little already.' He then went on to denounce Jesuits in much the same violent manner used in his Discourse. After that he referred to an amendment in the sections providing for priests or seminary scholars who might wish to recant and submit, where the Lords had added an additional safeguard in the form of the Oath of Supremacy. Perhaps Digges merely seized on the amendment as an excuse to express his opposition to having any truck with such dangerous characters; perhaps he merely objected to the Oath as an illusory guarantee and therefore dangerous. 'I like not', he declared, 'that they may submit themselves to a bishop or Justice of the Peace and take the Oath.' Who does not see that they have dispensations to free them from its obligations? 'Parry took the Oath, yet died a Catholic, as he called himself. This bill', he concluded, 'is a most dangerous bill. I pray God I be no prophet.'[1]

The Commons made some insignificant changes in the Lords' amendments, and there were consultations between the two Houses. But apart from misgivings and grumbles and a precedural dispute about amending amendments, there was no real difficulty. The bill passed both Houses.[2]

A third principal concern of the government, this Parliament, was money. Such, however, had been the absorption of the leaders of the House in other matters, that it was February 24th when Sir Walter Mildmay, Chancellor of the Exchequer, made his speech for supply.

He began by recalling his earlier speech and his comments on their many malicious enemies. 'As the waves of the sea do one follow upon another without intermission, so these men have no end of their practices whensoever opportunity may serve them; nourished with hope that at the length they may attain that they seek for.'

In addition to the laws already well forward, Parliament needed — said Mildmay — to provide forces by land and sea to defend the realm. This meant great charge. Ireland alone, since

[1] Lansdowne MS. 43, fol. 165.
[2] D'EWES, pp. 362, 365-7, 370; *L.J.* ii. 76, 83, 90-1, 95, 98, 104. The amendments are in two papers tied to the original Act at Westminster.

the last Parliament, had consumed the whole grant then made, and more. In addition, there were the charges for fortification at Berwick and upon the sea-coast. There was also the great provision of powder and munition lately made, 'the mass whereof is more than in any former time and is more to be accounted of than money itself, for such things cannot at all times be gotten for money'. Lastly, there was 'the new building and repairing of the navy, put now in better strength and better readiness than at any time before this: a matter of great importance, for the navy, being justly termed the wall of England, is a thing of all other principally to be cared for'.

By reason of these charges, the Queen had spent of her own revenue, for the defence of the realm, almost as much more as the aid granted by the last Parliament. I speak — he declared — not by conjecture but by view of her Majesty's receipts and payments. She has done this to avoid borrowing upon interest, a most perilous canker. It may seem strange to you that two fifteenths and a subsidy, so lately granted, should not suffice to meet these charges and leave a good surplus. 'This I myself would likewise marvel at, if two things did not move me, which I think will move you also: one, the costliness of the wars and the great increase of prices of all things in this age, far surmounting the times before; and the other, the easiness of the taxation [assessment] of the subsidies, which how favourable they be handled in all places no man can be ignorant. If I should tell you how meanly the great possessors in the country and the best aldermen and citizens of London and the rich men of the realm are rated, you would marvel at it . . . Thereby a very great deal less than is given to her Majesty is paid into her coffers: so much, as I dare assure you this last subsidy is far less than that which went before. And this I say, not to enhance men's taxations, but to let you see that subsidies thus favourably rated come short of that which you may think.'

All this and a great deal more of her own — he added — had been spent by her Majesty upon public affairs, 'and never a whit upon vain expenses for pleasure or delight, as other princes use'. As a result, Ireland, 'an ancient and precious jewel of the crown of England', had been saved. In the days of Queen Mary, 'by the ill government of a sort of priests that minded nothing so much as the restitution . . . of Popery', Calais had been lost: 'a mar-

vellous blow to this realm, and so is like to prove whensoever
wars shall happen between us and the French'. But if Ireland
were to fall into the hands of a potent prince, our enemy, it would
prove another matter than the loss of Calais. 'For Ireland, being
a whole region, furnished with so many notable havens, so
inhabited with many stout people, and so near our mainland,
would no doubt shake this whole state and every part thereof
more dangerously.'

Though our enemies' hatred is implacable and their desire to
overrun us insatiable, 'yet, seeing — as they have done — that by
her Majesty's provident circumspection they could not find her
unprepared, their enterprises have quailed and we have lived in
peace'. It behoves us — Mildmay concluded — to offer such aid
as may be answerable to the greatness of the charges, therein
showing ourselves 'dutiful to so gracious a Queen, that governs us
with justice and keeps us in peace'.[1]

The tax decided on was one subsidy and two fifteenths and
tenths, as before; and — be it added — as before, the yield
diminished. With her eyes on the calendar, the Queen wanted
the House to press on with the bill. She was disposed to have the
Lords adjourn for two days, hoping by the device to manœuvre
the Commons into haste. Burghley received a message from
Court to this effect on March 1st. At the same time, he learnt that
the Speaker was away ill and the House was therefore not sitting
that day. He was anxious to choose a Deputy-Speaker — which
would have been an interesting innovation if it had come to pass;
but the Speaker was back in his place the next day.[2]

It was not until March 12th that the subsidy bill received its
third reading and was passed by the Commons. Before being put
to the question, there was a characteristic incident, when one
of the many zealots moved that all Popish recusants should be
made to pay double rates, as 'strangers' did. 'Seeing they refused
to live according to the laws of the realm, they were not to be
accounted as subjects, but as foreigners'.

Mildmay dealt with this exuberant gentleman. 'The selfsame
matter', he said, 'was by the selfsame party mentioned the Parliament last going before this, but by a general consent rejected.'

---

[1] The text of the speech is in Fitzwilliam's diary; also in B.M. Sloane MS. 326,
fols. 83 seqq. D'Ewes, p. 355 has an epitome.
[2] S.P. Dom. Eliz. 177/1; D'Ewes, p. 361.

What objections were then made he had forgotten, but he propounded his own reasons for continued opposition. First, the bill was now ingrossed and at its third reading: such a motion 'was far out of season'. Next, while agreeing that recusants should be punished for their obstinacy, the punishment should be 'convenient', which this in no wise could be, both because the pain thereof is but little and also because a greater pain — namely, the recusancy fine of £20 a month — is already imposed upon them 'and maketh them to stoop'. Moreover, two great inconveniences would follow. First, by our eagerness to impose so small a grief on top of the present burden, we should 'be noted to leave the badge of the Gospel now preached — which is clemency and gentleness; and show the fruits of the contrary religion — which is sourness and cruelty, a thing utterly to be shunned of us and to be left wholly to' Catholics 'as the cognizance of their profession'. Secondly, 'in coupling them with the strangers we should give them cause to think that we had wholly secluded them from our society, not accounting them as natural-born Englishmen, and thereby drive a desperation into them: which is contrary to the course taken in our former laws — as namely, in the bill for the Queen's safety and the bill of Jesuits, wherein a liberty is given that such as will conform themselves to the due obedience that subjects ought to use may willingly be received.' In this way we show 'that we do not reject and refuse them as men unworthy of our company and fellowship, but be they never so ill, yet that we live still in hope to win and reconcile them.'

'This opinion', Fitzwilliam tells us, 'prevailed in overthrowing the other.' For our part, we might think it to savour of the unction of an Inquisitor.[1]

[1] D'Ewes, p. 366; Fitzwilliam's diary. The identity of Mildmay is revealed by the anonymous diary, which gives a brief account of the incident (Lansdowne MS. 43, fol. 166).

CHAPTER IV

RELIGION

THOUGH our sources depict Members of this Parliament more submissive and less talkative than their predecessors when dealing with the great government bills of the session, we find them as difficult to control as any assembly of the past when the subject was religion. Their appetite was whetted by the first bill of the session, read 'for order's sake' on the Speaker's return after confirmation of his election. Its object was 'the better and more reverent observing of the Sabbath Day': that is to say, the statutory enforcement of what in modern times has been called the English, as distinct from the Continental, Sunday.[1]

As a curtain-raiser to the grand drama that follows, the story of this bill is well worth telling. Who devised it and how it got priority we do not know: possibly some of the bishops, acting through Sir Walter Mildmay. It was not a Puritan bill. These zealots were of course thoroughgoing Sabbatarians, but desire for a more sober and comely observance of Sunday had a broader and older pedigree. Despite the earnest atmosphere of the new times, the Elizabethan Sunday was still spent in the customary, merry ways of pre-Reformation days. Two events in the previous year had stirred pious minds to fresh concern. One was the collapse of old scaffolding about the bear pit in Paris Garden when overcrowded on a Sunday. Eight persons had been killed: 'a friendly warning', as honest John Stow noted in his Chronicle, 'to such as more delight themselves in the cruelty of beasts than in the works of mercy, the fruits of a true professed faith, which ought to be the Sabbath Day's exercise'. The second event was the publication of Stubbes's *Anatomy of Abuses* with its attack on the violation of God's Sabbath.

The bill was read a second time the following day and committed to thirty-three Members, including such resolute Puritans as Beale, Lewkenor, Strickland and Turner, presided over by the Chancellor of the Exchequer, Sir Walter Mildmay. Evidently the rule was already established which permitted any other

[1] On this subject, see W. B. WHITAKER, *Sunday in Tudor & Stuart Times.*

Member of the House to attend and speak — though not vote —
at a committee meeting; and the subject, combined with the
novelty for newcomers to Parliament, seems to have attracted
many supernumeraries. 'The committees', reported Recorder
Fleetwood, 'amounted in number to sixty at the least, all young
gents; and at our meeting in the afternoon twenty at once did
speak. And there we sat talking and did nothing until night,
so that Mr. Chancellor was weary. And then we departed
home.'[1]

The odds are that these sombre enthusiasts found the bill too
moderate for their taste. At any rate, by December 3rd they had
drawn up a new one, which sailed through the House in three
days. No text survives, but we know that it forbade the holding
of markets or fairs or setting up of stalls on a Sunday, and banned
unlawful games, bearbaiting, wakes, hawking, hunting or rowing
with barges — these last, apparently, only during the time of
church-service. The Lords were as keen as the Commons about
the principle, but wanted to amend the text of the bill, perhaps
to tone down extravagances. They did their best to avoid a
collision by consulting with the Lower House. However, when
the bill returned to them, the Commons proceeded to amend the
amendments; whereupon a dispute arose between the two Houses
as to their right to do this, and progress was held up till March
while the battle over procedure and liberties was waged. In the
end the Commons prevailed. All was now harmony, and on the
suggestion of the Lords the much-altered bill was written out
anew in order that 'the record of so good and godly [a] law may
remain fair and perfect'.[2]

'Fair and perfect' the parchment may have become; 'remain' it
did not. They had reckoned without their Queen. In his final
oration the Speaker made special mention of the measure, giving
it priority in his request for the royal assent: 'Being persuaded
that all good laws of men ought to be grounded upon the eternal
law of God', Parliament, he declared, had thought — by providing for the right use of the Sabbath Day — 'to provoke' her
Majesty to give law concerning the Fourth of God's Command-
ments. The Queen was indeed provoked; but it was to veto, not
pass the bill. Her action may have been determined mainly by a

[1] D'EWES, p. 333; B.M. Lansdowne MS. 41, fol. 45.
[2] Cromwell's diary; D'EWES, pp. 335-69 passim.

resolve not to let Parliament interfere with any religious questions, but there can also be little doubt that she preferred a Merry to a Puritan England. What she had done was to veto a measure on which both Houses had set their hearts; and her chief statesman, Burghley, had been on the committee that steered it through the Lords.[1]

Welcome as it was to the Puritans, the bill about the Sabbath was no part of their campaign. We must turn to this major theme. The *classes* or organized groups of ministers — many of whose members found themselves at this time deprived, suspended or in trouble over Whitgift's three-pronged subscription — were fully alive to the opportunity presented by a meeting of Parliament. At Dedham on November 2nd they decided to hold a fast; also their members were enjoined each to 'stir up his people to earnest prayer for the good of the Church'. This was in preparation for the autumn sitting of Parliament. They prayed and fasted again for the post-Christmas sittings.

So much for prayer; now for militancy. At Dedham — also on November 2nd — they decided, 'so far as we could procure it', to arrange 'in every country . . . that some of best credit and most forward for the Gospel should go up to London to solicit the cause of the Church'. Perhaps they had in mind influencing parliamentary elections; certainly they meant to bring about a concentration in London, during this season of seasons, not only of Puritan ministers but of their keen friends among the country gentlemen. In London were the secretary of the Movement, John Field, and his ministerial brethren, meeting in *classis* monthly: an organized centre to co-ordinate activity throughout all the *classes* in the land, a cadre round which delegates from the provinces could gather and thus convert the London meetings into embryo national assemblies. There seems to have been an enlarged assembly during the autumn sittings of Parliament and a prolonged general conference in February. We are told — and can in essence believe it — that their agents 'were all day at the door of the Parliament House and some part of the night in the chambers of Parliament-men, effectually soliciting their business with them'.[2]

---

[1] Lansdowne MS. 115, fols. 38-9.
[2] USHER, *Presbyterian Movement* (Camden Soc.), pp. 40-1; FULLER, *Church History*, bk. ix. sec. vi (cf. BANCROFT, *Dangerous Positions*, ed. 1640, p. 81).

They planned their main campaign in continuation of the agitation in the two previous sessions of 1576 and 1581: a denunciation of the present state of the Church, inveighing against the number of unworthy, incompetent, non-preaching and non-resident ministers, and various other abuses. It was an indictment of episcopal discipline, and, by inference, an argument for substituting Presbyterian discipline. New emphasis was given to old complaints by the tale of able, godly and preaching ministers silenced or deprived by Whitgift's inquisitorial practices. To add substance to their argument, the Puritan *classes* had already begun a most remarkable investigation: a survey of the state of the ministry in various counties, listing the parishes and benefices along with the names of the ministers, appropriate, often scurrilous comments on their fitness, and other items of information. If evidence were needed of the precocious ability of Field and his fellow-organizers in the sphere of propaganda, it is here in this impressive co-operative work. Even allowing for a high degree of exaggeration, no one could read its factual, scathing tables without being deeply disturbed, not to say alarmed, at the unhealthy state of the Church: which, of course, was exactly the effect aimed at. We do not know how much of the survey was ready for use at this Parliament, but some of the statistical information evidently was, and in addition there were local petitions, signed by the gentry and others. In fact, the secret, co-ordinated activity of the *classes* had gone far enough to create an illusion of spontaneous, widespread discontent.[1]

The campaign opened in Parliament on December 14th. That morning, after one bill had been read, Sir Thomas Lucy, Member for Warwickshire, Sir Edward Dymock, Member for Lincolnshire and as eminent in that county as Lucy in his, and Mr. Geoffrey Gates, an Essex gentleman, nephew of Walsingham and stepson of Peter Wentworth, presented petitions from their respective counties. They were subscribed with the signatures of 'very many . . . of the gentlemen of the greatest worship in the same shires'. As well as complaining of the deplorable state of the clergy in their localities, they dealt with the restraint of 'so many good preachers'. Their sponsors urged the House to petition the Queen for reformation.

The House knew perfectly well that the Lord Chancellor, on

---

[1] *Seconde Parte of a Register*, ed. A. Peel, ii. 89.

the Queen's instructions, had placed a ban on the discussion of religious matters. Nevertheless, Members settled themselves and had the three petitions read. The atmosphere seems to have been so propitious that the eager Dr. Peter Turner was encouraged to go further. He called for 'a bill and book' which he had already introduced into the House: presumably meaning that he had handed them to Speaker or Clerk. They had been 'digested and framed by certain godly and learned ministers' — he declared — and tended 'to no other end . . . than the glory of God, the safety of her Majesty, and the benefit of the Commonwealth'. He wanted a formal reading to be given to them. The 'book' was the Genevan Prayer Book, and the purpose of the 'bill' was to establish this in place of the Elizabethan Prayer Book of 1559. The bill also set up a presbyterian system of ministers and elders to whom the jurisdiction of the Church was to be transferred. Archbishops, bishops and other existing officials do not seem to have been abolished: they were left as empty shells without any *raison d'être.*[1]

Although Dr. Turner's action may have been planned as an appendix to the general campaign, dependent on the reception accorded its opening move, it seems more likely that he represented an impatient wing of extremists determined to strike at once for Presbyterianism; for, even among the ministerial members of *classes*, there was a perceptible division between those who were not averse to a compromise with the bishops and those intent on immediate revolution. Whatever the explanation, this new move jeopardized the main petitionary strategy. Sir Francis Knollys rose. He spoke 'few words': indeed, this formerly garrulous Councillor, though senior in status to his colleagues, was receding from effective official leadership of the House before the growing authority of Hatton and Mildmay. What he said, we are not told: he must have opposed Turner's reckless motion. Sir Christopher Hatton followed. Less briefly, he so 'pressed and moved the House' that at length it was resolved not to read the bill and book and, as regards the grievances mentioned in the petitions, to trust that the Queen would take speedy order. As our diarist put it: 'In fine, the motion stayed, in respect the Queen had promised to have a care thereof'. No more was heard

---

[1] PEEL, op. cit. ii. 80-1. I am assuming that the undated bill, pp. 215-18, is Turner's.

of 'the bill and book' until the next Parliament: a mercy for the Puritans, since with such a Jonah aboard there would have been no prospect of reaching any port.[1]

Eased of this embarrassment, the House returned to the subject of the petitions two days later, on December 16th. There were 'some motions' and 'many arguments': they had a field-day. Mildmay spoke, and the Clerk of the House, Fulk Onslow, in the rough notes for his Journal, privately recorded his approbation: he 'spake exceeding well touching this business'. It was Mildmay — a Privy Councillor! — who, in flat contravention of his sovereign's command, proposed that they should appoint a committee to study the petitions, extract their points, and then approach the Upper House to join with them in further action. A committee of thirteen was appointed, men predominantly moderate in their views. Afterwards, 'conceiving the weight of this business required a greater number' — or, as we may strongly suspect, distrusting so respectable a committee — the House doubled its size and thus secured a solid core of inflexibles, among whom were Robert Beale, James Morice, William Stoughton, and Walsingham's secretary, Lawrence Tomson.[2]

The committee met that afternoon. A Member turned up, not one of the committee, who took upon himself to defend the bishops. Having disposed of this gentleman's arguments, they proceeded to set out their grievances in the form of a petition to the Lords, containing sixteen clauses: a moderate document on the whole, though certain Puritan demands and the constant stress placed on parliamentary statutes were bound to antagonize both the Queen and Whitgift. They asked for the removal or suspension of unqualified and unlearned ministers and for adequate provision against the future admission of such men, including — a central feature of Puritanism, this — participation of the parish in the placing of ministers. They also wanted no oath or subscription to be imposed on the clergy, other than those prescribed by parliamentary statute; no proceedings against ministers for omitting any mere portion or rite of the Prayer Book; the restoration of those suspended or deprived for refusing subscription to Whitgift's articles; no oath *ex officio*; the use of Exercises; in short, a Church safe for Puritans. A final group of clauses dealt

[1] D'Ewes, p. 339; Cromwell's diary; Fitzwilliam's diary.
[2] D'Ewes, p. 340.

with the abuse of excommunication and with non-residence and pluralities.[1]

On December 21st a delegation from the Commons, led by Sir Francis Knollys, delivered the petition to a committee of five Spiritual and twelve Temporal Lords. Mildmay was the spokesman. After recalling proceedings in the previous Parliament, he went on to say that complaints received this Parliament from sundry parts of the Realm and uttered in the Nether House showed that nothing had been done to remedy their griefs: indeed, they had increased. Rather than trouble her Majesty with a new petition, since they had received so gracious an answer in 1581, they now came to the Lords for help.

The seventeen peers had the petition read in their own House and then met Knollys and his group again to deliver their answer. At first they were for avoiding parliamentary action, on the ground — an episcopal criticism, maybe — that the grievances came from three counties only; but, on being told that 'by motions and speeches' in the House of Commons 'it well appeared to be the grief of the whole realm', their attitude changed. 'Their Lordships, having understood, did feelingly express how sensible they were of it, and how truly they did join with us of the House of Commons in wishing the reformation thereof.' They were as ready to lend their aid as they had been in earlier Parliaments, but, considering themselves to be under the same ban against dealing with matters of religion as the Commons, they wanted first to ascertain her Majesty's pleasure through the means of their Councillor-members.[2]

The Christmas recess now intervened and was evidently used by the Puritan party-managers to strengthen their attack and particularly to meet the criticism that their petitions came from only three counties. On February 15th William Stoughton started the business of the House by offering a parchment supplication about ministerial abuses and episcopal disorders in the county of Leicester. Edward Lewkenor promptly followed with a similar petition from the inhabitants of the east parts of Sussex, while John Moore, Member for Dover, produced a paper petition from the inhabitants of Folkestone. All three were read. The hunt was

[1] Fitzwilliam's diary. There are copies of the petition in Lansdowne MSS. 42, 396; B.M. Harleian MS. 158; B.M. Additional MS. 38492. It is printed in D'EWES, pp. 357-9; STRYPE, *Whitgift*, iii. 118-24.
[2] Fitzwilliam's diary; D'EWES, pp. 344-5.

on again. Perhaps at this juncture, the emotional George Ireland made another speech, briefly noted by our anonymous diarist. He was concerned about inaction in the two great matters of religion and the Queen's safety. 'We were very hot awhile,' he complained, 'but now cold again. Our petitions are not looked to; we do nothing. As Demosthenes did not believe one that told him he was beaten and wronged, because he did not speak earnestly enough, so we.' Then, talking — one supposes — about Mary Queen of Scots, he said: 'I would have her hopeless to reign and headless to live'.[1]

Sympathetic, prudent, and popular leader that he was, Mildmay let them run on for a time and then intervened to recall their earlier proceedings and persuade them to wait for an answer from the Lords, some of whom he had recently reminded of the business.

Mildmay promised an answer for the following day; but, as it happened, the Commons had annoyed their superiors by disrespectful treatment of one of their bills, and their Lordships refused to give the expected answer until they received satisfaction on this other point. It was February 22nd before the reply was given. Lord Burghley spoke first, telling the deputation sent from the Commons that some of the Privy Councillors in the Upper House had shown the Queen their petition, and that her Majesty had thereupon discussed the matter with Whitgift and the bishops. The outcome he described as follows: some of the reforms proposed in the petition were already under consideration (that is to say, Convocation was taking steps to prescribe them); others the Queen meant to carry out by her supreme authority; 'some were not fit to be reformed as requiring innovation and impugning the Book of Common Prayer'. Further, it was the Queen's wish that any offences should be dealt with in the diocese concerned, and only in the event of the bishop ignoring private representations was further complaint to be made: redress would then be given. In short, the Church was to be kept a distinct and self-sufficient sphere of power, free from the intrusion of Parliament.[2]

Whitgift followed Burghley. He took the sixteen clauses of the Commons' petition in order and dealt with each. In general, his answer accorded with Burghley's summary, except that he could not refrain from rubbing salt into the wounds he inflicted, as wit-

[1] D'EWES, p. 349; Lansdowne MS. 43, fol. 167.
[2] Cromwell's diary; D'EWES, pp. 351-4, 359.

ness the following quotations: it 'smelleth of popular election'; 'it was not tolerable in a settled state of the Church'; 'they that are deprived are justly deprived, that which is done is justly done and so will be avowed'; the *ex officio* oath was 'misliked first by Jesuits and Seminaries and from them derived to others that mislike government and would bring the Church to an anarchy'; some of the bishops against whom they were complaining 'had been preachers before some of us [that is, the Commons] were born — at the least, when we were in our swaddling clothes'.[1]

Whitgift had spoken at great length, from notes: a foolish procedure, for that no doubt helps to explain the caustic, insolent phrases of this proud prelate and the quality of the anger he aroused. 'In all the histories and records of time past', wrote Robert Beale, some years later, 'never any prince or subject gave such an insufficient and opprobrious answer.' After a preliminary report to the House by Mildmay, the delegates met to reconstruct from their joint memories a full account of the Archbishop's answer, which was read in the Commons on February 25th. 'Divers motions and sundry long speeches' followed. As our diarist succinctly remarks, 'the House was nothing satisfied'.[2]

Some tale-carrier seems to have jotted down a remark or two from the speeches of four Members: Henry Blagge, Member for Sudbury, Robert Beale, Lawrence Tomson, and Edward Lewkenor. Tomson described Whitgift's answer as 'rather a discourse than any resolution of a divine', adding 'that subscription was not used in any Church'; Lewkenor said of the bishops that 'they were rather deformers than reformers'; while Blagge scornfully referred to 'the Cardinal and Metropolitical answer'.[3]

As for Beale, we can probably get a very fair idea of his arguments from one of his papers, a Treatise, which, though couched in the form of a parliamentary speech made at this juncture, is much too long to have been delivered as written. It begins with an exordium on Magna Carta, which Puritan lawyers such as he were rediscovering in their fight for liberty against bishops. Beale describes himself as a petitioner, asking that from hence-

---

[1] Fitzwilliam gives the text compiled by the Commons' committee, which I have followed (cf. the disjointed text in D'EWES, pp. 359-60, where 'Archbishop of York' is an error for Canterbury). Whitgift's own (and naturally milder) version is in Inner Temple, Petyt MS. 538/38, fols. 79-82; copies in Lansdowne MS. 396, Lambeth Palace MS. 577; printed in STRYPE, *Whitgift*, i. 354-60.
[2] Additional MS. 48039 (Yelverton 44), fol. 67; D'EWES, p. 360; Cromwell's diary.
[3] S.P. Dom. Eliz. 175/51.

forth the Queen's subjects 'may be no otherwise dealt with in causes ecclesiastical than may stand with the said Charter and [the] laws and liberties of this Realm'. Since the clergy in Convocation were no part of Parliament, and the House of Commons represented the whole Realm except for the persons of the Lords Spiritual and Temporal, he concludes that the whole of the lower clergy were represented in the Commons and therefore that their grievances and complaints ought to be preferred and considered there: an ingenious, but thoroughly unconstitutional argument, repugnant to the Queen and to the main principle of the Reformation Settlement.

'The lamentable face of the Church at this day is not unknown unto you all', Beale continues: 'how the shires and boroughs from whence you come . . . are served with unlearned and insufficient ministers, and how that many of the learneder sort, for a refusal to a certain subscription, have been called up from far parts' and 'examined by corporal oaths'. Some have been put to silence, some imprisoned without bail, some suspended and deprived from their livings and ministry. All this 'is practised contrary to God's word, the laws and customs of England, the Canon laws, and her Majesty's Commission Ecclesiastical, which is used as a cloak for the maintenance of these said abuses'. Proceeding to justify his charge of illegality, Beale again challenges the official conception of the Reformation by subordinating the Church to parliamentary legislation. What is the ecclesiastical law of England? he asks. For answer he points out that it could be dispensed with or annulled by the Prince in Parliament, as was done in Henry VIII's reign, and new laws made, as in 1559, 1563 and 1571, 'all which were first begun in the Lower House'. In the detailed arguments that follow he has the audacity to suggest — and his contention was to become a favourite one with Puritans — that the Prayer Book then in use was not the one authorized by the Act of Uniformity. If his several points were sound — which they were not — then indeed Whitgift, in his proceedings against Puritans, and Matthew Parker before him, had acted illegally. In the spirit of Magna Carta, Beale goes on to assert that 'no spiritual person has the authority to imprison free men, except in cases specially granted to them by the law or their commission ecclesiastical; nor should they punish except by the same authority'. And while he has no objection to anything they did to Papists, he proceeds to argue that their authority did not extend against 'honest and godly ministers'. The bishops — men, he bitterly complains, who 'will never reform anything' — had in these proceedings of theirs committed 'a most manifest praemunire'. 'Albeit they will not make us in anything beholding unto them by helping us in our petitions, yet I beseech you let us requite good for bad'. Let us — following the precedent of the Statute for the Submission of the Clergy when Cardinal Wolsey and the clergy fell into a praemunire — be suitors to her Majesty to pardon them on the payment of a 'favourable and easy fine and ransom'. Such arguments and sentiments, coming from a royal official, a Clerk of the Privy Council and one in frequent diplomatic employment, may give us an idea of the difficulties confronting the Queen.[1]

Either on the morning of the debate, or perhaps the day before — at any rate, when the subsidy bill was under consideration — an anonymous 'burgess' expounded the classical strategy of linking supply with redress of grievances, 'thinking', as he said, 'the opportunity very fit, the rather for that her Majesty, expecting a benevolence from them, would the sooner yield to their lawful and necessary petitions'. 'Our case is most lamentable', he went on, 'that — having the word of God sincerely preached among us and His sacraments rightly administered' (thanks, under God's merciful goodness, to the great care and industry of our most virtuously and godly disposed Sovereign) — 'such ministers should be about her Highness as not only will not inform her' of the abuses and enormities that are crept into the Church, 'but also do keep from her gracious sight' our humble petitions lately exhibited to the Lords of the Upper House. Displaying, if not subtlety then a naivety passing understanding, he continued: 'Without all doubts, if her Majesty had once read them, she could not, considering her zeal towards the building of the Lord's house, but with all speed cut off those abuses . . . For how can it be that she, whose study hath ever been, like a most natural mother towards her tender children, for the preservation of her subjects' bodies in health and tranquillity' could 'pass over the ruinating and everlasting overthrow of . . . her subjects' souls?' He urged the House to choose a delegation for the sole

[1] Additional MS. 48116 (Yelverton 131), fols. 154 seqq.

purpose of asking the Queen to read their petitions. He was confident that she would speedily redress their grievances.

Had Peter Wentworth been a Member of this Parliament, we
might have suspected such infatuated innocence to be his. He
was not, however, the sole Elizabethan to think like that. Our
reporter, Fitzwilliam, tells us that the speech 'made a deep
impression' on 'the minds of the whole assembly'.

Guileless men! If they had been present at Court on February
27th, their illusion would have been shattered. On that day the
Queen, in the presence of her principal Councillors, gave audience
to Archbishop Whitgift, three bishops, and representatives of the
Lower House of Convocation who came to her in her Privy
Chamber at Somerset Place to offer their clerical subsidy. Having
received the bill, Elizabeth remarked that 'she did accept of it
thankfully, and the rather that it came voluntarily and frankly,
whereas the laity must be entreated and moved thereunto': an
outburst of spleen, perhaps provoked by the desire of the Commons
to link supply with grievances.

'Madam', interjected Burghley, 'these men come with mites,
but we will come with pounds.'

'I esteem more of their mites', retorted Elizabeth, 'than of your
pounds, for that they came of themselves, not moved, but you
tarry till you be urged thereunto.' 'Whatsoever you have bestowed upon me', she added, turning to the clergy, 'I am to
bestow it upon you again. God grant I may bestow it to His glory
and the benefit of this Realm.'

Changing the subject, she said to the bishops: 'We understand
that some of the Nether House have used divers reproachful
speeches against you, tending greatly to your dishonour, which we
will not suffer; and that they meddle with matters above their
capacity, not appertaining unto them, for the which we will call
some of them to an accompt. And we understand they be coun-
tenanced by some of our Council' — Mildmay and Knollys must
certainly have been in her mind — 'which we will redress or else
uncouncil some of them.'

'But', she continued, 'we will not charge the whole House with
this disorder, for although there be some intemperate and rash
heads in that House, yet there be many wise and discreet men,
who do find just cause of grievance against some of you. First, in
that you have not greater care in making ministers, whereof some

be of such lewd life and corrupt behaviour' as not to be 'worthy
to come into any honest company': a comment which might
indicate that she had seen or been told of the Puritan survey of
the state of the clergy. 'Again' — and now her diatribe once more
embraced the Puritans — 'you suffer many ministers to preach
what they list and to minister the sacraments according to their
own fancies, some one way, some another, to the breach of unity:
yea, and some of them so curious in searching matters above their
capacity as they preach they wot not what — that there is no Hell
but a torment of conscience. Nay, I have heard there be six
preachers in one diocese the which do preach six sundry ways. I
wish such men to be brought to conformity and unity: that they
minister the sacraments according to the order of this Realm and
preach all one truth; and that such as be found not worthy to
preach, be compelled to read homilies . . . for there is more
learning in one of those than in twenty of some of their sermons.
And we require you that you do not favour such men, being
carried away with pity, hoping of their conformity, and inclining
to noblemen's letters and gentlemen's letters, for they will be
hanged before they will be reformed.'

'Then', our report says, 'she told how she had received a letter
from beyond the sea, written by one that bore her no good will —
"Would you knew who it were", quoth she, "for I saw and read
the letter" — who wrote that the Papists were of hope to prevail
again in England, for that her Protestants themselves misliked her.
"And indeed, so they do", quoth she, "for I have heard that some
of them of late have said that I was of no religion — neither hot
nor cold, but such a one as one day would give God the vomit. I
pray you, look unto such men. I doubt not but you will look unto
the Papists, for that they not only have spit at me (and that very
nearly) but at the whole Realm . . . There is an Italian proverb
which saith, From mine enemy let me defend myself; but from a
pretensed friend, good Lord deliver me. Both these" ', she continued, ' "join together in one opinion against me, for neither of
them would have me to be Queen of England. And as for these
curious and busy fellows, their preaching tendeth only to popularity." '

The Queen bade the bishops see to private conventicles.
Noticing that Aylmer, Bishop of London, was not present, she
added: 'I miss my Lord of London, who looketh no better unto

the City, where every merchant must have his schoolmaster and nightly conventicles, expounding scriptures and catechizing their servants and maids: insomuch, that I have heard how some of their maids have not sticked to control learned preachers and say that such a man taught otherwise in our house.'

'Madam', said Whitgift, 'for mine own part I will look unto these things as well as I can, and I will take such order with my brethren as I trust they will look better unto such things.' However, it was the guilty, not innocent, bishops who should be charged with the faults.

'Truly, my Lord,' broke in Burghley, 'her Majesty hath declared unto you a marvellous fault, in that you make, in this time of light, so many lewd and unlearned ministers.'

Elizabeth hastened to Whitgift's defence: 'My Lord of Canterbury said well. Draw articles and charge them with it that have offended.'

'I do not burthen them that be here', Burghley hastily explained; 'but it is the Bishop of Lichfield and Coventry that I mean' — the worldly William Overton — 'who made seventy ministers in one day for money: some tailors, some shoemakers and others craftsmen. I am sure the greatest part of them are not worthy to keep horses.'

After a further exchange between Whitgift and Burghley, the Archbishop pointed out that it was impossible to have learned ministers in all of England's thirteen thousand parishes.

'Jesus!' exclaimed Elizabeth, 'thirteen thousand! It is not to be looked for . . . My meaning is not [that] you should make choice of learned ministers only, for they are not to be found, but of honest, sober and wise men and such as can read the scriptures and homilies well unto the people.' With that she rose, thanked the bishops, and bade them farewell.[1]

An intimate glimpse behind the public scene, and a rare treasure among Elizabethan documents! It makes clear how disturbing was the effect of propaganda upon everyone; how the Queen loathed Puritans; how inflexible her hostility to their ultimate aims; how frayed by agitation were her nerves. There could be no better preface to the story as it now unfolds itself.

[1] S.P. Dom. Eliz. 176/68.

CHAPTER V

RELIGION
(CONTINUED)

At the end of the debate on February 25th the Commons had decided that their committee, 'calling to them such other grave Members of this House, learned in divinity and in the Common Laws of the Realm and also in Canon Law, as they shall think good', should meet to set down the insufficiency of Whitgift's answer and confer about further proceedings. They met and prepared a statement which dealt with Whitgift's answer point by point, as he had dealt with the articles of their petition.[1]

At this juncture, it behoves us to remember that Knollys and Mildmay and other responsible Members were on the committee, for the statement they composed — echoing Robert Beale's subversive Treatise — tended to exalt parliamentary statutes into the main, even on occasions the sole, source of ecclesiastical discipline, and to discredit, if not destroy, the whole body of Canon Law which preserved the Church as a self-sufficient power. The immediate reason is obvious. These men wanted Parliament to be a protective cover for their Puritan, non-conforming friends. But deeper than this motive was the inevitable drift in the new modern State towards sovereignty; and, since the Church was now nationalized, it was bound to be a drift towards secular sovereignty, unless, indeed, the State were to become theocratic — which, oddly enough, their friends, the Presbyterian-Puritans, would have tried to make it.

Here are some excerpts from the committee's statement that betray its subversive intent: 'No such oath of canonical obedience is required by the laws of this Realm, either Common Law or Statute Law. If any such oath be appointed by law, the same — as we take it — is by the Canon Law, which is not to be allowed. Concerning subscription: since it is confessed that the same is not warranted by the statutes of this Realm, we desire to know by what law the same should be warranted.' Whitgift had tersely declared that the refractory Puritan ministers had been justly

[1] D'Ewes, p. 360; Cromwell's diary.

deprived. 'We would be glad to know by what law', retorted the Commons. 'For, as we take it, they are not deprived by any Common Law or Statute Law of this Realm.' To Whitgift's ill-tempered and arrogant gibe at their youthfulness — a mode of argument he employed much too frequently — they replied by beseeching him and his fellow-bishops not to esteem them 'according to our particular persons — against whom they may except for years — but as a part of the great Council of the Realm assembled in the name of all the Commonalty; and to consider these our requests, not as proceeding from any of us in particular, but from all the Commons of the Realm in general.' If only Whitgift had been sufficiently imaginative to detect the dignity and menace in this retort! As one thinks of Archbishop Laud's fate, it might seem that only a generation in time saved his predecessor. It was all very well for the Queen to abuse her devoted Commons: Whitgift had neither the mystical station nor the personality to be her understudy.[1]

This remarkable document, foreshadowing England's future history, was finished on February 27th, the day Elizabeth had her bellicose audience with Whitgift and the clergy. How dramatic the possibilities!

But the committee's statement never even got to the House. It was a Saturday. On the Monday morning — March 1st — the Speaker, Serjeant Puckering, having taken physic the day before, sent word that he was in bed and unable, 'without danger of greater peril of extremity', to be at the House. But, when at noon he received a command from the Queen to attend on her at once at Greenwich, extremity or no extremity he rose from his bed and went. Fitzwilliam believed that 'some false brother' had reported their proceedings to Elizabeth: hence her abrupt action.[2]

The following morning the Speaker reported to the House, having taken the precaution to jot down notes of the Queen's remarks: one set compiled in collaboration with Sir Christopher Hatton, another with the help of Walsingham. His jottings ran as follows:[3]

'As she well understood I was your mouth, so she well knew I was your mouth by her allowance': yet with this 'caution and exception, to deal in all causes fit, but not in causes forbidden or

---

[1] Fitzwilliam's diary.　　　[2] D'EWES, p. 361; Cromwell's diary.
[3] B.M. Harleian MS. 6853, fols. 285-7. My text is a conflation of both.

restrained'. They had been commanded not to 'meddle with
matters of the Church, neither in reformation of religion or of
discipline'. She 'blamed me for reading such bills . . . and allowing the reading of such articles and motions'. She hoped she had
well answered their petitions, 'both by the mouth of my Lord
Treasurer and by the Archbishop of Canterbury'.

'To you all she willed me to say: She knows — and thinks you
know — she is Supreme Governor of this Church, next under
God' and 'hath full power and authority both . . . by law of the
Crown as by law positive, by statute, to reform any disorders in
the same.' She 'hopes you doubt not' that 'as she hath power so
hath she good will to . . . examine and to redress whatsoever may
be found amiss'.

'By sundry complaints, which she hath heard of, she is of
opinion that there is some cause of redress . . . But her Majesty
cannot choose but marvel' at 'these courses of your proceedings':
namely, that having given you 'so loving commandment not to
meddle with these matters of rites and discipline of the Church',
yet, 'this notwithstanding, you would attempt to deal by receipt
of petitions and public reading of the same, and with such kind of
proceeding', thus breaking her commandment, distrusting her
promise, and derogating from her authority.

'These great enormities' follow: 'the adversary [Papists] may
say that either we want yet sufficient laws to maintain our Church
doctrine and discipline, or, having it, that you mistrust her
Majesty's good execution of it, or else that you show yourselves
very undutifully' in using 'these means to call her ecclesiastical
government into these suspicions.'

'Her Majesty is greatly grieved that she hath occasion to cause
this thus to be delivered unto you, whom she doth know and
affirmeth to be as loving subjects as any prince in the world hath.
And therefore, of her great and tender favour, she could not
choose but as a mother over her children eftsoons to warn you to
forbear any further proceedings in this course: the rather for that
. . . it pertained least unto them, being the lowest of the three
estates.'

'Resolutely, she will receive no motion of innovation, nor alter
or change any law whereby the religion or church of England
standeth established at this day'; 'but yet, upon due course of
complaint' will 'see the execution of any law already made, or

whatsoever else she may do by her supreme authority to reform
what shall be amiss'. 'Due course of complaint' she defined as
'first to the bishop of the diocese, next to the Metropolitan, then
to the Council, and at length to the Queen'.

'She finds not only a discontentation in the third estate of the
Realm against the clergy in general, but that they have with
most undecent terms used the chief bishops, the principal members of this State: which she thinks fit to be reformed in the
particular offenders.' Her Privy Councillors also came in for
rebuke: 'She doth greatly blame my masters of her Council who
have suffered thus far proceeding and hath not moved the House
to some other course, more agreeable to the furtherance of the
cause and to their duty.'

From the lengthy account which Fitzwilliam gives, it would
seem that the Speaker, in the actual delivery of his report, while
retaining the firm quality of Elizabeth's message, managed to
inject a little more reasonableness into it and make the most of
affectionate passages. Where the Queen stood in relation to the
Anglican Church was stated with harsh clarity: 'As she knew the
doctrine preached in this Church of England to be as sincere as
might be possible, so she knew the discipline thereof not so perfect
as might be, but blameable as we of the House had complained.
Yet to redress it in such open manner as we sought, whereby the
whole state ecclesiastical might be overturned, or at the least
defaced, that she most disliked. For as she found it at her first
coming in, and so hath maintained it these twenty-seven years,
she meant in like state, by God's grace, to continue it and leave
it behind her.' Cold comfort for Puritans![1]

There was an addendum to the message. The Speaker, records
our anonymous diarist, told us also 'how she found fault both in
our negligence in coming to the Parliament House and departing
before the rising of the House; and also that she heard how
Parliament-matters was the common table-talk at ordinaries,
which was a thing against the dignity of the House'.[2]

In an arresting passage Fitzwilliam describes the reaction of
Members. 'With this message the House found themselves so
greatly moved and so deeply wounded as they could not devise

---

[1] Fitzwilliam's diary. Cromwell and the anonymous diary have accounts of the
message. D'Ewes is silent.
[2] B.M. Lansdowne MS. 43, fol. 170b.

which way to cure themselves again: for so their case stood, as either they must offend their gracious Sovereign, towards whom, in respect of their singular benefits that they received by her most blessed and happy government, they durst not so much as to lift up one evil thought or imagination; or else to suffer the liberties of their House to be infringed, whereby they should leave their children and posterity in thraldom and bondage, they themselves by their forefathers being delivered into freedom and liberty.

'By this conceit a great amazement fell among them, and sundry times many of them met in private sort to devise how they might salve this sore so grievously inflicted upon them. Many ways were invented. Some thought best to have the Speaker displaced, for that he durst enterprise to go to the Queen without the privity of the House. Other thought better to have some one stand up and openly to refuse the accepting of any such commandment from her Majesty, because it touched the liberty and freedom of the House. But one other, misliking both these courses — for that thereby an open division would grow between her Majesty and the subject, whereby great mischief might follow to the general state of the Realm — wished rather that some way might be wrought underhand that should as forcibly restore the liberty of the House as any violent action openly used; and therefore thought best that some bill, containing matter for the reformation of the abuses of the Church — which were the things principally forbidden and whereby the liberties of the House were touched — might be drawn and presented; and that [such a bill], there read, would sufficiently restore the ancient liberties again to the House. This opinion was allowed.'

Fitzwilliam's commentary is worthy of place among the *morceaux choisies* of parliamentary history. Long might we ponder it: its revelation of an unofficial, and presumably substantial caucus, meeting in private to devise a policy — a misdemeanour akin to conspiracy in those days, and punishable; the novel, nay, the impudent doctrine that the Speaker should not obey a royal summons without the privity, and, one assumes, the assent of the House; the proposal to depose him from office; finally, the plan for rejecting, by formal motion, a command from the Sovereign. Paul and Peter Wentworth had not sown sterile seed. These startling ideas, though abandoned out of prudence and an idolatrous affection for their Queen, are profoundly significant.

WILLIAM FITZWILLIAM
The parliamentary diarist in later life

Even were we to assess them as no more than the vapourings of hot-headed youth, they nevertheless reflect the mentality and tactics of rebellion.

The rebels did, in fact, carry out their plan to launch a bill on religion. But if we are to savour their audacity to the full we must broaden our story and at this point tell also of other bills that they introduced this session. On February 22nd, the day they heard of Whitgift's unsatisfactory answer to their petition — doubtless having preliminary knowledge of its character — they had given a first reading to two anti-episcopal bills. The first compelled every archbishop and bishop to take an oath in Chancery for his due obedience to the Queen and for equal and due administration of his official duties, and forbade bishops to swear canonical obedience to an archbishop. It was evidently an attempt to give substance to their revolutionary theory that the Church should be controlled by the Common and Statute Law. What effrontery! The bill was read a second time and ingrossed on February 26th. Their second measure was directed against excessive fees in ecclesiastical courts. It prescribed a scale of charges, and by a further provision — where their brazenness was again manifest — forbade bishops to make visitations except in person, and that only 'upon just causes complained of'. In addition to these two bills, they had, on February 26th, read a third one, which permitted marriage at all times of the year. This was a favourite objective for Puritans, who bristled at every remnant of Papal practice left in their Church.[1]

If she had heard of the third bill, Elizabeth may have thought that she could afford to turn a blind eye to it. It passed the Commons. In the Lords it was not even read.[2] The other two bills, however, were too much for her stomach; and understandably so. In her message given to the Speaker on March 1st she ordered him not to accord them any further reading and commanded the House not to call for them.[3]

We are now in a position to appreciate the action of our rebel caucus. A general prohibition on ecclesiastical matters; a ban on two specific bills: what audacity to launch yet another religious bill! But they were astute in their choice of subject. The measure

[1] Cromwell's diary; D'Ewes, pp. 360-1, 371.
[2] D'Ewes, p. 367; Cromwell's diary (March 15th, 16th); *L.J.* ii. 99.
[3] Harleian MS. 6853, fol. 287; Cromwell's diary. The former appears to make the two bills into one; the latter leaves no doubt that both were banned.

was entitled, 'An Act for the better execution of a statute made in the 13th year of the Queen's Majesty's reign for reformation of certain disorders touching ministers of the Church'. It provided for the 'punishment of such as desire to be admitted to any benefice, not being qualified according to 13 Elizabeth': and the punishment? — it appears to have been the drastic one of a £20 fine, imprisonment for a year, and disablement for ever. While ostensibly a mere reinforcement of existing statutory law, it encroached upon the sphere of ecclesiastical discipline by using the machinery of the secular State to remedy one of the principal grievances in their sixteen-clause petition. As Whitgift later explained, it provided for the trial of a minister's sufficiency by 'twelve laymen': a subversive and horrifying proposal.[1]

The bill, Fitzwilliam tells us, 'was delivered to the Speaker with a full conclusion among themselves that, if the Speaker should refuse the accepting thereof, then that party who first devised this course should, with a speech which he had prepared, have maintained the liberties of the House to the uttermost'. In other words, the caucus was prepared to fight a pitched battle on this issue. The Speaker seems to have sat on the bill for a week or a fortnight, and we must conclude that he turned for advice to the Privy Councillors in the House. The test came on March 18th when the bill was called for and a motion was moved to read it. Thereupon an anonymous Member — 'a burgess' — objected that its title clearly indicated that it came within the Queen's prohibition and should not be read. This officious gentleman may well have been our old acquaintance Francis Alford, for later that year we find him successfully soliciting a lay prebend at Wells from its holder Toby Matthew, Dean of Durham, and the argument he used to obtain the consent of the Bishop of Wells to the transaction was his 'service to the Church the last Parliament'. The reaction to this discordant Member was notable, perhaps even terrifying. No one bothered to answer him, but 'with a general voice through the House the bill was called on to the reading, which it then received'.[2]

This was as near to rebellion as such ardent worshippers of their Queen could attain; and since nothing seems to have been hidden

---

[1] D'Ewes, p. 370; Cromwell's diary; Lansdowne MS. 43, fol. 166; STRYPE, *Whitgift*, i. 391.
[2] Inner Temple, Petyt MS. 538/10, fols. 16, 76, 78.

from Elizabeth, we can only conclude that she, as well as a distraught Speaker and the Councillors on the front bench, thought discretion the better part of valour.

The bill was read a second time next day and sent forward to a committee, Sir Francis Knollys in charge. Back the following day as a new bill, it was read twice, and at the next sitting, on March 22nd, was read a third time and 'after many arguments' passed. The rapidity, the instancy of this procedure! Apparently there were two debates: on the second reading of the original bill and on the third reading of the new one. Our anonymous diarist, whose jottings are undated and scattered, has preserved some fragments. Probably it was during the first debate that attacks upon the bishops brought Francis Alford to his feet. Referring to the incompetence of ministers, 'The bishops', he asserted, 'are not in the blame that is laid upon them, for it is the gentlemen that are patrons' of benefices. If the bishops refuse to induct their nominees, a writ of *quare impedit* lies against them. To this Sir Walter Mildmay retorted that the whole blame was not on gentlemen-patrons. The original fault was in the bishops, 'for the gentlemen can present none but ministers', and all ministers were of episcopal making. An unidentified speaker moved that patrons presenting unqualified ministers should be penalized. 'He did it', comments our diarist, 'upon no other intent but to overthrow the bill': that is to say, if a penalty had been imposed on lay patrons, many of the lukewarm Members of the House would, in defence of their own class, have turned against the bill.

The prolonged third-reading debate brought out our old friend, Recorder Fleetwood; and in view of the circumstances of the bill, the support of this influential, but by now conservative, leader is impressive. He had been on the committee. His speech was characteristic. 'I remember' — said he — about the first year of this Queen 'I was in commission to visit the English clergy, *tam in capite quam in membris*, and there we had four sorts:

> graduates — and all they were written in two lines;
> *pii et docti* [devout and learned] — and they in six lines;
> *penitus indocti* [wholly ignorant] — two skins of parchment —
> dizzards [fools] and idiots;
> *criminosi* — that is, drunkards, whoremongers.

And at that time we put out one bishop, the Bishop of Peterborough. Pius IV' — he went on, dragging in the inevitable anecdote — 'lying extreme sick, said, "I will tell you within these three hours whether there be a god or no; whether there be a soul or no; whether there be a hell and a heaven or no." This was one of their chief bishops. I pray you, Mr. Speaker,' he concluded, 'let us have a new commission. At least, let us pass this bill. If they stay it above, let them. *In magnis, voluisse satis est* [in great matters, it is enough to have wished to do right].'

The irrepressible, unchanging Alford got to his feet. 'We speak much of duty, but we do none. In other countries the sheep be so well taught and are so dutiful they will follow their shepherd through a market town. But our sheep will teach their shepherd. He cannot drive them before him; but if one fall a-leaping a ditch or hedge, all the rest will follow, though they break their necks for it. I like not of these verbal sermons', he said, turning his criticism to the Puritan emphasis on preaching. 'I dare boldly affirm it, one homily doth more edify than one hundred of these verbal sermons.'

James Dalton, no longer among the radicals, dissociated himself from the Puritan party: 'I am not of that faction.' The bill 'tends indirectly to thrust out two thousand ministers. Then what becomes of the sacraments, baptism, burial?'

'It will become of burial', interjected Alford, 'as one did that threw him into the earth and said, "Farewell Anthony!" ' 'That place' — he added, citing the scriptural passage, 'He that sets his hand to the plough' — 'is meant that none can be put out of the ministry.'

'He is worthy to be disabled for ever', retorted Mildmay, 'that will presume to intend himself into so high a calling, being unfit.'

'Where will you have sufficient number to supply [all benefices]?' asked Dalton.

'You may have a good many out of the Inns of Court', broke in Strickland.

'The livings of two thousand parishes in England', Alford replied, 'are but £8 by [the] year. How can you place a learned man there?'

'There is none of £8 in the Queen's books', retorted Mildmay, 'but is worth £20. Besides, who will not contribute to a learned minister? The law' — he seems to have added, presumably referring to this bill — 'would not be suffered to look back and put out such as were in.'

This cut and thrust of debate — a rare surviving specimen — might be thought more appropriate to the proceedings of a committee, but it looks as if it took place in the House. Indeed, it may have been the occasion of a note by our anonymous diarist: 'When two replied, one to the other', there was objection. 'It is against the order: you ought not to colloquy so'.[1]

The bill passed the Commons, probably by an overwhelming voice, and next day was given a reading in the Lords.[2] By great good fortune we are afforded a glimpse of what happened there. Fitzwilliam tells us that the bill 'was greatly inveighed against by the Archbishop of Canterbury, Dr. Whitgift, in the selfsame course that the burgess which withstood it at the first in the Lower House used'. In other words, he invoked the Queen's ban on such measures: typical of the working of his disciplinarian's mind.

And now we are given a unique historical item — an account of the famous Earl of Leicester in action in the House of Lords; and perhaps it may be taken as a measure of what we have lost by the silence that engulfs the Elizabethan Upper House. He replied to Whitgift, 'seeming much to mislike the Bishop's order of dealing in that nature, which rather tended to move her Majesty to offence towards the Commons than yielded any good reason why the same should not proceed. For, said he, evermore hath it been accounted a thing most necessary that when a statute, standing in force, hath any ambiguity in it or wanteth force for the better executing itself, the same should be explained or strengthened by another statute. Otherwise, the doubts that may thereby grow or the want of power to perform the intent will rather breed offence to the Commonwealth than good, contrary to the mind and intent of them that first invented the law. And that this bill now in hand importeth no other thing is most plain and evident.'

Not, alas, a very presentable summary of what was probably a vigorous, and may have been a venomous, attack on Whitgift, whom Leicester disliked, for a variety of reasons, some factious. But it shows how shrewd the caucus leaders had been in framing their test bill.

'This', Fitzwilliam added, 'was the last speech that was heard

---

[1] Lansdowne MS. 43, fols. 164, 166, 171, 173b.
[2] For the readings, see D'EWES, pp. 370-1; Cromwell's diary; L.J. ii. 105.

... touching that bill; wherewith the Lower House held themselves satisfied, who nothing so much regarded the consummating thereof ... as they joyed in its passage from their House to the Lords, whereby their wounded liberty had now received health and safety.'

However, the Commons had not finished being a nuisance to the bishops and a trial to the Queen. In her message, delivered by the Speaker on March 2nd, Elizabeth had ordered both Speaker and House to cease proceedings in the bill against excessive fees in ecclesiastical courts. They obeyed: but only temporarily. On March 22nd they revived the bill, giving it a second reading and committing it. This was indeed to emphasize their revolt against the Queen's ban. One can only conclude that the spirit of rebellion was so manifest that Speaker and Councillors were all paralysed. Perhaps, in their quandary, Councillor-Members stayed off the committee, hoping not to compromise themselves too deeply: at any rate, the committee was packed with Puritans — Beale, Strickland, Lawrence Tomson, James Morice — and it was a Puritan, William Stoughton, who brought the bill in again on March 26th and therefore may be presumed to have acted as chairman.[1]

This was not all. On March 24th a first reading was given to a bill which, as the diarist Cromwell describes it, enacted 'that preachers reading the Articles appointed to be read by [the statute of] 13 Elizabeth shall not be expulsed though they read them not before'. What appears to be the draft of this bill survives, showing that its purpose was to protect 'many able, godly and zealous ministers and preachers' deprived, or likely to be deprived for lack of proof that they had obeyed the statute. It was clearly an attempt to place the secular law behind Puritans who were willing to subscribe to the doctrinal Articles, as specified in the Act of 1571, but unwilling to obey Whitgift's demand for subscription to all thirty-nine Articles. It even empowered patrons of benefices to resist such deprivations. The bill was avowedly 'for the more security of the godly and learned ministers'. To countenance it by a formal reading was remarkable. But it got no further. In any case, there was hardly time left to go on with it.[2]

Everything points to the conclusion that the House had got

---

[1] D'EWES, pp. 371, 373; Cromwell's diary.
[2] Lansdowne MS. 105, fols. 195b-8.

quite out of control. Whitgift, watching events and presumably shaken by Leicester's trenchant criticism in the Lords, was afraid. On March 24th he sent a call for help to the Queen. 'May it please your Majesty', ran the opening phrase of his letter, 'notwithstanding the charge of late given by your Highness to the Lower House of Parliament for dealing in causes of the Church . . .' Evidently fearing from Leicester's speech that the bill about the qualifications of ministers might pass the Lords, he mentioned that measure first, pointing out that, besides handing over control to laymen, it had the 'inconvenience' that if passed by Parliament 'it cannot hereafter but in Parliament be altered'. Then he referred to the bill for marriage at all times of the year, criticizing it as 'contrary to the old canons continually observed among us'; and thirdly to the bill about fees in ecclesiastical courts, 'now in hand' in the Lower House. 'Continue your gracious goodness towards us', he begged Elizabeth.[1]

She did. By one means or another the three offending bills were stayed in their course. The close of the session was at hand, and may perhaps have been hastened to prevent further mischief. At any rate, the Commons (but not the Lords) received a royal command not to sit on Saturday, March 27th, and on the Monday afternoon the Parliament was prorogued. Only two bills concerning the Church had passed the Lords as well as the Commons. Elizabeth vetoed them both.[2]

[1] STRYPE, *Whitgift*, i. 391-2.   [2] D'EWES, pp. 373-4.

CHAPTER VI

OTHER BUSINESS:
END OF THE SESSION

THOUGH the main battle with authority was fought over the Church, there were other contests in which the Commons made a striking display of their prowess. Small matters, perhaps; but our narrative would be the poorer without them.

Our first story concerns a bill against fraudulent conveyances, the purpose of which was to give the Queen and her subjects protection and effective remedy against dishonest people who sold land without disclosing secret encumbrances upon it: a form of villainy facilitated by the excessively technical and complicated nature of legal practice in landholding. Mercifully, its details need not worry us. It was a government measure, drawn by the Queen's learned counsel and approved by Elizabeth, who, as Lord Burghley later told the Commons, 'used to call it her own bill'. It was introduced into the House of Lords in late November, committed on its second reading, with Burghley in charge, and reappeared as a new bill, which was duly read three times. As Burghley said, it had been 'very maturely and advisedly digested in the Upper House, with the privity and assistance of the judges there attending'. It was sent down to the Commons, 'specially recommended' by their Lordships. Could any measure have had weightier authority behind it?[1]

In the Commons it was read a first time on December 14th. Nothing was said. On February 8th it came to its second reading, and a storm broke. It was 'long debated and greatly impugned'. 'Away with it!' Members cried. Their angry demonstration was directed against an encroachment by the prerogative. For the bill provided that victims of fraudulent conveyances could complain in the Star Chamber and that the order or judgment of twelve members of that Court should be as effectual as any Act of Parliament. It meant transferring — or at any rate, extending — jurisdiction from the Common Law Courts to the Star Chamber; and though the latter was incomparably better able to probe

---

[1] *L.J.* ii. 65-72; D'EWES, pp. 338, 350.

questions of fraud, this particular type involved the ownership of property. By a fundamental principle of the constitution life, limb, and property were the preserve of the Common Law Courts. To allow the Star Chamber to trespass here — and, what is more, to do so with statutory authority and with its judgments binding on the Common Law Courts (for they were to be as effectual as any Act of Parliament) — would be political suicide: the spectre of Death stalking in the House of Liberty. It seems astonishing that Burghley — the presumptive parent of the bill — did not foresee the opposition. Perhaps he did, hoping, however, to bemuse the Commons with a show of authority. It was essentially an administrator's measure, not a statesman's: unless, indeed, the statesman were a 'prerogative-man', which Burghley was not.[1]

Fragments of the debate have come down to us. Recorder Fleetwood was one of the speakers. 'He that speaks of the sudden to a bill of weight', he began, 'may be gravelled, as I am like to be.' Thereupon he went off on one of his antiquarian perambulations: 'The Star Chamber is so called of a serpent called *Stellio* — so *Camera Stellionis*; and not of *Stella*, stars. For, as that serpent biting the finger, it must be cut off, so there must be speedy redress in causes.' What he said when he came to the point — as presumably he did — we are not told.

Dalton followed, surely happy in being for once with the majority: 'I see this bill is of great weight and therefore we had need to advise and advise again of it; and therefore neither let us commit it nor cast it away, but let it sleep till the next Parliament. I confess fraud is to be detected, detested and punished. But, as that is an ill medicine which cureth one disease and breeds ten worse in the body, so this bill. A man would be content to take a little poison to expel a great deal, but not the contrary.'[2]

Our witty and delightful diarist has left some drafts of speeches which he himself appears to have made this session. Alas! even in these his identity is masked, though he reveals that he sat on the higher benches in the lower part of the House: furthest from the Speaker, where lesser folk sat and the obstreperous young gentlemen from the West Country formed a Cave of Adullam. One of his speeches belongs to this debate. He had little to contribute,

---

[1] Cromwell's diary, December 14th, February 8th; S.P. Dom. Eliz. 176/34.
[2] B.M. Lansdowne MS. 43, fol. 165.

beyond asking, on his own behalf and for those sitting about him, that speakers would stretch their voices and speak as loudly as they reasonably could. 'Without hearing we cannot understand them, nor without understanding cannot give our consents; but shall be like those that hear service in a strange tongue and say "Amen" to that they understand not. When they think they pray to our Lord, they shall say "Amen" to a prayer made to our Lady . . . We see by experience that we are driven many times to rise, both to our distaste and disturbance of those that sit beneath us': presumably he meant that they had to leave their seats and stand on the floor to hear. 'We see, also, we are constrained many times . . . to cry "Speak out! Speak out!"': whereunto, as it hath been said that we must bring our ears with us, so they may better bring their tongues with them. It was moved', he went on, 'to know how far men might tell the secrets of the House: it is needless to us, for we can tell none, for we hear none.'

He then came to the bill. 'It hath been told us that it was drawn, perused, considered and passed [in the Lords], that it is a bill of great necessity and consequence to the Commonwealth. Again, it hath been told us' by others 'that it is very dangerous, full of inconveniences [and] impossibly great burdens to the subjects; [involving the] overthrow of the Common Law', and bringing 'as it were Westminster Hall into the Star Chamber . . . Where the truth is, that I trust every man desires to know.'[1]

As our diarist indicates, the bill did not lack weighty support. The Solicitor General, Thomas Egerton, was censorious: 'Many that spake to the bill understood it not; but much more they that cried "Away with it!" Therefore it was in them levity and rashness.' Let us commit it. To behave in this way stands not with the gravity of the House, nor with wisdom.

Egerton's recourse to the heavy hand brought the redoubtable mathematician, Thomas Digges, to his feet: 'I will not speak to the body [of the bill]: it is neither within my profession nor reach. I reverence, as becomes me, the Lords.' Yet, 'let us hold our liberties left us by our fathers; and when a number do cry "Away with the bill!" — as they may well — for any particular Member to say "This is levity and rashness in them", I say this is levity and rashness in him to say so. Therefore, put it [the bill] to the question.'[2]

---

[1] Lansdowne MS. 43, fol. 178b.   [2] Ibid. fol. 170.

Perhaps the speech by Digges ended the debate: a frequent happening. At any rate, it sustained the temper and temperature of the rebels. When the question was put, the bill was denied a commital by 156 voices to 140, and so lay moribund.[1]

A week later, on February 15th, the Lords asked for and obtained immediate conference 'in a matter of great importance'. In pontifical manner Lord Burghley addressed the delegation, saying — as it was afterwards reported to the Commons — that their Lordships of the Upper House, 'being of such quality and calling as they are known to be', were one member of Parliament, the knights and burgesses, representing the whole Commons of the Realm, were another, and her Majesty the head. These three estates were able to make laws, but neither of the two Houses without the other. 'Of ancient courtesy and custom' the Houses, in matter of doubt, had used mutual conference. A touch of caution now entered his censure: 'By speeches abroad, not out of this House (for they are not to take knowledge of anything in this House)' they had heard of their bill being denied a committal by the Commons; at which 'their Lordships do greatly marvel and think it very strange, not having known the like course used . . . before'. The offence was the greater because of the importance and the circumstances of the bill: which he proceeded to elaborate. He ended by requesting them to give further consideration to it, either by conference with the Lords or otherwise, and asked for an early answer. He was sure that they had misunderstood the measure and that the Lords could explain it to their satisfaction.

When, next day, the Commons tried to get an answer to their petition about the Church, they were told that it would be given after the Lords had received an answer about their bill; and it was this ultimatum which led Sir Walter Mildmay to give his fellow-Members a lead. In his opinion there were only two courses open to them: to give the Lords' bill a third reading and put it to the question for passing, without alteration; or to abandon that bill and frame a new one to their liking. His speech started a debate, which, 'the time being very far spent', was ultimately adjourned till the morrow.

Next day they were too busy, and it was not until February 18th that Mildmay managed to revive the matter with another speech,

[1] D'Ewes, p. 346.

in which he reviewed the whole situation. Though for his part —
as he confessed — he would have liked to see the bill committed,
he defended the action of the House and asserted their right either
to seek conference with the Lords, or not, as they thought fit.
This was the lead the Commons required, and they now despatched
their answer to the Lords. They declared they had 'in all parts
and points of their dealing . . . proceeded discreetly, gravely and
orderly, according to the liberties of this House, without any
errors . . . or cause of offence.' They wished to deal with the
subject of fraud, but not in the manner and form of the Lords'
bill; and therefore they purposed to frame a bill of their own.[1]

It was the answer Burghley might have expected. He might
equally have expected the form of the new bill that the Commons
proceeded to frame in committee. They took the Star Chamber
clean out of it. The Common Law Courts — Westminster Hall—
repelled the invader. When the bill reached the Upper House,
the Lords wanted to make some amendments, but did not dare
proceed without asking for a preliminary conference. Of these
amendments the only significant one was the proviso which comes
at the end of the statute: 'Provided that [neither] this Act nor
anything therein contained shall extend in any sort to restrain or
impair the jurisdiction, power or authority of the Court of Star
Chamber'.[2]

What had started as an assault on Westminster Hall ended in
what Burghley feared might prove a restraint on the Star Chamber.
The Commons could afford to give him his proviso. It remains one
of the minor monuments erected on the triumphal way of English
liberty.

Frustration was Burghley's lot in this Parliament. It is the
theme of our next story, and of subsequent ones also. Let us
recall what a to-do there had been in the Parliament of 1563 over
the Act establishing Wednesday as an extra fish day — 'Cecil's
Fast'; and what great difficulty had been encountered through
Puritan revulsion against a Popish practice, along with gastro-
nomic objection to government-inflicted abstemiousness. Let us
also recall that as soon as Cecil departed to the Upper House
the Commons, with eloquent celerity, had passed a bill 'against
Wednesdays'. Burghley had successfully blocked this in the Lords.

---

[1] D'EWES, pp. 349-53 passim.
[2] Ibid. pp. 361-3, 369, 371; Cromwell's diary; *Statutes of the Realm*, IV. i. 711.

Now the day of reckoning had come. The Act expired with the Parliament of 1584-85 and was among those which the government wished to be revived, continued, explained or perfected.[1]

The course of events is not without obscurities. However, on December 1st the Commons appointed a committee to consider this question of expiring statutes. It was composed of lawyers, and was singularly free from iconoclasts. The Solicitor General may have put across the government's plans — perhaps even a government-prepared bill — with little trouble. At any rate, their bill — which was given a first reading later that month — was in all probability a simple one, merely prolonging the required statutes, among them the Act of 1563.

It was February when we next find mention of the bill, then back in the hands of the committee. Three provisoes had appeared, including, it seems, the fatal one that abolished the Wednesday fish-day by repealing the appropriate provision in the Act of 1563. The Queen herself now intervened. In her message delivered on March 2nd there was a passage: that she thought 'the continuance of the Wednesday to be [a] fish-day was very necessary and commended it to the House'.

At this juncture Sir Christopher Hatton appeared on the committee; and it was he who brought in a new bill on March 5th. It seems likely that as a result of the Queen's message and his persuasive powers the Wednesday fish-day — whose tussle with death was becoming something of a comedy — was reprieved. At any rate, next day we find mention of a proviso by Strickland; which, surely, can only mean a renewed *coup de grâce* for 'Wednesdays'. On March 11th, when the bill was read a second time, back it was sent to the committee, with Strickland added to the membership. When it re-emerged next day, we know that it abolished 'Wednesdays', and in that form it passed the Commons.[2]

The diarist Fitzwilliam wrote a summary of the rival arguments voiced in the Commons, perhaps at the second-reading debate on March 11th. To the government's contention 'that thereby the navy of England was maintained', it was answered 'that the Wednesday was never kept and therefore the navy could not be thereby maintained'. The example of Holland and Zeeland being cited — grown 'mighty by sea' through fishing —

[1] Cf. my *Elizabeth I and her Parliaments, 1559-81*, pp. 114-16, 225.
[2] D'EWES, pp. 334, 340, 355-6, 363-7; Cromwell's diary.

the critics asked, Did they keep the Wednesday? No, it was
answered; and that argument collapsed. 'The trade of fishing bred
up the best mariners to serve by sea', it was urged. To which
came the reply, that when a great number of mariners were
pressed for naval service, most were taken from the wherry- and
barge-men and fewest from fishermen, who were 'weak and poor
creatures, not able to endure any long hardness' and unaccustomed
to the type of service in 'the greater vessels'. If the Wednesday
was put down, argued the government party, many fishing towns
would be utterly overthrown. Wednesday or no Wednesday,
retorted their opponents, dainty fish could be sold in London any
day of the week, witness 'our great feasts and banquets'; while
ordinary fish, being cheaper than flesh, would be bought by the
poor. There was a final, telling argument from the critics: many
of the inland shires, they said, were unable to observe the law
and thus laid themselves open to the blackmailing activities of
promoters.[1]

The omens were bad. However, when the Lords took up the
bill, they asked for a conference; and then Burghley, by way of
compromise, drafted a new proviso, maintaining Wednesday as
a fish-day, though only for places within twenty-five miles of the
sea and for the cities of London, York and Bristol. As a sop to the
critics, the penalties were drastically scaled down. The proviso
(or a new bill embodying it) was given a formal first reading in
the Lords on March 20th. If this be a sign that Burghley was
angry and inclined to stand no nonsense, a few days' reflection
must have taught him discretion. On the 24th, the Commons
having been summoned to a new conference, he did his best to
win them over. A debate must have taken place when the delegation reported back; but the Commons remained obdurate. No
option was now left to the Lords but to abandon Burghley's
'new bill' and pass the one from below.[2]

'Wednesdays' were at last abolished. Like previous Acts of a
similar nature, this one was to endure only to the end of the next
Parliament. When that time arrived — and again at the subsequent Parliament — Members showed that they had long
memories, for though the general text of the new bills, by continuing this Act of 1584-85, kept Wednesdays safely dead, a

[1] Northants Record Soc. MS. F.(M).P. 192.
[2] S.P. Dom. Eliz. 177/33; L.J. ii. 100, 103, 106; D'EWES, pp. 371-2.

special clause to that effect was inserted on each occasion, thus inflicting two mortal strokes, for good measure.[1]

Burghley was rebuffed over two other bills which had their origin in the Lords. They dealt with devices for defrauding the Queen of revenue from wardships. Being Master of the Court of Wards, presumably he was responsible for them. Only one has a story. All we know about the other is that it seems to have got no further than a first reading in the Commons.[2]

The bill we are to follow made land held from the Crown by knight service and leased for more than a hundred years liable to wardship.[3] It was to be retrospective in application. Why it aroused opposition can be readily understood. Wardship was a burden of a social as well as financial character, which became increasingly detested as the feudal age, to which it was appropriate, grew more and more remote. It was antiquated, irrational; a greater benefit to officials and speculators than to the Crown; an anxiety to parents, a breeding-ground of corruption. Since the possession of any portion of land, no matter how small, held by knight service of the Crown, subjected its owner and the whole of his estate to wardship, this form of tenure became an encumbrance, interfering with a ready sale. And land was the most common form of wealth, in which there was always an active market. People in the fortunate position of being immune from wardship were not likely to bring so malign a burden on themselves and their heirs, if they could avoid it. Consequently, owners of land thus encumbered hit on the device of disposing of it by way of a long lease, which left the purchaser unaffected. From the Crown's point of view the practice threatened to convert wardship from an expanding to a static, or even diminishing, source of income; and though socially such a result was most desirable, compensating revenue could not be found.

The Lords cannot have been enthusiastic about the bill. True, they were more or less all irredeemably subject to wardship, and in so far were less affected than many of the Commons. But as potential sellers of land their interests were the same. As a House, however, they were evidently incapable of resisting the pressure of the Crown and its spokesman, Burghley.

[1] 29 Eliz. cap. 5, sec. iii, 31 Eliz. cap. x, sec. ii (*Statutes of the Realm*, IV. ii. 770, 809).
[2] *L.J.* ii. 101-4; Cromwell's diary, March 23rd.
[3] For the gist of the bill, see Cromwell's diary, March 18th, etc.

In the Commons the bill ran into difficulty on its second reading. Mr. Williams — probably the Member for Brecon, and a lawyer with a distinguished career before him — was against it: whereupon — records our anonymous diarist — the cry went up, 'Away with it!' Richard Kingsmill, Attorney of the Court of Wards, rose in defence, among other arguments declaring that it was no more than an explanation of the Common Law and therefore not a new burden. To this Fleetwood replied. Kingsmill, he said, 'spake good reason but it was not law', for if it was, what need was there for the bill? He did not like 'these bills that look backward . . . None of your old statutes look back'. With that, he went off on an antiquarian discourse, pointed by a merry tale and a reminiscence: a gross irrelevance, though the House loved it. 'I think you would be content to hear me these two hours', he appreciatively added. 'Many', he went on, 'do not make leases so much to avoid wardships as [to avoid] fines for alienation, for upon years they pay none. Leases for years forfeits in [case of] outlawry . . . : then set the hare's head against the geese-giblets.' A noncommittal speech, it seems. The Solicitor General, as became him, was for the bill. He wanted it committed. It had been digested by the judges; and 'we must consider what is justice and equity in the case'. He then dilated upon the history of wardship, and told how in the past men had hit upon a device to defeat it 'by enfeoffing their son and heir fraudulently: whereupon a statute [was] made'. Why should not we now provide a remedy when a new kind of fraud arises? 'I see no reason', he added, 'why a statute might not look back if there be reason why it should.'[1]

The bill was committed, with Hatton and Mildmay on the committee to watch over the government's interests; there was a conference with the Lords; a new bill was drawn. This in turn being committed and amended after a first reading, came in due course to its final reading.[2]

We have some notes which appear to be of the debate on that occasion. Richard Grafton, Member for Tregony, was against the bill. It was 'beneficial to officers of the Court', he said. This brought Kingsmill to his feet. 'I trust I shall be accounted an honest, poor man', he pleaded. 'For any profit I get in my office, more than the dignity of serving her Majesty, I would another

[1] Lansdowne MS. 43, fol. 166.   [2] D'EWES, pp. 370, 372-3; Cromwell's diary.

had it. I have gotten no lease since I was officer.' It was the sort of lament customary with Elizabethan officials, whose not inconsiderable gains were never commensurate with their great expectations.

Francis Bacon spoke: the first parliamentary speech by this immortal of which there is any record. 'Many rather mislike of jealousy and are timorous of that they conceive not': the authentic voice of the essayist. Our diarist evidently disliked the young prig. 'I will open plainly to you that this bill is harder in some point', said Bacon. 'If', exclaims our diarist, 'he had as substantially answered that as he confessed it plainly!' Speaking of the Queen's worthiness to be respected, Bacon, by way of illustration, remarked that 'his father had received, by her, ability to leave a fifth son [enough] to live upon. But', he added, 'that is nothing to the matter'. 'Then', the diarist caustically remarks, 'you should have let it alone.' Perhaps the generality of the House reacted in the same way to this *début* of a genius.

Recorder Fleetwood added a characteristic speech, beginning with the remark that the bill had been spoken to by many, very learnedly, and then wandering off into irrelevancies, in the course of which he praised the Court of Wards for its justice, its discretion and its mercy. 'I have found it so in mine own case, or else I might have had that laid on my back [which] would have made it crack.' 'Let us give her Majesty her due revenue, or else she must have subsidies and fifteenths.' 'I could put you a thousand cases upon this point', he concluded; 'for I was a moot-man thirty years together. But I'll let it go and tell you plainly, Mr. Speaker, the bill is a very good bill.' The Solicitor General added his persuasion: 'If I did think it would wrong or prejudice the subject any way, I would not allow of it or give my consent. For, though I am an officer of her Majesty, yet I have children and may have land to leave them.' Mr. Edmund Saunders, a Surrey gentleman, followed: 'I will not speak against the bill, but I see many doubt of it. It is of great weight. It toucheth every man's lands.' It was now the last real day of business for the House, and, as Sanders pointed out, the majority of the lawyer-Members were absent. He was therefore for leaving the bill in suspense and telling the Lords so.[1]

Despite this face-saving suggestion, the bill was put to the

[1] Lansdowne MS. 43, fol. 175.

question and was dashed, 75 voting for and 95 against it. All the government's efforts, and the modifications made in committee, had been vain.[1]

Our theme is continued in the instant hostility shown by the Commons to two bills concerned with printing. The first may have come from the Stationers' Company, which by royal letters patent possessed very nearly a monopoly control of printing. The bill sought to strengthen the privileges and orders of the Company by giving them statutory authority. In any case, a measure which could weight the scales more heavily against the clandestine Puritan press was unlikely to be welcomed in the House of Commons; but there seems also to have been a preamble referring to books critical of the Church, and that certainly rang the alarm bell.[2]

Our anonymous diarist, not unfavourable to the measure, composed, and probably delivered, a speech about it. 'And please you, Mr. Speaker', he began, 'I heard a good old Parliament-man say once, that many penal statutes are very like unto nets, which being made to catch crows, do often times take pigeons.' Some Members, he went on, are afraid that a like effect would follow from this bill. If its preamble were retained and censors were not marvellous men of great knowledge and conscience, a book might be adjudged 'a disturber of the Church' which in fact tended to 'the propagation of the Church'. 'It was said by Ahab to Elias that he troubled and disturbed Israel: he answered, "Nay, it is thee and thy father's house that disturb Israel." ' Our speaker wanted 'this quarrelling head cut clear off and some other framed, fitter for the body'.[3]

Other Members were not so acquiescent. Against his entry of the bill, Thomas Cromwell notes: 'first read and very much misliked'. Apparently, it progressed no further.[4]

After their experience with this bill, government leaders ought to have been prepared for the fate of the other one. It dealt with slanderous books and libels. There had been a bill 'against slanderous libelling' introduced in the Lords in December, perhaps occasioned by the infamous libel against the Earl of Leicester, known as *Leicester's Commonwealth*, which was published abroad in

---

[1] D'EWES, p. 373.   [2] Cromwell's diary, February 10th.
[3] Lansdowne MS. 43, fols. 181, 182 (two drafts of the speech).
[4] Diary, February 10th.

1584. It had been committed on its second reading but had not re-emerged, possibly because the government had already decided upon a bill of its own, to be started in the Lower House. This bill, which we may fairly confidently identify with certain 'articles' surviving in the Attorney General's hand, was not introduced until March 17th. It consisted of three clauses, dealing with the writing, printing, dispersing or importing of any book, ballad or libel: first, those tending to the slander of the government, for which the penalty was felony; secondly, those slandering and defacing 'the religion here professed' or the laws, the penalty being praemunire for the first offence, and treason for the second, if the book were in English; and thirdly, those slandering any of the Queen's Council, for which the penalty was imprisonment for life and a fine at her Majesty's pleasure.

No doubt *Leicester's Commonwealth* and Catholic propaganda in general were in the mind of the government when commissioning its legal officers to draft the bill; but in the hands of authority — especially Whitgift and some of the judges — such an Act would have become a deadly weapon against Protestant radicals. Puritan propagandists were as busy as could be 'defacing the religion here professed', and they were not averse to slandering Privy Councillors. Here, in fact, was a net, set to catch crows, which would inevitably take pigeons. The threat was so obvious that one is amazed at the crudity of Councillors: unless they were merely obeying royal orders. The House of Commons responded as might have been expected. They rejected the bill on its first reading — the grossest contumely a measure could receive — and it was delivered back to the Attorney General by the Speaker. Certainly, these gentlemen earned the rating that they were soon to receive from the Lord Chancellor.[1]

In the afternoon of Monday, March 29th, the Queen came to end the session. Serjeant Puckering, the Speaker, had prepared himself for the occasion with two draft orations: one, a rather conventional composition, written by Burghley, perhaps to serve as a model for a diffident friend; the other, an independent and more specific speech, presumably composed by himself. If we may judge from the long résumé given by Fitzwilliam, when the time came Puckering did not read his speech but spoke freely, following

[1] *L.J.* ii. 72, 74; D'EWES, pp. 368-9; Cromwell's diary; S.P. Dom. Eliz. 176/34.

in the main his own draft, though with an odd borrowing from Burghley's.[1]

He began with the accustomed self-depreciation and then dilated on the benefits they received by the assembling of Parliament: among them, 'that it hath pleased your Majesty to cheer us therein with the presence of your most royal and gladsome person, than the which nothing (under God) can be more comfortable unto us'. After rendering thanks for the Act of General Pardon, he craved both for himself and the House 'a favourable construction of the whole proceedings in this session . . . ; in the which, all in general, from the first to the last (one only wretched caitiff — Parry — excepted, upon whom due punishment had lighted', yet not 'such as they wished . . .) bare towards her Majesty such faithful, dutiful and reverent hearts, that if anything had passed from them wherein her Highness might find herself discontented . . . he durst in all their names protest and avow that it was never so meant among them.' In handling the bill for her Majesty's safety, they had 'intended a course far beyond that which was now set down; yet, finding the same to dislike her clement and pitiful nature, held themselves contented with that which was delivered to them as best liking to her Highness'. As for their petitions about the Church, 'they straight surceased from meddling with them' — declared Puckering, with better intentions than veracity — 'after her commandment was once delivered, giving such reverent regard thereunto that, receiving from her mouth an absolute commandment no further to proceed in them, not one man stood up to impugn the same; led thereunto with this reason — that her Majesty, having supreme authority over all such causes, both had given order to the clergy for the well looking unto them, and also would see the same duly and sincerely executed.' He wished 'most vehemently that such ability of speech were in him as thereby he might make known to her Majesty their careful endeavour towards her service'.

In asking the Queen for her assent to their bills — as Fitzwilliam records the speech — Puckering used a phrase about the Act for the Queen's safety that reveals the sacrifice they made in yielding to her wishes: 'whereby she may perceive what little regard they have to themselves for the future, in respect to continue the

[1] Lansdowne MS. 104, fols. 150-4 (copy, ibid. 43, fols. 189 seqq.); ibid. 115, fols. 33b-46; Fitzwilliam's diary.

present still among them, which is her Majesty'. For peroration he wrote as follows: 'May the King of Kings and God of Glory that so brightly shineth . . . assist your Majesty's counsels, continue His favourable spirit with you, establish your royal seat and estate, preserve you from all your enemies, reveal and frustrate all their wicked practices and devices, and grant you long to live and reign over us and ours here, and take you late (but at length) from us forth of this mortal kingdom unto Himself, into His heavenly kingdom, there to reign with Him in glory for ever. Amen.'[1]

The Lord Chancellor, Sir Thomas Bromley, speaking as the mouth of the Queen, rehearsed the four sections of Puckering's speech, adding appropriate comments. When he came to the behaviour of the Commons, there was little felicity. The Queen, he said, might easily pardon the Speaker of any offence, 'being a man that had nothing at all offended. And so likewise such contempts as by the body of the Lower House in general hath been committed, she may easily remit, because she knows none by them to be committed. But . . . some particular persons there were among them, whom her Majesty could not suffer to escape, but would see them punished as the case requireth. For they, in a heady and violent course, forgetting the bounds of modesty and good manners, most audaciously and arrogantly did forerun their elders . . . to the derogation of her Majesty's authority, to the contempt of the honourable assembly of the Upper House, and to the breach of the orders of their own House: all which manifestly appeared by two several matters happening in this session.

'The one, in that they would meddle with causes concerning the Church and religion: a thing by reason of the perfection of the same (for no Church in the world is better governed than ours) altogether needless, and also at the beginning of the session by her Majesty expressly forbidden. Yet was that commandment of hers so lightly esteemed' that her Majesty was forced, by the Speaker's mouth, to forbid the same again. A strange example this was; and, save with so clement a prince, not so quietly to be endured.

The other offence consisted in this: 'that they contemptuously and disdainfully rejected such matters as came from their betters, the Lords of the Higher House, whose proceedings they ought with

---

[1] My account is mainly from Fitzwilliam, with borrowings from Lansdowne MS. 115, fols. 33b-46.

all reverent and dutiful manner to have received'. As one, among many examples, the Lord Chancellor cited 'the arrogant using of the bill of fraudulent conveyances: a cause first deeply considered of by her Majesty's own person, with the advice of her judges, the greatest learned men of the Realm; digested afterward by the wisdom of her nobility of the Higher House and learned counsel there; and lastly, being by their Lordships, with her Highness's commendation, sent down, was so scornfully and despitefully received by the Commons . . . as upon the first reading they spurned it out of doors, not vouchsafing it so much as a committal, the usual course in all matters, be they never so base of condition.

'This wayward and perverse dealing, his Lordship said, was so far unlike to be committed by any wise men, as . . . her Majesty could not impute the offence to the generality of' the House, 'but to some number among them, and yet such a number as *major pars vicit meliorem* [quantity overcame quality]. Wherefore, being apparent by the example of this disorder that no grave consultation could ever follow in Parliament, unless good remedy were provided for the eschewing of the like hereafter, . . . her Majesty intended severely to punish the authors of these misdemeanours, for the example of others.'

Bromley referred to two bills — for the Queen's safety, and the subsidy: 'two such tokens of true and loving subjects as greater could not be'. He trusted that the former would never be put in proof. As for the subsidy, her Majesty did most graciously accept it. If it only concerned herself, she would return it to them. But in giving to her, every man gave to himself. She would retain the money 'as a storer, until such time as occasion . . . offered to lay out both that and her own for the public commodity'.[1]

The titles of bills were then read and the royal assent given. Cromwell notes that nine were vetoed, but in fact the number appears to have been fifteen: the largest slaughter of the reign.[2]

---

[1] Fitzwilliam's diary.

[2] Cromwell notes the following: for the Sabbath Day; for the armour of recusants; for disappropriating of parsonages impropriate; for maintenance of navigation; against making of glass by aliens; for keeping the sessions at Carnarvon; for keeping the county court at Morpeth and Alnwick; against moor-burning; for naturalizing children of certain Englishmen. In addition, the following were evidently vetoed: for maintenance of Rochester Bridge (cf. *L.J.* ii. 90); for Orford haven (ibid. p. 97); for Sir Thomas Barrington (ibid. p. 104); the haven at Chichester (ibid.); highways in Kent (ibid.); sea-banks in Norfolk (ibid.).

In addition to the two bills about the Church, Elizabeth vetoed one for the safe-keeping of the armour of obstinate recusants. This had originated in a motion by the Lieutenant of the Tower that 'the armour of the Papists might be committed to the custody of some others, lest it might be employed against her Majesty upon any exploit'. The speed with which the Lords dealt with the bill in order to pass it in time — they gave it three readings in one day — demonstrates that they too were enthusiastic about it. The Queen's veto is another illustration of her calm, merciful and independent judgment. She maintained herself above the conflict of passions, preferring to trust in the fundamental loyalty of her ordinary Catholic subjects; and by so doing she was largely justified in her faith. [1]

This ritual ended, Elizabeth herself addressed the assembly. John Stow, antiquary and chronicler, preserved the speech, and, judging by the style, it looks as if he may have had the authentic text. [2] The Queen began:

'My Lords and ye of the Lower House, my silence must not injure the owner so much as to suppose a substitute sufficient to render you the thanks that my heart yieldeth you: not so much for the safe-keeping of my life — for which your care appears so manifest — as for the neglecting your private future peril, not regarding other way than my present state. No prince herein, I confess, can be surer tied or faster bound than I am with the link of your good will; and can for that but yield a heart and head to seek for ever all your best.

'Yet one matter toucheth me so near, as I may not overskip: religion, the ground on which all other matters ought to take root, and, being corrupted, may mar all the tree; and that there be some fault-finders with the order of the clergy, which so may make a slander to myself and the Church, whose over-ruler God hath made me, whose negligence cannot be excused if any schisms or errors heretical were suffered.

'Thus much I must say, that some faults and negligences may grow and be, as in all other great charges it happeneth: and what vocation without? All which, if you, my Lords of the clergy, do not amend, I mean to depose you: look ye therefore well to your

---

[1] Cromwell's diary, December 8th; D'Ewes, p. 337; *L.J.* ii. 106.
[2] Printed in Stow's *Annals*; Holinshed's *Chronicles*. My text is from Harleian MS. 540, fols. 115 seqq., written in Stow's hand. There are several manuscript copies. All texts derive from Stow.

charges.' Then, turning her shaft at the Commons: 'This may be amended without heedless or open exclamations'.

'I am supposed to have many studies', she continued, 'but most philosophical. I must yield this to be true: that I suppose few, that be no professors, have read more. And I need not tell you that I am so simple that I understand not, nor so forgetful that I remember not.[1] And yet, amidst my many volumes, I hope God's book hath not been my seldomest lectures; in which we find that which by reason (for my part) we ought to believe — that, seeing so great wickedness and griefs in the world, in which we live but as wayfaring pilgrims, we must suppose that God would never have made us but for a better place and of more comfort than we find here. I know no creature that breatheth whose life standeth hourly in more peril for it [i.e. religion] than mine own; who entered not into my state without sight of manifold dangers of life and crown, as one that had the mightiest and greatest to wrestle with. Then it followeth that I regarded it so much as I left myself behind my care.

'And so you see that you wrong me too much, if any such there be as doubt my coldness in that behalf. For, if I were not persuaded that mine were the true way of God's will, God forbid I should live to prescribe it to you. Take you heed lest Ecclesiastes say not too true: they that fear the hoary frost, the snow shall fall upon them. I see many overbold with God Almighty, making too many subtle scannings of His blessed will, as lawyers do with human testaments. The presumption is so great, as I may not suffer it. Yet mind I not hereby to animate Romanists (which, what adversaries they be to mine estate is sufficiently known), nor tolerate new-fangledness. I mean to guide them both by God's holy true rule. In both parts be perils. And of the latter, I must pronounce them dangerous to a kingly rule: to have every man, according to his own censure, to make a doom of the validity and privity of his Prince's government, with a common veil and cover of God's word, whose followers must not be judged but by private men's exposition. God defend you from such a ruler that so evil will guide you.

'Now I conclude, that your love and care neither is nor shall be bestowed upon a careless Prince, but such as, but for your good will, passeth [i.e. careth] as little for this world as who careth least.

---

[1] i.e. There is no reason to think me so simple, etc.

With thanks for your free subsidy, a manifest show of the abundance of your good wills: the which, I assure you, but to be employed to your weal, I could be better pleased to return than receive.'

How marked a contrast with the Lord Chancellor's censure! There was policy, instinct, temperament in the difference. Her anger raged and then cooled. Both the sting and the balm were hers: reason and affection. And affection was not false, either in her or her subjects. The Lord Chancellor (on her instructions) threatened punishment for the rebels. Whether they were touched, we do not know. There is no evidence that they were.

The Parliament was prorogued until the following May. If times had been normal, we cannot doubt that Elizabeth would have dissolved this perverse assembly as deliberately as she did the Parliament of 1571; but with plot, assassination and invasion in the air, as also the question of aiding the Netherlands, it had to be kept in being and on short prorogation.

PART TWO

THE PARLIAMENT OF 1586-87

CHAPTER I

MARY QUEEN OF SCOTS

THE assassination of William the Silent in 1584 created a void in the Netherlands; and, if the rebellion of those territories against Philip II was to be kept going, this had to be filled by outside help. The pattern of a world in ideological conflict was working itself out. Foreseeing the grave consequences of open intervention, and unstirred by the crusading instinct of Protestant zealots, Elizabeth was loth to act. All the same, facts were too strong for her. By the autumn of 1585 she was committed to a treaty with the rebel States and to sending an army. Further delay occurred before she would consent to the dramatic gesture of naming the Earl of Leicester as general of her forces; but in December 1585 he too crossed to the Netherlands. It was tantamount to an act of war, and indeed marks the opening of the war-period of the reign. War on the formal plane was not, however, Elizabeth's intention. Nor was Philip II averse to informality. His mind turned with favour to the Catholic Enterprise against England. He was ready to encourage Catholic schemes for Elizabeth's murder.[1]

In certain Catholic circles, concentration of thought and hopes on the assassination of that 'monster of the world', Elizabeth of England, is a striking feature of the extant letters of this period. It is very understandable, if we enter into the mentality of the times, recognizing the Catholic view that the eternal destiny of so many human souls was at stake. Nothing can be more misleading than to project back into those days our own moral standards and attempt to explain away or reduce to trifling significance the plots against Elizabeth's life and throne. Earnest and devout men were as convinced of the virtue of ridding the world of this 'impious

---

[1] Cf. *Spanish Cal. Eliz.* iii. 614-15.

Jezebel' as we should be today of destroying the most infamous enemy of society. It follows that we should not be surprised at the reaction of English Protestants. Mary Queen of Scots was the destined Queen of Catholic conspirators. It became increasingly obvious that so long as she lived Elizabeth's life would be in jeopardy. This had been the passionate conviction of Council and Parliament in 1572, when they clamoured for Mary's death; and while the Queen had been able to defy her advisers on that occasion, such a personal feat seemed — as it proved to be — incapable of repetition in the heightened dangers of these later years.

As was inevitable, events repeated themselves. In 1572 it had been the Ridolfi Plot: in 1586 it was the Babington Plot. The Act for the Queen's Safety, passed in the previous Parliament, had been devised for just such an occasion; and when the Plot broke in August 1586, and after the main conspirators had been dealt with, the Commission of peers, Councillors, and judges, provided for by the Act, was sent to Fotheringay to try Mary Queen of Scots for her knowledge of the Plot and complicity in it.

Thanks to the subtle web which Sir Francis Walsingham had spun about Mary's activities, the government possessed, in the text of her letter to Babington, and in other documents, conclusive evidence that she had lent herself with cordial approval — and pathetic optimism — to the design of killing Elizabeth. Having no doubt about the Commission's verdict, Privy Councillors began to think of summoning Parliament. 'We stick upon Parliament, which her Majesty mislikes to have', wrote Burghley to Walsingham on September 8th; 'but we all persist, to make the burden better borne and the world abroad better satisfied.' They anticipated difficulty with their Sovereign over putting Mary to death, and wanted the overwhelming pressure of Parliament behind them. The same thought, but an opposite reaction, was evidently in Elizabeth's mind. For a variety of reasons — not least because delay engendered new doubts or strengthened old in their mistress — Burghley and his colleagues desired speed; and since the Parliament of 1584 stood prorogued until November 14th, 1586, which they regarded as too late, they had it dissolved and a new one summoned.[1]

It is beyond question that any Elizabethan Parliament would have reacted in only one way to the issue raised by the Babington

[1] *Scottish Cal.* viii. 701.

Plot; but as a result of Council instructions the new Parliament contained a larger proportion of former Members than any other since 1559. Rather more than half those in the Lower House had sat in 1584-85, and in addition there were some thirty, reappearing from earlier Parliaments. Among the latter were Robert Bainbridge, Anthony Cope, and the redoubtable Peter Wentworth — a host in themselves. One of the newcomers was William Davison, of Puritan outlook, recently appointed colleague to Walsingham, as second Secretary, and destined — predestined, the cynic might think — to be the unfortunate scapegoat for the tragedy that was to follow. Another newcomer was Job Throckmorton, an explosive Puritan, who turned the town of Warwick upside down by his election tactics, and was later to be closely connected — how closely, we shall have occasion to suggest — with the Marprelate tracts. Altogether it was a House worthy of comparison with the great assemblies of 1566 and 1572.[1]

Parliament was summoned for October 15th, but delays over Mary's trial led to its meeting being put off until the 27th and then the 29th. Its extraordinary character was emphasized at once by the absence of the Queen. She remained at Richmond during the dramatic sittings of the next five weeks: aloof, more than usually a prey to her own thoughts, subject to less responsible advice, adding considerably to the worries and fatigue of her principal Councillors. 'These hard accidents', complained Burghley from London when letters were unaccountably delayed, 'happen by her Majesty's being so far from here.' 'I am come home after daylight', he wrote, on his return from a special visit to Richmond, 'as also I passed through the City and Southwark afore daylight — which served me to small purpose, for though I came [to the Court] about 8 a.m. yet her Majesty did not stir from her bed afore 10 a.m.' 'Thus you see', he ended another letter, 'I cannot but utter my opinion, long afore daylight, for I have been up since 5 a.m.' To complete the picture, it must be added that the poor man suffered constantly from gout.[2]

The Queen's absence was due to decorum: her desire not to associate herself publicly with proceedings against a cousin and Queen. Her safety was not the reason. Though, as she told Parliament, there was good cause for her to know the peril of com-

---

[1] Cf. my *Elizabethan House of Commons*, pp. 291-2, 251-4.
[2] S.P. Dom. Eliz. 195/25, 41, 22.

mitting her person 'into the presence of the multitude, yet in truth there was in her no such fear; but being loth to hear so many foul and grievous matters revealed and ripped up, she had small pleasure to be there present'.[1]

A Commission of three, including Whitgift and Burghley, deputized for the Queen at the opening ceremonies; and both the Bishop of Salisbury, in the sermon at the Abbey, and the Lord Chancellor, Sir Thomas Bromley, in his subsequent oration in the Parliament Chamber, spoke of the dangers to England and their Queen. Her Majesty, declared Bromley, has not summoned this Parliament to make laws — of which there were more made than were well executed; nor to have a subsidy — although subsidies were very convenient as occasion should require. 'The cause was rare and extraordinary, of great weight, great peril, and dangerous consequence.' Then he declared what 'practices had been contrived of late, and how miraculously the merciful providence of God had, by discovery thereof, beyond all human policy, preserved her Majesty, the destruction of whose sacred person was most treacherously compassed and imagined'. Of the conspirators, 'one remained that, by due course of law, had received her sentence'. Her Majesty required their faithful advice thereon.[2]

When the Commons returned to their House, the desire of the government to preserve continuity was emphasized by the re-election of Serjeant John Puckering as Speaker. He was presented to the Commissioners on Monday, October 31st. Perhaps he, too, marked the unusual nature of the occasion by making a short speech instead of an ornate oration. Our rather brief account of events would also suggest that the Commissioners omitted to mention the usual limitations placed on the privilege of free speech. It may well be that the Queen was not then contemplating a post-Christmas resumption of Parliament: in which case the only business foreseen was that of Mary Queen of Scots, and the question of limitations did not arise. For form's sake, the Commons read their usual bill on returning to their House. They then adjourned for three days.

Though 'the great cause' was to dominate these sittings, even

---

[1] Exeter Coll. Oxf. MS. 127, fol. 53b; cf. Camb. Univ. Lib. MS. Gg. III. 34, p. 302.
[2] B.M. Additional MS. 5758, fols. 83-4; *L.J.* ii. 117; *Eng. Hist. Rev.* xxxv. 106; Camb. Univ. Lib. MS. Gg. III. 34, p. 302.

to the extent of determining whether the House met or not on particular days, it left periods of leisure, which — contrary to the Chancellor's injunction — the House utilized to read private bills and deal with other business. So it was on November 3rd. They began the morning by reading two bills, presumably while waiting for Privy Councillors. When Sir Christopher Hatton arrived, he immediately intervened, stopped the debate, and then, after giving a résumé of the Lord Chancellor's opening speech for the benefit of those who had been absent, proceeded to inaugurate the main business of the session by expounding the case against Mary Queen of Scots.

In his speech, Hatton described Mary as 'the hope of all idolatry', conceived by 'a number of subjects terming themselves Catholics . . . to be a present possessor of the crown of England'. The manner of her life and her practices had been from the beginning 'most filthy and detestable'; 'her ambitious mind, grounded in Papistry' had 'thirsted after this crown . . . and our overthrow'. Pursuing this thesis, he 'very excellently, plainly and effectually' — as the Clerk noted in his rough Journal — made relation of her 'horrible and wicked practices', beginning with 1559 when she was in France, and expanding into a detailed indictment when he came to her part in the Babington Plot. For himself, he thought speedy consideration should be had 'for the cutting of her off, by course of justice'. Otherwise, 'the Queen's Majesty's most royal person cannot be continued with safety'. '*Ne pereat Israel, pereat Absalom*' (Absalom must perish, lest Israel perish). [1]

Sir Walter Mildmay followed with another of his model orations. He set himself to consider, first against whom this horrible conspiracy was intended, next by whom, and thirdly to what end. 'First, it was intended against our most gracious Queen Elizabeth: a Queen anointed, the daughter of that most noble and famous King, Henry VIII; against the lawful and rightful inheritor of this crown, that entered peaceably into her kingdom and was received with great joy and acclamation of all her people.' Continuing, he built up a description of their Queen in felicitous language, recalling his moving orations in previous Parliaments. 'This is that royal and excellent person, against whom this most treasonable conspiracy hath been devised.'

[1] Bodleian Lib. MS. Tanner 78, fols. 14-15; D'EWES, p. 393.

A contrasting picture followed of 'the principal conspirator and the very root from whom all the other lewd weeds do spring': her 'horrible and odious crimes', especially the murder of the Lord Darnley, her late husband; her flight for safeguard of her life to England; her honourable entertainment here at the Queen's cost, with all courtesy and humanity; her successive conspiracies, culminating in the Babington Plot, for which she had received sentence and judgment. She has been 'heard at large, both patiently and favourably, to say for herself anything she could in answer of the matters alleged against her; yet the force of the proofs and the force of the truth was such as she could by no means avoid them, except her single negation, without any other ground, should have been taken against the direct confessions' of Ballard, Babington and her secretaries. 'Whether it be reasonable to believe her bare denial in her own case, being *pars delinquens*, against those direct and manifest proofs, let all men that are indifferent judge.' 'Such is the nature of ambition and desire of a kingdom' that her eyes were blinded and she was unable to see the danger she was like to fall into. Nor could she remember 'the great benefits and favours which our gracious Queen hath many ways and many times showed unto her'. These favours Mildmay enumerated, starting with the expulsion of the French from Scotland in 1560 — an odd view of that episode! — and ending with the less dubious service rendered to Mary in the Parliament of 1572. Her Majesty thought thereby to reclaim her from the evil course she held and to win her love unfeignedly for ever.

He continued. The purpose of these practices is evident enough: 'to advance this Scottish lady to the present possession of this crown, and thereby to overthrow the church of God, not only here but in all other countries where the Gospel is professed, and so to restore Popery and to bring us again under the bondage of the Pope'. Dilating at length on this rousing theme, he commented on 'those Jesuits and seminary priests that of late years have swarmed in this realm; a rabble of vagrant friars and false hypocrites, who pretend — as they say — nothing here but the saving of souls, but indeed their errand is to destroy us both in body and soul and, by secret practising of this conspiracy, to bereave us of our dear Sovereign and so to kill us all at one blow'. There is no end to it all: 'as the waves of the sea, without stay, do one rise and overtake another, so the Pope and his lewd ministers be never at rest, but as fast as one enterprise faileth they take another in hand without let of time, hoping at the last to prevail'.[1]

The Chancellor of the Duchy of Lancaster, old Sir Ralph Sadler — now in his eightieth and last year of life, a man whose parliamentary experience went back through many assemblies to that of 1541 — spoke next, and spoke bluntly. 'You have heard by these honourable and grave gentlemen the manner and circumstances of the late most rare and abominable conspiracy.' The 'root and ground' is the Queen of Scots; 'who living, there is no safety for our most gracious Sovereign'. 'God, for his mercy, put a willingness, yea even to the performance', into her Majesty's heart 'to take away this most wicked and filthy woman . . . who from the beginning hath thirsted for this crown, is a murderer of her husband . . . [and] is a most detestable traitor to our Sovereign, and enemy to us all.' In parenthesis, after describing Mary as 'a murderer of her husband', he alluded to the second Casket Letter — that centrepiece of modern Marian controversy — where, he said, 'I have seen [proof] by her own letter and hand to the Earl of Bothwell, with whom she wrought his death'. 'If the Queen's Majesty', he continued, 'do not justice upon her, assuredly it will be thought and said that either her Majesty loveth insecurity — regarding nothing the wealth and quiet of this Realm and subjects — or else plainly that she is afraid to do it.' Much else this ancient statesman said, in 'a long and great discourse'.[2]

John Wolley — Latin Secretary and Privy Councillor, and son-in-law of a fine old English gentleman, Sir William More of Loseley — followed Sadler: a practical speech, one infers, winding up this front-bench eloquence. The time was now 'far spent', and further debate was postponed till the morrow.[3]

Next day, November 4th, the debate was resumed. The Clerk mentions eleven Members as speaking: there may have been more. Two Privy Councillors opened: Sir James Croft, the Comptroller, and Sir Francis Knollys, Treasurer. Young Francis Bacon spoke; and so did James Dalton, who in August last had made a notable oration to the citizens of London before reading the affectionate and moving letter sent by the Queen to thank them for their demonstration of loyalty. Job Throckmorton and Robert Bainbridge were also among the speakers: men who did

---

[1] B.M. Sloane MS. 326, fols. 95 seqq.   [2] Bodleian MS. Tanner 78, fol. 16.
[3] Ibid.; D'Ewes, p. 393.

not mince their words. As it happens, the text of Throckmorton's speech has survived. It is all we possess of the debate.

'I thank God with all my heart for these good beginnings', were his opening words. 'No question but the cause is a very worthy cause, and my hope is — though great be the corruption of our time and though Satan do wondrously bestir himself in this last age — yet that this House will not afford us' a voice in opposition. 'Let Rome and Rheims, with that viperous brood of our conspiring Jesuits; let France and Spain and those kingdoms that are already drunk with the lies of that antichristian beast . . . have the praise and privilege of this work. Why! Hath not, I pray you, the very sink of the stews found out her patrons among these: a Harding, a Stapleton, a Parsons, and I know not who? . . . Such is the kind humour of our Romish crew that, were the case ten times more desperate than it is; yea, were the fact in that height and degree of iniquity as the horror thereof might go near to darken the sun; yet should it not want by their good wills an orator to smooth it, an advocate to plead for it, nor a champion to avow it in any court whatsoever.'

Turning his eloquence against Mary Queen of Scots: 'In a kingdom of the gospel', he adjured them, 'where both Prince and people, through the mercy of God, have long felt the sweetness of a holy and religious peace, let it never be said for shame that there was found a man that durst once stain his mouth in defence of her whom I protest unto you I know not how to describe. If I should term her the daughter of sedition, the mother of rebellion, the nurse of impiety, the handmaid of iniquity, the sister of unshamefastness; or if I should tell you that which you know already — that she is Scottish of nation, French of education, Papist of profession, a Guisan of blood, a Spaniard in practice, a libertine in life: as all this were not to flatter her, so yet this were nothing near to describe her. Ye have seen her anatomy already, ye have heard her whole life and practices reasonably laid forth unto you by an honourable personage, to whose worthy speech yet this one thing may be added: that were his gifts and sufficiency redoubled . . . yet would her wickedness . . . still surmount his description . . . Such a creature whom no Christian eye can behold with patience, whose villainy hath stained the earth and infected the air.' To destroy her would be 'one of the fairest riddances that ever the church of God had'.

'Oh! but mercy, you will say, is a commendable thing and well beseeming the seat of a Prince. Very true, indeed: but how long? Till it bring justice in contempt, and the state of the Church and Commonwealth in danger?' Throckmorton then recalled the Parliament of 1572 and Elizabeth's veto of the bill against Mary. 'And what got her Majesty, I pray you, by this her lenity? Even as much as commonly one shall get by saving a thief from the gallows: a heap of treasons and conspiracies, huddling one in the neck of the other, sufficient to affright both Prince and people . . . It is now high time for her Majesty, I trow, to beware of lenitives and to fall to corrosives . . . and to lance an inch deeper than ever she did, if she mean to sit quietly in her seat . . . For ambition (you know) is like a quick eel in a man's bowels that never giveth rest, and no julep can quench the thirst of a kingdom, but only blood . . . She ought indeed to die the death.'

Then this gifted stylist turned to the question, who should be her judges and executioners? Was a parliament of princes needed to do the feat? 'Thanks be to God', he answered, 'there is redress enough at home . . . May not one write upon the doors of this House, *Quid non*? . . . Under the warrant of God's law, what may not this House do? I mean the three estates of the land. To deny the power of this House, ye know, is treason: therefore, to say that this House is not able to cut off ten such serpents' heads as this is, not able' — and here we note the incorrigible Puritan dragging in his propaganda — 'to reform religion and establish succession, it is treason . . . The issue then . . . is that we be all joint suitors to her Majesty that Jezebel may live no longer to persecute the prophets of God . . . ; that so the land may be purged, the wrath of God pacified, and her Majesty's days prolonged in peace, to the comfort of us and our posterity.'[1]

The Clerk of the House of Commons tells us that the burden of all the speeches was that the Scottish Queen should immediately 'suffer the due execution of justice, according to her deserts'. Mary must die.

Following the precedent of 1572, a large and impressive committee was appointed, to meet that afternoon, confer about a petition to the Queen, and seek the co-operation of the Higher House.

For two or three days activity was concentrated in committee,

[1] Pierpont Morgan Lib., New York, MS. MA. 276, pp. 3-9.

but the following morning in the House George More, son and heir of Sir William, voiced a common fear. 'After sundry great and weighty reasons first showed', he concluded 'that only Popery is the chief and principal root of all the late horrible and wicked treacheries . . . and the Queen of Scots a principal branch issuing from the same root' — 'the most perilous and full of poison'. It was not out of affection to her person — since most of them did not know her — that the Papists wished her to have the crown, but because she would set up Popery. They 'either wish, or could easily bear, the death of our Sovereign Lady, the Queen's Majesty, though perhaps they would not show themselves to be actors or dealers therein'. In brief, no Catholic could be trusted: a reasonable thesis in the circumstances. He wanted the House, when petitioning the Queen, to ask her to retain no servant about her person except 'such only as may be well known to profess the true and sincere religion and also to be every way true and faithful subjects'. He further wanted the existing laws against Papists put in execution.

The speech might well have started a passionate, non-stop tirade against Catholics if the Speaker had not intervened to remind Members that the committee was the place for such suggestions. Even so, three days later Dr. Peter Turner, a man with an itch for action as well as words, reopened the subject. He was 'fully persuaded that her Majesty's safety cannot be sufficiently provided for by the speedy cutting off of the Queen of Scots, unless some good means withal be had for the rooting out of Papistry — either by making of some good new laws for that purpose, or else by . . . due execution of the laws already in force'. 'No Papist', he averred, 'can be a good subject.' Thereupon he offered the House a bill to effect his purpose. Unfortunately, no description of it survives: otherwise we might have learnt the new extremes to which such men as Dr. Turner — perhaps, indeed, a majority of the House — were prepared to go in order to extirpate Catholicism. The Speaker once more intervened to direct these zealots to the committee; and after speeches by More himself, Sir Henry Knyvet, Sir Francis Knollys, and Francis Hastings — a predominantly Puritan group — the Speaker's procedural ruling was accepted and it was decided not to read the bill 'as yet'.[1]

Meanwhile the House of Lords had also been discussing the

[1] D'EWES, pp. 393-5.

great cause. On November 5th the Lord Chancellor, 'at good length', had opened the business in a speech similar to that made by Sir Christopher Hatton in the Commons two days earlier. He was followed by Lord Burghley, who, as one to whom the whole proceedings were better known, 'excellently and more fully' dilated on the subject. At the next sitting, on November 7th, the Lords' debate was being continued, when the Commons, who had that morning received an interim report from their committee, sent up a delegation. A joint-committee of both Houses was now constituted and its first meeting fixed for that afternoon.[1]

Next morning, as a result of this meeting, each House, before hearing and approving of a petition prepared by the committee, listened to the reading, in part or whole, of the official account of Mary's trial, followed by the judgment of the Commissioners: a proceeding which seems to have taken longer in the Commons than the Lords. There was unanimity in both Houses. The record states: 'After long and advised deliberation and consultation' the Commons 'did all, with one full consent, conclude and agree' that the sentence and judgment of the Commissioners 'was in all things most honourable, just and lawful'; while the Lords, 'with one assent', agreed 'to use all humble and instant means, so far as might stand with their duties, to move and press her Majesty to proceed' according to the statute of 1584-85. On this occasion, unlike 1572, there was not even a single voice in favour of lenity. Mary must die.[2]

This was also the burden of their petition. After a preamble recalling their intolerable grief at the Scottish Queen's 'execrable practices' and Elizabeth's persistent clemency in face of parliamentary and other pressure, followed by a detailed recital of the facts of the Babington Plot and Mary's subsequent trial and sentence, the petition proceeded: 'Now forasmuch as we, your most humble, loyal and dutiful subjects, representing to your most excellent Majesty the universal state of your whole people of all degrees in this your Realm . . . are fully satisfied that the same sentence and judgment is in all things most honourable, just and lawful' and 'find that if the said Lady should now escape . . . death . . . your Highness's person shall be exposed to many more, and those more secret and dangerous conspiracies than before,

---

[1] *Eng. Hist. Rev.* xxxv. 107-8; MS. Lords Journal at Westminster (deleted passages).
[2] D'Ewes, pp. 397-8; *Eng. Hist. Rev.* xxxv. 108-9; *L.J.* ii. 120-1.

and such as shall not or cannot be foreseen and discovered . . .';
we beseech your Majesty 'that declaration of the said sentence and
judgment be made and published by proclamation, and thereupon direction be given for further proceeding against the said
Scottish Queen according to the effect and true meaning of' the
statute of 1584-85. Should this not be done, they would 'be
brought in utter despair'.[1]

The petition being 'short' — or so thought these ardent gentlemen, who had a hundred and one other invincible arguments in
their minds — it was agreed that, at the audience with the Queen,
the Lord Chancellor and the Speaker should reinforce the petition,
each with an array of verbal persuasions. In 1572, misled by a
plausible piece of sophistry, they had relied on the written word:
now they determined to employ both. The Speaker asked for
assistance; and the great committee was therefore instructed to
meet that afternoon to employ its imagination, an invitation being
extended to any and every Member to join in the exercise. It is
both a pity and a mercy that we have no record of the meeting.
The Speaker sought another indulgence — a day off, to 'bethink
and prepare himself' for his task. The House adjourned from the
Wednesday till the Friday.

On the Friday, Hatton informed the House that an audience
with the Queen, at which twenty peers and forty of themselves
were to be present, had been arranged for the following day at
Richmond, between 1 p.m. and 2 p.m. Then followed a striking,
if humourless display of pedantry. There had been a disputed
election in Norfolk, in consequence of which the two county
Members and eight of the borough Members had not taken their
seats until this day. To make their petition the indubitable voice
of all England, the House now had it re-read so that the Speaker
might solemnly 'put the question' to these ten Members.[2]

After this, Hatton again intervened, with a motion behind which
lies a curious story. It looks as if Elizabeth, though she was later
to sustain the pretence that she had not seen the petition, had in
fact been shown an advance copy and had noticed that it contained no reference to the Bond of Association: a strange, perhaps
a deliberate, omission, since Burghley seems to have been mainly

---

[1] B.M. Cotton MS. Caligula C. IX. fols. 616-17. A draft, with Burghley's amendments, is in the Huntington Library, U.S.A. (Ellesmere MS. 1191).
[2] D'EWES, pp. 398-9.

responsible for the drafting. From Elizabeth's point of view it was vital that Mary's death — if it was to come — should appear to the world as the act of an indignant nation: in other words, that it should appear in the perspective of the Bond of Association, which, as modified by the Act of 1584-85, bound all signatories under the most solemn oath — and permitted all subjects — to pursue the guilty party to the death, once her sentence had been proclaimed. It is not impossible that the Queen was already hoping — as she certainly was a month or so later — that someone or other, bound by the Oath and protected by the Statute, would solve her agonizing problem by lynching Mary. It was not a hope that most of her Councillors either encouraged or believed in: perhaps because they were men and remorselessly logical; perhaps also because as advisers they never experienced the finer doubts of ultimate responsibility; certainly because they were neither sovereigns nor relatives of Mary.

From a cryptic letter of Burghley's it seems that Elizabeth sent to ask that reference be made in the petition to the Bond of Association. He replied that it was no longer possible to alter the wording, since the House of Lords had adjourned until the following Tuesday, but that Hatton could arrange with the Lower House, which was sitting that morning, to include an allusion in the speech to be made by the Speaker at the forthcoming audience. Hatton, in fact, did this; and the Speaker was instructed to urge the 'necessity of the late Instruments of Association, respecting especially the consciences of a great number of her Highness's good and loyal subjects, which cannot be dispensed with by laws'.[1]

The following afternoon — Saturday, November 12th — the deputation of Lords and Commons waited on the Queen in her Withdrawing Chamber at Richmond. They had with them their petition, ingrossed on parchment, which the Lord Chancellor presented, after a speech of moderate length, epitomizing its contents. The Speaker followed. He was not brief. His task was to supplement the petition, 'with very great and weighty reasons' devised by his colleagues. We possess the draft marshalling of the arguments, written in his own hand. They were arranged as items under three headings: the danger to the Queen's person; risk to the true religion; and peril to the happy estate of the

---

[1] S.P. Dom. Eliz. 195/12; D'Ewes, p. 399.

Realm. There were no peradventures, no gradations. All was inspissated gloom — disaster certain, if speedy execution were not inflicted on Mary. 'Since the sparing of her' in 1572, 'Popish traitors and recusants have multiplied exceedingly. If you spare her now again, they will grow both innumerable and invincible.' 'She is only a cousin to you in a remote degree. But we be sons and children of this land, whereof you be not only the natural mother but also the wedded spouse. And therefore much more is due from you to us all than to her alone.' As instructed, the Speaker brought in the Oath of Association: 'Either we must take her life from her without your direction, which will be to our extreme danger by the offence of your law; or else we must suffer her to live against our express oath, which will be to the uttermost peril of our own soul, wherewith no Act of Parliament or power of man whatsoever can in any wise dispense'. His 'lastly' — rivalling a preacher's — opened with the assumption that her Majesty was 'duly exercised in reading the book of God', and then (as in 1572) recited Old Testament precedents to warn her of God's vengeance for sparing the life of a wicked prince.[1]

Calling her audience near to her, Elizabeth replied. She must of course have cogitated in advance on her speech, but there is good reason for thinking that she spoke extempore. If so, it was a *tour de force*, delivered, as the Lord Chancellor later told the Upper House, 'in so eloquent and goodly sort, and with words so well placed', that he 'would not take upon him to report it as it was uttered by her Majesty'.[2] There are several accounts of the speech. Each is open to criticism; but it would be an artistic outrage to blend them. The following text is a report which the Queen herself heavily amended in her own hand. It represents the speech as she was content for the world to read it.[3]

'The bottomless graces and immeasurable benefits bestowed upon me by the Almighty are and have been such, as I must not only acknowledge them but admire them, accounting them as well miracles as benefits; not so much in respect of His Divine Majesty — with whom nothing is more common than to do things rare and singular — as in regard of our weakness, who cannot sufficiently set forth His wonderful works and graces, which to me have been

---

[1] Cotton MS. Titus F. I. fols. 282-6; HOLINSHED, *Chronicles* (1587), iii. 1580-2.

[2] MS. Lords Journal, Westminster, November 15th (using deleted words).

[3] My text is from Lansdowne MS. 94, fols. 84-5, aided by the text in HOLINSHED, iii. 1582-3.

so many, so diversely folded and embroidered one upon another, as in no sort am I able to express them.

'And although there liveth not any that may more justly acknowledge themselves infinitely bound unto God than I, whose life He hath miraculously preserved at sundry times (beyond my merit) from a multitude of perils and dangers, yet is not that the cause for which I count myself the deepliest bound to give Him my humblest thanks, or to yield Him greatest recognition; but this which I shall tell you hereafter, which will deserve the name of wonder, if rare things and seldom seen be worthy of account. Even this it is: that as I came to the crown with the willing hearts of subjects, so do I now, after twenty-eight years' reign, perceive in you no diminution of good wills, which, if haply I should want, well might I breathe but never think I lived.

'And now, albeit I find my life hath been full dangerously sought, and death contrived by such as no desert procured it, yet am I thereof so clear from malice — which hath the property to make men glad at the falls and faults of their foes, and make them seem to do for other causes, when rancour is the ground — as I protest it is and hath been my grievous thought that one, not different in sex, of like estate, and my near kin, should be fallen into so great a crime. Yea, I had so little purpose to pursue her with any colour of malice, that as it is not unknown to some of my Lords here — for now I will play the blab — I secretly wrote her a letter upon the discovery of sundry treasons, that if she would confess them, and privately acknowledge them by her letters unto myself, she never should need be called for them into so public question. Neither did I it of mind to circumvent her, for then I knew as much as she could confess; and so did I write.

'And if, even yet, now the matter is made but too apparent, I thought she truly would repent — as perhaps she would easily appear in outward show to do — and that for her none other would take the matter upon them; or that we were but as two milk-maids, with pails upon our arms; or that there were no more dependency upon us, but mine own life were only in danger, and not the whole estate of your religion and well doings; I protest — wherein you may believe me, for although I may have many vices, I hope I have not accustomed my tongue to be an instrument of untruth — I would most willingly pardon and remit this offence. Or if by my death other nations and kingdoms might truly say that this Realm had attained an ever prosperous and flourishing estate, I would (I assure you) not desire to live, but gladly give my life, to the end my death might procure you a better Prince. And for your sakes it is that I desire to live: to keep you from a worse. For, as for me, I assure you I find no great cause I should be fond to live. I take no such pleasure in it that I should much wish it, nor conceive such terror in death that I should greatly fear it. And yet I say not but, if the stroke were coming, perchance flesh and blood would be moved with it, and seek to shun it.

'I have had good experience and trial of this world. I know what it is to be a subject, what to be a Sovereign, what to have good neighbours, and sometime meet evil-willers. I have found treason in trust, seen great benefits little regarded, and instead of gratefulness, courses of purpose to cross. These former remembrances, present feeling, and future expectation of evils, (I say), have made me think an evil is much the better the less while it dureth, and so them happiest that are soonest hence; and taught me to bear with a better mind these treasons, than is common to my sex — yea, with a better heart perhaps than is in some men. Which I hope you will not merely impute to my simplicity or want of understanding, but rather that I thus conceived — that had their purposes taken effect, I should not have found the blow, before I had felt it; nor, though my peril should have been great, my pain should have been but small and short. Wherein, as I would be loth to die so bloody a death, so doubt I not but God would have given me grace to be prepared for such an event; which, when it shall chance, I refer to His good pleasure.

'And now, as touching their treasons and conspiracies, together with the contriver of them. I will not so prejudicate myself and this my Realm as to say or think that I might not, without the last statute, by the ancient laws of this land have proceeded against her; which [i.e. the statute of 1584-85] was not made particularly to prejudice her, though perhaps it might then be suspected in respect of the disposition of such as depend that way. It was so far from being intended to entrap her, that it was rather an admonition to warn the danger thereof. But sith it is made, and in the force of a law, I thought good, in that which might concern her, to proceed according thereunto rather than by course of common law. Wherein, if you the judges have not deceived me,

or that the books you brought me were not false — which God
forbid — I might as justly have tried her by the ancient laws of the
land.

'But' — continued the Queen, at this point 'presenting herself
nearer the Speaker' — 'you lawyers are so nice and so precise in
sifting and scanning every word and letter, that many times you
stand more upon form than matter, upon syllables than the sense
of the law. For, in this strictness and exact following of common
form, she [i.e. Mary] must have been indicted in Staffordshire,
been arraigned at the bar, holden up her hand, and then been
tried by a jury: a proper course, forsooth, to deal in that manner
with one of her estate! I thought it better, therefore, for avoiding
of these and more absurdities, to commit the cause to the inquisition of a good number of the greatest and most noble personages
of this Realm, of the judges and others of good account, whose
sentence I must approve.

'And all little enough: for we Princes, I tell you, are set on
stages, in the sight and view of all the world duly observed. The
eyes of many behold our actions; a spot is soon spied in our gar-
ments, a blemish quickly noted in our doings. It behoveth us,
therefore, to be careful that our proceedings be just and honourable.

'But I must tell you one thing more: that in this late Act of
Parliament you have laid an hard hand on me — that I must
give direction for her death, which cannot be but most grievous,
and an irksome burden to me. And lest you might mistake mine
absence from this Parliament — which I had almost forgotten:
although there be no cause why I should willingly come amongst
multitudes (for that amongst many, some may be evil), yet hath it
not been the doubt of any such danger or occasion that kept me
from thence, but only the great grief to hear this cause spoken of,
especially that such one of state and kin should need so open a
declaration, and that this nation should be so spotted with blots
of disloyalty. Wherein, the less is my grief for that I hope the
better part is mine; and those of the worse not much to be accounted of, for that in seeking my destruction they might have spoiled
their own souls.

'And even now could I tell you that which would make you
sorry. It is a secret; and yet I will tell it you (although it be
known I have the property to keep counsel but too well, often

times to mine own peril). It is not long since mine eyes did see it written that an oath was taken within few days either to kill me or to be hanged themselves; and that to be performed ere one month were ended.' 'Her Majesty', a marginal note to the manuscript says, 'referred the further knowledge hereof to some of the Lords there present, whereof the Lord Treasurer [Burghley] seemed to be one, for that he stood up to verify it.' Elizabeth continued: 'Hereby I see your danger in me, and neither can or will be so unthankful or careless of your consciences as to take no care for your safety.

'I am not unmindful of your oath made in the Association, manifesting your great good wills and affections, taken and entered into upon good conscience and true knowledge of the guilt, for safeguard of my person; done (I protest to God) before I ever heard it, or ever thought of such a matter, till a thousand hands, with many obligations, were showed me at Hampton Court, signed and subscribed with the names and seals of the greatest of this land. Which, as I do acknowledge as a perfect argument of your true hearts and great zeal to my safety, so shall my bond be stronger tied to greater care for all your good.

'But, for that this matter is rare, weighty and of great consequence, and I think you do not look for any present resolution — the rather for that, as it is not my manner in matters of far less moment to give speedy answer without due consideration, so in this of such importance — I think it very requisite with earnest prayer to beseech His Divine Majesty so to illuminate mine understanding and inspire me with His grace, as I may do and determine that which shall serve to the establishment of His Church, preservation of your estates, and prosperity of this Commonwealth under my charge. Wherein, for that I know delay is dangerous, you shall have with all conveniency our resolution delivered by our message. And what ever any Prince may merit of their subjects, for their approved testimony of their unfeigned sincerity, either by governing justly, void of all partiality, or sufferance of any injuries done (even to the poorest), that do I assuredly promise inviolably to perform, for requital of your so many deserts.'

In the actual delivery of the speech, the passage explaining her absence from Parliament came as an afterthought. As a reporter says: 'She arose and went down from the cloth of estate (where she sat) to retire herself; but presently returned, saying that she had almost forgot one thing she meant to tell them'. She then made the explanation. 'And so' — the report continues — 'they most affectionately praying unto God for her long and happy reign over them, she for the same yielding great thanks departed'.[1] Burghley told a correspondent that her speech 'drew tears from many eyes'.[2]

[1] Exeter Coll. Oxf. MS. 127, fols. 51b-53. There are also reports of the speech in B.M. Harleian MS. 158, fols. 156-7 (cf. Camb. Univ. Lib. MS. Gg. III. 34, pp. 302 seqq.), and B.M. Stowe MS. 361, fol. 2.

[2] *Scottish Cal.* ix. 154.

CHAPTER II

MARY QUEEN OF SCOTS
(CONTINUED)

ON the Monday — November 14th — Mr. Speaker reported to the Commons about Saturday's audience. Sir Christopher Hatton followed in confirmation, warmly commendng the Speaker's performance on that day, and asking the House to extend their hearty thanks to him; 'which they so then did in very loving and courteous sort'. There was more Hatton had to say: something forgotten by Elizabeth on Saturday, but which she had commanded him this morning to signify to them. It was that her Majesty, 'moved with some commiseration towards the Scottish Queen, in respect of her former dignity and great fortunes in her younger years, her nearness of kindred . . . and also her sex, could be pleased to forbear the taking of her blood, if by any other means, to be devised by her Highness's Great Council of this Realm, the safety of her Majesty's own person and of the State might be preserved . . . without peril or danger of ruin and destruction; and else, not'. The Queen left them free to proceed as they wished. She would willingly listen to any device or reasons from individuals; and Members were told that they could impart their private conceits either to their Privy-Councillor colleagues or to the Speaker for transmission to her.

Hatton went on to remind Members of the prohibition against making new laws this session and announced that the Queen did not intend to be present at the end of the session to give her royal assent to any bills. Consequently, he advised adjournment of the House till Friday, by which time the Queen might be ready to answer their petition, which as yet — so he said — she had not read.

When the Commons met again on the Friday there was no response to their petition: the Queen, in fact, was waiting for an answer to the message which she had addressed both to them and to the Lords on Monday. A debate began. The Clerk names seven as speaking, including Sir Edward Dymock, Sir Thomas Scot, Dalton, Mildmay and Hatton: 'grave speeches, sound arguments and forcible reasons' — as our very human Clerk noted in his rough Journal — each of the speakers 'resolutely concluding that no other device, way, or means whatsoever could or can possibly be found or imagined'. The speedy execution of the Queen of Scots was the sole road to safety. Mary must die.

Hatton spoke last. Apparently, some of the speakers — recalling, one supposes, the proceedings in 1572 — had imagined the Queen's message to be 'a peremptory proposition', excluding them from continuing their suit for Mary's death: a misapprehension which heightens our regret that on this occasion we have no Cromwell reporting the debate, for the sentiment may have been rebellious. Hatton assured them that the message was not so. Her Majesty had left them full liberty. For his own part he agreed with the other speakers; and he suggested that, after considering in committee what answer to make to the Queen, they should seek joint action with the Lords. The former grand committee, with the addition of this day's speakers, was ordered to meet next morning, and any others who wished were authorized to attend. The House adjourned till Monday.[1]

On the Monday it was Sir Francis Knollys, who for form's sake, as the senior Privy Councillor, opened the committee's report to the House, but it was the impressive Hatton — who had quite eclipsed him and every other Councillor in leadership of the House — who took charge of the business: 'very excellently, plainly, and aptly', noted the Clerk, perhaps in his mind contrasting Hatton with the rather senile Knollys. Apparently, the committee, in deference to the Queen's wish, had considered 'all such arguments and objections as could be by them devised against the executing' of Mary.[2] But, to leave no doubt about the result, Hatton now repeated the invitation for any Member to suggest a device by which execution might be avoided. There was a pause. No one spoke. Thereupon, 'it was resolved by the whole House to insist only upon' their former petition. Mary must die.

After some speeches, in which emphasis was laid on the Oath of Association, the committee was instructed to confer with the Lords the following day and seek audience with the Queen.

The Comptroller, Sir James Croft — that dim and dubious

---

[1] D'EWES, pp. 402-3.
[2] Camb. Univ. Lib. MS. Gg. III. 34, p. 309.

Councillor, who seems to have been a *gauche*, unpopular figure in Parliament and who apparently had made some discordant speeches this session — rose to explain that he had been misinterpreted. He affirmed his 'earnest and devout prayer to God to incline her Majesty's heart' to their petition. Perhaps with a view to improving his reputation in that godly assembly, he moved that 'some apt and special course of prayer to that end' might be devised by Members and said daily in the House and privately in Members' lodgings. Sir Francis Knollys — surely meaning to snub his colleague — replied that such prayers were in print and already used in the House: maybe he was referring to 'An Order of Prayer and Thanksgiving for the preservation of her Majesty and the Realm from the traitorous and bloody practices of the Pope and his adherents', printed that year.[1]

There seems to have been time to spare that morning, and tongues were voluble. Sir John Higham stressed the burden of the Oath of Association and wanted the House to urge the Queen to speedy execution. Recorder Fleetwood, 'bending many speeches and reciting many precedents' — the Clerk's charitable description — very earnestly persuaded them to insist on their petition. Anthony Cope advocated an addition of the words, 'with all good and fit speed', to their former resolution. Gently, Sir Walter Mildmay brought the talk to an end.[2]

Meanwhile, the House of Lords, meeting on the Tuesday, had received a report of the audience with the Queen and of her subsequent message. They met again on the Saturday, when there were 'many wise and grave speeches', which all 'tended to one effect: that their Lordships, after long consultation and great deliberation thereupon had, could not find any other way than was already set down in their petition. Then the Lords agreed that the matter should be put to the question; and, being particularly asked, every one his several voice' — 'from the lowest to the highest', as the Lord Chancellor later told the Queen — 'they all answered (not one gainsaying) that they could find none other way of safety for her Majesty and the Realm.' Mary must die.[3]

On Tuesday, November 22nd, both Houses received a report from their joint-committee. In the Commons, Hatton explained

---

[1] *Liturgical Services*, ed. W. K. Clay (Parker Soc.), p. 595.
[2] D'EWES, pp. 404-5.
[3] *Eng. Hist. Rev.* xxxv. 110-11; Camb. Univ. Lib. MS. Gg. III. 34. p. 310.

that the Lords had decided to arm themselves with arguments
against any reasons the Queen was likely to urge at their forthcoming audience, but only to use them if, in fact, she raised objections to their petition. He proposed similar tactics on their part
and wanted a committee to prepare arguments: fresh ones, not
already used by the Speaker at the previous audience. The grand
committee was set to do this, a civil lawyer, Dr. Lewin, being
added to their number, evidently because they felt themselves
weak on that side.

Next day, Wednesday, the Speaker reported on two meetings of
the committee. Very many and sound reasons — 'to very great
depth' — had been delivered, some verbally, some in writing:
too many for his memory, but he had asked the Solicitor General,
Egerton, who was responsible for the most important, to note
them down. Egerton then expounded his memorandum, proving
'by invincible reasons, that neither by expectation of reformation
in the disposition of the Scottish Lady, if the Queen's Majesty
should spare her life; nor yet by safer or stronger guarding of her
person; nor by her promise upon word or oath; nor by the hostages
of other Princes, her allies; nor by her banishment; nor by the
revocation of the Bull of Pope Pius V; nor yet by the bonds or
word of a Prince, or of any or all the Princes, her allies; nor by any
other way or means whatsoever, other than only by the speedy
execution to death of the said Scottish Queen' — could true religion,
the most royal person of the Queen's Majesty, and the peaceable
state of this Realm be provided for. The 'devices' which this
statement rejected were in fact similar to those which the representatives of Henry III of France and James VI of Scotland had
already or soon were to put forward in the diplomatic *démarches*
they were making to save Mary's life.

Thomas Knyvet, in his ardour, wanted a paper of his own
conceits read to the House. Hatton pointed out that it ought to
have been handed to the committee. He then went on to say that
audience with the Queen was arranged for the morrow, between
1 p.m. and 2 p.m. at Court; that her Majesty would receive as
many as the House pleased to send; and that she accepted 'in
most gracious and loving part' their 'exceeding great and especial
care' for her, 'reposing next under God' — as she commanded
him to signify — 'her own safety to be greater in the dutiful love
and obedience of so faithful and loving subjects (an inestimable

blessing of God unto her Majesty) than in their riches, abilities and forces; rehearsing this sentence — *fide quam ferro tutius regnant reges*' (kings reign the safer by loyalty than the sword). Hatton also informed them that the Queen did not intend to conduct a debate on the morrow. He therefore suggested that the Speaker incorporate their battery of arguments in his speech.[1]

Thursday, November 24th, came. The delegation from both Houses arrived at Richmond, and the Lord Chancellor and the Speaker delivered the reply of their assemblies to the Queen's message, each stressing the unanimity of the decision. The Lord Chancellor seems to have kept to his compact and was brief. The Speaker also kept to his; but this involved an exposition of those 'invincible reasons', devised with such heartfelt concern by both committee and House.[2]

The Queen then addressed them. Once more it seems that she spoke extempore. Once more our text is a report, elaborately amended by the Queen herself. It is not easy reading, but its introspective, almost confessional mood compensates for that.

'Full grievous is the way whose going on and end breeds cumber for the hire of a laborious journey. I have strived more this day than ever in my life whether I should speak or use silence. If I speak and not complain, I shall dissemble; if I hold my peace, your labour taken were full vain.

'For me to make my moan were strange and rare, for I suppose you shall find few that, for their own particular, will cumber you with such a care. Yet such, I protest, hath been my greedy desire and hungry will that of your consultation might have fallen out some other means to work my safety, joined with your assurance, than that for which you are become so earnest suitors, as I protest I must needs use complaint — though not of you, but unto you, and of the cause; for that I do perceive, by your advices, prayers, and desires, there falleth out this accident, that only my injurer's bane must be my life's surety.

'But if any there live so wicked of nature to suppose that I prolonged this time only *pro forma*, to the intent to make a show of clemency, thereby to set my praises to the wire-drawers to lengthen them the more, they do me so great a wrong as they can hardly recompense. Or if any person there be that think or imagine

---

[1] D'Ewes, pp. 405-6.
[2] Holinshed, iii. 1583-5; Camb. Univ. Lib. MS. Gg. III. 34, p. 310.

that the least vainglorious thought hath drawn me further herein, they do me as open injury as ever was done to any living creature — as He that is the maker of all thoughts knoweth best to be true. Or if there be any that think that the Lords, appointed in commission [i.e. the Commissioners who tried Mary], durst do no other, as fearing thereby to displease or to be suspected to be of a contrary opinion to my safety, they do but heap upon me injurious conceits. For, either those put in trust by me to supply my place have not performed their duty towards me, or else they have signified unto you all that my desire was that every one should do according to his conscience, and in the course of these proceedings should enjoy both freedom of voice and liberty of opinion, and what they would not openly, they might privately to myself declare. It was of a willing mind and great desire I had, that some other means might be found out, wherein I should have taken more comfort than in any other thing under the sun.

'And since now it is resolved that my surety cannot be established without a Princess's head, I have just cause to complain that I, who have in my time pardoned so many rebels, winked at so many treasons, and either not produced them or altogether slipped them over with silence, should now be forced to this proceeding, against such a person. I have besides, during my reign, seen and heard many opprobrious books and pamphlets against me, my Realm and State, accusing me to be a tyrant. I thank them for their alms. I believe therein their meaning was to tell me news: and news it is to me indeed. I would it were as strange to hear of their impiety. What will they not now say, when it shall be spread that for the safety of her life a maiden Queen could be content to spill the blood even of her own kinswoman? I may therefore full well complain that any man should think me given to cruelty; whereof I am so guiltless and innocent as I should slander God if I should say He gave me so vile a mind. Yea, I protest, I am so far from it that for mine own life I would not touch her. Neither hath my care been so much bent how to prolong mine, as how to preserve both: which I am right sorry is made so hard, yea so impossible.

'I am not so void of judgment as not to see mine own peril; nor yet so ignorant as not to know it were in nature a foolish course to cherish a sword to cut mine own throat; nor so careless as not to weigh that my life daily is in hazard. But this I do con-

sider, that many a man would put his life in danger for the safeguard of a King. I do not say that so will I; but I pray you think
that I have thought upon it.

'But sith so many hath both written and spoken against me, I
pray you give me leave to say somewhat for myself, and, before
you return to your countries, let you know for what a one you
have passed so careful thoughts.[1] And, as I think myself infinitely
beholding unto you all that seek to preserve my life by all the
means you may, so I protest that there liveth no Prince — nor
ever shall be — more mindful to requite so good deserts. Wherein,
as I perceive you have kept your old wont in a general seeking
the lengthening of my days, so am I sure that never shall I
requite it, unless I had as many lives as you all; but for ever I will
acknowledge it while there is any breath left me. Although I may
not justify, but may justly condemn, my sundry faults and sins to
God, yet for my care in this government let me acquaint you
with my intents.

'When first I took the sceptre, my title made me not forget the
giver, and therefore [I] began as it became me, with such religion
as both I was born in, bred in, and, I trust, shall die in; although I
was not so simple as not to know what danger and peril so great
an alteration might procure me — how many great Princes of the
contrary opinion would attempt all they might against me, and
generally what enmity I should thereby breed unto myself.
Which all I regarded not, knowing that He, for whose sake I did
it, might and would defend me. Rather marvel that I am, than
muse that I should not be if it were not God's holy hand that con-
tinueth me beyond all other expectation.

'I was not simply trained up, nor in my youth spent my time
altogether idly; and yet, when I came to the crown, then entered
I first into the school of experience, bethinking myself of those
things that best fitted a king — justice, temper, magnanimity,
judgment. As for the two latter, I will not boast.[2] But for the two
first, this may I truly say: among my subjects I never knew a
difference of person, where right was one; nor never to my
knowledge preferred for favour what I thought not fit for worth;
nor bent mine ears to credit a tale that first was told me; nor was

---

[1] I omit a clause here, which Elizabeth evidently forgot to delete. It is omitted in
the Holinshed text.
[2] The printed text here inserts: 'my sex doth not permit it'.

so rash to corrupt my judgment with my censure, ere I heard the cause. I will not say but many reports might fortune be brought me by such as must hear the matter, whose partiality might mar the right; for we Princes cannot hear all causes ourselves. But this dare I boldly affirm: my verdict went with the truth of my knowledge.

'But full well wished Alcibiades his friend, that he should not give any answer till he had recited the letters of the alphabet. So have I not used over-sudden resolutions in matters that have touched me full near: you will say that with me, I think. And therefore, as touching your counsels and consultations, I conceive them to be wise, honest, and conscionable; so provident and careful for the safety of my life (which I wish no longer than may be for your good), that though I never can yield you of recompense your due, yet shall I endeavour myself to give you cause to think your good will not ill bestowed, and strive to make myself worthy for such subjects. And as for your petition: your judgment I condemn not, neither do I mistake your reasons, but pray you to accept my thankfulness, excuse my doubtfulness, and take in good part my answer-answerless. Wherein I attribute not so much to my own judgment, but that I think many particular persons may go before me, though by my degree I go before them. Therefore, if I should say, I would not do what you request, it might peradventure be more thàn I thought; and to say I would do it, might perhaps breed peril of that you labour to preserve, being more than in your own wisdoms and discretions would seem convenient, circumstances of place and time being duly considered.'[1]

Behind our text of the Queen's speeches this session lies a curious story. Shortly after their delivery a tract with a long title was printed: *The Copie of a Letter to the Right Honourable the Earle of Leycester . . . With a report of certeine petitions and declarations made to the Queenes Majestie at two severall times, from all the Lordes and Commons lately assembled in Parliament. And her Majesties answeres thereunto by her selfe delivered, though not expressed by the reporter with such grace and life, as the same were uttered by her Majestie.*[2] The author, designated by the initials R. C., was Robert Cecil.[3] The tract

---

[1] B.M. Lansdowne MS. 94, fols. 86-8. There are other reports in B.M. Harleian MS. 158, fols. 158-60; Camb. Univ. Lib. MS. Gg. III. 34, pp. 310 seqq. There is also the printed text in Holinshed.

[2] It is reprinted in HOLINSHED, iii. 1580 seqq.

[3] This is established by a statement of Robert Beale's in B.M. Additional MS. 48027 (Yelverton 31), fol. 396.

purported to be 'written before, but delivered at', Leicester's return from the Netherlands: a mere literary pretence, for Leicester arrived back at Court at 10 p.m. on November 24th, whereas the draft of the tract — if, as seems likely, an enigmatic letter from Robert Cecil refers to this business — was not ready before December 1st. The letter reveals Secretary Walsingham, that master of secret arts, in charge of this piece of propaganda.[1]

Propaganda it was. Translated into several languages, including Latin, its function was to ease the inexpressible shock to the world at large of a Queen's execution, and to furnish an apology for Elizabeth's part in it. Her speeches, with their moving theme — 'If this cup can be taken from me' — appear against a background of irresistible argument and pressure: as a Greek tragedy with a fatal parliamentary chorus incessantly chanting Mary's doom.

In the title, in the preface, and again before the text of the first speech, the author asserts his incapacity to report the speeches 'answerable to the original, which the learned call *Prototypon*': 'I might incur great blame by my slender manner of report, so to have blemished the excellency of her Majesty's speeches'. We know, however, that it was not Elizabeth's way to permit her speeches — or for that matter her portraits — to be blemished. And so to the unfolding of a singular secret.

In the British Museum are manuscript copies of the texts Cecil proposed to print.[2] They are profusely amended by the Queen herself. In the main the changes are stylistic. The most pernickety author could scarcely expect to produce a more dishevelled manuscript. They offer a fascinating and unique opportunity of studying the niceties of Elizabeth's literary style. Her involved, regal language may be far from modern taste, but many of her corrections, especially the inversions of words and phrases, would win approval from a master of style.

However, what chiefly interests us is that the text as corrected

---

[1] B.M. Cotton MS. Faustina F. X, fol. 256.

[2] Lansdowne MS. 94, fols. 84 seqq. In due course I hope to publish these, showing the Queen's alterations. In Lansdowne MS. 103, fol. 64 are 'Extractions taken by the Queen's order in reformation of some errors' in the reports of her two speeches. Robert Cecil may have been responsible for the basic 'report' of the second speech; but as he was not placed on the 'great committee' until November 21st (D'EWES, p. 404), he was presumably not present at the first audience and would have been unable to write the 'report' of the speech on that occasion. A (? unique) copy of this 'report' for November 12th is in Francis Alford's papers (Inner Temple, Petyt MS. 538/10, fols. 6b-7). Can Alford have been the reporter in this instance?

by the Queen is that of the tract. In other words, Elizabeth knew about this piece of propaganda and revised her speeches for publication. Perhaps the idea was hers, though she clearly did not wish to be associated with it. Cecil's apologies for blemishing the speeches were therefore a subterfuge: though there is this to be said for them, that his original texts were almost certainly reports; and if reports, then it would seem that Elizabeth possessed no text of her own and must have spoken extempore.

Both Houses met again on Friday, November 25th, the day after the audience. In the Upper House the Lord Chancellor gave an account of that event and of the Queen's speech. So no doubt did the Speaker in the Lower House, though we are not told this. We are, however, told that Mr. Grice of Great Yarmouth — a Puritan, one of the radical 'choir' of 1563, friend of Thomas Norton, and follower of the Earl of Leicester — had something to say about the recently arrived special ambassador from France, sent by Henry III to exert pressure on Elizabeth and save Mary's life. Mr. Grice had heard that he was to be granted audience the next day, and 'fully persuading himself' — with the hearty prejudice of an Englishman against the French — that he 'cometh not for any good, either to her Majesty or to the Realm; and knowing that their manner is in such cases to be attended for the most part with a company of rascals and basest sort of people of their nation, and all the rabble of them accustomed to thrust into the presence of the Prince with their master'; he wanted the Privy-Councillor Members of the House to procure that the ambassador was heard by the Council and received his answer at their hands, and was on no account granted access to the Queen. Sir Christopher Hatton answered that at the last meeting of the joint-committee of both Houses this question had been discussed, and that the Lord Chamberlain and others at Court had been warned to take precautions.[1]

Attention now centres on the vacillations and uncertainties of Elizabeth's mind. Two formal acts of hers were essential before Mary could be executed. The first was proclamation of the sentence against her, as required by the statute of 1584-85. Burghley hoped for this before Parliament was ended; but on the day of the audience he was evidently informed that the Queen intended to have Parliament prorogued the next morning. No

[1] *Eng. Hist. Rev.* xxxv. 112; D'Ewes, p. 406.

proclamation, and prorogation till March 6th, was her plan; and, knowing his mistress, he must have been near despair. She was yielding nothing and getting rid of parliamentary pressure. Left with her doubts, paralysis would be the result. It seemed to be 1572 over again. Burghley wrote to Secretary Davison, who was functioning at Court. He told him to remind the Queen to send in writing the manner of the speech that the Lord Chancellor was to use at the prorogation next day: an interesting sidelight on procedure, though the occasion of course was exceptional. Burghley knew that she meant to thank the Lords and Commons for their pains and care for her safety; 'but if', he bitterly added, 'they have not some comfort also to see the fruits of their cares . . . the thanks will be of small weight to carry into the countries; and then the Realm may call this a vain Parliament, or otherwise nickname it a Parliament of Words'. If the sentence against the Scottish Queen is not published at once, it 'will be termed a dumb sentence', and Commissioners and Parliament will repent the time spent on it. He wanted the Queen to sign the proclamation that day: she could then face James VI's ambassador with an act done at the importunity of Parliament; and to-morrow the Lord Chancellor could declare it to Parliament. He went on to express his hope for the final step — execution: that the Queen would allow it to be said that she would not take the advice of foreigners rather than of her own people. 'And to that hope' (the hope of execution), 'I beseech God give full perfection'.[1]

His letter had no immediate effect. Elizabeth sent the brief for the Lord Chancellor's speech. Burghley received it at 6.30 p.m. on the 24th. The Lord Chancellor, besides being annoyed at so sudden a warning of prorogation, 'could not read one half line' of Elizabeth's writing — which is a consoling thought! — so that Burghley was constrained to copy it out for him.[2]

And then — evidently in the night watches, when reflection habitually troubled her — the Queen changed her mind. In the morning she sent Burghley instructions to postpone the prorogation. They arrived only in the nick of time. Both Houses adjourned for a week. Burghley now had the proclamation of Mary's sentence prepared and ingrossed. Elizabeth thought it too brief and formal, and wanted to add an explanatory, propa-

---

[1] S.P. Dom. Eliz. 195/22 (undated, but clearly November 24th).
[2] Ibid. 195/25 (November 25th).

gandist setting. It had to be recast. Burghley was at Richmond on December 1st, and, in the main, found his Sovereign pliant.[1]

The next day, December 2nd, Parliament met in formal session with the Queen's Commissioners presiding. The Lord Chancellor made a speech, thanking them all in her Majesty's name for their labours, and announcing that she was content to yield so far to their petition that the sentence against Mary would be immediately proclaimed under the great seal of England. The Speaker followed with humble thanks for the concession, but desiring both Commissioners and Privy Councillors 'to be earnest mediators to her Majesty to grant also ... the residue of their said petition'. He further asked that both the petition and the proceedings of Parliament in this great cause should be entered of record in the Rolls of Parliament: a request that pleased their Lordships, if the Queen would consent. In fact, proceedings and petition were enrolled upon a special parliament roll; but this extraordinary record now reposes, not at the Public Record Office but among the Cecil Papers at Hatfield House. We must conclude, either that Elizabeth refused to allow it to be deposited with the records of Parliament, or that it was withdrawn as an infamous memorial when Mary's son succeeded to the throne.[2]

The Commissioners ended the sitting by adjourning — not proroguing — Parliament until February 15th. This early date was a victory for Burghley. It gave Elizabeth ten and a half weeks in which to do one of two things: put Mary to death, or dissolve a Parliament she would not dare to face again.

The sentence against Mary was duly issued two days later and was proclaimed in county and town 'with great port and stateliness'. The citizens of London thronged to hear it proclaimed. They rang their bells, made bonfires, and sang psalms 'in every street and lane of the City': tribute to Elizabeth's flair for publicity in giving the proclamation its long, explanatory setting.[3]

Councillors hoped that the proclamation would be followed rapidly by a warrant for Mary's execution: before the effect of parliamentary pressure had time to wear off. Indeed, Walsingham had already drafted such a document, which bears Burghley's endorsement that it was to be dated the day after the proclama-

[1] Ibid. 195/25; ibid. 195/28, 41; D'Ewes, p. 406.
[2] It was printed by me in *Eng. Hist. Rev.* xxxv. 103-13.
[3] Holinshed, iii. 1586. There is a long account of the proclamation in the city records of Winchester, which Mr. Tom Atkinson kindly showed me.

tion. The wording — quite different from that ultimately adopted — is interesting. Closely pursuing the statute of 1584-85, its operative words were as follows: 'We, therefore, do hereby direct . . . that the same Mary shall and may be pursued unto death, according unto the said statute'; for the convenient doing whereof the commissioners were instructed 'immediately' to 'cause the head of the same Mary to be cut off'. To remind the Queen of the lynch-law element in the statute and the Bond of Association hardly seems the height of ministerial wisdom. But perhaps Elizabeth did not see this draft. [1]

Not only was the Council ready with a warrant: on December 10th Burghley drafted the necessary letters patent to Mary's keeper, Sir Amias Paulet, authorizing him to surrender her person for execution. And, further evidence that they expected rapid action: on December 11th Walsingham was telling a correspondent of the Queen's continued resolution to proceed to execution. However, abroad in the Netherlands Thomas Wilkes, Clerk of the Council, was not so optimistic: 'God send our great cause at home a good issue', he wrote to Walsingham on December 14th; but 'I fear her Majesty will hardly be wrought to assent to the execution of the Scottish Queen to be done according to justice'. He evidently thought that the proclamation might lead to a solution of the problem by lynching, though in his opinion it would be no small blemish to their Queen's honour and the justice of England. Not everyone — not Elizabeth — thought so. [2]

For the moment, however, action was out of the question, unless precipitated by a new crisis. The Queen had to deal with ambassadors from Henry III of France and James VI of Scotland, who were in London in December, exercising pressure, uttering threats, offering all manner of guarantees to save Mary's life: alas, any dispassionate critic must acknowledge the futility of their guarantees. Councillors fretted at the delay; but it was a sound instinct that led Elizabeth to grant audience after audience. In her interviews she was on the whole firm, maintaining her right to put Mary to death and the expediency, nay the necessity, of doing so. When James VI wrote a tactless letter, saying 'King Henry VIII's reputation was never prejudiced in anything but in

---

[1] MURDIN, *Burghley Papers*, pp. 576-7; and cf. with the later warrant in *Scottish Cal.* ix. 262-3.

[2] MURDIN, pp. 574-5; *Scottish Cal.* ix. 196; *Foreign Cal. Eliz.* XXI. ii. 274-5.

the beheading of his bedfellows', Elizabeth's fury disconcerted ambassadors and master.

James was intent on preserving both his mother's life and his own title to the English succession. His honour bade him intervene for his mother. So did the pressure of his subjects. The Scots, who in 1567 had demonstrated against Mary with the cry, 'Burn the whore!', were beside themselves with anger, vowing to march on England and causing their poor King to fear for his throne. Elizabeth was now 'the whore'. Among the libels daily set up in open street after the execution was one with a little cord of hemp tied halter-wise, and this epigram:

> To Jesabell that Englishe heure
> receyve this Scottish cheyne
> As presagies of her gret malhouer
> for murthering of oure quene.[1]

As for James, there was no doubt where his heart and soul really were: in the succession to the English throne. And he made this clear. 'How fond and inconstant I were if I should prefer my mother to the title, let all men judge', he wrote on December 15th, in reply to a warning message from the Earl of Leicester. The supreme wisdom shown by Elizabeth in the Parliament of 1584-85 — wisdom that had already paid a valuable dividend in the league with Scotland of July 1586 — revealed itself. It was she, personally, who had prevented the Act for the Queen's Safety (and, in consequence, the Bond of Association) from involving James in his mother's downfall. But for her, his title would now have been forfeit. Scotland in consequence would have been thrown into the arms of France and maybe of Spain, and arrayed against Elizabeth's England. As it was, the Scottish King's vehement *démarches* were reduced to sound and fury: indeed, what else could he have expected after his shocking letter to the Earl of Leicester? Elizabeth allowed him to send fresh delegates at the end of December, listened to their representations, countered their arguments; but when, on January 10th, they asked for a further delay of fifteen days to communicate with their King, she refused. They craved eight days. 'Not an hour!', she answered, and left the room.[2]

[1] RAIT & CAMERON, *King James's Secret*; *Warrender Papers*, ed. Cameron (Scottish History Soc.), vol. i; *Scottish Cal.* ix. 331.
[2] Cf. RAIT & CAMERON, p. 102 and passim.

When, at long last, the ambassadors were got out of the way, Elizabeth was left to face the most distressing decision of her life. At the time of the Duke of Norfolk's execution in 1572, she had told Burghley that the hind part of her head (the seat of the affections) would not trust the forward side of the same (the seat of reason). The same conflict was repeated now. The Queen's Councillors — wrote Burghley, a few months afterwards — continuing to demand justice, 'were dismissed, all unsatisfied, with no other reason but that it was a natural disposition in her, utterly repugnant to her mind'.[1]

The Court moved to Greenwich before Christmas, and there the rest of the drama was played out. Tension was acute. It was feared that some desperate attempt would be made to murder the Queen or rouse disturbances in the country and rescue Mary; and the expected happened. Early in January a crude — and, for the historian, mystifying — plot came to light to kill Elizabeth, in which the French ambassador was involved. It appears to have been partly, perhaps wholly, bogus. The simplest explanation would be the cynical one that it had been provoked by Walsingham or other Councillors in order to parry French intervention for Mary and scare Elizabeth into action. But, if we believe Councillors capable of that stratagem, then more credence must be given to the Queen's version of what subsequently happened over the warrant for Mary's execution.

At the end of January and beginning of February there was alarm throughout the country. 'False bruits were spread abroad', wrote Walsingham: 'that the Queen of Scots was broken out of prison; that the City of London was fired; that many thousand Spaniards were landed in Wales; that certain noblemen were fled; and such like . . . The stir and confusion was great: such as I think happened not in England these hundred years past, for precepts and hue and cries ran from place to place, even from out of the north into these parts, and over all the west as far as Cornwall.'[2]

In late December, Elizabeth had authorized Burghley to draw up the warrant for Mary's execution: probably to be prepared against sudden crisis. It was entrusted to Secretary Davison to

---

[1] *Scottish Cal.* ix. 394.
[2] READ's *Walsingham*, iii. 60-2; *Foreign Cal. Eliz.* XXI. i. 241; J. MORRIS, *Letter Books of Sir Amias Poulet*, pp. 354-6.

secure her signature at the right time. The story now centres on this unfortunate gentleman, who had only recently been made Secretary. At the crucial juncture Walsingham was away from Court, conveniently or providentially ill.

Two contradictory accounts exist of what followed. According to Davison, after he had kept the warrant in his possession for five or six weeks, on February 1st the Queen sent for him. Alarmed by the rumours then spreading throughout the country and by the danger to public quiet and her life, she was fully resolved to proceed with Mary's execution. She signed the warrant, ordered him to have it sealed with the great seal at once, and then, with a flash of caustic wit, bade him show it to Walsingham: 'The grief thereof would go near to kill him outright'. Davison immediately went to Burghley and told him the news: perhaps a conspiratorial, perhaps merely a natural action, but one for which he had no specific authority. Next day, after the warrant had passed the seal, Elizabeth frightened him by asking, why the haste? and by other remarks, indicating that she was averse to taking responsibility for Mary's death. Foreseeing his fate, and determined not to be left isolated, Davison went to Hatton, who brought him to Burghley. The result was that the whole of the Council then at Court assumed responsibility, holding that the Queen had done as much as could be expected. They took the warrant, wrote the necessary Council letters to accompany it, and sent them all off in the reliable custody of Robert Beale. Mary was executed at Fotheringay on February 8th.[1]

When Elizabeth heard the news she was overwhelmed with grief and anger: whether genuine or feigned, it is for us to judge. Her wrath was directed against those involved in the dispatch of the warrant, particularly Davison and Burghley. She asserted that she had given Davison express charge to keep the document secret, and that, after learning it had passed the seal, she had charged him on his life not to let it go out of his hands until he knew her further pleasure. Davison was sent to the Tower and subsequently tried in the Star Chamber, where he was sentenced to a fine of ten thousand marks and imprisonment during the Queen's pleasure.

Of the two conflicting stories, Davison's appears so honest and circumstantial that one might be inclined to agree with his

[1] *Scottish Cal.* ix. 287 seqq. Cf. N. H. NICOLAS, *Life of Wm. Davison* (1823).

biographer and pronounce Elizabeth a hypocrite and liar: with, however, the qualification that she was forced into that sorry role by political necessity. Political necessity, because she had to provide an excuse for James VI and Henry III to maintain relations with England. It was the position in which Catherine de Medici had found herself after the Massacre of St. Bartholomew. Elizabeth told her story in a personal letter to James, and back came the message: so far, so good, 'but to confirm it to be true — I speak plain language — *necesse est unum mori pro populo*'. There had to be a scapegoat. It was Davison.[1]

The thesis is plausible. Scotsmen and Frenchmen believed it. In retrospect, Robert Beale believed it; and he was among the persons of the drama. 'It was thought meet to put' the blame 'from the Queen upon Mr. Davison', he notes in some private jottings, written not earlier than 1594. He attributes the idea to the Earl of Leicester, stating — and here, surely, he must be wrong — that the first plan was to imprison Burghley; 'but her Majesty thought that to commit him to the Tower would kill him'. 'Mr. Secretary Walsingham', he adds, 'was thought too stout, and would utter all. Therefore, Mr. Davison must bear the burden.' The Queen's subsequent treatment of Davison — as Beale emphasizes — points to the same conclusion. He was secretly released from the Tower and placed in private custody, pending full freedom, in October 1588: as soon, in fact, as the defeat of the Armada gave final assurance against a Spanish-Scottish alliance. What is more, the Tower officials were forbidden to charge him the fees customarily paid by prisoners on their release. Then, about June or July 1589 his Star-Chamber fine was remitted by privy seal. He kept his fee as Secretary, and in 1594 was granted land worth £200 per annum, which he sold for £5000.[2]

The thesis certainly is plausible; but it fails in being too simple. It ignores the complexity of the problem; the psychology is false. Knowing Elizabeth's actions in the Parliament of 1572, we need not be cynical about her speeches to the Parliament of 1586, expressing distress at the thought of Mary's death. Leicester had no doubt of her genuine emotion. 'There is a letter from the

---

[1] *Scottish Cal.* ix. 285; *H.M.C. Hatfield MSS.* iii. 230.
[2] Additional MS. 48027 (Yelverton 31), an unfoliated paper, and fol. 576. Cf. *Eng. Hist. Rev.* xliv. 104-6, xlvi. 632-6.

Scottish Queen that hath wrought tears', he wrote to Walsingham on December 23rd, reporting the effect of Mary's last letter to Elizabeth; 'but I trust [it] shall do no further herein: albeit, the delay is too dangerous.' What disturbed Elizabeth most profoundly — more profoundly than pity — was the sacrilege of subjecting an anointed Queen to public execution. After the tragedy, the English ambassador in Paris reported the reaction in high circles there: if only, he wrote, 'a hangman had not touched the head of a Queen of France'. It was the manner of the death that mattered. And later it was reported, both from the Count of Aremburg in the Low Countries and from the King and others in France that it would have been better to have poisoned Mary or choked her with a pillow, than to have put her to so open a death. 'The Queen of England' wrote Henry III in a message to James VI, 'has offended all the sovereign princes and kings in the world . . . subjecting a sovereign Queen to that from which God has by special privilege exempted kings, who cannot be judged except by Him'. In a letter to Elizabeth before the execution James had delivered a homily on this theme: it was doubtless more impressive than all his hectoring. The doctrine was a central one in the political thought of the great Reformers of the sixteenth century. Both as a Protestant and as a Sovereign, Elizabeth shrank from the infamy: 'that she, of all Christian princes, should be the first author of so strange a precedent'. Could she have foreseen the execution of Charles I in the following century, her distress would have been the greater.[1]

There were those about Elizabeth who counselled her to have Mary murdered. Beale picked out Leicester as the principal advocate and associates Whitgift with the plan. 'The Archbishop of Canterbury', he notes, was 'sent from the Queen to Mr. Secretary Walsingham to persuade him': perhaps not an incredible statement, though Beale's word by itself is not sufficient authority. Says Beale: 'One Wingfield (as it was thought) should have been appointed for this deed; and it seemed that her Majesty would have had it done so, rather than otherwise, pretending that Archibald Douglas, the Scottish ambassador, had so advised her: . . . [also] alleging the [Bond of] Association, whereby men

[1] Harleian MS. 285, fol. 268; *Foreign Cal. Eliz.* XXI. i. 252, 254; Additional MS. 48027 (Yelverton 31), fol. 529; *Scottish Cal.* ix. 346, 363; RAIT & CAMERON, op. cit. p. 180.

seemed bound to such a thing, and promising pardon'. 'Both the Secretaries misliked thereof; and so did Sir Amias Paulet and Sir Drue Drury' — Mary's custodians.[1]

Elizabeth, as Davison relates, after signing the warrant had clutched at the murder plan, just as he was leaving her: as though in a desperate, last-minute effort to avoid a greater evil. She insisted that he and Walsingham should write to Mary's custodians, reproaching them for failing, 'in all this time', to shorten Mary's life, and urging that there was warrant for both conscience and credit in their Oath of Association. The two gentlemen replied in great distress, refusing to 'make so foul a shipwreck' of their consciences, or leave so great a blot to their posterity, or shed blood without law and warrant. Noble words, they have been called; but there was at least some excuse for Elizabeth's bitter complaint of their 'daintiness' and of the 'perjury' of men, who, contrary to their Oath, would cast the burden upon herself.[2]

During this final episode, Elizabeth's mind seems to have veered, with increasing preference, towards murder. At least three times she spoke to Davison of it: 'of a course that had been propounded unto her underhand by one of great place'. And when he argued against it, she told him that wiser men than he were of other opinion. It is very hard, in the face of these facts, recorded by Davison, not to conclude that, in dispatching the warrant, Councillors were conscious of forcing the Queen's hand. But other, arresting evidence comes from Beale. In his notes, he records that when he arrived at Fotheringay with the warrant he was told by Paulet and Drury 'that they had been dealt with by a letter' to know 'if they could have been induced to suffer' Mary 'to have been violently murdered by some that should have been appointed for that purpose'. The plan was thereupon discussed, and, from another note of Beale's, one might possibly infer that the two commissioners for the execution, the Earls of Shrewsbury and Kent, as well as Beale, Paulet and Drury, were parties to the discussion. Having considered the precedents of Edward II and Richard II, says Beale, 'it was not thought convenient or safe to proceed covertly, but openly according to the statute' of 1584-85. In other words, these men as good as took on themselves the crucial

---

[1] Additional MS. 48027 (Yelverton 31), unfoliated sheet, and fol. 529.
[2] MORRIS, *Poulet Letter Books*, pp. 359-62; NICOLAS, *Davison*, pp. 86-7, 100-1, 245.

decision between murder and execution. They hesitated before
acting on the royal warrant. Surely we may infer that the Councillors at Court were also aware of reasons for hesitating.[1]

Elizabeth's behaviour after hearing of the execution is worth
examining. There seems little doubt that she was genuinely
shocked. Her Councillors, in an apologetic letter written on
February 12th — meant for no eye but her own — expressed 'with
sobbing hearts our desire to have your grief of mind to cease, and
to give yourself to your natural food and sleep, to maintain your
health'. The night before, she had reprimanded them 'exceedingly'. Burghley was unfortunately away from Court at the time,
having hurt his leg in a fall from his horse. After Davison, her
wrath fell most heavily on him. She refused to see him and would
not receive letters from him.[2]

And now for a remarkable piece of evidence: a document
worthy of place among the curiosities of our history. On February
25th Burghley wrote a secret letter to someone unnamed: so secret
that he employed ciphers or blanks, and masculine for feminine
pronouns, to conceal its purport, and asked for its immediate
return to him. It survives in a copy made by his secretary, with
a sheet of clues. 'I doubt not', he wrote, 'but you understand her
Majesty's great displeasure for the execution of the Scottish
Queen, though justly done and most profitable for her Majesty's
surety, if by mishandling since . . . it be not impaired. Poor Mr.
Davison is, as you know, in the Tower, whose conscience doth only
comfort him; and though her Majesty hath shown her offence to
her Council that were privy to the execution, yet her offence is to
me so further in some degree, as I, not having been able to appear
before her with the rest, by reason of my hurt, am forbidden, or not
licensed, to come to her presence to answer for myself . . . She
(I know not how) is informed that by her prerogative she may
cause Mr. Davison to be hanged, and that we all may be so convicted as we shall require pardon. Hereupon, yesterday, she,
having Mr. Justice Anderson with her and demanding question
whether her prerogative were not absolute, he answered, as I
hear, "Yes".' She had turned on Lord Buckhurst for saying that
she could not hang a man against her laws, rebuking him bitterly,

---

[1] *Scottish Cal.* ix. 299, 291; Additional MS. 48027, fols. 528b, 529 (printed in part in
Eng. Hist. Rev. xl. 234-5).
[2] *Hatfield MSS.* iii. 221; WRIGHT, *Q. Elizabeth & her Times*, ii. 332; *Foreign Cal. Eliz.*
XXI. i. 242; STRYPE, *Annals*, III. i. 539 seqq. ii. 404-11.

and citing Justice Anderson. She has since 'declared the judgment of Mr. Anderson to serve her purpose', and intends to consult the other judges. Burghley asks his correspondent to warn
certain of them, secretly, to be careful what they reply. 'The
goods of men may be lost by their answers.' 'I would be loth to
live to see a woman of such wisdom as she is, to be wrongly
advised, for fear or other infirmity; and I think it a hard time if
men, for doing well afore God and man, shall be otherwise
punished than law may warrant, with an opinion gotten from the
judges that her prerogative is above her law.' He was fearful
for Elizabeth's reputation if the proceeding should become
known.[1]

What are we to make of this strange document? Undoubtedly
Burghley was distraught at the time: witness his fearful letters to
the Queen on his own fall from grace, and his readiness to sacrifice
Davison on the eve of the Star-Chamber trial. His letters are
abject: partly, no doubt, in deference to convention, but probably
also because such a situation, in the sixteenth century, was often
the prelude to ruin, if not to death. The odds are that stout
Walsingham would not have panicked at the tantrums of a
woman: as he drily told Leicester, he knew quite well that the
Queen would not use his services if she could do without them.
Nevertheless, there was substance behind Burghley's letter.
Walsingham told a correspondent of the Queen's 'great passion
against Mr. Davison', and of her consulting the judges. Beale
records — on the authority of Davison himself, who received a
message to this effect from Sir Walter Mildmay — that the
Attorney General and Solicitor General both said plainly that
they would rather lose office than deal against Davison otherwise
than in the Star Chamber, 'where somewhat might be done to
countenance the matter and satisfy her Majesty, and [afterwards]
be remitted by her, as was in this case'. It looks as if the Court,
united in wanting Mary's death, was in a subdued mood of revolt
against their Queen's reaction to it. Nonetheless, they deserted
Davison, and cringed before the wrath of the Prince.[2]

At last, our portrait has acquired its lineaments, and a solution
of our problem seems possible. Though Elizabeth's foreign policy

[1] Lansdowne MS. 108, fol. 90.
[2] *Scottish Cal.* ix. 344, 347; WRIGHT, op cit. ii. 335; *Foreign Cal. Eliz.* XXI. i. 241-2;
Additional MS. 48027, unfoliated sheet.

certainly demanded a scapegoat for Mary's death, we cannot believe that she was merely playing—or even preposterously overplaying—a game of diplomatic expediency. The execution was a national, not a personal act. Those final days at the beginning of February were a period of decision and indecision, Councillors taking advantage of the former, the Queen falling back on the latter. If ministers had proved responsive to her moods — as duty enjoined — she might have proceeded from delay to delay until the crisis eased: as she had done in 1572 and as was her habit when possessed by doubt. And then the pattern of events would have repeated itself: Ridolfi Plot; Babington Plot; anon some new Plot. This was precisely what Councillors feared. It was also what she feared. She must surely have known that the fatal deed was in train; though she probably hoped, or maybe thought, that murder would be the means employed. Equally, Councillors must have been conscious that they were forcing her hand: a highly dangerous game, akin to touching the sceptre. When news of the execution arrived, the Queen was overwhelmed by a sense of irrevocable tragedy and the infamy of a sacrilegious deed. Her doubts cleared, her deep-seated, persistent instinct seemed right. But it was too late. In unreasoning anger she heaped her own responsibility on that of others. Such a reaction, in its irrational complexity, is not outside human experience at any time.

Sir Christopher Hatton had ended one of his speeches: *Ne pereat Israel, pereat Absalom*. David and Absalom! The parallel proved to be closer than Hatton can have anticipated. In retrospect, her Councillors were wiser than the Queen. *Mortui non mordent*: 'the dead do not bite', they had argued. Mary's death assured the safety of Elizabeth and Protestant England.[1]

Our narrative has strayed from its parliamentary focus; but not fruitlessly, for we have acquired a principal clue to the theme that follows. When Parliament reassembled in February, the Puritan party was to stage its great effort to revolutionize the Church. And at that time the Queen, its inflexible opponent, was unrestrained at Court and in a flamboyant humour. Burghley — the voice of caution — was not at hand. He remained in disgrace for about two months, and was absent from Parliament until the last day of the session, though he carried on his functions as

[1] *Bardon Papers*, ed. Conyers Read (Camden Soc.), p. 95.

minister and Councillor. As for the rest of the chief Councillors, they were in no fettle to restrain their mistress. They were cowed: brought to heel by her prolonged anger over the execution of Mary Queen of Scots.[1]

[1] Cf. Strype, *Annals*, III. ii. 410; *Hatfield MSS*. iii. 242; Wright, ii. 335; attendance lists in *Lords Journals*.

CHAPTER III

RELIGION

THE bitter struggle of the Puritan ministers against Archbishop Whitgift had not abated. Their parliamentary programme may have failed in 1584-85, but their organization had been tried out and its power demonstrated. Bishops, Councillors, even the Queen had been shaken by what seemed a widespread and spontaneous outburst of lay and clerical discontent. For nonconforming ministers the obvious moral was to extend and strengthen their organization. United, there was some hope of resisting the pressure being put on them: isolated, there was none. In 1585 their leaders had turned their minds to the preparation of a Book of Discipline — an outline of the presbyterian form of church government — to be subscribed by party-members after scrutiny in their *classes* or conferences. The Northampton *classis* — we are told — agreed that it was necessary in conscience to practise the discipline privately, seeing that the Queen would not establish it publicly; and that each preacher should endeavour to increase the number of converts. Presumably the policy of other *classes* was much the same.[1]

Since there was no place in their philosophy for religious toleration, 'the godly brotherhood' — as they termed themselves — were in process of creating a revolutionary situation. John Field, their central secretary, 'a great and chief man amongst the brethren of London, and one to whom the managing of the discipline . . . was especially, by the rest, committed', deliberately willed this result. 'Tush, Mr. Edmondes!', he said to a brother who was arguing against popular methods, 'Hold your peace. Seeing we cannot compass these things by suit nor dispute, it is the multitude and people that must bring the discipline to pass, which we desire.' The examples of Scotland and the Netherlands may have been in his mind. He was the principal man among a group of extremists who — as was noted on the eve of this Parliament — were 'of mind to ask a full reformation and to accept of

[1] SCOTT PEARSON, *Thomas Cartwright*, pp. 252-3; P.R.O. Star Chamber, Eliz. A 49/34, John Johnson's depositions.

none, if they had not all'. In contrast, there were others who thought 'some reformation' might be accepted, 'if it were granted'. This difference in outlook among the brethren needs to be kept in mind. Among Puritan sympathizers in the House of Commons the difference was even greater. Some were zealots of the Field school of thought, some moderate presbyterians, while others were 'fellow-travellers', ranging themselves behind extremist leadership out of earnest concern for the religious state of the country, or from predominantly patriotic or anti-clerical motives.[1]

In times of passion a middle-of-the-way policy is hard to pursue; to pursue it with vigour still harder. The ordinary Member of Parliament saw his Queen, country, and faith in dire peril from Catholic forces, which were prepared to stick at nothing in order to reimpose a detested tyranny. He also saw a dour and donnish Whitgift, aided by the unpopular, and by some, despised Bishop of London, John Aylmer, silencing or depriving so many of the most ardent Protestant ministers that the bishops might be thought more eager to root out Puritans than Papists, and less tolerant of excessive zeal than of ignorance, incompetence and moral turpitude. The situation lent itself to skilful propaganda. John Field and his godly brotherhood continued the compilation of their remarkable statistical and descriptive 'Survey of the Ministry'. By November 1586 they had ready disturbing, tendentious studies of more than 2500 parishes, covering eleven counties and the City of London, for which, by way of preface, they wrote an enormously long Supplication to Parliament. Together, these documents presented the argumentative and factual case for the 'full reformation' desired by Field and his group; and the 'reformation' was to be accomplished by an accompanying Bill and Book.[2]

These were not the only Puritan documents got ready for Parliament. There were other bills and other supplications. Moderates as well as extremists had been busy. One brother, of the latter persuasion, who dipped his pen in vitriol, wrote a 'Request of all true Christians to the most honourable High Court of Parliament', showing the iconoclastic contempt of such men for everything connected with episcopacy: for 'the titles and names of

---

[1] BANCROFT, *Survey of the Pretended Holy Discipline* (ed. 1663), p. 295; Star Chamber, Eliz. A 49/34, depositions of Thos. Edmondes; USHER, *Presbyterian Movement* (Camden Soc.), p. 59.
[2] PEEL, *Seconde Parte of a Register*, ii. 70 seqq.

Antichrist — as Lord's Grace, Lord Bishop, Dean, Archdeacon' — through which 'tyranny reigns'. 'Let cathedral churches be utterly destroyed', was his advice. They are 'much like the sinful houses of Friars that were sometime amongst us . . ., very dens of thieves, where the time and place of God's service, preaching, and prayer is most filthily abused: in piping with organs; in singing, ringing and trolling of the Psalms from one side of the choir to another, with squeaking of chanting choristers . . . ; in pistelling and gospelling with such vain mockeries . . ., imitating the manners and fashions of Antichrist the Pope, that man of sin and child of perdition . . . Dumb dogs, unskilful, sacrificing priests, destroying drones, or rather, caterpillars of the Word . . . Dens of lazy, loitering lubbards.' Their revenues, he argued, should be turned over to the maintenance of learned preachers and other good purposes.[1]

Parliamentary elections were another concern of the brotherhood. It was evidently on the eve of the elections to this Parliament that the leader of the Dedham *classis* wrote as follows to John Field: 'I hope you have not let slip this notable opportunity of furthering the cause of religion by noting out all the places of government in the land for which burgesses for the Parliament are to be chosen, and using all the best means you can possibly for . . . procuring the best gentlemen of those places, by whose wisdom and zeal God's causes may be preferred. Confer amongst yourselves how it may best be compassed.' That firebrand, Job Throckmorton, probably owed his election at Warwick to Puritan pressure; perhaps Anthony Cope was similarly persuaded to re-emerge at his borough of Banbury after being absent from the last Parliament; and in one way or another the party may have had a hand in the election of other Members. But the letter suggests far more than can have been accomplished. It is chiefly significant for the idea: another sign of the strange modernity of the Puritan story.[2]

The ministers probably held a general conference or national synod in London in November, when they hoped to launch their parliamentary campaign. Perhaps they managed to circulate some of their papers and do a little discreet propaganda; but the complete absorption of Parliament in the business of Mary Queen

---

[1] Ibid. pp. 208-11; and cf. other papers in this collection.
[2] BANCROFT'S *Survey*, p. 294.

of Scots compelled them to postpone action till after Christmas. In February, when Parliament reassembled, we know for certain that there was a synod, attended by 'many of our godly brethren and fellow-labourers'; and these men were in contact, probably through John Field and other leaders, with a group of Members of Parliament, including Peter Wentworth, Cope, Lewkenor, Hurleston, and Bainbridge, who met together 'before the Parliament', — as doubtless during it — to plan the parliamentary campaign.[1]

The extremist or root and branch party had apparently carried the day in the synod's confabulations. At any rate, it was their policy that this group of Parliament men sponsored; and the person chosen to make the initial move was Anthony Cope, stepson of George Carleton and friend of Peter Wentworth.

On Monday, February 27th, by which day the business of supply was temporarily out of the way and room left for other interests, Cope opened the attack, rising from his seat about 9 a.m., after two bills had been read and three hours remained for debate. The Clerk notes that he first used 'some speeches touching the necessity of a learned ministry and the amendment of things amiss in the ecclesiastical estate'. Probably the Puritan Survey of the Ministry and its prefatory Supplication served as his brief. He then offered to the House a Bill and a Book, explained briefly their purport, and asked that the Book might be read.[2]

We have the text of the Bill. Its preamble opened with a historical review of the English Reformation. Henry VIII, it stated, had done well enough for his time. Edward VI, blessed with a further increase of heavenly light, had travailed worthily, but had been handicapped by the immensity of his task and shortness of his reign, and could not effect a clean purge of former infections and errors. As for Elizabeth, at her accession she had been compelled, by the necessity of sudden change, merely to revive the reforms of her father and brother; but, since that time, 'the light of God's glorious gospel', increasing daily, had revealed the imperfections and conflicts with the word of God contained in the order, discipline and Prayer Book of the Church. There followed an exposition of the perfect, the Presbyterian Church — 'approved by the general judgment and practice of all the best-

---

[1] USHER, op. cit. p. 98; my article, 'Peter Wentworth', in *Eng. Hist. Rev.* xxxix. 50.
[2] D'EWES, p. 410.

reformed Churches' — contrasted with the perverted and corrupt episcopal Church now established. A further advancement of the gospel would be 'a sweet and acceptable sacrifice to Almighty God for His late most wonderful and gracious deliverance' of the Queen from the Babington Plot.

After the long preamble came two brief enacting clauses. The first authorized the use of the annexed Book of Common Prayer: a revised version of the Genevan Prayer Book, recently published, which incorporated a Presbyterian form of Church constitution. The second declared 'utterly void and of none effect' all existing 'laws, customs, statutes, ordinances and constitutions' so far as they affect the government of the Church as well as its services. The whole existing hierarchy, the ecclesiastical courts with their canon law, the royal supremacy, and every relevant Act of Parliament, old and new, including the Acts of Supremacy and Uniformity and even some of the Acts against Catholic recusants, so acceptable to Puritans: all were swept away by this astounding essay in naivety. *Tabula rasa*; stark revolution. Its like was never seen before in English Parliament.[1]

Whether Speaker or assembly grasped the full implications of the motion may be doubted. With memories of previous trouble, the Speaker begged Members not to proceed, reminding them that 'her Majesty, before this time, had commanded the House not to meddle with this matter', and that she had promised to take order for the reform of abuses, to the good satisfaction — he did not doubt — of all her people. He pleaded in vain. The organized group for whom Cope spoke called for the Book to be read, and were supported, vocally or silently, by the great majority of Members. Overwhelmed, the Speaker gave the Clerk instructions to proceed with the reading. Hereupon, James Dalton — the renegade radical — intervened. The Book, he told them, appointed 'a new form of administration of the sacraments and ceremonies of the Church, to the discredit of the Book of Common Prayer and of the whole State'. They would bring on themselves her Majesty's indignation for daring to deal with matters belonging to her own charge and direction.

For such opposition, Cope and his friends were ready. Edward Lewkenor rose to answer Dalton, showing 'the necessity of

[1] PEEL, op. cit. ii. 212-14. (The text of the final clause here is faulty: the correct one is in S.P. Dom. Eliz. 199/2.)

preaching and of a learned ministry', and declaring it very fit that
Bill and Book should be read. Job Throckmorton spoke in support
of Lewkenor, as also did Ralph Hurleston and Robert Bainbridge.[1]

The speech that Throckmorton wrote for this occasion survives: a lengthy document. After an opening apology, he complained of the restrictions upon Members, who, greeted with 'a
show of freedom' on entering the House, in the sequel found
themselves threatened with bondage. 'Ye shall speak in the
Parliament House freely, provided always that ye meddle neither
with the reformation of religion nor the establishment of [the]
succession . . . In these causes . . . that reach so high and pierce
so near the marrow and bones of Church and Commonwealth, if
any of the inferior sort here amongst us do happen in some zeal
to overstrain himself, surely ye that are honourable [i.e. Privy
Councillors] . . . ought in equity to bear with them, because the
fault is in yourselves. I have heard it often said that the next [i.e.
the quickest] way to put the fool to silence is for the wise man to
speak in the cause himself . . . When grey hairs grow silent, then
young heads grow venturous . . . It is wondered at above that
simple men of the country should be so forward; and it doth amaze
us in the country that wise men of the Court should be so backward. If it be more than need in us to fear everything, it is less
than due in them to sit down with *omnia bene* [all's well] and fear
nothing. Is it a fault in a private man to be too busy, and can it
be excused in a Councillor to be too sleepy?'

The surest way for the safety of her Majesty — the chief cause
of all their consultations — is, he declared, 'to begin at the house
of God and to prefer the reformation of Jerusalem before all the
fleeting felicities of this mortal life'. 'It was (out of all question)
a very worthy act that was late done at Fotheringay — the cutting
off from the earth of that wretched Athalia . . . It was well and
worthily done of her Majesty to execute justice upon that Guisian
imp, one of the principal sheet anchors of all our discontented heads;
but yet, by your favour, to reform the house of Goddan to settle
the Crown to the bliss of posterity shall be ten times better done.'

Turning specifically to Cope's Bill and Book, to which he had
evidently anticipated opposition when preparing his speech, he
continued: 'If it be true that this plot here laid before us be
indeed warrantable by the law of God, justifiable by the power of

[1] D'EWES, p. 410; B.M. Harleian MS. 7188, fol. 92b (an anonymous diary).

the Word, and already unanswerably proved to the view of the
world, let us take good heed, I say, that this our wilful rejecting
of it . . . be not fearfully punished upon us and our posterity.' He
protested against the epithet 'Puritanism' applied to all righteous
intentions. 'To bewail the distresses of God's children, it is
puritanism. To reprove a man for swearing, it is puritanism.
To banish an adulterer out of the house, it is puritanism. To
make humble suit to her Majesty and the High Court of Parliament for a learned ministry, it is puritanism . . . I fear me
we shall come shortly to this, that to do God and her Majesty
good service shall be counted puritanism . . . It pleased good
Mr. Babington to bestow this name and title' on my Lord of
Leicester and Sir Amias Paulet. 'The Lord send her Majesty store
of such Puritans.'

He dwelt on the deformities of the Church and the perils of
Catholicism, in particular of Jesuits. As 'ancient Father Augus-
tine', being asked the chief point of Christianity, replied 'Humility,
humility', 'even so must I, if I were asked what is the bane of the
Church and Commonwealth, answer make, "The dumb ministry,
the dumb ministry"; yea, if I were asked a thousand times, I must
say, "The dumb ministry".' A learned ministry was the remedy;
and Parliament should deal in it, not 'the grave fathers' — the
bishops — who, hitherto, had been 'as a northern wind that
seldom bloweth good to the Church of God'.

The speech gives us a hint of that flair for organized political
agitation which made the Puritan classical movement so very
dangerous. In 1585 — as we have noticed — their agents were
said to have been 'all day at the door of the Parliament House'.
In 1589 — as one of their ministers deposed in the Star Chamber
— 'many were sent to attend at the said Parliament, from the
most parts in England'. In other words, they exploited the modern
art of parliamentary lobbying, copying and extending a practice
which began with — and, so far as we know, had hitherto been
confined to — the promoters of private bills. It seems clear from
Throckmorton's speech that they were using the same tactics in
1587, for he urged Members to open their ears and admit into
their presence 'the lamentable outcries of the poor distressed souls
of the land, whose humble suit and grievances shall be laid before
you when you please. And it may be' — he added — 'some of
them stand now at your door, thirsting for relief.' In all likelihood

there were at that moment Puritan agents in the Lobby, equipped with their petitions, their surveys of the ministry, and other papers.

'Alas!', continued our speaker, criticizing the effect of Whitgift's disciplinary drive, 'is there law to expel out of the ministry a learned man of life untainted, and is there no law to banish thence an adulterer, an incestuous person, a drunkard, a dumb hireling, a swearer, a blasphemer, or such like? whereof, if it come to examination I fear me ye will blush at the number. Surely, if there were such a brack or lameness in the law, can there come any greater honour to this High Court of Parliament than to reform it with speed, that thereby the Lord might have cause to bless us still in the mighty preservation of our Theodosia?'

Assuming Cassandra's role, he foretold dire happenings if reform were not undertaken. But if their Queen's — their Theodosia's — heart were awakened, then 'the Lord may be moved to bless us still with her . . . that her days may be aged, her reign prosperous, her bliss endless; that the last day of her life may (if so please Him) be the last day of this earth; that when she fleeteth hence to our earthly discomfort, we may then behold His son Jesus, sitting in His throne of judgment, to our endless and everlasting comfort.'[1]

This, we need to remember, was a speech for revolution. How innocent, how plausible: how little the audience was really told about that cataclysmic bill! The other speakers may have been just as careful to exhort without alarming. At any rate, they carried the House with them: a profoundly significant fact. But godliness and brevity dwelt not together: our zealots had talked the hours away. Agreeing to read the Bill and Book 'tomorrow', the House rose, probably very late.[2]

There was no 'tomorrow'. Elizabeth acted instantly. From Greenwich, where she was still in residence, she sent to Mr. Speaker for Cope's Bill and Book and also for the Bill and Book put into the House by Dr. Turner in 1585. When the House met the following morning the Speaker announced that he had sent them to her Majesty, by her express command.[3]

---

[1] Pierpont Morgan Lib., New York, MS. MA. 276.

[2] D'EWES, p. 410; Harleian MS. 7188, fol. 92b.

[3] D'EWES, p. 410, states that the House did not sit this day, as the Queen sent for the Speaker. D'Ewes is using the rough notes kept by William Onslow, acting as deputy for his sick cousin, Fulk Onslow (a very unsatisfactory substitute, from our point of view). D'Ewes is certainly wrong, for our anonymous diarist gives the proceedings narrated above.

One might have expected an abashed silence. Instead there was a debate on the state of the Church. It was Edward Dounlee, Member for Carmarthen and a Justice of the Peace in that county, who started it by presenting a supplication to Parliament on behalf of the country of Wales, written by the young Welsh preacher, John Penry. Penry, whose passionate outbursts and indiscretions brought him ultimately to the gallows, had hastened the printing of his treatise in order to get it before Parliament. In his speech Dounlee spoke 'of the great idolatry begun again in Wales to an idol; of the number of people that resort to it; of the solitary [character] and closeness of the place, amongst bushes, where they abuse other men's wives; of the service . . . said in neither Welsh nor English tongue; and of the superstition they use to a spring-well, in casting it over their shoulders and head; and what ignorance they live in for lack of learned and honest ministers'. [1]

Dounlee was followed by that curious, sadistic gentleman, Richard Topcliffe; a man of birth, education and religious zeal, who revelled in his official task of torturing Catholics. His strange character remains portrayed for us in marginal comments written in his copy of an Italian history of the English Reformation, [2] where from time to time he drew pictures of gallows, 'for the author and William Allen and for his Pope, Clement VII'. 'The viper'; 'the villain'; 'the bastard'; 'I wished that I had this Doctor in Westminster Hall without weapon, and the author of this book in St. John's Wood with my two-handed sword': these are samples of his private exuberance. In his speech on this occasion Topcliffe backed up Dounlee by mention 'of the like superstitious use of Buxton's well, and how they brought children to christen them in the well; of the ignorance for lack of learned ministers'. He 'wished every man might give a particular note of all the disorders in his country, which he himself offered to justify'. It looks very much as if Topcliffe was one of that Puritan group, whose part in this astonishingly well organized agitation was so obviously prearranged. Certainly it is true of the next speaker, Bainbridge, now on his feet again. In our diarist's succinct comment — by no means a pointer to original brevity —

[1] Harleian MS. 7188, fol. 93b. Dounlee was later removed from the Commission for the Peace, partly because of this action (cf. B.M. Additional MS. 48064, fols. 144-5).
[2] L'Historia Ecclesiastica della Rivoluzion d'Inghilterra (Rome, 1594), now belonging to Professor Gordon of Reading University, who most kindly allowed me to see it.

he is noted as 'also for reformation, to divert God's plague from us'.

Next came Mr. Francis Hastings, one of five brothers of the Puritan Earl of Huntingdon, an able, responsible parliamentarian, who is hardly likely to have been one of the conspirators. He had been at strife with himself — he said — whether to speak or hold his peace; 'but, considering his duty to God, loyalty to the Queen, and love to his country, he could not be silent, but in [a] place of free speech [was] willing and ready to deliver his conscience'. The issue was the safety of her Majesty and strengthening of our country. As we daily pray for it to God, so now in our assembly let us do what may be most to His Glory. We must not thrust God out of doors. Our ministers are blind. There is necessity for preaching. Idleness, duplicity, non-residence hinder salvation. The people are untaught, God dishonoured, the Word contemned. Catholic seminarists abound. With better laws, her Majesty would be better obeyed.

Mr. John Aldred, a former mayor of Hull and Member for that borough, followed. The clipped sentences of our diarist convey the flavour of his speech. 'Speaking as a poor labourer in the building of the Temple. Something wanting we wish to be amended. With many examples out of the Bible.' Francis Alford then rose, and — strange fact, unless our diarist's jottings are misleading — seemed almost accommodating in his conservatism. Nonetheless, he thought there was already remedy by course of law. Perhaps others spoke. Time was left for reading the subsidy bill; but it was the only business accomplished that day.[1]

Next day, March 1st, was Ash Wednesday, and our diarist absented himself to hear the Dean of Paul's preach at Court. We could have better spared him on almost any other day, for this was Peter Wentworth's occasion. The Puritan group, meeting to determine their tactics and perhaps recalling the discussions of the parliamentary caucus in the previous Parliament, so strikingly described by Fitzwilliam, had evidently assigned to him the task — undeniably his — of raising the question of freedom of speech, should their initial move meet official obstruction. He had his speech ready, and on March 1st opened the proceedings of the day by rising to deliver it:

'Mr. Speaker, Forasmuch as such laws as God is to be honoured

[1] Harleian MS. 7188, fols. 93-4.

by, and . . . such laws as our noble Sovereign and this worthy realm of England are to be enriched, strengthened and preserved by from all foreign and domestical enemies and traitors, are to be made by this honourable Council; I, as one being moved and stirred up by all dutiful love, and desirous (even for conscience sake) and of a mind to set forward God's glory, the wealth, strength and safety of our natural Queen and Commonweal, do earnestly desire . . . to be satisfied of a few questions to be moved by you, Mr. Speaker, concerning the liberties of this honourable Council.' Both he and 'many godly, faithful and true-hearted gentlemen in this honourable assembly' were 'fearful and loth to give or offer any offence to her Majesty or unto her laws, the which we presume we shall not do if we keep ourselves within the circle of them . . . Wherefore, I pray you, Mr. Speaker, eftsoons to move these few questions', one by one, 'whereby every one of this House may know how far he may proceed . . . for I am fully persuaded that God cannot be honoured, neither yet our noble Prince or Commonweal preserved or maintained, without free speech and consultation . . . And so, here are the questions, Mr. Speaker . . . The Lord direct our tongues that we may answer them even with His spirit.'

Among Wentworth's questions were the following: 'Whether this Council be not a place for any Member . . . freely and without controment of any person or danger of law, by bill or speech to utter any . . . griefs . . . touching the service of God, the safety of the Prince and this noble Realm? . . . Whether it be not against the orders of this Council to make any secret or matter of weight which is here in hand known to the Prince or any other? . . . Whether the Speaker or any other may interrupt any member of this Council in his speech? . . . Whether the Speaker may rise when he will (any matter being propounded) without consent of the House? . . . Whether the Speaker may overrule the House? . . . Whether the Prince and State can . . . be maintained without this Council of Parliament, not altering the government of the State?' In another version of the questions — whether later or earlier, we cannot tell — are these significant items: 'Whether it be not . . . against the law that the Prince or Privy Council should send for any Member . . . and check, blame, or punish them for any speech used in this place, except it be for traitorous words? . . . Whether it be not against the . . . liberties of this

House to receive messages either of commanding or prohibiting, and whether the messenger be not to be reputed as an enemy to God, the Prince and State? Whether it be not against the . . . liberties of this House to make anything known unto the Prince that is here in hand . . . and whether the tale-carrier be not to be punished by the House?'[1]

In these questions — comparable, in the secular sphere, with the theses posted on the church door at Wittenberg by Martin Luther — the radical and the prophet spoke. By entrenching Parliament in the fundamental constitution of the country, by claiming for it, as an essential quality, freedom of speech and action according to his own far-reaching description, and by his more detailed and specific contentions, Wentworth was robbing the Crown of its prescriptive right of control and discipline and leaving it defence-less, except for the House of Lords and the royal veto, neither of which could be an adequate and lasting protection for personal monarchy. In truth, through the plottings of the godly brother-hood and their organized group of parliamentary agents, Queen Elizabeth was menaced with revolution in both Church and State.

When Wentworth handed his questions to the Speaker, this embarrassed gentleman 'required him to spare his motion' until the Queen's pleasure was known about Cope's Bill and Book. Unyielding, Wentworth insisted on his questions being read. And here, it seems, Mr. Butler of Essex — John Butler, Member for the Puritan borough of Malden and friend of Lord Rich, a patron of Puritans — should have risen in support. There exists a speech on the theme of liberty, clearly composed by Wentworth for this occasion, which had presumably been written for Mr. Butler to use. But the faint-hearted gentleman 'brake his faith in forsaking the matter'. Asserting a right recognized in connection with bills, the Speaker said he would first peruse the questions and then do what was fit. He 'pocketed them up' and after-wards showed them to the courtier, Sir Thomas Heneage, with consequences that we shall see.[2]

Perhaps some stalwarts would have stepped into the breach left by Mr. Butler, and the Speaker would have been subject, once

---

[1] B.M. Cotton MS. Titus F. I, fols. 289-90; B.M. Lansdowne MS. 105, fol. 182 (printed by me in *Eng. Hist. Rev.* xxxix. 48).

[2] D'Ewes, pp. 410-11 (the footnote about Mr. Butler is not in the Cotton MS. and I have not found its source); *Eng. Hist. Rev.* xxxix. 52-3.

more, to irresistible pressure. But, apparently at this juncture, a
message arrived summoning him to go immediately to the Court.
The House rose. No other business was done that day. Since
Greenwich was too far away for the Queen to hear of Wentworth's motion and act so rapidly, we must conclude, either that
Privy Councillors had taken fright at a developing crisis and
(relying on the Queen's approval) had invented the message, or
that the summoning of the Speaker was Elizabeth's reaction to
yesterday's debate.

Discipline was now in the ascendant. The Queen's instinct
about the danger from Puritanism was clear and sound; and,
with Burghley in disgrace at Court and other Councillors in
trepidation, the normal restraints on her policy were weakened.
Wentworth may have been summoned before certain Privy
Councillors that afternoon. He was sent to the Tower. Next day,
Cope, Lewkenor, Hurleston and Bainbridge were also imprisoned
there. Somehow the authorities had got wind of their conferences
about the Bill and Book, held out of Parliament: an offence not
protected by privilege. It may well be that there were others who
had been at these meetings, and yet escaped either detection or
punishment. That the Queen herself was behind this display of
discipline, we need not doubt.[1]

At the opening of proceedings on March 2nd the Speaker
reported on his audience at Court. 'Her Majesty', he said, 'had
sent for him and noted great negligence in him that he suffered so
great disorder in the House. That for matter of reformation, at
the beginning of this Parliament' — she was probably thinking of
the previous Parliament — 'she charged my Lord Chancellor
nought should be said of religion', without first being made privy
herself. 'That he [the Speaker] had before told her pleasure to the
House. That notwithstanding, they had broken it. That again
she commanded, no more should be said.' Sir Christopher Hatton
reinforced the Speaker's warning, telling them 'that they did
great hurt to the good and orderly proceeding in reformation to
meddle now so busily in it.'[2]

The House turned submissively to routine business, while their
Puritan leaders — if we may guess from their tactics last Parliament — took time to think of their next move.

Two days later, on March 4th, they were ready. Sir John

[1] D'EWES, p. 411; *Eng. Hist. Rev.* xxxix. 49-51.   [2] Harleian MS. 7188, fol. 94b.

Higham — Member for Suffolk, a Deputy Lieutenant in that county and a keen, influential Puritan — was their spokesman. Waiting until a bill had been read and so securing a full House, he made his speech and motion. 'He would not — nor thought none of the House would — once open his mouth for any disloyal subject, such as Parry was, that was taken out from amongst them [in the last Parliament] and worthily committed. But, encouraged by the liberties of the House, he was more bold to beseech the House to join with him as humble suitors to her Majesty for the enlargement of some of the House he heard to be lately committed to the Tower for speaking of their conscience; not well seeing how the House could further proceed . . . without its Members.' After this covert suggestion of a parliamentary strike, he proceeded to talk about the state of the Church, with particular reference to his county of Suffolk, where, he said — or the diarist reports him as saying (and one or the other was hopelessly wrong) — there were three thousand parishes and few preachers. He ended by proposing that the House should petition the Queen for the release of their imprisoned colleagues. It was possibly a substantial, set speech, calculated to revive the whole religious agitation — though now with a moderate programme — as well as secure the freedom of Wentworth and his group.

The invaluable Hatton rose to reply, taking care to draw a distinction between actions subject to parliamentary privilege and those that were the exclusive concern of the Crown. 'Of these gentlemen committed', he declared, 'I assure you I know nothing.' In other words — and it may be an indication of the Queen's personal hand in this business — he had not been one of the Councillors set to examine the offenders. 'But,' he continued, 'knowing her Majesty's princely disposition, favouring all men, I stay at the matter, and think it necessary we all stay, to be first informed further before we presume to sue.' 'If the gentlemen were committed for matter within the compass of the privilege of this House, then there might be a petition; but if not, then we should give occasion of her Majesty's further displeasure.'[1]

Hatton then opened a massive counter-attack on the Bill and Book, the obvious aim being to expose their revolutionary character and reveal to fellow-travellers the dangerous and irresponsible company they had been keeping. Her Majesty, he

[1] Harleian MS. 7188, fols. 95-6; D'EWES, p. 412.

explained, had thought good to suppress these documents, but, in her concern for their contentment, was willing to give reasons for her action, and had accordingly charged Mildmay, Egerton, and himself with the task. The moment was cleverly timed, the choice of speakers masterly: Hatton, the respected, the supreme parliamentary manager; Mildmay, a great orator, who was notorious for his Puritan sympathies, who had now come — and how many of that assembly would follow him? — to the parting of the ways; Egerton, whose analysis of the legal and constitutional issues would carry the authority of an exceptionally able Solicitor General.

In his exordium Hatton explained that he had taken no further pains in the word of God than became a true Christian man. He deemed it an especial part of Christian sobriety for everyone to contain himself within the bounds of his own vocation, not presuming upon his own knowledge to dispute about ecclesiastical matters, which properly pertained to the learned Doctors and grave Fathers of the Church. However, a great part of the reformation desired in the Bill and Book came within the compass of his profession, which was matters of state.

He reviewed, as did the preamble to Cope's Bill, the history of the English Reformation, 'fined and refined', with gladness at home and congratulation from abroad. The enemies of man, he declared, are in his own house; and 'amongst all the assaults made hitherto by sundry sectaries against this our Reformation, there was never any, to my knowledge, comparable to this late Bill and Book.' 'First, my masters — I will speak but like a politic man — will you alter the whole form and order of your [church] service? Will you take the book from us which we have been persuaded to think both good and godly? . . . Might it not have sufficed to have reformed the errors? If you answer that there were so many, it could not be otherwise done, will any man believe you?' Commenting on certain features of the Puritan Book, he contrasted its extempore prayers and its emphasis on the sermon — 'which is, indeed, the whole service' — with the set prayers of the Anglican Book, which the illiterate common people could learn, by often hearing, and thus comfort themselves out of church. 'For anything I see, although to please us withal there be in show a Book presented, yet . . . all or the most part is left to the minister's spirit.' 'Trust me' — our diarist reports him as adding — 'you shall know it fitter to be suppressed than to be debated. And this I deliver you from her Majesty, that no further argument be used in it.'

He proceeded to examine the effect of the new order on the laity, the clergy, and the Queen. As regards the laity, he pointed out that the patronage of church livings — so much of which was in the hands of country gentlemen — would be transferred to the presbyteries. It 'toucheth us all in our inheritances'. Moreover, every parish would be burdened with 'one pastor at the least, a doctor, two deacons at the least, besides I know not how many elders'. If poor, they must be paid for their work. Neither Bill nor Book mentions this: wherein cunning is shown. 'For indeed their meaning is to draw from us, maugre our heads, our impropriations.' Bishops and cathedral churches were to be spoiled; and if — as was certain — these proved insufficient, then 'we are bound to surrender . . . our Abbey lands and such other possessions as have at any time belonged to the Church . . . They call us Church robbers, devourers of holy things, cormorants, etc.' This section of the speech was a shrewd appeal to the self-interest of Members. Had not even Catholic M.P.s in Mary Tudor's reign feared for their possessions?

He touched only briefly on the fate of the higher clergy, probably reflecting that his audience had little sympathy for bishops. But he denounced the new order as 'a barbarous equality', and pointed his argument with 'a pretty story' from the history of Carthage.

The Queen's estate received closer study: it touched them most of all. He examined the statutory elements of her royal supremacy. They were 'in a manner wholly abrogated by this Bill and Book'. What, he asked, was left to her Majesty when all the affairs and business of the Church were committed to pastors, doctors and elders in their presbyteries and synods? Moreover, the Queen's revenues were injured. 'First fruits, tenths, [clerical] subsidies, all gone; yet the Crown still bound to defend the Realm . . . It must all come out of your own purses.' In addition, the Queen was made subject to censure and excommunication by their presbyteries. What might emerge from this she knew only too well from certain contemporary tracts on rebellion: the notorious *Vindiciae contra tyrannos*, and writings by Buchanan and Beza.

'I pray you', he concluded, 'wherein differ these men . . . from the Papists?' A series of parallels followed. There was a final appeal to deluded fellow-travellers: 'Out of my heart, I think the honest, zealous gentleman of this House' — Anthony Cope — 'hath been slily led into this action'. *Sermonis finis*, notes our diarist: which may mean that one Member at least was beyond persuasion.[1]

Mildmay followed: an admirable speech. He directed attention to the second of the two brief enacting clauses in Cope's bill. 'To cancel and cut off at one blow so many laws, made so many years past, even from the statute of Magna Carta, is a thing that hath never been offered in this House.' He cited the Acts of Elizabeth's reign that would go, including those against Catholic recusants. Disannul spiritual jurisdiction, and what, he asked, would become of testaments and wills, tithes, contracts of marriage, questions of bastardy? The devisers of this plan were men of small judgment and experience. Cope, its sponsor, was honest; but it 'was put into his hands'.

He doubted whether a 'mere popular' election of ministers would produce more worthy men. It would create factions and confusions among the vulgar people, and in many places an evil lord or chief of the town would have his way. According to the Book, elders were to be godly and wise men; and, indeed, they had need to be, in view of their authority. How will such be found in country towns and small villages? Mildmay made many other points, some anticipated by Hatton. His Puritan outlook left him only too conscious of things amiss in the Church: 'would to God there were no cause to complain'. But, like many another moderate, he had evidently been shocked into a con-servative frame of mind by the extravagance of his friends: perhaps also by the reaction of his Sovereign. He was for counting present blessings: 'We live here under a Christian Princess, in a Church that professeth [the] true religion of the Gospel'. And for redress of shortcomings, his advice was 'to follow that course . . . with all humility, which is fit for us and is most like to prevail'.[2]

Egerton's speech, with its colder, analytical quality, was a suit-able climax to the persuasive eloquence of Hatton and Mildmay.

[1] Lambeth Palace MS. 178, fols. 48-51 (and in S.P. Dom. Eliz. 199/1). In delivery, Hatton must have departed slightly from his prepared text. I have inserted excerpts from the summary in the anonymous diary (cf. also Bodleian MS. Tanner 79, fols. 133-8).
[2] B.M. Sloane MS. 326, fols. 112 seqq.; anonymous diary (Harleian MS. 7188).

He had drawn up a set of notes, containing item after item of drastic change contained in the presbyterian programme; exposing in particular the consequences of sweeping away the whole legal and customary framework of the Church. He left no illusions and must surely have disconcerted all but fanatics. It is a pity that Fitzwilliam did not, this Parliament as last, leave us some comment on the reaction of the House.

That this impressive, triple exposure had been effective may perhaps be inferred from an addendum by Hatton. He rose to tell the House briefly that it was her Majesty's pleasure they should look at certain Puritan tracts that he named, giving his audience, as it were, a bibliography for further study.

As for the normal, legislative business of Parliament: only one bill had been read this day. Religion was a creeping paralysis in Elizabeth's Parliaments.

At the beginning of his speech, when replying to Sir John Higham's motion, Hatton seems to have promised early news about their imprisoned Members. Perhaps it was this remark which encouraged the intrepid Dr. Peter Turner, at the next sitting, on Monday, March 6th, to move 'for the liberty of the gentlemen committed to the Tower, pleading the liberties of the House'. The rest is mystery. Our diarist states that Sir Henry Knyvet spoke, saying that he thought 'our knights were sent for for that purpose', and that the House should therefore 'stay till they returned'. There is nothing to help us elucidate this. Presumably a delegation had been summoned either to wait on the Queen or on the House of Lords; but why, we neither know nor can guess. Certainly, the Members remained in prison.[1]

If a remark by Sir Christopher Hatton prepared the way for Dr. Turner's motion, it may be that certain passages in Mildmay's speech played a part in encouraging moderate Puritan leaders, now that their extremist brethren had been discredited, to try again, on restricted and reasonable lines. Their spokesman was once more Sir John Higham. On March 8th he moved a two-pronged motion: 'to have the amendment of some things whereunto ministers are required to be sworn' — an attempt to bridle Whitgift's disciplinary proceedings; and 'that some good course might be taken to have a learned ministry'. He carried the House with him: a remarkable fact, proclaiming anew the essen-

[1] S.P. Dom. Eliz. 199/2; Harleian MS. 7188, fol. 99.

tial sympathy and insubordination of Members. An impressive
committee was appointed, consisting of Privy Councillors and
thirty other Members, 'to confer upon some reasonable motion
to be made unto her Majesty for redress in these things'. The
committee included Higham himself, Beale, Francis Hastings, Sir
Richard Knightley and James Morice: all men of conviction and
grit. Anglicanism had its experts in Dr. Cosins and Dr. Lewin. [1]

Alas! once more our deficient sources close down on us. However, we may presume that the committee set about drafting a
petition to the Queen; and at Lambeth there is a copy of a document in the hand of Whitgift's secretary which could be fitted into
our story at this point, but seemingly nowhere else. It is a
message from the Queen, headed 'Why you ought not to deal
with matters of religion'. The odds are that Whitgift, hearing of
the committee and its task, called on Elizabeth for help, as he did
in 1585, and that her response was this message, delivered to the
committee by some Privy Councillor before the petition could even
be submitted to the House.

The message left no ambiguities: 'Her Majesty is fully resolved,
by her own reading and princely judgment, upon the truth of the
reformation which we have already . . . Her Majesty hath been
confirmed in her said judgment . . . by the letters and writings
of the most famous men in Christendom . . . Her Majesty
thinketh it very inconvenient and dangerous, whilst our enemies
are labouring to overthrow the religion established, as false and
erroneous, that we by new disputations should seem ourselves to
doubt thereof. Her Majesty hath fully considered, not only of the
exceptions which are made against the present reformation —
and doth find them frivolous; but also of the platform which is
desired — and accounteth it most prejudicial to the religion
established, to her crown, to her government, and to her subjects.
Her Majesty thinketh that though it were granted that some
things were amiss in the Church . . . ; [yet] to make every day new
laws . . . were a means to breed great lightness in her subjects,
to nourish an unstaid humour in them of seeking still for exchanges
. . . If anything were amiss, it appertaineth to the clergy . . . to
see the same redressed . . . Her Majesty taketh your petition
herein to be against the prerogative of her crown: for, by your
full consents, it hath been confirmed and enacted (as the truth

[1] D'EWES, p. 413.

therein requireth) that the full power, authority, jurisdiction and supremacy in church causes . . . should be united and annexed to the Imperial Crown of this Realm.'[1]

Silenced at last on religion, Members were still restless over the continued imprisonment of their colleagues; and if, as seems fairly certain, another of their company, the master-stylist and wit, Job Throckmorton, had recently been sent to the Tower for a speech containing 'lewd and blasphemous' criticism of James VI, then their feelings may have been dangerously inflamed. On March 13th, the moderate Thomas Cromwell, by now one of the most influential and respected of independent Members, moved a motion, 'to have some conference with the Privy Council of this House' and with others, concerning those gentlemen lately committed to the Tower. The House appointed a committee, consisting of all Councillor Members along with nine others, among whom were Beale, Hastings, Higham and Recorder Fleetwood.

Cromwell prepared himself for this committee with the thoroughness of the antiquary. He searched the statutes, the rolls of parliament, the journals, law reports and chronicles, from Edward III's days to Elizabeth's, for precedents, and seems to have distributed copies of his resultant paper to fellow-members. Beale's copy survives, described by him as 'Gathered by Mr. Thomas Cromwell in the Parliament of 28 *Reg. El.* when certain of the Lower House were committed to the Tower'; and to this copy Beale himself added further precedents and notes. In the hands of these men, the precedents were made to prove that the Queen had no right to imprison Wentworth and the rest. A series of irrelevant statutes were quoted to establish certain theses: that it was 'lawful for every Member of the House to open that which he conceiveth to be a grievance, and withal to offer that which he taketh to be a remedy, and also to consider and confer thereof'; that the 'dignities, liberties and privileges' attached to membership included 'the liberty of speech and of the body, of the which the body [is] the principal, for where the body is restrained, the speech is also restrained'; that a Member of the House 'should not be withdrawn' from his service. The Henrician Act about Richard Strode is in the collection, with as gross a misinterpretation as Stuart parliamentarians put upon it; and there is a string of precedents to show that, by 'ancient custom', the Commons

[1] Lambeth MS. 178, fol. 88.

themselves punished offending Members. Cromwell used his intimate knowledge of Elizabeth's Parliaments to recall the occasions when the Queen rescinded disciplinary orders. In some respects it is as significant a document as the famous Commons' Apology of 1604; and its historical sense is just as wretched.[1]

What happened as a result of the committee, we do not know. Probably nothing. Nor do we know when the imprisoned Members were released. Apparently, not before the end of the session. Hatton and his colleagues must surely have been disturbed by the rebellious mood of the House and by the uncompromising leadership of such a man as Cromwell. But they dared not whisper together — as was done over Strickland in 1571 — and arrange for the release of the offenders. The shadow of Mary Stuart lay between them and their mistress. *Ira principis mors est*: the wrath of the Prince is death. They were too mindful of this contemporary aphorism to curb their angry Queen.[2]

[1] Northants Record Soc., Finch-Hatton MS. 16, fols. 547-50.
[2] D'EWES, p. 415. For the discord between Elizabeth and her Councillors as late as April, see Walsingham's letters, quoted in MOTLEY, *United Netherlands* (1875), ii. 200.

CHAPTER IV

FOREIGN POLICY

THERE had been compelling reason for reassembling Parliament in February 1587. War-clouds were gathering, and more money was needed, though the last subsidy had been granted only two years before. Assistance to the Netherlands had been a great drain on the Queen's finances — and on her temper. Much had been spent: more, perhaps, than prudence warranted. Little had been accomplished. Dutch agents were again in England, trying to persuade Elizabeth to sink even more men and money in their struggle; offering her once more, as they had done before, the sovereignty of their country. In addition, England had to face the imminent prospect of a Spanish invasion. The short-term effect of the execution of Mary Queen of Scots had been to increase the menace from Catholicism. As though to emphasize the critical character of the occasion, the government chose Sir Christopher Hatton to make the principal speech in the House of Commons.

The House had reassembled on February 15th; and on that day Thomas Cromwell voiced the mood of the assembly when he moved that they should tender their humble thanks to her Majesty for responding to their petition by doing justice upon the Scottish Queen. Anything more welcome, yet at the same time more injudicious, it would be hard to conceive. It was of course 'well liked'; but, as we are also told, it 'proceeded no further'. Those near to the Queen must have shuddered at the thought of her probable reaction; and Hatton may have smothered the motion by reciting his instructions to have both Houses of Parliament adjourned for a week, owing to the absence of many of the nobility and principal gentlemen.

Consequently, serious business did not begin until February 22nd; and it was then that Hatton rose to make his speech on the dangers confronting the country. Alas! the text has not survived, though the deputy-Clerk — an otherwise laconic and most unsatisfactory recorder — was inspired to jot down in his rough notes an impressively long, but disjointed summary. The delivery may have occupied between one and two hours.[1]

The speech began with a message from the Queen. It was her Majesty's pleasure, said Hatton, to have the dangers of the country disclosed and to have the Commons know that she thanked God for their goodness. She wished the Parliament to be short, so that Members might return home and attend to matters of government, hospitality, and defence. Only essential bills should be handled.

He then turned to discuss the dangers confronting the country: 'the Catholics abroad, the Pope, the King of Spain, the Princes of the [Holy] League, the Papists at home'. Probing into the roots, he gave a long survey of contemporary history, from the Council of Trent to the King of Spain's present preparations for the invasion of England and Ireland. These, he said, consisted of '360 sail of Spain; 80 gallies from Venice and Genoa; one galliass with 600 armed men from the Duke of Florence; 12,000 men maintained by Italy and the Pope; 6,000 by the Spanish clergy; 12,000 by his nobility and gentlemen of Spain. It is reported that 10,000 of these be horsemen. I think it not all true, but something there is. We must look to the Papists at home and abroad', who practise to frame subjects against all duty. They teach that it is lawful and meritorious to kill the Queen, 'and have sent their instruments abroad to that purpose'.

Proceeding to discuss defence, Hatton devoted considerable attention to assistance for the Low Countries, describing their sufferings at the hands of Spain, and the diplomatic and other ties which bound England to them. The Queen's intervention was warranted by God and essential to the safety of her dominions. 'It may not be suffered that a neighbour should grow too strong', he added, uttering these words — noted the Clerk — 'as though it were not meet another Prince should have' that country (the Netherlands), and enforcing his point by historical examples, including Henry VII's aid to the Duke of Brittany. Whether, by such deliberate stress, he meant to provoke the House into an attempt to dictate foreign policy to their Sovereign, is not clear. But that, as we shall see, was the result; and to a section of the Council, including himself, a welcome result.

He went on to explain and excuse Elizabeth's past behaviour

[1] D'EWES, pp. 407-9.

towards Spain: a distorted story. 'The great grief', he reiterated — and his diagnosis here was sound as well as acceptable — 'is religion, and . . . all godly ones are bound to defend it.' He commended the Queen's courage against 'their malice', esteeming it not less than that of 'the stoutest kings in Europe'.

Sir Walter Mildmay followed, with a shorter, felicitous speech, playing on the patriotic sentiment of Members, their love for a most noble and precious Queen and their detestation of Popery, in phrases and arguments that echoed the moving speeches he had made in previous Parliaments: 'England, our native country, one of the most renowned monarchies in the world, against which the Pope beareth a special eye of envy and malice: envy for the wealth and peace that we enjoy through the goodness of Almighty God . . . ; malice for the religion of the Gospel which we profess, whereby the dignity of his triple crown is almost shaken in pieces'. Our enemies shoot at both England and Ireland. 'Their scope is by invasion and rebellion to subdue and conquer all, with purpose, as it seemeth, to root out from them the English nation for ever. And if it fall not out according to their desires — as, with God's help, it never shall — yet at the least they will do their best to trouble the Queen and her State, to burn, to spoil, to kill, to rob.' Mildmay also spoke of assistance to the Low Countries.

Great and strong preparations, he told them, must of necessity be made by sea and land. 'By sea is one of the things we ought chiefly to regard, being rightly termed the wall of England; for which her Majesty, with her provident care, is so furnished with great and good shipping . . . as in no age the like, and such and so many as no Prince in Christendom may compare with.' Money was needed. Members might think it too soon to grant another subsidy. But the tax assessments were so mild, being every time less than the previous, that 'not the sixth part of that which is given . . . doth come to her Majesty's coffers'. The grant given in the last Parliament did not amount to much more than half the charges of defence. This being so, 'let us lift up our hearts and stretch out our hands'. 'If it be thought that this present charge, coming so soon after the last, will be over-burdenous to the Realm', consider how intolerable yet unavoidable the charge would be if the enemy 'should take hold of any part of England or Ireland, or if he should be wholly master of the Low Countries'.[1]

[1] B.M. Sloane MS. 326, fols. 105-11. It is misdated February 24th.

In response to these two solemn orations, the House appointed a grand committee to prepare the subsidy, and for 'other great causes'.

Mildmay had no need to worry: so far from being reluctant to grant another subsidy, the assembly — or, at least, its vocal section — was anxious to do more. Next day they started a debate. Perhaps patriotic and religious exaltation, coupled with commercial interests, is sufficient to explain the agitation which then began. Perhaps, if we knew more, we might perceive a concerted operation, inspired by the Earl of Leicester, who still aspired to be viceroy in the Netherlands and had many followers in the Lower House, especially Puritans. Among the speakers that morning was the turbulent young Warwickshire squire, Job Throckmorton, one of the Earl's admirers. By good fortune we possess the speech he wrote for that occasion.[1]

To Throckmorton, as to most of his audience, the world about him was filled with the struggle between darkness and light. He began his speech with a review of that contest, starting from the famous conference at Bayonne in 1565, when Catherine de Medici and her son, Charles IX, met the Queen of Spain and the Duke of Alva. There — as Protestant myth reported and Throckmorton phrased it — had been hatched 'a pestilent conspiracy against the Church of God and the professors of holy religion', one incident in which was the infamous Massacre of St. Bartholomew. 'Mark what king it was', said Throckmorton: 'it was the same king that wept to the Admiral [Coligny] overnight, and gave him up to the butchery to be cut in pieces in the morning.' They plotted 'the rooting out of the House of Bourbon, with all the Huguenots in France; . . . the sacking of the city of Geneva; . . . the bringing of the free estates in Germany into an absolute subjection of the Empire; . . . the pacifying of the troubles in the Low Country, with the pruning out of such as were suspected to be of the religion; . . . the restoring of the pseudo-catholic religion in England by deposing of Queen Elizabeth and setting up the Scottish Queen.'

Having outlined the historical perspective of twenty years, he described the frustration of these plans, ending with 'the Scottish Dame, by the good providence of God brought low to the dust . . . The kings and princes of the earth assembled themselves and laid

[1] Pierpont Morgan Lib., New York, MS. MA. 276, pp. 28-51.

their heads together against the Lord and His anointed; but He that sits on high, even our Jehovah, hath laughed their devices to scorn'.

'*Our* Jehovah'! Throckmorton told how, 'some fourteen years ago', a *valet de chambre* of Charles IX — 'I might have said, varlet *de chambre du roi* well enough, for a wretched, irreligious varlet he was indeed' — passing through England with a message to the Scottish king, and hearing at Berwick of the fall of Edinburgh castle, defended by Mary's adherents, rapped out an oath and struck his hand on his breast: ' "I think", saith he, "God be sworn English, there is nothing will prosper against the Queen of England!" ' 'With what affection that wretched man spake it, I know not', said Throckmorton. 'But sure', he added, giving expression to the mystical inspiration of his generation, 'we that have lived in the eyes of all men, so choked, as it were, with blessings of God beyond desert, we that have lived to see her Majesty's life, so dear unto us, pulled out, as it were, even out of the lion's jaws in despite of Hell and Satan, may truly — not in any pride of heart, but in humbleness of soul to our comforts — confess that indeed the Lord hath vowed himself to be English . . . It is an argument unanswerable, to prove the Pope to be that man described in the Apocalypse — I mean that man of sin, that beast with the mark in his forehead — to prove him, I say, to be Antichrist . . . that look! where he curseth the Lord continually blesseth, and on the contrary, where he blesseth the finger of God's wrath is never from thence. Mark it, I pray you, well.'

From the Pope, he turned to delineate the judgment of God 'upon those kings, and in the kings upon the kingdoms'. 'For France, Catherine de Medici (I hope I need not describe her) hath not many (thanks be to God) left of her loins to pester the earth with. And those that she hath yet living, truly — to speak indifferently — she may have as much comfort of them as the adder hath of her brood. Whether they sucked their mother's breast, I know not; but sure, if they did not, it seemeth their nurses were greatly to blame, instead of milk to suckle them up with blood from their infancy . . . Queen Mother may . . . brag above all women in Europe, that hath brought us into this world such a litter (to her praise be it spoken) as few women have done . . . ; whose principal delight . . . hath been in nothing almost but in hypocrisy, filthiness of life, and persecuting of the church of God.

As to him that now holdeth the sceptre there [Henry III], do ye not see him smitten [with] barrenness? Is that all? Nay, do ye not see him stricken with a fearful kind of giddiness, as it were a man in a trance or ecstasy', drawn sometimes to the Guisan faction, sometimes underhand to the King of Navarre? It may truly be said of him, 'He is afraid of shadows that feareth not the Lord'.

Philip II was next anatomized: his profession superstitious, 'his religion idolatrous, his life some think licentious, his marriage we all know incestuous, great-uncle to his own children'. Can there come any greater plague to a Prince than this — to leave his dominions 'to be possessed by an incestuous race of bastards'; to sit down in his chair in his old age 'and behold the ruin of his house before his face'? He possesses 'many rich countries, populous nations, golden mines, and I know not what'. Mighty as he is, 'the Lord hath put a snaffle in his mouth for all that'. His dominions are rather a burden than a defence; his receipts do little more than answer his disbursements; 'maugre his head', he is forced to make peace with the sworn enemy of all Christendom. 'Have we not lived to see him stricken with a sottish kind of madness', yielding 'to the drawing of the heart blood of his own son', and suffering 'his wife to be in the house of [the] Inquisition?'

'A man with half an eye may easily behold the judgment of God upon both these kings, notwithstanding the blessing of the Holy Father. Whether any of them hath the leprosy of the body, I know not; but we are well assured both of them have the lethargy of the soul — that is, the sleeping sickness'.

Throckmorton warned Members against a sense of security, bred by the rare and blessed peace they had enjoyed under her Majesty's government — a government 'in wisdom equal, in mildness and mercy superior' to that of all her progenitors. Coming to his principal point, which was to urge acceptance of the sovereignty of the Netherlands, he described this offer as 'an evident sign that the Lord hath yet once more vowed himself to be English, notwithstanding all our former unthankfulness and wretched deserts'. He pictured God addressing them from Heaven: 'Though your sins do swarm in abundance . . . if ye will reform your church and lives in time, I will here offer you a means whereby ye shall be able to stand alone, yea, and to withstand all the foreign invasions of your ungodly enemies'.

If we neglect this offer of the Low Countries, where else, he asked, is there any other anchor-hold of safety? 'Our dear brother of France . . . howsoever we league it or temporize it with him', is in far deeper league with our sworn and professed enemy, Spain. 'In whom there is no religion, in him there is no trust. A Frenchman unreformed is as vile a man as lives, and no villainy can make him blush.'

Such unrestrained vituperation against a continental king, whose good will Elizabeth was anxious to maintain, was bad enough. But there was an even more delicate and vital strand in England's foreign policy — the league with James VI of Scotland, which had already been strained almost to breaking point by the execution of Mary Stuart. Throckmorton blundered into that. 'Whither, then, shall we cast our eye?' he asked. 'Northward towards the young imp of Scotland? Alas! it is a cold coast (ye know) and he that should set up his rest upon so young and wavering a head might happen find cold comfort . . . Ye knew his mother, I am sure: did ye not? Then I hope ye will all join with me in this prayer: that whatsoever his father was, I beseech the Lord he take not after his mother . . . How he may degenerate from the humour of his ancestors, I know not.' As a boy, I heard it said that falsehood was the very nature of a Scot. It may be that religion and good education have saved him from corruption: we hope they have. But her Majesty should keep a jealous and watchful eye on him. The Catholic leader, Dr. Allen, has commended him. 'When a man of Allen's humour falls a-praising of him . . . can he be an ill-minded subject amongst us that thereupon . . . feareth some mischief?'

Throckmorton continued: 'We see no hope of Spain, no trust in France, cold comfort in Scotland. Whither then shall we direct our course?' The very finger of God directs us to the Low Countries, as though to say: 'There only is the means of your safety, there only is the passage laid open unto you, there only, and nowhere else, is the vent of your commodities.' The action is lawful. These countries never were an 'absolute government'. The King of Spain has lost the right of his sovereignty 'by tyranny and blood, or rather, if ye will, by the just judgment of God.' Throckmorton was sure that the people there 'desire, even from the bottom of their hearts, to live under the obeissance of her Majesty, before any other prince or potentate of the earth', having tasted 'the sweetness and equality of her Majesty's government under an honourable general [the Earl of Leicester], who, by his wisdom, hath emblazoned her name there and renowned her sceptre to posterity'. The Queen's purpose had been 'to succour the afflicted for the cause of religion'. The Romans, for their own glory, had written 'in their ensigns', *parcere subiectis et debellare superbos*: may the Lord, not for her glory but for His, vouchsafe that Elizabeth in her ensigns write, *sceptrum afflictae ecclesiae consecratum* — my sceptre dedicated to the afflicted Church.

To those who might object that this policy would 'pull Spain on our heads', he answered: Better that, than 'pull the wrath of God on our heads'. As Elisha was saved from the Syrian army by the host of Heaven, so might they be. It was not Spain nor France they had to fear, but the lack of true Christian discipline. 'Our bodies are in England, our hearts are at Rome.' Mere outward conformity is what our spiritual governors seem to desire and our carnal gospellers to practise. If it would please the Lord so to work on her Majesty's heart that this was reformed, 'then should we not need to fear either the fury of Spain, or the treachery of France, or the hosts of the Assyrians, or all the power of Hell and darkness.'

Our diarist has a brief reference to this speech: 'Mr. Job Throckmorton spake sharply of princes, and after [was] rebuked covertly by Mr. Vice-Chamberlain [Hatton]'. The word 'covertly' replaces 'openly'. It may have been both, for two days later — probably on instructions from Court — Hatton rose to make what our diarist terms 'a motion to admonish'. 'This other day in proceeding' — he said — 'divers spake very well . . ., but one, a gentleman of noble blood, zealous in religion . . . spake sharply of princes and laid indignities on them. The reverence to princes is due by God . . . We are bound to obey good princes. God doth correct by ill princes.' All of which — be it interpolated — was good orthodox Reformist theory. 'We should,' he continued, 'use great regard of princes in free speech.' It was 'hard and intolerable to use ill speeches of the King of France, continuing in league and friendship with us. Neither ought we to upbraid him with his ancestors. God is to judge. Matter nearer than this [was] glanced at also: yea, and touched a little against the King of Scotland, a prince young, of good religion, a friend, and in league with her Majesty, both offensive and defensive.' It was a 'sin then to speak ill of him, and shame to detract him: rather, to pray for him.' A king presents the image of God to men; lower than Him, but above all others.[1]

Hatton hoped that his motion might 'avail to make some repair': from which we might infer that the authorities — maybe, even the Queen — would have been content to allow an egregious example of licentious speech, threatening vital foreign friendships and alliances, go at that. But reports of the speech reached Archibald Douglas, James VI's ambassador or agent in London; and at such a delicate moment in their relations Elizabeth dared not let Scotland be further provoked. James was relying on the English succession as the price to be paid him for his mother's execution. Little prospect there would be of enjoying his side of the bargain if the Commons of England thought and talked like Throckmorton. Burghley wrote to Douglas on March 2nd: 'I have caused her Majesty to be informed of the lewd and blasphemous speeches used in the Commons House by one, Job Throckmorton, against the honour of the King of Scots, for which cause he shall be committed tomorrow to the Tower as a close prisoner, and shall thereby, for the rashness of his tongue, feel smart in his whole body. His fault is not excusable, and therefore the sharplier to be punished . . . And so I wish your advertisement of the punishment [to James] may accompany or prevent [i.e. precede] the report of the fault.'[2]

Presumably, Throckmorton was sent to the Tower. He wrote a letter to Burghley on April 3rd asking him to mediate with the Queen: 'I have read indeed long ago, but I never felt it by experience till now, that the indignation of the Prince was death.' His fault, he wrote, sprang from unadvisedness, not contempt; rashness, not disloyalty; from 'the privilege of the place [the House of Commons], apt enough to bring a young head into a distemperature'. He was evidently still in prison, though Parliament had by then been dissolved.[3]

In modern eyes, Throckmorton's punishment may seem tyrannical. It was not. The privilege of free speech did not extend to licence, as the Commons themselves were only too ready to assert when it suited their humour, and as they demonstrated when, for example, they sent Wentworth to the Tower in 1576.

[1] B.M. Harleian MS. 7188, fols. 89, 92.
[2] *Illustrations of Scottish History*, ed. Margaret Warrender, p. 32.
[3] B.M. Lansdowne MS. 53, fol. 148.

Hitherto, so far as we know, the Queen had limited her discipline, where speech alone was concerned, to reprimands; and if she was responsible for Hatton's admonitory speech on February 25th, then initially she intended no more on this occasion. She had little option in acting as she did when the incident threatened her strained relations with Scotland.

It is evident from Hatton's remarks on February 25th that Throckmorton's speech two days earlier was one of several. Our diarist only notes two: one by Francis Alford, urging the continuance of action in the Netherlands; the other by Hatton, justifying this policy. Hatton, who described Philip II as greater than Alexander the Great, may even have favoured accepting the sovereignty of that country. As for the House, though warned that they would have to pay for their fancy, over and above the subsidy then in hand, they followed the lead of their speakers and appointed a committee to confer about a loan or benevolence to be offered to the Queen: a committee of phenomenal size, having the grand committee on the subsidy as its core. Job Throckmorton was one, and seems to have been among the first named: surely a sign that his speech had been popular.[1]

Before the committee met, another opportunity for debate arose when, on February 24th, the subsidy articles were read. Sir Thomas Scott of Kent discussed the dangers to England, both inward and outward. He struck a congenial note when he declared that there was 'more danger by advancing Papists into place of trust and government than by anything'. Discoursing on defence by ships, he stressed the wisdom of resisting the enemy at sea or while landing on the beaches, citing the resistance to Julius Caesar. Mr. Wroth, the wealthy Member for Middlesex, seized the chance to advocate accepting the sovereignty of the Low Countries. For his own part, he would give £100 a year towards the maintenance of that war. If the loss of Dunkirk had done so much harm, what would the loss of such places as Flushing, Brille, and Holland do? Francis Bacon then intervened: a cold, prudent mind, untouched by the fire of youth, immune from infection by his audience; already a prerogative-man. Our diarist jotted down these points of his: 'All speeches placable and good. Not liking a committee, but to leave it to her Majesty. But if her Majesty stick

[1] Harleian MS. 7188, fol. 89; D'EWES, p. 410 (and cf. the original MS. of this, Harleian MS. 74, fol. 277b).

to take it, for want of treasure, then to put it to committees. Preposterous the vale to judge of the hill: etcetera.' Alford spoke again, evidently as a counterblast to Bacon — a strange role for him. He favoured a committee to agree on a bill, moving her Majesty to undertake the Low Countries. It may have been now — rather than at the end of the previous day's debate — that the House set up its committee.[1]

The debate, however, was not yet ended. One after another our Puritan zealots got up to pursue Sir Thomas Scott's attack on Papists and excite minds only too responsive to witch-hunting. Of course, they spoke as they felt; but, familiar as we now are with the revolutionary's technique of promoting fear and hatred against some enemy of society, we cannot but reflect that belling the Papist provided a propitious setting for what these conspiring gentlemen were about in Church affairs. Mr. Grice and Mr. Beale — as our diarist notes their speeches — wanted all weapons and furniture of war taken from Papists. Dr. Turner desired 'that by some token a Papist may be known': can he have had in mind a distinctive badge? Bainbridge wanted 'detracting Papists' to be looked to. And then came Mr. Topcliffe — *experto crede!* — to stampede their fears. He told them of 'weapons and all massing trumpery, with books papistical', found 'in the very next house joining to the Cloth of Estate by the Parliament House. The owner's name, one Mr. Ingam of Kent, a principal of an Inn of Chancery'. When searching his house, this man had offered him money to spare him. He found 'prayers for King Philip, etcetera'. Peter Wentworth at once rose to move that the man be sent for; and, though the Commons had neither right nor jurisdiction to warrant their action, they appointed Sir Thomas Scott, Sir Henry Knyvet, Mr. Thomas Knyvet and Mr. Topcliffe — godly gentlemen all — 'to search certain houses in Westminster suspected of receiving and harbouring of Jesuits, seminaries, or of seditious and Popish books and trumperies of superstition'. We do not know the sequel. But how needful and appropriate was the role Elizabeth played of restraining, affectionate, on occasions stern mother to her excitable children![2]

That afternoon — February 24th — the committee met to con-

[1] D'EWES, p. 410 (following the Clerk's rough notes) gives February 23rd for the committee. Neither D'Ewes nor the Clerk is reliable.
[2] Harleian MS. 7188, fol. 90; D'EWES, p. 410.

sider the question of the Netherlands. It is interesting to learn that
the Speaker, Puckering, was there: the occasion, like the committee,
was extraordinary. He jotted down notes of the debate in law-
French, spattered with English, using this medium because its
abbreviations provided him with a form of shorthand. Mildmay
started the discussion, suggesting that, in order to encourage the
Queen to deal effectively with the Low Countries, they should
offer a benevolence, as a voluntary subsidy for two, three, or more
years, if the war continued so long. On the central issue of accepting the sovereignty of the country, he would leave the decision to
the Queen: a sentiment becoming him as a Privy Councillor.
Wroth then spoke. 'His meaning was that she should accept [the]
sovereignty.' Sir Thomas Cecil, Burghley's eldest son, uttered
some platitudes, and then Sir Francis Knollys spoke. He, too, was
a subdued Councillor: they might express the opinion that
sovereignty was the better way, but they must not offer their
benevolence with that tying condition. Bainbridge spoke: a
strangely temperate speech. Since England was divided in religion, there could be no peace at home should Spain re-establish
herself in the Netherlands. Therefore it is better to support wars
against Spain abroad; and let the Queen accept the sovereignty
if she wishes. Francis Bacon gave much the same advice.

Two others spoke, and then Sir Christopher Hatton made a
major speech, reported at considerable length by Puckering.
Referring to the treaty made with the Low Countries preparatory
to sending an army in 1585, he remarked: 'The matter was debated
before the Queen herself by her Councillors, arguing on both
sides; and at last [it was] agreed to be undertaken as honourable,
just, and necessary for profit'. If we neglect the Low Countries, we
lose dominion of the narrow seas and put into a mighty monarch's
hand that which all the world cannot give him — navigation. He
will be able to bring his silver from the Indies and stop our trade.
'Whither shall we carry our commodities if he has the Low Countries?' Spain is richer than England in wool and wishes to sell its
wool there. To defend these countries is to have an open market,
with good and quick return: to lose them is to lose all. Hatton
warned them that the French were equally conscious of the value
of the Low Countries. He then turned to the financial problem.
The Netherlands could not defend themselves, nor could the
Queen continue, 'if we go no further than a subsidy'. They had

offered us the sovereignty as their contribution to the cost of defence; alternatively, the status of protector; or, if neither of these was acceptable, then they asked for assistance. They have neither the forces nor means to resist the enemy. If they are not given aid, they may want to slip away from us.

Hatton had apparently been content to give no lead about sovereignty. Mildmay now tried to bring the discussion to some conclusion. He suggested a humble petition to the Queen, setting forth the importance of the cause to her and to the kingdom, with the need 'to embrace it more roundly'. To encourage her, they should offer a benevolence. They could express their desire for one line of policy — clearly he meant sovereignty — rather than another; but he deprecated any present discussion of relative merits. They must be clear about the manner of raising the benevolence: better no offer than fail to implement it and so reveal to the King of Spain a want of good will in the country.

Alford then spoke. Picking up Mildmay's hint, he was for stating their opinion in favour of sovereignty: men, he remarked — and what he said was true for mercenaries of all nations — would more willingly enter the Queen's service and pay than that of the States. If it is odd to discover Alford consorting with radicals, it is stranger still to find Sir Francis Knollys acting the canny realist. If the Queen, he said, takes the sovereignty, then the States would know that, though they furnished little or even no assistance, she would nevertheless maintain the war: which is what they desire. Whereas, if she merely assists, then she is not tied to them should they give insufficient support. Hatton intervened again, speaking also as a realist, but with a wholly different emphasis: 'If we enter in strength, we shall have the sovereignty when it pleases us, or make such a peace as we ourselves desire.' He was clearly delighted with the way things had gone both in the House and in committee: 'These days' doings, well known and continued, will mightily further the enterprise. It is such a consultation as this Realm has not known these hundred years'. But in his enthusiasm Hatton forgot his mistress; he was blind to the serious practical and constitutional issue involved in dictating foreign policy to the monarch. He ought to have been wiser, especially in the aftermath of Mary Stuart's execution.

Discussion now turned mainly on the form of the benevolence. Puckering notes a further seven speeches. Mr. Saltonstall, a wealthy

London merchant, pointed out the dependence of Philip II on
the safe arrival of his treasure fleets. At that moment, he said,
there were five coming from different places. Intercept them,
and the war would be ended, with a good peace. Sir Henry
Knyvet distrusted the Dutch. To be sure of them, we must take
the sovereignty and be there in greater strength than they. He
also advocated help to Don Antonio, claimant to the Portuguese
throne, thus raising rebellion in that country and closing both
ports and seas.

Puckering's jottings are followed by outline notes for a petition
to the Queen: possibly the concluding item of the committee's
work. It selected the principal points from the discussion, and
offered, in the name of 'all the nobility, gentry, and men of
ability', a large benevolence, while the war lasted, for the maintenance of the Queen's sovereignty in the Low Countries. 'Note'
— Puckering wrote in the margin — 'question whether sovereignty
or aid.' It was not the only uncertainty. The nobility were
included in that offer; and they had not yet been consulted.[1]

The committee met again on Monday, February 27th, when
Mildmay defined their business as deciding what they would give
'toward this and all other her Majesty's so great charges', and also
how to raise the money. Hatton spoke; and from a brief note of his
speech made by our diarist, it seems that his rapture of the other
day was evaporating. Evidently, the sentiment for sovereignty, and
nothing but sovereignty, was strong; while Hatton had probably
been to Court and found the omens there threatening. It was 'not
fit', he told the committee, 'to design and direct the Queen how
she shall use' the benevolence. But, he said, the money was 'not
to be taken, if not used': that is, he favoured a conditional grant.
Egerton, the Solicitor General, seems to have been less purposeful.
He viewed the benevolence as an aid 'for peace and the protection
of religion'. He would 'put in all, and refer the distribution of all
[to the Queen] and her wise Council'.[2]

If we may rely on the date, 'February', endorsed by Speaker
Puckering on two of his papers, then at this meeting, or at another
on the following day, the committee prepared for an approach to
be made to the Queen. Puckering wrote down — this time in
English — 'points of a petition' to be exhibited to her Majesty.
They were to offer — 'if now or at any time after, it shall please her

[1] Harleian MS. 6845, fols. 34-9.   [2] Harleian MS. 7188, fol. 93.

Highness to accept the sovereignty of the countries of Holland and Zeeland' — that they would 'most willingly and largely yield a voluntary yearly contribution', which, joined to her Majesty's treasure, 'may well defray the burden and charge of the said wars'.

In addition, someone — a Councillor, maybe — drafted a speech for Puckering to deliver to the Queen. It has occasional marginal notes, explaining allusions — for example, who Pluto, Aeolus, and Neptune were; that a line of Latin verse was 'Vergil's verse to the Queen Juno — which you may omit if you will'; and so on: a curious reflection on Puckering's cultural limitations! The speech approached its purpose through a choice preamble of grateful adulation. If the Queen were to forsake the Low Countries — ran the argument — and they were subdued by the King of Spain, 'then shall it come to pass that, even as his Indies have already made him Pluto of all the silver and gold, so the Low Countries shall crown him Aeolus and Neptune of the winds and narrow seas. Then shall it lie in his power, either to starve the Germans with cold and nakedness for want of that cloth which they have now from us, or else to put them into his own cloth and livery, and thereby to cloy and glut us with the overflowing store and plenty of that for which we shall find no vent at all. Then shall our stately ships, that now be the wooden walls and wings of the Realm, become unserviceable to us. Then shall our treasure [and] riches, that be maintained, not by mines but by merchandise alone, continually fade, diminish, and decay. Yea, then shall the ancient glory and renown of this your Majesty's kingdom be eclipsed; the bright candle of the word of God shall be extinguished; the hearts of the English nation shall be appalled; and they and their land together, thus enfeebled, shall be an open booty and unbloody conquest, either to himself or to any other.'

The speech went on to ask the Queen to accept the sovereignty of the Low Countries, or any other arrangement with them, as her wisdom prompted. Politeness inserted a sentence: 'The affairs of your royal estate are not to be directed by us, but to be managed by yourself'. A dutiful, tactful statement; but its lack of sincerity and the desire of the Commons to direct their Sovereign were revealed in the conditional character of their financial offer. If the Queen would take on herself the sovereignty, then they promised and vowed to follow and feed this holy war with a yearly benevolence, to be levied among the wealthier persons of the Realm.[1]

At this point, when they were almost ready to report back to the House, something happened to paralyse the committee: evidently a command from the Queen not to meddle with the question of sovereignty. Let us recall that it was on March 1st that Elizabeth interrupted the sitting of the Commons by summoning the Speaker to Greenwich. Her main purpose was to forbid action or discussion about the Church. But this desire of the Commons to interfere with foreign policy also touched the prerogative, and it also drew much of its inspiration from Puritan sentiment. What with the successful Autumn pressure that had procured the execution of Mary Stuart, the present agitation over Cope's Bill and Book, Peter Wentworth's subversive questions on the constitution, and this business of the sovereignty of the Netherlands, Elizabeth must have been alarmed and outraged. The monarchy was in danger, its intimacies profaned. Probably it was on this occasion that she pronounced the veto which brought the committee's deliberations to an end.

However, these fellows were a resilient lot. On March 6th 'it was moved by a gentleman — and good hold taken of it — for benevolence above the subsidy'. Mildmay picked up the suggestion and told sorrowfully of the committee's fate: 'many meetings, no good. Pity it should die.' He proposed that the committee should meet again that afternoon.[2]

When the committee met, Hatton had encouraging news. The clergy in Convocation had come into this business of bribing the Queen in the hope of influencing her foreign policy, and had agreed to levy a benevolence, equalling half their subsidy grant, without, however, any condition, even without any allusion to the Netherlands in the text of the grant.[3] After Hatton had given this news, Mr. Wroth spoke. He had offered £100 for the Queen to take the sovereignty; and although her Majesty would not do this, 'yet he would mend his subsidy'. Hatton spoke again, stressing that the Queen had expenses in many places. They must think on this and decide whether they give anything or nothing; though the position remains, that 'we may not meddle with sove-

---

[1] Harleian MS. 6845, fols. 30-1, 40-2.
[2] Harleian MS. 7188, fol. 100; D'Ewes, p. 412.
[3] The text of this grant is in S.P. Dom. Eliz. 199/10. Cf. Harleian MS. 6994, fol. 58.

reignty'. Mildmay then urged them to consider how much more they should offer, and how to rate it. Many other Members spoke. James Morice and Sir Henry Knyvet were doubtful if the people could bear a further levy on top of the subsidy. Their faith, able before to remove mountains, was feeble now that they could not bribe the Queen to do their will. Morice, who loathed bishops, pointed out that prelates were better able to bear this expense, because they were free from the burden of musters. Knyvet was inclined to wait and give a new subsidy when the present one was exhausted: to which Hatton retorted that the present subsidy would be spent in sixteen months. In the end, they seem to have agreed to petition the Queen, asking her to appoint commissioners to raise a benevolence, in this following the precedent of Henry VIII's reign, which Sir William More had commended.[1]

Here our diary fades out. The next we hear of the subject is on March 11th, when it was before the House and Sir Francis Knollys was asking whether they should approach the Lords for joint action, or proceed on their own. They decided on joint action. There were several conferences between delegations from both Houses. At last, on March 15th, the Lords decided, 'for divers reasons', that it was 'not fit' to join with the Commons, but that each House should proceed on its own. We are not told their reasons; but they may have been afraid of the precedent, disliked subordinating themselves to the Commons in a liberal gesture, and above all wished to avoid any suspicion of dictating to the Queen on foreign policy. On March 16th they decided to grant a benevolence equivalent to half the subsidy rate, in this following the lead of the clergy. They instructed their Councillor-members to inform the Queen of their decision.[2]

We can only guess what the Commons did; but, taking a hint from a comment of Hatton's at the committee-meeting on March 6th — 'That this benevolence should grow voluntary, without constraint . . . chiefly from the wealthiest and most zealous, well-affected to her Majesty' — and coupling this with a suggestion by Mr. Wroth — that it should 'be by law, from £10 upwards to give 2s. in the pound' — it seems likely that the House followed the same plan as clergy and Lords, offering a benevolence at half the subsidy rate, but confining the levy to those more highly assessed.[3]

[1] Harleian MS. 7188, fols. 100b-102.   [2] D'Ewes, p. 414; L.J. ii. 134, 137-8.
[3] Harleian MS. 7188, fol. 101.

The Queen was probably informed of their decision by Privy Councillors, and perhaps audience was sought to make the offer in petition-form: an innocuous petition, for they knew that nothing else would be acceptable. On Saturday, March 18th, the Clerk recorded that Mr. Speaker delivered a message from her Majesty: 'She thanked God', he reported, 'understanding of their great love unto her in regard of her charges sustained in the Low Countries, and . . . was contented this afternoon that some convenient number of them should have audience before her Majesty'. The House appointed twelve Members, in addition to their Councillors, to wait on the Queen.[1]

Of the audience we know nothing. We know only that Elizabeth, though accepting the unconditional clerical benevolence, refused any benevolence from Lords and Commons.[2] Desperate as her need of money was, she valued independence above bribes. True, all conditions had by now been dropped from the offer. Nevertheless, the background of debate and action made it tainted money. She was inflexibly and wisely opposed to accepting the sovereignty of the Low Countries. Unlike so many of her subjects, she found little or no pleasure in assisting the Dutch. She had no confidence in their ability to wage successful war. She disliked their treatment of herself, her general — the Earl of Leicester — and her soldiers. Finally, she did not share the crusading instinct of her radicals, and consequently did not accept the inevitability of war à outrance with Philip of Spain. She and Burghley were in fact, at that very time, encouraging informal peace-feelers. To accept the sovereignty of the Low Countries would have involved a drastic change in her foreign policy. To allow Parliament to dictate that policy would have undermined the constitution.

---

[1] D'Ewes, p. 416.
[2] Cf. Dietz, *English Public Finance, 1558-1641*, p. 53. The clerical benevolence was evidently not refused (cf. Strype, *Whitgift*, i. 540, and S.P. Dom. Eliz. 199/10).

CHAPTER V

END OF THE SESSION

A FEW minor incidents deserve attention before we end the story of this Parliament. The first takes us back to the beginning of the session in the autumn, and concerns an episode of some notoriety in our text-books — the county election in Norfolk.

In this faction-ridden community, two enemies, Thomas Farmer and Christopher Heydon — the latter provoked to stand for election by 'the immoderate brags' of the former — were rivals for one of the two county seats. Farmer won in a contest where three thousand persons are said to have been present. But the election writ only reached the sheriff on the eve of the county-day, when by law he was compelled to execute it; and, though it is quite clear that people generally knew there was to be an election, he was in fact prevented through lack of time from giving the usual formal warning by proclamation. On this ground, and on others, Heydon and his friends complained to the Privy Council, alleging disorderly procedure by the sheriff; whereupon the Council inadvisedly prompted the Lord Chancellor to issue a new writ. At the second election Heydon carried the day, helped by the wording of the new writ and by a reprimand administered to the sheriff for choosing Farmer. Naturally, Farmer's party was not prepared to accept this result and therefore two returns were delivered into Chancery, one favouring Farmer, the other Heydon. Complaint was made to the House of Commons, and thus the question arose whether Chancery or the Lower House of Parliament was the proper authority to decide a disputed election case.

There can be no doubt as to where, by constitutional theory, jurisdiction lay. It was with the Crown in Chancery. Equally there can be no doubt about the practical issue involved. If the Crown — through Council or Chancery, or both — could quash elections displeasing to itself and order new ones, then, when hard-driven and unscrupulous, it could take steps to exclude trouble-some critics from Parliament. Charles I's device of pricking his opponents for sheriff in 1625 was later to demonstrate the reality of such a danger.

Theoretically, the Commons had no right to question the list of its Members, compiled in Chancery at the beginning of a Parliament and certified into their House as the Clerk of the Crown's *Liber Parliamenti*. Before they became politically mature and critical of the government, the issue could hardly have arisen. True, they had precedents for taking an interest in, and even passing judgment on, points of membership. When an institution is young and its latent power unperceived, and before authority is alerted about the ultimate bearing and importance of a principle, it may well happen that precedents are created which turn out to be embarrassing. But never before had the matter been so clear-cut and decisive as in the Norfolk election case. The claim made on this occasion by the House of Commons — details of which we shall shortly examine — is barely conceivable before the 1580s; and one is reminded, not only of such pioneers as the Wentworth brothers, but of that more widespread, deliberate thought about constitutional principles which Fitzwilliam's diary revealed in startling clarity in the Parliament of 1585.

The agitation began in the House of Commons on October 31st, after Members had returned from the ceremony of confirming the Speaker's election. Farmer's friends were presumably behind it. The Clerk has no entry in his Journal, but at the next sitting, two days later, he tells us that the Speaker delivered a 'commandment' from the Queen, conveyed to him through the Lord Chancellor. 'Her Highness', ran the message, 'was sorry this House was troubled the last sitting thereof with the matter touching the choosing and returning of the knights for the county of Norfolk: a thing, in truth, impertinent for this House to deal withal, and only belonging to the charge and office of the Lord Chancellor, from whence the writs . . . issued out, and are thither returnable again.' Her Majesty had ordered the Lord Chancellor and judges to confer together, and, after examining the returns and the sheriff, to decide as 'justice and right' indicate.

That ought to have settled the matter. The Queen had commanded; she was within her rights; and there was no reason to expect any other than a just decision from the judges. But on November 8th, towards the end of the morning, the subject was raised again, in 'sundry speeches' about 'the liberties of this House'. Some argued one way, some another. They talked the time away without a decision. At the opening of business next morning, they were at it again: 'motions and speeches', and the issue once more 'the liberties' of the House. A committee of fifteen was set up, including two Councillors and such authorities on parliamentry lore as Recorder Fleetwood and our former diarist, Thomas Cromwell.

Had this been an ordinary session of Parliament, the Queen in all likelihood would now have intervened a second time, with a peremptory prohibition in defence of her prerogative. But it was out of the question to risk a struggle over parliamentary liberties while the delicate problem of Mary Queen of Scots was under discussion. One party or the other had to give way: if not the Commons, then the Queen. Consequently, the Commons were able to establish a precedent which, though not sustained in later Elizabethan Parliaments, ultimately filched from the Crown power essential to the evolution of parliamentary government.

The committee duly met on November 10th, eleven members being present; and, with the Clerk of the Crown and the Under-Sheriff of Norfolk attendant, they reviewed the story of the two writs and elections. They had no hesitation in deciding for the first election, and were highly critical of the injunction in the second writ to elect 'two *others*' — a loose form of wording, presumably. It might, they justly said, 'be a perilous precedent for the time to come to the liberty and privilege of this House to admit or pass over any such writ or return'. The Clerk of the Crown told them — and this was confirmed by Recorder Fleetwood, who had it from the Chief Justice — that the Lord Chancellor had already ordered him to accept the first return. That is to say, Chancellor and judges had come to the same conclusion as the committee.

Sir Francis Knollys, while agreeing with the rest, and agreeing also, so he said, that jurisdiction in the case belonged to the House of Commons — an opinion flatly opposed to his Sovereign's — nevertheless wanted the committee to send to the Lord Chancellor and ascertain what he had done in the matter. In rejecting his proposal, the committee formulated certain celebrated points. First, they thought it very prejudicial to the privileges and liberties of the House to have this cause decided or dealt in by any except Members of the House. Secondly, though the Lord Chancellor and judges were to be respected, and their competence in their proper place acknowledged, yet they were not 'judges in Parliament in this House' — that is, they were not Members of the House of Commons — and so were incompetent to deal with the case.

On November 11th, Thomas Cromwell reported the committee's proceedings to the Commons, concluding with a motion that Mr. Farmer and Mr. Gresham — the two gentlemen elected on the first writ — should be received into their assembly, as 'allowed and admitted only by the censure of this House, and not as allowed of by the said Lord Chancellor or judges'. Nothing could have been more explicit. 'The whole House' agreed, and ordered the Clerk to enter the report in his Journal, thus recording a precedent, as an advancing army might dig a trench in newly-won ground.

Sir Francis Knollys then spoke, affirming his agreement with the committee's views, announcing that he had already administered the Member's oath to Mr. Farmer, and then going on to explain and excuse his lonely motion in committee. Fleetwood followed, 'making a large and plentiful discourse of the ancient privileges and liberties of this House, furnished with recital of sundry precedents and examples'. The occasion, indeed, fitted the man. It is a pity we do not have his speech, to see how the antiquary murdered history. He told how Chief Justice Anderson had that morning informed him of the Chancellor and judges' decision: to which he had replied that 'the censure thereof belonged unto this House and not unto them, and that he, for his part, would take no notice . . . of their so doing'. He concluded by approving the wisdom of the House in recording their judgment. And so, no doubt, everyone was happy, except the Queen, who had been compelled by the tactical situation to let the invader advance. Sir Christopher Hatton intervened to get Members off their hobby-horse and back to the business of Mary Queen of Scots.[1]

In the post-Christmas sittings, the Commons made yet another attempt to control Court purveyors, those harpies whose corrupt and tyrannous exactions when gathering provisions for the royal household were a constant source of grievance and anger. The great statute on purveyance of 1555, if observed, should have kept them in order; but, human nature and Elizabethan times being what they were, it was flagrantly broken. On March 2nd a bill

[1] DASENT, *Acts of the Privy Council*, xiv. 241-2; D'EWES, pp. 393, 395-9. The two accounts of Cromwell's report in D'Ewes are (pp. 396-7) from the Clerk's finished Journal, and (pp. 398-9) from his rough notes. The correct date for both is November 11th. The summary on p. 397 is by D'Ewes and carries no authority.

was introduced into the Commons 'concerning the great abuse of purveyors'. It imposed a penalty of £20 for taking goods other than as allowed by the statute, and attempted to put a stop to the tyranny of officials by forbidding the summoning of anyone to answer at Whitehall, on complaint of purveyors, unless two neighbouring Justices of the Peace sanctioned it — a salutary device, but a weakening of the prerogative. One might have expected Elizabeth to intervene with a message; but she had enough on her hands at that moment, and evidently preferred delayed action.

Sir Walter Mildmay spoke on the first reading. He shared the Commons', not his mistress's view: another instance of a Privy Councillor acting as a good House of Commons man rather than an official. The vexation of subjects — he seems to have argued — was a hindrance to their readiness to pay subsidies. Where exactions were proved, offenders should be well punished: but, he added, some people complained 'for private displeasure'. Next day, the bill was read a second time, debated — in the course of which much was said about the evil practices of purveyors — and committed. Back in the House on March 6th, Mildmay now asked for a recommittal and a new bill. On this occasion, Fleetwood, by way of jest — undoubtedly a popular one — suggested that they should make a law, 'that who hinders the bill of purveyors to be in case of praemunire'. The new bill was passed on March 11th. It passed the Lords on March 13th, receiving two readings on one day: eloquent testimony to its acceptability there. The will of Parliament was emphatic. The Queen nevertheless vetoed the bill. Where her prerogative was concerned, she was adamant.[1]

An episode in the relations of the two Houses ends our miscellany. There was a private bill 'for the sale of Thomas Hanforde's lands, towards the payment of her Majesty's debts', introduced into the Lords and passed quickly through its stages, apparently without committal. Reaching the Commons, it was twice committed, and a new bill emerged, devised — so the Clerk noted — by Hanforde himself, who appeared before the House and subscribed every sheet with his own hand. It passed through all its stages the same day. There must be a story behind this strange procedure, but we do not know it: certainly, it seems as if Hanforde

---

[1] Anonymous diary (B.M. Harleian MS. 7188, fols. 89 seqq.); D'Ewes, pp. 412-14; L.J. ii. 134-5.

was finding a sympathy in the Commons that he had failed to obtain in the Lords.

When the new bill came to the Upper House, there was much ado. The Clerk — usually a reticent and negligent journalist — became, for once, quite wordy: 'Having before passed a bill to the same effect, and sent it down to the Commons' House, and there rejected without conference with some of the Lords of this House; the Lords thought it a precedent so strange, and so far different from the orders of this House . . . that they did resolve to put it to the question whether this new bill should, by the orders of the House, be read here or not.' Each peer, being asked his opinion, agreed not. It was the penultimate day of the session, and time, as well as exasperation, may have imposed the deadlock. The Commons had certainly not displayed due reverence for their Lordships.[1]

The closing ceremony of the Parliament took place on March 23rd, 1587. The Queen was not present. Officially, her absence was explained in a trite, formal phrase: 'for divers great and urgent causes'. Perhaps a sense of propriety kept her from the closing, as well as the opening, of a Parliament concerned with the death of Mary Queen of Scots: though the long Christmas break and the character of subsequent business make this explanation seem unreal. Or maybe her absence was a symbol of mourning for a tragedy she deplored. But there were some odd features about the occasion that suggest a broader explanation. In the first place, Lord Burghley, who had been the senior commissioner for the opening of Parliament in October, was omitted from the commission for ending it. He had been absent from all the business sittings of the Upper House since Christmas, but was present for this last sitting. Present, and not on the commission! It seems a deliberate humiliation. What is more, Elizabeth ordered the Parliament to be dissolved. Surely this was deliberate also, for since the perils of the reign became threatening, it had become the practice, by short adjournments, to keep a Parliament readily available; and if ever that policy was needed, it was at this juncture, when the perils were clearly more serious and imminent.

Perhaps we are being fanciful — there is no means of telling — but it seems as if Elizabeth was so at odds with her Councillors and so thoroughly disgusted with Parliament that, though her instincts

---

[1] *L.J.* ii. 134-6, 141; D'EWES, pp. 415-17.

as publicist and actress usually prompted her to exploit a ceremonial sitting of the Estates of the Realm, she took advantage
of a slender excuse and of the fact that she was at Greenwich, not
Whitehall, to stay away. Had she been present, she might have
found herself listening to the Speaker urge either the cause of the
Netherlands or reform of the Church. She would surely have felt
impelled to trounce the Commons for their behaviour this session;
and at a time when her people might, any moment, have to face
ordeal by battle, a silent thought was preferable to a stormy
harangue.

When both Houses assembled in the Upper Chamber, there
were two commissions under the great seal to direct their proceedings. The first authorized Sir Edmund Anderson, Chief
Justice of the Common Pleas — who, during the whole of these
post-Christmas sittings, had presided in the Upper House in
place of the mortally-sick Lord Chancellor — to give the royal
assent to ten bills named in the commission. It was a poor legislative output, both in number and quality. Almost all were
government bills: only one a private measure. Though the commission itself carried no mention of the veto, three — or possibly
four — bills, including the one about purveyors, appear to have
met this fate.[1]

After this commission, a second was read, giving the Archbishop of Canterbury and seven other peers — including Leicester
but not Burghley — authority to dissolve Parliament. We must
presume that the commissioners thereupon presided over the
closing ceremonies. We have the text of the speech made to them
by Speaker Puckering: a laboured, uninspired oration; as though
the absence of the Queen had taken out of him such little virtue
as he possessed. A 'rude and unpolished action', he called it: so it
was. He referred to the behaviour of Members this session:
though 'some very few of them have fallen and offended, rather
by infirmity of judgment and through a preposterous zeal, than
of any either disobedience to her Majesty or intention of dis-

---

[1] The vetoed bills were: an act about fines and recoveries (cf. *L.J.* ii. 132); the
purveyors bill (ibid. p. 135); an act appointing the width of fishing nets (ibid.). In
the draft of his final oration, Speaker Puckering mentions, among the bills awaiting
the royal assent, one 'taking away such delays [in justice] . . . as by pretence of errors
have lately crept into the courts'. This seems to refer to a second bill about fines and
recoveries, entered as rejected in *L.J.* ii. 140. Either this entry is an error of the
Clerk's: in which case Elizabeth vetoed four bills. Or Puckering may have written
the draft speech before the Lords rejected the bill.

turbance to our better proceedings; yet, generally, the whole number hath from time to time no less readily assembled than quietly conferred and painfully travailed . . . for the glory of God, the service of her Majesty, and the common good of the Realm'.

In his descriptive reference to the bills that had passed both Houses, Puckering made no reference to the one about purveyors: perhaps he knew its impending fate. The final paragraph of his speech was devoted to the Netherlands, and was an anti-climax. The benevolence was dead: so was any ambitious dream of sovereignty. They were offering 'one usual subsidy' to help the Queen in her assistance to afflicted neighbours. True, he added a feeble — and dully phrased — hint: the subsidy was 'an earnest penny and pledge of our hearty devotion and readiness to employ whatsoever we do possess besides, at her Majesty's commandment and disposition'. Presumably, Sir Edmund Anderson replied to this oration on behalf of the Queen's commissioners; but we have no report of his speech.[1]

It makes a dull end to a lively, but — in its latter phase — frustrated Parliament. Every Elizabethan Parliament acquired a character of its own. Comparison can be misleading; but in its positive result — the execution of Mary Queen of Scots — and in its negative — the exposure and defeat of the Puritan revolution — the Parliament of 1586-87 yields in interest and significance to none. The perennial surprise is that however their masterful Queen thwarted them, Members of the House of Commons, and not least the irrepressibles, maintained their devotion to her. We might reflect that worship they must; and they had no other earthly god to adore. But it is an inadequate explanation of a mystical phenomenon.

---

[1] *L.J.* ii. 142-3; Harleian MS. 6846, fol. 17.

PART THREE

THE PARLIAMENT OF 1589

CHAPTER I

INTRODUCTORY

In the second edition of Holinshed's *Chronicles*, published in 1587, the editor alluded to an ancient prophecy, 'now so rife in every man's mouth'. It concerned 'the year of wonders, gathered to be 1588', and foretold that 'either a final dissolution or a wonderful, horrible alteration of the world is then to be expected.' The Chronicle ended with a prayer, asking God 'to bless the realm of England; and the precious jewel of the same — even good Queen Elizabeth — to save, as the apple of His eye', from 'all the pernicious practices of Satan's instruments . . . We beseech God . . . that the gospel . . . may be glorified in the commonwealth of England: a corner of the world, O Lord, which Thou hast singled out for the magnifying of Thy majesty.'[1]

Wonderful the year 1588 proved to be, and the majesty of God, as exalted Elizabethans conceived it, was gloriously magnified in the defeat of the Spanish Armada. While the nation rejoiced in that Providential miracle, its governors thought of the Exchequer and the inordinate strain placed upon it. Money — an exceptional amount — was needed; which meant summoning Parliament, a prospect that the Queen must have faced with a good deal of distaste and anxiety. The Armada was defeated and destroyed in July to August. Writs for a new Parliament went out in September. From a letter of Burghley's we learn that Elizabeth 'finding a great want of noblemen for Parliament' — death had thinned their number — was 'minded to create some earls and some barons'. It is characteristic of the Queen's rigorous and prudent economy, even over honours, that, on reflection, five of the seven potential barons named by Burghley were not ennobled.

[1] HOLINSHED, *Chronicles*, iii. 1356-7, 1592.

Her Majesty — wrote Burghley — 'had some speech with me, to call me to some other degree, but I have showed her Majesty just cause to leave me as I am', being too old and too poor for higher honour. 'Too poor'! a characteristic wail. He was to die a very rich man, worthy of his wealth, but not of such humbug.[1]

So far as we can tell, there was nothing unusual about the elections to this Parliament. Prevailing social factors operated, without government intervention. Even the Puritan *classes* do not seem to have taken concerted action: at least, there is no trace of it. A normal proportion of Members — rather less than half (220 out of 462) — were newcomers. The great lawyer, Edward Coke, was one. Among those not reappearing from the last Parliament was that colourful, remarkable man, Job Throckmorton. Probably he was too much involved with Martin Marprelate's activity to venture exposing and immobilizing himself at Westminster. Bainbridge and Hurleston, who had been sent to the Tower in 1587, did not sit again. Nor did Dr. Peter Turner or Edward Dounlee. Sir John Higham, the Puritan stalwart from Suffolk, was also absent, as was Richard Topcliffe. The House must have been a duller place without them. But other Puritan leaders came back: Peter Wentworth, Anthony Cope, Edward Lewkenor, Sir Richard Knightley, and, above all, Robert Beale and James Morice, whose constitutional approach in the campaign against bishops was to be an outstanding feature of this and the next Parliament. A Puritan newcomer, and one who seems quickly to have made his personality felt, was John Stubbs, brave author of *The Gaping Gulf*.

Parliament was summoned to meet on November 12th, 1588, but by October 15th the government had changed its mind. Perhaps some wise person reflected that the last payment of the subsidy granted in the previous Parliament was only now being collected; and that to seek — as they were to do — a new grant, double in amount, before the payment of the old was finished, would be asking for trouble. The assembly was prorogued till February 4th following.

The Lord Chancellor who made the opening oration on that day was Sir Christopher Hatton. He had been given the office

[1] Burghley to Shrewsbury, January 18th, 1589, in Baskerville's MS. calendar at the P.R.O. of the Talbot MSS. (Longleat).

in April 1587 on the death of Sir Thomas Bromley; and, though the Queen had had her misgivings about the appointment, both before and immediately afterwards, it was — on political grounds, at any rate — a fitting climax to distinguished service. How fitting, may be judged by his oration at the opening of this, his first Parliament as Lord Chancellor, and his last.

The theme was the state of the nation; the occasion, the morrow of a resounding victory in one of Europe's decisive wars. In the course of the centuries our English Parliament has listened to many famous speeches, and in our own time war has inspired oratory of immortal quality. For its eloquence, its emotion, and its stirring, confident patriotism, as well as a withering contempt for the enemy, Hatton's speech is not unworthy of place in the treasury of England's best. Sycophant though Francis Alford was, he wrote but the truth when he referred to 'the great wisdom and natural excellency of speech that was in him'. The indefatigable Burghley had sent Hatton a brief, to aid him in composing the speech. One can only comment that, if use was made of it, the philosopher's stone could not have transmuted common metal more wonderfully.[1]

Hatton began his review with the Papacy. 'You cannot forget how Clement VII and Paul III, breaking out into fury against her Majesty's father, spared not even then to smite at her honour. Afterward, her Highness being possessed of the crown, what a raging bull did that monster Pius V bring forth, whereby he laboured every way to wound her: in her soul, by denouncing her an heretic; in her honour, by his slanderous calumniations; and in her most royal dignity, by deposing her, by absolving her subjects from their duties of obedience, and by cursing of all such as should any way acknowledge their allegiance unto her . . . Immediately after him, Gregory XIII, beginning where he had left, attempted to the same purpose an invasion in Ireland.

'In both which enterprises, perceiving they wanted number to effect their designments, and that their instruments, whereby they wrought, through the providence of this government were intercepted and cut short . . . they devised another most pernicious and dangerous complot. And it was, that the litter of seminary priests, from nine days old and upward, tag and rag, should be

---

[1] Inner Temple, Petyt MS. 538/10, fol. 54; B.M. Lansdowne MS. 104, fols. 62-3 (Burghley's brief, in his own hand).

sent hither, pell mell, thick and threefold, under pretence of planting of Popery to increase this number and to reconcile such again to his Holiness as had neglected their duties in not assisting of the foresaid rebellions.'

'Whilst this number was thus preparing — but not with such success as was expected — divers other ways, far more compendious, were greatly urged and commended. And hence it was that divers pictures were made and sundry enchantments used, you know to what purpose; that Somerville undertook that villainy against her Majesty's person with his dag [i.e. pistol]; that Parry was set on by the Cardinal of Como with the Pope's consent to have committed the like unnatural cruelty with his dagger; and that both Savage and Babington, with the rest of those traitors . . . should have accomplished the same.'

Frustrated in their expectation and weary of delay, the Pope that now is, Sixtus V, 'exceeding all other that went before him in tyranny and cruelty . . . will needs have a bridge of wood made over our seas. He will no more bend his wits only against her Majesty — although, indeed, as in the heart is contained the life of the body, so is our happiness in her Highness's safety; but now he voweth the utter subversion and destruction of us all, Queen, people, and country, and to make our land a prey to foreign enemies. To this end he hath renewed the bull of Pius V, fraughting the same with most villainous slanders; he hath abrogated his predecessors' toleration; he hath cursed us all and blessed our enemies; he hath taken upon him to give and dispose of the crown of this realm as it pleaseth him best; he hath solicited divers kings and princes, according to their oaths in the Holy League, to be the executioners of this intended cruelty; and hath, at the length, with his charge of two millions, found a man, according to his own heart and disposition, who hath been content to be so wickedly employed.

'This necessary soldier and priestly champion is the King of Spain, one of all the kings of Europe that had least cause so to do: were it not that, like a most ambitious tyrant, forgetting all the honour he hath received amongst us, he thought like a conqueror to take this occasion for our utter subduing. And accordingly you know he hath proceeded. For, what preparations he was able to make, either by sea or land, what forces he could procure from all his confederates — the Venetians, the Florentines, the Genoans, the Bavarians, and the Germans — he hath assailed us with them. He came late against us like thunder. Indeed, God be thanked, he feared more than hurt us.'

These things are 'sufficient to show to all posterity the unchristian fury, both of the Pope (that wolfish bloodsucker) and of the Spaniard (that insatiable tyrant) in that they never bent themselves with such might and resolution against the very Turk or any other infidel, as they have done against a Virgin Queen, a famous lady, and a country which embraceth without corruption in doctrine the true and sincere religion of Christ. But yet, that which moveth her Majesty most is this: to think that ever any of her own subjects, mere Englishmen, born and brought up amongst us, should combine themselves — as some have done — with her so deadly enemies.'

Hatton then passed in rapid review the names of Catholic traitors, from 'that proud Cardinal Pole' in Henry VIII's reign, to Babington and his company recently. He lingered over Cardinal Allen, who, in sure trust of a Spanish victory, had published a tract against Elizabeth, distilled from scandal's cesspool. If 'tit for tat' be a sound principle, then Hatton was justified in his vituperation. 'Of all the villainous traitors that I think this land ever bred or brought up', he declared, 'that wicked priest, that shameless atheist and bloody Cardinal Allen, he indeed excelleth. Look what late dangers have been anyway towards us, and you shall find him a chief dealer in them . . . He was the procurer of this last bull, and, it is very apparent, the penner of it. He, like a proud and an impudent varlet, dareth by his letters to solicit the nobles and commonalty of England to join with the enemy. He is not ashamed to confess — and that in writing that the memory of his villainy may never die — how this Spanish hostility hath been greatly furthered by his and the rest of these fugitives' endeavours . . . O savage and barbarous priest! It is much to have such cruelty attempted by any foreign enemies. It is more that priests should so delight in blood. But that English subjects, being priests, should take upon them to be the workers of such an extremity, and that against their own country! before this devilish brood was hatched, I think it was never heard of amongst the very Scythians. It is said that the snakes in Syria will not bite nor sting the people that are born there; but these most venomous snakes, you see, do not only labour to bite and sting us, but, as a generation of cruel vipers, to tear us in pieces and to feed themselves with our blood.'

Such was the wrath — the *saeva indignatio* — of Hatton's generation for the Quislings and Fifth Column of their day.

Parliament met while Martin Marprelate's disturbing tracts were coming from their secret press, and it says much for the concern caused by this latest activity of the extreme Protestant wing that in the middle of his speech Hatton turned from his scathing attack on England's mortal enemy to pronounce, in no less certain fashion, the Queen's inflexible opposition to Puritans. The Catholics — said he — rage and they rail; and yet her Majesty, because she ever accounted them her enemies and never looked for any better at their hands, is not so much grieved about them as she is 'that there are divers, of latter days risen up, even amongst her friends, who, being men of a very intemperate humour, do greatly deprave the present estate and reformation of religion, so hardly attained to, and with such her danger continued and preserved; whereby her loving subjects are greatly disquieted, her enemies are encouraged, religion is slandered, piety is hindered, schisms are maintained, and the peace of the Church is altogether rent in sunder and violated.

'These things, her Majesty confesseth, do indeed very greatly trouble her, and [she] hath given me particularly in commandment, touching those manner of persons . . . to intimate this her pleasure unto you . . . Her Highness, upon certain trial, doth know most assuredly that those kinds of platforms and devices which they speak of are most absurd, that they tend to intolerable innovation, that they want all grounds of authority . . . that they effect an unspeakable tyranny, and that they are most dangerous to all good Christian government.' She is 'most fully and firmly settled in her conscience, by the word of God, that the estate and government of this Church of England, as now it standeth in this reformation, may justly be compared to any church which hath been established in any Christian kingdom since the Apostles' times; that both in form and doctrine it is agreeable with the scriptures, with the most ancient general Councils, with the practice of the primitive church, and with the judgments of all the old and learned fathers.'

A more direct and dogmatic refutation of the points of Presbyterian-Puritanism it would be hard to conceive. 'Her Highness, therefore', continued Hatton, 'in respect of your loving affection towards her, doth as a most gracious Lady very heartily desire and entreat you; but, if that will not serve' — and what light this saving clause throws on her expectation of indiscipline! — 'then doth she, as your Prince and dread Sovereign, most straitly charge and command you, upon your allegiance, that — the premises considered, and seeing that all authority for dealing in these causes is by all your consents (as by right it ought to be) invested into her imperial Crown — you do not in this assembly so much as once meddle with any such matters or causes of religion, except it be to bridle all those, whether Papists or Puritans, which are therewithal discontented: assuring you further, in the word of a Prince, that, as better opportunity shall be offered and occasion shall require, there shall such order be taken for the reformation of any abuse as to equity, conscience and good religion shall any way appertain.'

Trusting to his listeners' great wisdom and loyalty, and expressing a final hope that the present state of religion would prove a stumbling block only to the Queen's enemies, Hatton resumed his attack on Catholics. 'And here I may not forget those vile wretches, those bloody priests and false traitors, here in our bosoms, but beyond the seas especially. They will not cease to practise both at home and abroad . . . And concerning the Pope: . . . may we look for any better dealing from him? It were madness to think so . . . Winds, a little before their fall, are ever most boisterous. He seeth his ruin at hand, except he bestir him . . . He hath been at the charge of one million already; but when I consider . . . with what villainous fury he is inflamed in his said Bull, how he rageth, how he foameth, how he lieth, how he slandereth, how he thundereth against her Majesty and this estate: notwithstanding that he blasphemously alleges for himself that he is moved thereunto by the Holy Ghost, I am fully of opinion that, rather than this invasion should not go forward, if that might serve the turn he would give his soul to the devil.'

As for the King of Spain, he will not give us over. His ambitious nature 'is like a vessel with the bottom upwards, and will never be full . . . It cannot be denied that he is a great and mighty Prince; but yet, as Briareus had a hundred hands, so had he to feed with them fifty bellies. Though the Spaniard hath under him many kingdoms and countries, yet is he thereby drawn, we know not to what exceeding charges. His success of late years in many places hath wrapped up his estate in darkness; but, as it is in men's bodies — whilst they are in health they feel no pain in any part, but if they grow to be sick all infirmities and weaknesses of every member doth show itself — so fareth it with him.' 'Considering his oath in the League, his promise to the Pope, his brags throughout the world, his peremptory distribution both of this crown and country, his vows, protestations, attempts, and invincible preparations (as he termed them) for our utter extirpation: if now, notwithstanding, either through want of power and ability or upon any other consideration, he should be driven to put up such great loss, so open a foil, so public a shame, and so great a dishonour as, to the admiration of all Europe, he hath received at our hands . . . assuredly he should make himself a byword to all posterity; his weakness or cowardliness must needs be manifest, and the provinces under him, which are in tyrannous subjection and do hate him with a deadly hatred — as the Indians, the Neapolitans, the Milanese, and such other — they will begin to examine their strength and to shake off the yoke of their servitude and subjection. So we are all fully to assure ourselves that what he is able to do, either by his friends, by his credit, by his money, or by his uttermost force, power and strength; what the Pope or any English traitor can any ways work by sorcery, cursing, practices, cruelty, or any manner of persuasions; what they can severally, everyone of himself, or jointly all together, devise to bring to pass, all shall be employed to our invasion.'

'It is true that God hath mightily hitherto defended her Majesty and this realm from the hands of her enemies by detecting their conspiracies and making the very birds of the air, as it were, to reveal them. He hath blessed where they have cursed, and multiplied His innumerable benefits upon us. Their bulls He hath caused to gore themselves, and given us of late a most notable victory. But yet, notwithstanding, we may not be secure. Means for our defence must diligently be cared for. An enemy is never so much to be feared as when he is contemned . . . We have lopped off some of his boughs; but they will sooner grow again than we think of.'

'We are bound to defend ourselves, our wives, our children, our

friends: it is by an instinct of nature. We are bound to defend
our country, our prince, our state, our laws, our liberties: it is
agreeable to the laws of all nations and toucheth us all in honour.
We are bound to defend our possessions, our liberties, our goods,
and our lands: it wholly concerneth our profit . . . In times past
our noble predecessors have been able to defend this realm, when
they wanted such means as we may have; and shall we now
disable ourselves and through our negligence lose it? They, upon
occasions offered, have been as you know most worthy con-
querors; and shall we now suffer ourselves with all dishonour to be
conquered? England hath been accounted hitherto the most
renowned kingdom for valour and manhood in all Christendom;
and shall we now lose our old reputation? If we should, it had
been better for England we had never been born.'

'Our enemies make great preparation to assail us by sea: our
navy must be made fit to encounter them. They have great
strength to invade us by land: a correspondency of force must be
had to withstand them. They are caring for means to continue
their offence: we must likewise consider of good means to continue our defence. Our duties towards God, her Majesty, and our
country doth require all this at your hands.'[1]

We can imagine — to know, we are denied — the effect of this
most stirring of Elizabethan parliamentary orations on its
audience.

When the Commons retired to their Chamber at the close of
the ceremony they duly elected as their Speaker Serjeant Thomas
Snagge,[2] a choice already determined upon by the Queen in the
previous September. He was a distinguished lawyer, a Bedfordshire gentleman who, having sat for his county in 1571 and 1586,
now represented the borough. He was formally presented to her
Majesty on February 6th. We possess a draft of Hatton's reply to
his disabling speech: a polished gem, but as artificial and empty
as the occasion. Gladly would we exchange this schoolroom
exercise for some account — other than the brief, formal, and
utterly misleading entry in the Lords Journal — of what Hatton
afterwards said in reply to the Speaker's main oration, with its
petition for privileges. There can be little doubt that the clearest

---

[1] Lambeth Palace MS. 178, fols. 75-81.
[2] D'Ewes (p. 428) erroneously names him 'George': an error I repeated in the index
to my previous volume. The printed *Lords Journal* names him 'Jonas'.

warning was given about freedom of speech, and an emphatic
ban placed on all discussion of religious questions. The Queen
was too afraid of Puritan agitation to leave that matter in the
slightest doubt.[1]

---

[1] NICOLAS, *Sir Christopher Hatton*, p. 482; Lambeth MS. 178, fols. 88-9 (undated,
but I think clearly Hatton's speech for this occasion).

CHAPTER II

THE SUBSIDY: THE PREROGATIVE

THE Commons made a leisurely start this Parliament. Only one bill seems to have been read on the first full morning. Their initial action was to set up a standing committee for privileges. The idea of such a committee had arisen casually in 1585, in circumstances that suggested no conscious procedural innovation. Recalling the precedent early in the 1586 Parliament, Recorder Fleetwood then had it repeated; and now in 1589, by appearing as the first item of business, this provocative device — another of the many signs of institutional maturity — could be regarded as permanently established.[1]

The rest of the morning went in calling the House — attendance this session seems to have been poor — and in hasty, ill-considered decisions to issue warrants for the election of new Members in place of two who were ill. Fortunately, an opportunity of reviewing the principle involved was afforded when next day a committee was appointed to consider 'sundry abuses' and errors in election returns. It looked like a roving commission to enquire into parliamentary elections: an application of the subversive doctrine enunciated by the Commons in the Norfolk election case of 1586. And so, perhaps, the mover of the motion intended it to be. He was Sir Edward Hoby, a young gentleman of twenty-eight, highly connected, a nephew of Burghley, and of scholarly and radical inclination: a man liable to run into trouble. The Clerk of the Crown, who happened to be a Member of the House, was ordered to bring to the meeting the election returns, of which he was the custodian, along with his official list of Members.

Whether reflection on the Norfolk election case had led such procedural authorities as Recorder Fleetwood and Thomas Cromwell to doubt the validity of their arguments in 1586; whether, being detached from an evident threat to electoral independence, the issue was now seen more dispassionately; or whether it was simply that, in the post-Armada atmosphere, more deference was paid to the Crown's rights: whatever the cause, the

---

[1] D'EWES, pp. 349, 393, 429.

committee, reporting through Sir Francis Knollys next day, abandoned the revolutionary principle of their 1586 decision. They concluded that the House ought not to concern itself with the electoral conduct of sheriffs, or anyone else, but should accept the names of Members certified to them by the Clerk of the Crown. This meant that decisions on disputed or disorderly elections were left to the Crown and Chancery: sound, historically and constitutionally. However, they went on to say that in cases where no return was made at all, the House should direct a warrant from Speaker to Chancery for the issue of a writ; thus leaving a remnant of authority with the House, from which they could later recover the position of 1586, and even progress further. As a matter of fact, the committee violated its own principle by scrutinizing one of the original election returns and pronouncing it invalid. The committee also decided that a seat could not be vacated on the ground of sickness, unless thought to be incurable, 'as frenzy or such like'.[1]

After these decisions had been confirmed, the Speaker reminded the House that it had already infringed the ruling about sick Members; and the assembly was in process of spending still more time discussing this dilemma when Sir Walter Mildmay — who saw the morning slipping away — interrupted the business and, with an apology, launched the great speech on supply which he had planned for that day.

In his rough Journal — which, at second-hand, is nearly all we have for the day-to-day proceedings of this Parliament — the Clerk left 'almost three entire blank pages', intending, no doubt, to write a long résumé of the speech, after borrowing the text. But even Fitzwilliam — Mildmay's son-in-law — seems on this occasion to have secured only the notes that formed its framework: a most orderly document. Possibly, Mildmay had by now become so practised a hand, that he did not trouble to write out the speech. At any rate, the notes show that it followed his standard pattern, adapted to the year 1589. Like Sir Christopher Hatton's opening oration, it was a survey of foreign dangers, partly historical in treatment. One heading — 'The means' our enemies 'have used against us' — was followed by another — 'The means we had against them'. Under the latter, both the items and their order are illuminating: 'The mighty hand of God;

[1] D'EWES, pp. 429-31.

the providence of the Queen's Majesty — her invincible courage; the magnanimity and constancy of the nobility; the fidelity and readiness of the people; the Queen's forces by sea; the forces by land; the goodness of the quarrel; the defence of the Gospel and the Realm; the prayers of good people; the honourable and good dealing of the King and Realm of Scotland, tied unto us with the band of religion'. It was Mildmay's anatomy of the great Armada victory. In the end he brought his speech carefully to its purpose: the provision of money.[1]

The oration ended, a grand committee was appointed, consisting of close on a hundred Members, with a knight from every shire: an exceptionally large body. The government, in fact, was intending to confront them with an extraordinary demand. To meet war expenditure, nothing less than a double subsidy was needed; and while Elizabethans were ready enough to adventure their lives for their country, they were less eager to empty their pockets. It was sound psychology to give a substantial section of the House a chance to air their fears and misgivings in committee instead of stampeding the full assembly into irresponsible criticism. Some members of the committee were slack in attendance, but four meetings were held and obviously a great deal was said. Convinced of the necessity for granting two subsidies instead of the usual one, they yet remained afraid of the precedent. Consequently, Francis Bacon was charged with drafting a passage for the preamble of the bill, which they imagined would safeguard the future. Mercifully, the future was hidden from them, and they little thought that they would find themselves granting three subsidies in the next Parliament, and four in 1601. We do not know what Bacon wrote. The very mild, ineffective words finally incorporated in the preamble appear to have been composed by Burghley.[2]

Mildmay reported on behalf of the committee on February 17th. The House gave its ready approval, remitting the drafting of bill and preamble to the Queen's learned counsel. After that, their concern was to delay the passage of the bill. Once through its stages, they expected the Queen to end the session and be rid of them and their less palatable projects. At the second reading, on February 27th, they deliberately postponed having the usual

[1] Northants Record Soc. Fitzwilliam of Milton Papers, 147.
[2] D'EWES, pp. 431, 433-4; B.M. Lansdowne MS. 58, fols. 182-4.

question put for ingrossing, mainly on this ground; and when, next day, the matter was raised again, there was a debate before the government got its way. The third reading did not take place until March 10th, and, even then, forcing tactics seem to have been needed.[1]

At this third reading — assuming, as we probably may, that a speech we possess was delivered — there was at least one discordant voice. The speaker was Henry Jackman, Member for Calne, Wiltshire, and a newcomer to Parliament: a London cloth-merchant and a man of parts, who jotted down a number of Latin and English passages for use in this and another speech that he composed. He was opposed to the levying of a second subsidy. If the Queen herself — he declared — had asked for a double subsidy, or if the danger of invasion — 'the principal and almost only persuader for the bill' that he had heard — had required it, he would have acquiesced in its necessity. But they had received no commandment from her Majesty; and 'our country is at this present in no such desperate or dangerous case . . ., the teeth and jaws of our mightiest and most malicious enemy having been so lately broken'. Moreover, the first instalment of the second subsidy was not to be paid till the end of three years. It would be too late for defence. The knowledge of such a tax, coming on top of recent financial burdens — of burdens such as arming against the Armada, paying the final instalment of the 1587 subsidy, and contributing to the forced loan being raised at this very time — would breed discontent in the minds and hearts of the people. To most Members of the House, it might seem a fleabite: they were able to pay, and educated to understand. But to the poor and needy countryman and the artificer, 'whose treasure is always in his hand', it would appear a punishment. 'The suits, exclamations, complaints and lamentations of the commons of this realm, well known to the most part of this House, which they make either at the assessing or collection of these subsidies' sufficiently testify to this. 'The precedent, besides, may be dangerous both to ourselves and our posterity, for we commonly see that in all counsels and deliberations a precedent is a forcible and persuading argument.' Jackman then went on to cite precedents from the reigns of Henry III and Henry VIII in

[1] D'EWES, pp. 440-1, 444.

which the House of Commons refused to grant as large taxes as were demanded.[1]

Our courageous gentleman — who, as his other speech indicates, was of a liberal cast of mind — may have had few or none to keep him company at this late stage of the bill; but there were surely others who thought as he did, and some may have voiced similar misgivings in committee. Several decades were yet to elapse before Englishmen reluctantly accepted the idea that taxation must form a regular and substantial part of the Crown's revenues.

The subsidy bill caused no real trouble: the House after all was patriotic, and as yet the medicine they had to swallow was not over tart. But there were two bills about which there was much ado: the one 'concerning process and pleadings in the Court of Exchequer'; the other concerning purveyors. Both appeared on the same day, February 14th. The first — centred on the tyrannous use of the writ *quo titulo ingressus est* — revived an old grievance that the Commons had attempted to remedy by Act of Parliament in 1571. On that occasion the bill had lapsed in the House of Lords, stopped, possibly, by the Queen's command: it trespassed on her prerogative. She promised remedy. Exchequer officials, however, seem to have continued their time-dishonoured practices. As for purveyors, we hardly need reminding of them. The Queen, as we have seen, had vetoed a bill about them in the last Parliament.

It was Sir Edward Hoby who 'brought in' the Exchequer bill, accompanied, we infer, by a biting attack on the officials concerned. Next morning, he was on his feet at the commencement of the sitting, asking the Speaker to admonish Members against infringing the secrecy of debate: speeches were being turned into table-talk, and written notes on them disseminated. The admonition was duly given. Clearly, Hoby's criticisms had been repeated in Court circles; and no wonder, for there were Exchequer officials in the Commons. At the following sitting, Hoby complained again. 'Some great personage' — perhaps his uncle, Lord Burghley, who as Lord Treasurer was head of the Exchequer — had 'very sharply rebuked' him for what he was reported to have said. Hoby was now concerned to correct these untrue and sinister reports, and, in defence of 'the ancient liberties' of the

[1] Lansdowne MS. 55, fols. 180-3, 186-7. The speaker's name is revealed by the handwriting, which is that of Lansdowne MS. 83, fols. 199-206, identified on fol. 206b.

assembly, to have the House both justify him to 'the said great personage', and name the errant reporter of his speech. He concluded by once more commending his bill and asking for it to be given a second reading at once.

Here was a hare likely to set Members chasing excitedly after it for the rest of that morning. But Mildmay immediately rose, interrupted the business, and made his report about the subsidy. As an old campaigner he knew the virtue of cooling tempers by a diversion. He was unable, however, to suppress the complaint. His report on the subsidy ended, Sir Henry Knyvet got up to speak in vindication of Hoby. Others spoke, but, thanks no doubt to Mildmay's diversionary tactics, the House seems to have concluded that the best way to confirm its faith in Hoby was to give his bill an immediate second reading: which was done. Goodness knows what folly the hotheads would have run into otherwise. The debate on the second reading and the championing of Hoby were resumed next day. Quite a number of Members seem to have spoken, including an important Exchequer official, Peter Osborne. The bill was committed, and, in cautionary mood, the committee received authority to consult with the Queen's learned counsel.

The measure re-emerged as a new bill on February 24th, when on behalf of the committee the Chancellor of the Exchequer, Mildmay, reported in its favour. He was not the only Exchequer official to give it his blessing. Mr. Osborne, whose department had caused most of the fuss, had been at the meetings of the committee and pronounced his assent and good liking, welcoming the bill because it would give him authority to change the procedure of his department. On Mildmay's suggestion the bill was immediately given two readings and sent to be ingrossed. Next day it was passed and sent to the Lords. Such expedition was its surest commendation. All interests now seemed satisfied: with one exception. That exception was the Queen, with her instinctive and theoretical aversion — an aversion profoundly right from the Crown's point of view — to limiting the royal prerogative by statutory action. It was to prove fatal to the bill.[1]

Meanwhile, the bill about purveyors had been running its course. Its sponsor was Mr. John Hare, one of a pair of brothers who together occupied the two Horsham seats in several Parlia-

[1] D'EWES, pp. 432-9.

ments. He was a London lawyer and was to become Clerk of the Court of Wards: a client of Burghley's. He spoke about the abuses of purveyors and offered his bill on February 14th. It was read the next day, and, though this was only the first reading, provoked a debate which appears to have occupied practically the whole morning. Elizabethans needed no interval to marshal their thoughts on the subject, particularly just then. Since the agitation in the last Parliament, the Armada preparations had concentrated large numbers of soldiers in the counties near to London, creating an extraordinary problem of food-supplies; and in such circumstances the activities of purveyors must have seemed less tolerable than ever. Little wonder that this Parliament brought the climax of discontent. The Clerk noted a dozen Members as speaking. Perhaps there were more.

The bill, in preamble and elsewhere, seems to have been scathing: it blamed the officials of the royal Household, and by inference might be thought to blame the Queen. Its provisions were in part a repetition of those of 1587; in part, probably new. In an attempt to stop notorious and acknowledged abuses, it undoubtedly hindered the Queen's service and clipped the authority of her Household court, known as the Board of Greencloth. The prerogative was threatened.[1]

The first speaker in the debate was Sir Francis Knollys, who, as Treasurer, was the senior officer of the Household. He was aware of the abuses; he was aware also that the proper, in fact the only remedy, short of abolishing purveyance, was the radical one of substituting composition by counties for the forays of individual purveyors. He sympathized with the victims of the present, antiquated system; but he was concerned to maintain the Queen's prerogative, on which depended the business of feeding the Court without a vast and unbearable increase in royal expenditure. We have no report of the debate, though we cannot doubt that it was bitterly critical. The bill was immediately read a second time and sent to a committee, which — a sign of responsibility — was authorized to give audience to any of the officers of the Household and Court of Greencloth who wished to be heard.

The committee reported on February 19th, through the mouth of Sir Thomas Heneage, a courtier whom we have already met,

---

[1] A note of the bill's provisions is in a fragmentary diary by Henry Jackman, Lansdowne MS. 55, fols. 184-5.

now aged about forty-five; one who had risen, through various offices and the more significant role of Queen's 'favourite', to become Hatton's successor as Vice-Chamberlain. He was an efficient man, but lacked the poise, understanding, and independent outlook which had made such good Parliament-men of Knollys, Mildmay, Hatton and other Councillors in the high Elizabethan period. Perhaps he was too wholly the courtier: one of the legacies in his will was a jewel, valued at a thousand French crowns, which he bequeathed to the Queen, 'who, above all other earthly creatures, I have thought most worthy of all my heart's love and reverence'.[1]

Heneage reported that they had conferred with some of her Majesty's officers of the Greencloth and had amended the bill and added a proviso. He did not say that they had secured these officials' good will and approval. In the nature of things that was impossible; and we know that Sir Francis Knollys was aggrieved, that Burghley was critical, and that the purveyors themselves cried doom and threatened resignation. It 'hath much nettled all the officers of the Greencloth', wrote a Member to his father. A long debate followed, which went on until, 'the time being far spent', they were prompted to rise by the call of their stomachs. If only we had an account of the speeches, we should be in a better position to judge the temper of this Parliament. Perhaps the hotheads were protesting against concessions; perhaps the official party were arguing their case: probably both. Two days later the proviso and amendments were formally read, and the following day — February 22nd — the bill was passed and sent to the Lords.[2]

Thus, by February 25th the Lords had before them two bills, both specially recommended to them by the Commons; bills which, from the Queen's point of view, were explosive. Knowing this, the Lords appear to have refrained deliberately from reading them. Royal action followed. On February 27th the Commons were informed that the Lords had received a message from her Majesty, delivered by two Privy Councillors, and wished to impart it to a delegation, meeting a select number of peers. At the meeting, Burghley acted as spokesman. He told them that the

[1] R. C. GABRIEL, 'Members of the House of Commons, 1586-87' (London M.A. thesis).
[2] D'EWES, pp. 432-9; Lansdowne MS. 56, fols. 85, 87; ibid. 58, fols. 111-12, 113-22; B.M. Egerton MS. 2804, fols. 67-8.

SIR THOMAS HENEAGE

Queen's message concerned the passing of these two bills: 'a thing misliked of her Majesty'. The one touched 'the officers and ministers of her own Household'; the other, 'the officers and ministers of her own court of her own revenues'. In both matters, if any officials demeaned themselves unlawfully or untruly, 'her Majesty was of herself both able and willing to see due reformation', and would do so, to the public example of others. In brief, the command was, 'Hands off the prerogative!' The bills were dead. We catch a glimpse of all three parties to the episode in a letter from Lord Talbot to his father, the Earl of Shrewsbury, written on March 3rd. After mentioning that the Queen had taken offence, he went on: 'Some stir' has been bred 'by her Majesty's especial dislike of certain young gentlemen who have been much busier — both in these bills and others — than they needed'; also, 'by them in the Nether House who think that we in our [the Upper] House deal somewhat hardly with them' in refusing to read whatever bills they pass and send to us.[1]

On returning to their chamber, it was Sir Francis Knollys who made the report. There followed sundry motions, speeches and advices as to what might best be done to satisfy her Majesty about their actions, 'either by way of excuse, or confession, or otherwise'. The triple mode of approach may be taken to represent the varying reactions of the speakers. The 'busy young gentlemen' whom the Queen disliked were obviously opposed to surrender: hence Lord Talbot's reference to 'some stir'; hence also the injunction to the committee, set up at the close of the debate, 'to search such precedents as might best serve' their purpose.[2]

John Fortescue, Privy Councillor and Master of the Wardrobe, seconded by the lawyer, Edward Coke, delivered the report of the committee. We possess a paper, endorsed 'Reasons for proceeding in the bills touching the Exechequer and purveyors'. It is probably Fortescue's report, which we must conceive as having been elaborated and fortified with precedents by Coke — a rival to Recorder Fleetwood in his antiquarian learning.

On the purveyors bill it answered three criticisms which must have been made when Burghley remitted the Queen's message. The first was that the procedure had not been by way of preliminary complaint to her Majesty. 'This form of proceeding' — the

---

[1] Baskerville's calendar at the P.R.O. of the Talbot MSS. (Longleat).
[2] D'EWES, p. 440.

Commons unrepentantly answered — 'is and hath been in all times very usual: that the King by the petition of his Commons, assembled in Parliament, provided remedy in Parliament for the grievances of his subjects; which is most agreeable to his princely authority and most acceptable to the subjects.' What the Commons conveniently ignored in this comment of theirs was the distinction between a petition, pure and simple, and a petition in the form of an Act of Parliament. The former was unobjectionable, but was more appropriate to the procedure of a medieval than a modern Parliament, and, in point of fact, was likely to achieve nothing. The latter was a legal process, and, in constitutional theory, when the prerogative was involved, ought not to proceed *rege non consulto* (without the consent of the Crown).

The second of the criticisms delivered by Burghley was that her Majesty herself had the 'skill, will and ability' to reform her Household. This the Commons confessed, but they pointed out the desirability, nay the necessity, for parliamentary legislation, in the interests of the people. The third criticism was that the bill touched the Queen's prerogative. To this the Commons made answer that abuses only were restrained, and 'her Majesty's purveyance or prerogative ... nothing thereby impeached'. Considering the provisions of the bill, the answer can only be described as naïve, false or sinister.

In criticism of the Exchequer bill, Burghley had said that it was concerned with the revenues and prerogatives of her Majesty's crown, where it was in her power to prescribe reform; and that it was prejudicial to her Majesty's 'tenures, wardships and revenues'. To this the Commons gave answer: 'There are many precedents by Act of Parliament ... and therefore this bill importeth no strange or rare matter'. They went on to justify the bill's provisions, pointing out that the Queen's learned counsel had been consulted and that the Exchequer official chiefly concerned [Mr. Osborne] had given his assent.

As the historian reflects on these answers, he cannot but be conscious that the Tudor constitution was by now standing on uncertain foundations: on little more than the masterful nature and unique personality of an ageing Queen.[1]

The committee recommended 'that in most humble and dutiful wise this House, by their own mouth, Mr. Speaker, do exhibit

[1] Lansdowne MS. 86, fols. 144-5.

unto her Majesty the causes and reasons moving' them 'to proceed
in the two said bills'. Sundry speeches followed. In the end, the
committee's recommendation was adopted, as 'best to stand with
the liberties and the honour of this House': prophetic words, when
used against the Crown. They decided to inform the Upper House
of their resolution, hoping — over-optimistically or diplomatically
— to have their Lordships' good favour; and they instructed Sir
Thomas Heneage to seek audience with the Queen. Elizabeth sent
her reply, conceding the audience, *via* the House of Lords instead
of through Heneage: surely a calculated gesture, meant to remind
the Commons of their place. She also imposed a stint on the
number she would receive: ten, besides the Speaker, two of whom
must be Privy Councillors. The audience was to have been on
Thursday afternoon, March 6th; but that morning, her Majesty,
having been abroad in the air, took a little cold and put the interview off till next day.

The Speaker had been ordered to make 'most humble petition
and suit . . . that her Majesty would vouchsafe her most gracious
favour' in allowing the two bills; and to explain 'that this House
would willingly and most gladly have taken . . . any such other
course whatsoever' in passing them, as they might have known
to stand with her good liking. Presumably he framed his speech
along these lines.

When, on March 8th, he duly made his report to the House on
the course of the audience, he explained that 'they received from
her Majesty most comfortable and gracious speeches — in far
better sort and measure than he was any way able to repeat or
open unto them — of her Highness's great and inestimable loving
care towards her loving subjects: yea, more than of her own self, or
than any of them have of themselves'. Coming to their petition,
and first to the abuses of purveyors, the Queen explained that 'of
her own princely care towards her subjects' she had ordered the
late Lord Steward — the Earl of Leicester — to write to all the
shires of the realm causing enquiry to be made into the misdemeanours of purveyors, in order to devise redress. But, 'before any good
order could well be taken . . . the Spaniards, upon a sudden,
attempted the invasion of this realm'. She had 'as much skill, will
and power to rule and govern her own Household' — she added —
as any subject to manage his, without the aid of his neighbours.
Out of her own 'great love and affection towards her dutiful and

loving subjects — whose most faithful and approved good love and fidelity towards her she more esteemeth than all the treasures of the world besides' — she intended, before the close of this session of Parliament, to have a collection made of all the laws already in force about purveyors, as also of her Household regulations, and then, by the advice of her judges and learned counsel, to set down a plan of reform, 'as good or better, for the ease of the subjects, than that which this House had attempted without her privity, and in which they would have bereaved her Majesty [of] the honour, glory and commendation of the same'. 'Touching the Exchequer, she said it was her Chamber, and so more near unto her than the Household.' She added that in the tenth year of her reign, she had caused certain regulations to be set down for the proper procedure in these matters that now seemed to be causing grievance.

The odds are that the affectionate passages of the speech were qualified by much more vigorous criticism than the Speaker's report suggests. Lacking the original text, we may have lost an Elizabethan gem. The Queen's determination to prevent trespassing on her prerogative is clear. She was right about the enquiry she had ordered the Earl of Leicester to make after the agitation in the last Parliament. Also, she kept her promise to take action before this present Parliament ended, for on March 17th the Speaker had another royal message to report to the Commons. It was to signify her gracious pleasure that four of the House should be chosen to have conference with a group of Privy Councillors and Household officials about convenient regulations to be made for purveyors.

The wisdom, the magnanimity, the statesmanship of her action in allowing Members of the House to participate in devising these regulations command respect. She had preserved the sanctity of the royal prerogative and yet reconciled it with Parliament's urge to redress grievances. She was to employ a rather similar strategy over the grievance of monopolies in her last Parliament. It was the only — the slender — hope of preserving the Tudor constitution in a changing society.

The Commons immediately appointed a committee — probably a strong one — to prepare a brief for their four representatives. Next day Heneage reported their deliberations. They had received information about the abuses of purveyors, which, said

Heneage, 'were very many and foul, and some of them offered to be proved true in such sort as the same had been reported unto them'. The House then chose its four representatives: Sir Henry Knyvet, Thomas Cromwell, John Hare, Robert Wroth — independent men, and Hare the originator of the agitation. What is more, all Members of the House were authorized to supply any of these four with instructions and information, the better to accomplish their task. The Queen's plan seems to have succeeded. Purveyance did not recur as a grievance in the later Parliaments of the reign; and, under Burghley's leadership, the years from 1590 on were marked by a rapid extension of county compositions, the soundest method of distributing the burden equitably.

Two days after these events, the Clerk made a cryptic entry in his rough notes: 'Sir Edward Hoby, Mr. Shirley, Mr. Francis Moore and Mr. Morice for the Exchequer matter'. From this we might infer that the Queen also set up a commission to reform the practices of the Exchequer, and invited the House to choose four Members to act as consultants. If she did, our respect deepens. The pity is that the problem of the Church could not be handled in the same way. But in that sphere, grievances were inextricably mingled with dogma. Even on the basis of exploring abuses and causes of inefficiency, religious colloquies were therefore doomed to failure. The only solution was the toleration of non-conformity; and that was a philosophy far in advance, not only of practical politics but also of mental horizons.[1]

---

[1] D'EWES, pp. 442-4, 446, 448. Cf. ALLEGRA WOODWORTH, *Purveyance in the Reign of Elizabeth*.

CHAPTER III

RELIGION

BOTH at the time and in the retrospect of later years the defeat of
the Presbyterian Puritans in the Parliament of 1586-87 seemed
decisive. But it was only defeat — the defeat of an extremist programme — in Parliament. The secret Classical Movement among
the clergy continued active, improving its organization, clarifying
its views and policy, refining its discipline, and expanding. Much
mystery envelops it; but in 1591, when the leaders were prosecuted
in the Star Chamber, the testimony of witnesses threw considerable, if wavering, light on these years; particularly the testimony of Mr. John Johnson, late vicar of All Saints, Northampton,
then aged thirty-six. Mr. Johnson was a 'brother' who had left
the Movement in a huff after being subjected to an admonition, or
fraternal censure: a 'party' practice of some interest to students of
our own contemporary scene.[1]

In these years, 1587 and 1588, the Directory of Church Government, or Book of Discipline, had been circulated for comment and
subscription, a number of important General Conferences had
been held, at which Cartwright and other leaders were present,
and steps had been taken to turn meetings of ministers into *classes*,
conforming to the pattern of the Directory. There were three or
four *classes* in every shire, said one witness, which sent their
resolutions to greater assemblies at Cambridge and London. The
statement is no more than a rough generalization; but the Puritan
county of Northampton, to take one example, was organized in
three divisions, each with its *classis*, and these were capped with
frequent provincial or county assemblies. Mr. Johnson told of
a free-lance Puritan minister, Mr. Fludd, who, 'like an Apostle or
Patriarch', rode about the country, giving instructions. On his
advice, the ministers of Northamptonshire set about making a
survey of the state of all the churches in their county, as other
counties had done on the eve of previous Parliaments. According
to this renegade informant, one of the delegates charged with the

---

[1] The documents in the Star Chamber case (A 27/33, A 39/23, A 49/34, A 56/1) are
very many and lengthy. I have used the transcripts made by my former student, the
late Edna Bibby, kindly given me by her father.

task brought 'a most railing discourse against every minister who was not of that fraternity'. If Mr. Johnson can be trusted about his dates, it seems that the party was aiming at perfecting its survey of the clergy in time for the 1589 Parliament.[1]

There were further plans. Northamptonshire, in common with other counties, was to send, and did send, accredited representatives to London during the meeting of Parliament, to confer and take joint action. Johnson said that many went from most parts of England. One device propounded by the busy Mr. Fludd and agreed to by this general assembly was that some twenty or thirty of their company of ministers should go 'in their gowns, with all gravity', to the door of the Parliament House, and there deliver a petition asking for a disputation. It would seem that they entertained the hope of persuading the Queen, through petitions directed to her, the Privy Council, and the Bishops, to permit another Westminster debate, comparable to that between the Catholic and Protestant divines in 1559: a debate which on this occasion would usher in the new, the Presbyterian Reformation.[2]

Such projects remained vain hopes: why, we shall understand in due course. But what a startling picture all this makes! If we reflect on the nature and tactics of revolutionary movements in our own times, we may arrive at a better appreciation of the Queen's implacable opposition to Puritans. Neither she nor Whitgift, however, was insensitive to those defects in church life which lent substance to propaganda. On the eve of this Parliament Whitgift sent a circular letter to his bishops, demanding a certificate of the number of persons admitted to the ministry since 1584, and the number who were preachers. He expected parliamentary agitation and needed to know how far Convocation's reforming articles of 1587 and their canons of 1584 had been observed. By the Queen's express command similar returns were required before the Parliament of 1593; and agitation in 1597 was to evoke another circular letter on the eve of the last Parliament of the reign. We must not think that the only royal answer to Puritanism was the parliamentary veto; though, with a bench of bishops such as Whitgift had, and with the corruptive forces of contemporary society ever active, gospel standards were far out of reach.[3]

It looks as if the national synods or general assemblies of Puritan

[1] Examinations of Richard Hawger (A 27/33), John Johnson (A 49/34).
[2] Cf. Thomas Stone's Star Chamber depositions (A 49/34).
[3] Lambeth Palace MS., Whitgift's Register, i. fols. 151, 199b; iii. fol. 135.

ministers were more radical in their decisions when meetings took place in London. Quite understandably, for there tended to be a concentration of extremists in the capital, including deprived or suspended ministers, who were sustained by being given lectureships or aided by the alms of wealthy citizens. Whether they attended the synods or not, their influence was bound to be felt. Their man of genius — the general secretary of the party, John Field — died in March 1588. He was an irreparable loss to the movement; and so, in a quite different way, was the Earl of Leicester, who died in September that year. But there were others who, if they did not have Field's organizing ability, shared his revolutionary spirit. Also, there were extremists outside London. Our depositions tell — and tell plausibly — a story of Mr. Edmund Snape, the minister of St. Peter's, Northampton, talking at this time to a few of his flock in the great pew of his church: 'How say you if we devise a way whereby to shake off all the antichristian yoke and government of bishops, and . . . jointly together erect the discipline and government [of Presbyterianism] all in one day; and that in such sort as they that be against it shall never be able to prevail to the contrary? But', he added, 'peradventure it will not be this year and a half.' Our optimist must have been counting on so rapid and extensive an advance of their movement that the structure of the Anglican Church would collapse before a concerted push, administered, perhaps, through the House of Commons. He probably made his prophecy when the country was agog over the Marprelate Tracts, the culmination of the Puritan literary campaign.[1]

Throughout its story, from the publication of the *Admonition to Parliament* in 1572, there had been a literary background to this religious controversy. Some of the tracts had been sprightly and vituperative; most were exceedingly dull. To the latter class belonged an Anglican tract by Dr. John Bridges, *A Defence of the Government Established*, published in 1587: 'a portentous quarto of over fourteen hundred pages'. It evoked puritan replies. There was nothing electrifying in the first two; but about October 1588 there appeared *An Epistle to the terrible Priests*, written 'by the reverend and worthy Martin Marprelate, gentleman', and printed — it facetiously proclaimed — 'oversea in Europe, within

---

[1] Star Chamber depositions of Thomas Barber (A 49/34); documents connected with Snape (A 27/33).

a furlong of a bouncing priest'. 'Oh! read over Dr John Bridges',
says the title page, 'for it is a worthy work'. This was the first of
seven Martinist tracts which appeared at intervals in the next
eleven months, ending with *The Protestation*, a final gesture of
defiance, printed in Spetember 1589, a month after the secret press
used by Martin had been discovered at Manchester, and while the
printers were awaiting the rack to extort from them information
that might lead to the identification and arrest of the author. In
these eleven months the authorities, and in particular Whitgift,
with his fellow-officials of the Church, had been disturbed as never
before by the prospect of domestic unrest. They almost feared —
as Mr. Snape of Northampton hoped — that revolution was round
the corner. Feverishly they searched for the elusive secret press.
They tried to put up an episcopal counterblast by employing the
unfortunate Bishop Cooper of Winchester to write *An Admonition
to the People of England*: only to be met by a rollicking retort from
Martin in his *Hay any work for Cooper*, a tract whose title, adopting a
London street-cry, was in itself devasting. They turned to the
professional literary hacks, as more skilled and less scrupulous, to
meet humour with scurrility and obscenity. Even the stage was
invoked in an effort to counter genius by any — and, too frequently, quite disgraceful — methods.

It must be emphasized that Martin Marprelate's tracts represent no departure in Puritan policy. As the author's pseudonym
indicates, they were directed against bishops and the episcopal
system. All Presbyterian-Puritans thought the system erroneous,
if not unlawful. Again, the scurrilous personal attacks merely
echoed what the brethren thought about Whitgift, Aylmer, and
other merciless persecutors. Similar sentiments had often been
expressed in print. In all respects save one the Marprelate tracts
were typical products of the extremist wing of the movement. The
sole novelty was the genius of the author. Today we recognize him
as 'the great prose satirist of the Elizabethan period', a forerunner
of the master of satire, Dean Swift. It was this quality — the wit,
humour, buffoonery and scurrility, set in a prose extraordinarily
direct and vigorous for those days, and suffused with an earnest
and lofty purpose — that gave the tracts their notoriety and made
them seem so dangerous. They were eagerly read in Court, town
and country. Legend has it that when the Queen was speaking
to the young Earl of Essex about her proclamation, forbidding

possession of them, he pulled out a copy of the latest one, remarking, 'What then is to become of me?'

The identity of Martin Marprelate eluded contemporaries and has remained a mystery to this day. John Penry and Job Throckmorton are known to have been most closely associated with the printing of the tracts. Both denied being Martin. That need weigh very little. Other arguments rule out Penry, and, as the evidence now stands, Throckmorton seems most likely. On purely literary grounds the case for him is strengthened by the hitherto-unknown speeches — already noticed in our narrative — which he made in the Parliament of 1586-87. All three display the qualities of the Marprelate tracts; and of the best it is tempting to say that either Throckmorton was Martin Marprelate or Martin was not unique. If in these striking parliamentary speeches we have found the answer to an ancient riddle, it explains why Throckmorton did not become a Member of the 1589 Parliament.[1]

To present-day readers, the Marprelate tracts seem good fun. They shocked the Elizabethan world: except, of course, the extremist wing of the Puritan party. Cartwright and many others condemned and deplored them, as responsible leaders generally — and, as a rule, rightly — deplore support that flagrantly exceeds the bounds of respectability. Undoubtedly, the tracts did their cause more immediate harm than good: though, if we reflect on the mood of early-Stuart England, the balance-sheet may not be so clearly drawn. In Court, Church and official circles they were regarded as sedition of an alarming and dangerous kind; and it is interesting to note that the statute under which the printers were tried — for lack of the government bill rejected in 1584-85 — was the Act of 1581 against seditious words, which the Puritan House of Commons had tried — vainly, as this occasion proved — to render impotent against brethren of their persuasion. In her proclamation of February 13th, 1589, the Queen denounced the writings as tending by their scope to bring in a monstrous and apparent dangerous innovation: their rash and malicious purpose was 'to dissolve the estate of the prelacy, being one of the three ancient estates of this realm'. Said the Earl of Hertford: 'As they shoot at bishops now, so will they do at the nobility also, if they be suffered.'

[1] Cf. WM. PIERCE, *Historical Introduction to the Marprelate Tracts*; *Martin Marprelate Controversy*, ed. Arber; ante, pp. 110-11, 150-2, 169-73.

Yes, he that now saith, 'Why should bishops be?'
Will next cry out, 'Why Kings? The saints are free'.

Or, to quote Shakespeare:

> Take but degree away, untune that string
> And, hark! what discord follows. [1]

Parliament met in the middle of the disturbance created by
Marprelate. On the first Sunday of the session, February 9th,
Richard Bancroft — organizer of the search for the secret press,
and soon to be the instrument of destruction for the Classical
Movement — was put up to preach the sermon at St. Paul's. He
took for his text the passage: 'Dearly beloved, believe not every
spirit, but try the spirits whether they be of God. For many false
prophets have gone out into the world'. It was a vigorous attack
on Presbyterian-Puritanism as a subversive, revolutionary movement. In defence of episcopacy, he uttered words which were construed as a claim that the authority of bishops over their inferior
brethren existed by divine right. Just as the medieval theory of the
divine right of kings had been formulated to resist high papal claims,
so in reverse this conception of the divine right of bishops was being
used to combat the prevalent argument of Puritan lawyers that all
ecclesiastical authority was subject to the supremacy of Parliament
and the secular law. The sermon was hurried into print and
acquired fame and notoriety. It sharpened the conflict with the
Whitgift party and stimulated the anti-clericalism of Englishmen.
Sir Francis Knollys denounced Bancroft's claim as an affront to
the royal supremacy, and the fearful word *praemunire* was on
lawyers' lips. [2]

Whatever plans the Puritan party may have had for this Parliament, the outlook for them was gloomy in the extreme, what with
a natural exaltation of patriotic sentiment after the glorious naval
victory of 1588, and the revulsion of moderate minds against
Martin Marprelate's extravagance. 'We expect no good in the
cause of religion', wrote one of the London ministers to a brother,
after the opening of the session: 'we rather fear some evil.' Indeed,

[1] Cf. my *Elizabeth I and her Parliaments, 1559-81*, pp. 393-8; ARBER, op. cit. pp.
109-11; PIERCE, op. cit. p. 182; H. M. DEXTER, *Congregationalism*, p. 170, quoting
A Whip for an Ape; SHAKESPEARE's 'Troilus and Cressida'.
[2] R. G. USHER, *Reconstruction of the English Church*, i. 50 seqq.; S.P. Dom. Eliz.
223/23.

the Queen's injunction through the mouth of Lord Chancellor
Hatton, made first as an appeal to Members' affection, but, failing
that, as a command upon their allegiance, was so emphatic and so
sweeping — 'You do not in this assembly so much as once meddle'
with matters of religion — that if Puritans had remained dumb,
it would not have been surprising. This thought should linger in
our minds as we follow their story. [1]

The first attempt to defy the Queen's taboo came on February
25th. The spokesman was Humphrey Davenport, who sat for
Brackley, probably as the Earl of Derby's nominee: a young lawyer
aged twenty-two, still a student at the Inns of Court. How he
came to be the instrument of a planned operation — for that it
certainly was — we do not know. His youth must explain much.
'Mr. Davenport' — the Clerk noted in his rough Journal — 'moved
neither for making of any new laws, nor for abrogating of any old
laws, but for a due course of proceeding in laws already established,
but executed (he thinketh) by some ecclesiastical governor[s]
contrary both to the purport of the same laws and also to the minds
and meanings of the law-makers, to the great hurts and grievances
of sundry her Majesty's good subjects.' He offered particulars in
writing, praying that they be read and then sent to a committee
for further consideration.

Official reaction was prompt. Mr. Secretary Wolley rose to
remind the House of the Queen's 'express inhibition'. They would
run into contempt of her Highness if they dealt in this matter, he
said. And so the writing was received but not read; and on the
last day of the session the Speaker handed it back to Mr. Davenport. [2]

In all probability, Davenport's writing was a document we
possess, entitled 'Certain motions whereupon a conference is
humbly to be desired before the Lords of the Higher House and a
committee of the Lower House, in the presence of the Bishops and
all the Judges of the land'. The motions were many, the document
long and significant. By way of preamble, the petitioners gave an
assurance that they did not mean to call in question either the
royal supremacy or the ecclesiastical laws of the Realm, but
merely to reform abuses committed by the bishops and ecclesiastical commissioners, 'against the word of God, the prerogative [of
the] Crown, the laws, liberties and customs' of England. They

[1] STRYPE, *Whitgift*, i. 537.   [2] D'EWES, pp. 438-9.

declared that according to sundry statutes no ecclesiastical law or canon was to be executed in this realm that was repugnant to statute law or custom; and they referred to statutes of Edward III's reign to prove that Parliament was the place where remedy should be sought for infringement of the great charter or other laws of the land. The argument was clear, its implications shattering to the Church, and, in the long run, to the Crown.

Then came a number of 'points' on which conference was desired: items of episcopal procedure which, they contended, were illegal. The whole *ex officio* process was there; silencing of ministers for failure to subscribe to Whitgift's articles; imprisonment for trifles, 'without a lawful cause'; deprivation 'for causes not expressly appointed by law'. A long series of questions probed the legality of the offences for which Puritan ministers had been deprived. Was not the Act of Uniformity, being a penal law, to be interpreted strictly? As the Prayer Book was first authorized in the House of Commons and did not receive the assent either of Convocation or the bishops, and it being a maxim of law that the makers of the law are its best expositors, should not the opinion — Parliament's opinion — prevail that it was directed against Papists and not Puritans? Another item questioned the legality of the Prayer Book because it differed from the description in the Act of Uniformity. Whitgift's notorious articles of 1583 were challenged on the authority of two Henrician statutes, forbidding the bishops to enforce any constitution or article without the royal assent. One by one Puritan practices were cited, with a view to justifying or excusing them. There had been toleration of such divergences in Edward VI's reign: it would be well, for the sake of peace and unity, to have similar toleration now. Despite the obvious danger of echoing Martin Marprelate, the document went on to arraign particular bishops for questionable doctrine or practices. Page followed page, each with several theses. The penultimate one suggested that the bishops had 'fallen into the high offence of a praemunire': let Parliament sue for their pardon and for the establishment of a better order of things.

The final section of our document is headed, 'Means of Unity'. It may perhaps belong to a subsequent chapter of the story, when the compilers approached Archbishop Whitgift. Wholly moderate, it asks the bishops for a series of reforms to secure better qualified ministers, a better regulation of church life, and the toleration of

Puritan — but not Presbyterian — non-conforming practices. Had the peace of the Church been attainable, we might agree that they formed a reasonable basis for it. But one of the theses in the earlier part of the document — 'Whether the desire of a further and better reformation in the Church of England, in dutiful manner, be not warranted by the word of God and law of England?' — betrayed the ideologue speaking a language capable of infinite wrangle.[1]

The arresting feature of this document is its legal and constitutional character. Robert Beale had compiled the first great manifesto along such lines in the Parliament of 1585. He and James Morice were to be dominant in the Parliament of 1593; and we may suspect that both — certainly Beale — were behind the scenes on this occasion. The Puritan ministers, meeting in their national synod, may also have been involved; but if so, it was their moderate wing. The doctrinaire group, with their Bill and Book, had been discredited and decisively beaten in the Parliament of 1587, thus leaving the way open for a new leadership, which, with its constitutional and practical cast of thought, made a stronger appeal to the House of Commons and was more congenial to the English nation.

Secretary Wolley's intervention stayed the development of the campaign in the House of Commons, but its sponsors decided to confront the arch-enemy himself — Whitgift — with their 'motions'. The Journals give no hint that the House was responsible for the move; and almost certainly it was not. No change was obtained from Whitgift. He apostilled his answers on their document, and — as Beale later informed Hatton — told the gentleman who brought it to him that he 'should take heed how he were addicted to that side, for that they were like to Jack Straw that would have suffered but the order only of begging friars'. A typical remark of this proud, humourless prelate; and the more typical if the emissary was young Humphrey Davenport.[2]

Davenport's motion was made on February 25th. Two days later, Mr. Henry Apsley — Member for Hastings, a young lawyer who in the following Parliament got into trouble for associating with Peter Wentworth — started the principal religious disturbance of the session when he spoke about the evils of pluralities (the

---

[1] B.M. Lansdowne MS. 119, fols. 94-101.
[2] Thynne MS. lxxvi, at Longleat ('Certain motions', with Whitgift's answers in the margins); B.M. Additional MS. 48039 (Yelverton 44), fol. 67.

holding of several benefices by one minister) and non-residence, offering a bill to remedy them. We may surmise that the bill came out of the synod of Puritan ministers and the speech out of their tendentious survey of the clergy. Both clearly contravened the Queen's command, and someone — if only the Speaker — must have said so. But the vocal majority of the House evidently thought there were limits to true obedience. They ordered the immediate reading of the bill: which may be interpreted as a clue to the reluctance with which they had previously abandoned Mr. Davenport's motions.

At the second reading, which took place on March 1st, there were — the Clerk tells us — 'sundry arguments, many with the bill and some against it'. Lord Talbot mentioned the debate in a letter to his father. 'Divers pure fellows', he wrote, 'are very hot and earnest: amongst whom, Mr. Beale hath made a very sharp speech, which is nothing well liked by the bishops'. The bill was committed to Sir Francis Knollys, James Morice, Robert Beale, Sir Robert Jermyn, and Francis Hastings: Puritans all, though there were other members whose names are not given. Jermyn, a Suffolk gentleman, had been in hot dispute with his bishop, some years back, over the latter's treatment of Puritan ministers, and had complained to Walsingham that the bishop was preventing the gentry from reforming the Church. Our committee prepared a new bill, which Sir Francis Knollys reported to the House, asking that it be given an immediate reading. This done, some of Talbot's 'pure fellows' demanded a second immediate reading, and Knollys, in the name of the whole committee, supported them. This also was accorded, and the bill was sent to be ingrossed. Presumably, the friends of Whitgift and the Queen, having had their say before the committee stage, did not dare to open their mouths in stay of its irresistible march. A few days later the bill was passed and sent to the Lords.[1]

One minister, one benefice was its basic principle: though in a proviso a somewhat illusory concession was made by permitting two benefices to be held, if distant no more than three miles from each other and not exceeding the value of £8 per annum apiece. The bill did not venture to oust existing pluralists; but they were restrained by the provision that acceptance of any further benefice would vacate the original one. Residence — with a sole

<hr>

[1] D'EWES, pp. 441-4; P.R.O. Baskerville's calendar of Talbot MSS. (Longleat).

exception for anyone in the Queen's service — was made obliga-
tory, and absence for an aggregate of three months in the year
incurred a penalty of £10 a month. Pluralists were obliged to
maintain preachers where they did not reside, the penalty being
£5 for every month's default. Finally, all dispensations against
these provisions were declared void.[1]

To us, the bill may seem entirely reasonable and commendable,
but in the circumstances of the time it was hopelessly visionary.
John Fortescue, Master of the Wardrobe and Privy Councillor,
was one of those who had spoken on the subject, probably during
the second-reading debate on the original bill. Be rid of doctrinaire assumptions and look at the problem historically and
practically, sums up his approach. If this matter had its foundation from God, there was no more to be said — it was inviolable:
if from men, then it could be altered by man. But how could the
former be the case when there were no parishes in the Apostles'
time, and no tying of men to parishes? Having thus disposed of
a priori reasoning, he reviewed the historical setting of the problem,
starting with the Henrician Reformation, which dealt with the
evil of pluralism and non-residence in a statute of 1529. Its
principle was the same as that of the bill before them, but it
permitted dispensations in the interests of the Crown, the Church,
the nobility and learning. Turning to the actual administration
of this law, he compared the number of dispensations issued in
Archbishop Cranmer's time with those of Parker and Grindal.
Grindal had effected a remarkable reduction: more than some
Councillors had thought wise. His severe policy had been continued by Whitgift and had been embodied by Convocation in a
constitution, carrying the royal assent. Indeed, the grievances
now being aired were not caused by recent but by old dispensations, and could not be remedied until the beneficiaries died.
Was it wise, because dispensations had been too liberally granted
in the past, to overthrow the present moderate regulations; to
infringe the Queen's supremacy and take revenue from her?
Was it wise to prevent the Queen from rewarding her chaplains,
usually men of special gifts? Would the nobles and great officers
of the realm — unable to keep resident chaplains or present them
to two competent livings — be content to have their privileges
taken away? Again, was it wise to deprive bishops of the assistance

[1] Lansdowne MS. 104/3; Inner Temple, Petyt MS. 538/52, fol. 32.

of learned divines? Was no greater respect to be paid to a Doctor
or Bachelor of Divinity of thirty years' standing in the University,
than to the merest preacher in the land? Deans of cathedral
churches and Masters of colleges in the university could not continue their residence and duties without the financial aid of some
benefice.[1]

Whitgift's supporters, by now becoming in their turn something
of a party, were far from idle. To marshal opposition, they prepared papers with arguments similar to those used by Fortescue.
The egalitarian nature of the bill came under criticism. So did its
disregard of problems created by the great number of benefices,
the extreme poverty of some, and the small value of most: there
were said to be about 9000 benefices, ten per cent of which were
insufficient to maintain 'a mean person', while less than five per
cent were worth more than a clear £30 per annum. Item after
item analysed the ill effects of the bill. One paper survives containing a protagonist's answers to some of these criticisms: they
are not impressive.[2]

The bill was given a first reading in the House of Lords on
March 13th and there was a debate.[3] Someone wrote a summary of three of the speeches, evidently for Whitgift, thus preserving for us a precious glimpse at that august assembly. Burghley
spoke. He was moved to do so, he said, by conscience and country.
Extolling the objects of the bill as set out in the preamble, he
then, like Fortescue in the Lower House, embarked on a historical
survey, commencing with the Henrician Act of 1529, which, he
said, made good provision, though corruption afterwards set in.
This he blamed on the Mass, 'which, being a hawking or hunting
Mass, was very short'. The Act of 1529 made exceptions in
favour of noblemen and others, but their chaplains took advantage
of the statute and did no service even in their lords' houses: they
merely 'put all in their purses'. His historical survey continued
and broadened, with praise for Grindal's restraint and also Whitgift's. At this point he brightened his speech with 'a merry tale'
of Dr. Chambers, a physician, and Dr. Butts, Henry VIII's
physician. Alas! the tale — clearly, an unedifying one — is not

---

[1] Petyt MS. 538/52, fols. 34-6 (another copy in Lansdowne MS. 396, fols. 59-66).
[2] S.P. Dom. Eliz. 223/14; St. Paul's Cathedral Add. MS. vii. 8 (31); Lansdowne
MS. 68, fol. 92. Strype is not to be trusted in his dating of papers about this bill.
Some belong to 1601.
[3] *L.J.* ii. 159.

recorded. Then, 'with some hard terms', he attacked the bishops as a body for their insufferable slackness and greed. The Queen, he said, was acquainted with the matter and was very forward to redress the faults. He urged the bishops 'not to hinder her good and gracious purpose' when she conferred with them, adding that the Purveyors Bill merely touched the food of the body, 'but this concerned the food of the soul'.

In conclusion, Burghley — whose mind, by long training, worked in pros and cons — declared himself not so scrupulous as to like the bill absolutely, without any exception. He favoured learning, and wished it a competent reward. Consequently, he was in favour of allowing a learned man to have two benefices, provided they were both in one diocese.

Whitgift seems to have answered this speech. He was followed by Lord Grey, who declared that after hearing Whitgift he was more in favour of Burghley's opinion than before. The Arch-bishop had evidently said that it would be impossible to find enough learned ministers to serve all the benefices: Grey was optimistic. The Archbishop had claimed that there were now more learned ministers in the Church of England than ever before, more, indeed, than in all the reformed churches in Christendom: Grey retorted that this was attributable to God, not the bishops. Probably we should assume that Whitgift had been charged to deliver a message from the Queen, taking the problem into her own hands and announcing that she would confer with the bishops, thus, incidentally, killing the bill. At any rate, our bishop-baiting peer — as the report narrates — 'seemed to wonder greatly at her Majesty, that she would make choice to confer with those who were all enemies to reformation, for that it nearly touched their freeholds'. He thought the House should choose some lay peers to join the bishops in that conference. 'Last of all, he wished the bishops might be served as they were' in King Henry VIII's days, 'when, as in the case of praemunire, they were all thrust out of doors'.

Burghley intervened to lend weight, without heat, to Grey's suggestion: 'If they were wise', he said, the bishops 'would them-selves be humble suitors to her Majesty to have some of the temporal Lords joined with them'.

Lord Hunsdon, the Lord Chamberlain and cousin to the Queen, 'utterly disliked the Lord Grey's motion'. They should leave it to

the Queen to choose whom to consult, and not dictate to her. He
went on to attack the bill at length, in a manner and with arguments similar to Whitgift's, invoking Plato in criticism of its
egalitarianism. 'Not to every man alike, but to everyone according to the measure of his desert'.[1]

It is a pity that not even on this occasion are we granted a full
savouring of a Lords' debate. How many, we ask, were like Lord
Grey, who would have been thoroughly at home in the House of
Commons? Burghley's speech was a courageous one for an
instinctive trimmer. No one knew better than he the views and
temper of his mistress. The bill proceeded no further than a first
reading in the Lords. Undoubtedly, the Queen stayed it; and in
view of her sweeping prohibition of such topics, we can only
register surprise that the Lords dared to go so far.

A cloud now descends on us, with occasional peeps that hint at a
landscape lost to view. The Puritans were certainly more active
in and out of Parliament than our evidence reveals. Two documents among Robert Beale's papers suggest how propaganda
went on among Members. One is a petition from the inhabitants
of South Farnham, Surrey — the original of which was 'subscribed with many hands' — complaining of the state of their
parish. The living was wealthy enough to support a preacher,
but the vicar was a foreigner-born, a 'silly man', who could not
read plainly and distinctly, an immoral man and a drunkard to
boot; and of four curates serving various villages, three were
common drunkards and the fourth 'a modest man, but altogether
unlearned'. They had petitioned the bishop, and even used the
mediation of Sir Francis Walsingham: all in vain. They now
approached the Council through Sir William More, with a
suggestion that Parliament might be told of their 'most miserable
and hard case'. Perhaps the pluralities bill gave More an opportunity of airing this scandal. At any rate, he showed the petition
to Beale (who took a copy of it), and presumably he showed it to
other Members. Another document, casting a baleful light on
episcopal corruption, was even more disturbing. It was a petition,
apparently to some Councillors, asking them to compel the Bishop
of Lichfield — the notorious William Overton — to continue

---

[1] The best, but incomplete, text is St. Paul's Add. MS. iv. 137. The full text is in
Inner Temple, Petyt MS. 538/52, fols. 32b seqq. and Lansdowne MS. 396, fols.
59 seqq.

paying the petitioner an annuity of £20 for moving the Earl of
Lincoln to get Overton's *congé d'élire* sealed — a service which the
Bishop had described as greater than that of another person to
whom he had paid 1000 marks 'to help him to the bishopric'.
Beale has written in the margin, '1588 in Parliament': meaning,
presumably, that the document went the round of the House of
Commons.[1]

We ought probably to imagine other documents in circulation:
for example, the enlarged Puritan survey of the state of the clergy,
now covering an appreciable part of England; and selections
from the vast collection of papers made by John Field before he
died, which, incidentally, seem to have been at Martin Marprelate's service. Some of these papers were to be secretly printed as
A Parte of a Register in 1593. A more extensive 'Seconde Parte'
was intended for publication. It remained in manuscript and —
significant fact — passed into the possession of Sir John Higham,
the Suffolk Puritan and parliamentarian. Field took care to
preserve in his Register many dramatic dialogues between
Puritan 'martyrs' and their episcopal 'persecutors', probably in
imitation of Foxe's *Book of Martyrs*. Even today they are capable
of arousing one's indignation; and doubtless it was this type of
indoctrination which explains, at least in part, the mood of
Elizabethan Members of Parliament. These Puritans were skilled
beyond measure in the arts of revolution.

One, Anthony Bridgeman, of Mitchell-Dean, Gloucestershire,
a gentleman whose simple mind was exalted by Puritan ideas, was
prompted to help the revolution on its way. On Sunday, January
5th, he had been at Court, and — probably as the Queen went
through to chapel — had proffered a petition, which he entitled,
'A New-Year's gift', having 'thirteen branches to the dozen, to be
planted in this your Highness's garden of England'. It suggested
twelve religious and social reforms of a radical character, adding,
as branch 13, 'the body and service of myself, your most humble,
poor subject and daily orator to command at your Highness's
pleasure'. A Master of Requests took the paper and suppressed it.
A month or so later, disappointed but not discouraged, this most
worthy gentleman sent Walsingham a copy of a bill, which he
proposed, though not a Member of Parliament, to 'prefer into the
Parliament House upon Wednesday next'. It calmly dissolved

[1] B.M. Additional MS. 48064, fols. 72-3, 48.

every collegiate and cathedral church within the realm, turning their revenues over to the Crown. From the consequent windfall, the Queen was asked to provide and pay three ministers in each of the dissolved cathedrals and give £200 per annum for the relief of the poor in each diocese or county. God would be more zealously served, the people better edified, and the Queen's revenues increased by more than £20,000 of unimproved rents. Needless to say, nothing came of the proposal: it is not even in a list of unread bills in the Speaker's custody. Walsingham, we suppose, mercifully suffocated it: and so might we have done, except that naivety is often a mirror — albeit a distorting one — to its surroundings.[1]

On March 3rd Lord Talbot told his father: 'Divers articles are preferred unto the Nether House for reformation of the Book of Common Prayer and such like matters; but the Speaker dare not read them'. He was probably referring to Mr. Davenport's 'motions'; but he may also have had in mind two bills which appeared as 'not read' in a list of bills in the Speaker's possession on March 15th. One was entitled, 'A Bill for a learned ministry'. Its pedigree is obvious: more we cannot say. The second carried the innocent but arresting title, 'for confirmation of a branch of *Magna Charta*'. On this occasion we are lucky. The original draft survives; and arresting it indeed is. The bill, which in effect gives legislative expression to one of the theses in Davenport's 'motions', must surely have emanated from the Beale-Morice group of Puritans. 'Whereas' — runs the preamble — 'the bodies of sundry her Majesty's subjects, without any suit or lawful process or arrest, or without sufficient warrant or ordinary and due course and proceeding in law . . . have been committed to prison and there remain, to their grievous and intolerable vexation and contrary to the great Charter and ancient good laws and statutes of this Realm . . .' The enacting clause lays down that no person be hereafter committed to prison except by sufficient warrant and authority and by due course and proceeding in law, on pain of treble damages to the victim, to be recovered in the Common Law Courts. The justices of any of these courts are authorized to direct a writ of Habeas Corpus for the delivery of every person so imprisoned, with ruinous penalties against the gaoler if he fails to obey the writ. Though quite general in wording, it was clearly

[1] S.P. Dom. Eliz. 222/70.

meant to arm the Common Law Courts against the Court of High
Commission, and with their aid to wreck episcopal practices
against the Puritans.[1]

The bill was not even read. Perhaps other moves were equally
abortive. But the future is often built on present failure; and who,
reading this fugitive bill about *Magna Carta*, would not pause to
salute it?

[1] P.R.O. Baskerville's calendar of Talbot MSS. (Longleat); S.P. Dom. Eliz. 223/17;
B.M. Harleian MS. 6847, fols. 64-5.

CHAPTER IV

END OF THE SESSION

THE Clerk of the House of Commons, Fulk Onslow, was in poor health again this Parliament and obtained permission to use one of his servants as his deputy when illness incapacitated him. Consequently, the rough Journal of the House — which, through the imperfect medium of the early Stuart antiquary, Sir Simonds D'Ewes, is our staple authority for the proceedings — was badly kept. We become very conscious of this as we now turn to pick up a few stray threads and end our story of a Parliament that was clearly more intransigent, and therefore more interesting, than our sources permit us to know.

Philip Gawdy, Member for Thetford and an attractive letter-writer, gives us a glimpse of the scene. 'Let them all know', he told his brother on February 22nd, 'that my second speech in the Parliament House is yet to make. It may be as wise as any that hath yet [been] spoken, for I am untried and therefore it hangs in suspense. Sweet brother, I will make convenient haste to come to thee, but no leave will be given to any that I yet hear of. But the continuance of the Parliament will not be long. Monsieur Bacon [i.e. Francis Bacon] is very silent in the House: he restoreth for a further time.' Five days later, when religious questions were stirring, Gawdy was no longer optimistic about a speedy end, and by March 13th he thought the Parliament would 'continue very long', the current expectation being an adjournment over Easter.[1]

For one reason and another the pace of legislation was slow. On March 17th the Lords tried, by a message, to speed the passage of five of their own bills, already specially recommended to the Commons. One had provoked a great debate on its first reading; another — against excess in apparel — was also misliked. Later, in a desperate attempt to get these two particular bills through in time, the Lords asked for a conference about them, although they were still *sub judice* in the Lower House. The Commons passed neither. It would seem that they simply refused to give a further

[1] B.M. Egerton MS. 2804, fols. 65, 67-9.

reading to the bill on apparel; and they probably treated the other bill in the same way. About a third bill they were more accommodating, trying to get the Lords' approval in advance to the amendments they wanted to make. This time the Lords stood on their dignity: they told the Commons to do what they liked, and they, for their part, would do as they pleased. When the bill came back to them, they left the amendments unread, and so it foundered. Only two of these five bills, desired so keenly by both government and peers, got through the Parliament. At Court there was anger, as we learn from Francis Alford, who was wrongly blamed for opposing one of them.[1]

On Friday, March 21st, the Lords informed the Commons that the Queen wished to end the Parliament before Easter, and earnestly hoped this could be done on Wednesday next. Wednesday came: still there were bills unfinished that the government wanted. Rather than face an adjournment over Easter — as Philip Gawdy expected — and thus present the Commons with leisure for further agitation, the Queen kept them at it till the Saturday, the eve of Easter Day. Parliament was then dissolved.

On this last morning, March 29th, the Lords asked for a conference between delegates from both Houses, and there proposed that they should all join in petition to the Queen, asking her to declare open war against the King of Spain, 'if it so shall seem good unto her', and 'to use all honourable means, as well offensive as defensive' against him and his adherents, as time and occasion offered. The Speaker was to make the petition in the name of both Houses, immediately after the offering of the subsidy bill in the closing ceremonies that afternoon. Needless to say, the Commons readily agreed to exert pressure on their sovereign; and no doubt the petition included an offer — which we find in a tentative draft by Burghley — of 'their bodies, their lives, lands and goods to serve her Majesty': choice words, even genuine sentiment, but an unsubstantial foundation for policy.[2]

Speculation must now direct our narrative. It seems that in these last days of the session — probably after the intimation on March 21st that Easter would bring the Parliament to an end —

[1] D'Ewes, pp. 439-53; Inner Temple, Petyt MS. 538/10, fols. 53-4.
[2] D'Ewes, pp. 450, 454; S.P. Dom. Eliz. 223/34 (a copy of the entry in the lost, finished Journal of the Commons); B.M. Lansdowne MS. 104, fol. 55 (Burghley's draft, before the Lords decided on a joint petition).

the Beale-Morice group of Puritans took the bit between their teeth again. Their 'motions' had been suppressed in the House and rejected with needless contumely by Whitgift; their bill about *Magna Carta* remained unread; and yet their romantic faith in the Queen — a faith passing all understanding — persisted. Encouraged by her 'comfortable and gracious speeches' at the audience about the purveyors and the Exchequer bills and by the statesmanlike and magnanimous action that followed, they decided to have another try to stop the proceedings of the bishops against Puritan ministers. Our Journals are utterly silent on the subject, but we must, I think, conclude that the House agreed to take action, and appointed a committee to draft a petition.

The texts of two petitions survive. One was written by the redoubtable John Stubbs. 'This supplication', wrote Beale on his copy of it, 'was drawn by Mr. Stubbs to be exhibited in Parliament, March 1589': a note which would date the document between March 25th and 29th, if it can be interpreted strictly. Its opening words are worth quoting: 'Having now one and thirty years' most happy experience of God's tender and watchful eye over your princely care and study to protect and govern us in piety, peace and justice; thereto receiving lately by our Speaker your good pleasure answerable to your wonted clemency; and forasmuch as for most real accomplishment of your word, and whatsoever may be expected from a good prince, your Majesty is renowned above all princes of the earth . . .' One hears again — not without emotion — the voice that cried 'God save the Queen!' as the hangman severed his right hand on the block.[1]

Possibly Stubbs was responsible for initiating the business in the House, and had his 'supplication' drawn up in readiness. The appointment of a committee would supplant his document; and the phraseology of our second petition, which is both broader and narrower in scope, does in fact suggest the work of a committee. It begins — perhaps for tactical reasons — on a theme seemingly remote from religious grievances. After reminding the Queen that they are granting a double subsidy and must justify themselves to constituents who had recently been heavily burdened with taxes and the charges of war, and who now were impoverished by the interruption of foreign trade, they ask her to fulfil her declared intention of repealing unnecessary penal laws. The background

[1] B.M. Additional MS. 48101 (Yelverton 110), fols. 136-7.

to this plea is probably to be found in action taken by the Privy Council at the end of 1588, when four lawyers from each of the four Inns of Court were commissioned to meet, along with the judges, once or twice weekly until the beginning of Parliament and review existing statutes. They were to suggest the repeal or amendment of old laws: a seemingly large-scale and striking scheme for legal reform. All that appears to have come out of their labours in this Parliament was a bill to repeal certain statutes of an economic character.[1] It was a modest beginning. Even so, it came to nothing, because the Queen vetoed the bill: probably because the Commons had added obnoxious amendments. The full story would doubtless be interesting; but, alas, it evades even intelligent guessing. In their petition, the Commons ask that the penal statutes which they had planned to rescind, but could not now deal with owing to the imminent end of the session, should be suspended by the Queen until the next Parliament; and that this be done by proclamation before Parliament dispersed, thus giving Members something with which to content the people.[2]

By this avenue, the petition naturally and quickly reached its destination: religious grievances. For many years — it points out — the Commons in Parliament had been complaining of ecclesiastical disorders. The Queen had referred their complaints to the bishops for redress, but the disorders continue, displeasing God, destroying the peace and unity of the Realm, and causing a marvellous increase of Popery and atheism. 'Albeit our meaning be not to intermeddle any whit with your Majesty's prerogative royal', yet we serve 'as mouths, in the name of all the people of this land, to crave and desire a reformation at your Majesty's hands'. Then follow the familiar arguments against the legality of *ex officio* proceedings. 'We most humbly beseech your Majesty to take order that your Highness's commission ecclesiastical may not be so abused as hitherto it hath been ... We are no schismatics, no libellers, rebellious or disordered persons.' After thus dissociating themselves from Brownists and Marprelatists, they complain of Whitgift, Bancroft, and others — those who 'would mingle and couple us with recusants, sectaries, and other like offenders. We hold no conventicles or unlawful assemblies, but detest them. We desire to live under your Majesty's laws and not the laws of the

[1] I assume that the contents of this bill were as in Lansdowne MS. 55, fol. 184b.
[2] DASENT, *Acts of the Privy Council*, xvi. 416-18.

Pope or innovations of private men's opinions ... We desire that by a preaching ministry all the people of your kingdom may be taught to obey and serve your Highness.' Since the bishops confess 'that the disagreement between them and many good and learned ministers is not in any substance of doctrine, but only in some ceremonies and indifferent things, whereto the Apostle teacheth us that every man's conscience is not to be forced ...', they beseech the Queen to permit 'a Christian and peaceable toleration, not contrary to the law': such a toleration as was used in Edward VI's time and also at one period (clearly Grindal's) in the Queen's own happy reign. They ask that good and peaceable men, who pray daily for her and are ready to lose all for her weal, 'be no otherwise judged nor proceeded against than according to your Highness's laws of England'.[1]

The petition assumes the voice of moderate men, outraged by the tyranny of Whitgift and his colleagues and perturbed by its harmful effect on national wellbeing. It can hardly fail to engage our sympathies, as Whitgift's practices alienate them. Unfortunately, the problem was not so simple as that.

What action was taken, we do not know. There was probably no time left to seek audience to present the petition: nor, if time had permitted, was the Queen likely to have granted audience. It may well be that the Speaker was ordered to incorporate it in his closing speech before Queen and Parliament. If so, he had two petitions to make in his oration.

Parliament assembled for the final ceremonies in the afternoon of Saturday, March 29th. No account survives of the proceedings and not a hint of the character of the Speaker's oration. Fortunately, however, we have the text of a letter from Francis Alford to one of Sir Christopher Hatton's servants, in which he comments on the Lord Chancellor's reply. 'My Lord, your master', he wrote, 'gave us so good a lesson at our farewell that I trust will be remembered while any of us live which served in this council ... You know how much I ever honoured his Lordship for the great wisdom and natural excellency of speech that was in him; but in this conclusion I did wonder at him — wherein he surpassed himself and the best-learned men that ever I heard in that place, which have been divers of great note and fame. For the service of God and preservation of His holy religion amongst us, his Lord-

[1] Inner Temple, Petyt MS. 538/36, fols. 327-9.

ship did with great zeal reprehend the fanatical humour of the
Precision and the Puritan, most impure; whom he divided in his
tender consideration of the Church, but, in truth, they be all one
in faction and action. And, as he noted unto us her Majesty's
benign inclination, in love of the peace of Christ's Church, to
suppress them, and her clemency not to persecute them; so, if
they be not utterly put down, and that with speed, I fear they will
trouble the whole state. He did gravely advise young men: but
not without offence to them. The elders' — Alford obviously
counted himself among these — 'thought it most needful. And
surely, to report truth, the Parliament had young gentlemen of
worthy calling, which will prove good servitors in their commonwealth, who would not be discouraged; but the admonition will
do them great good. His Lordship handled divers other points,
necessary for the government.'[1]

The special attention which Hatton gave to Puritans, his
announcement — no doubt on Elizabeth's express command —
of the Queen's deliberate resolve to suppress but not to persecute
them, his grave advice to young men: all these points would be
compatible with — indeed, they almost suggest — the inclusion
in the Speaker's speech of that final Puritan petition. Alford, no
doubt, was obsequiously minded in his letter, but his high praise
of Hatton's speech is nonetheless impressive. He knew, as we
know, the superlative quality of the Lord Chancellor's opening
oration; and if the closing speech surpassed that, then indeed it
deserved such eulogy. Hatton had submitted his speech beforehand to Burghley. Returning it, on March 27th, the latter
praised its division into three parts and remarked that he had
'unneedfully' made some suggestions to prove that he had read it.
'Unneedfully', we can well believe.[2]

Hatton's speech is lost: a great loss. An even greater loss may be
the Queen's speech, for Elizabeth herself seems to have addressed
the assembly before it ended. We learn this from an allusion by
Edward Coke in the next Parliament, who referred to her remark,
'Many come hither *ad consulendum, qui nesciunt quid sit consulendum*':
many come hither to counsel, who are ignorant what counsel
means. 'A just reprehension to many', added Coke. Presumably,
Elizabeth replied to the petition about declaring war on Spain.
Perhaps her caustic comment merely referred to that particular

[1] Petyt MS. 538/10, fols. 53-4.   [2] S.P. Dom. Eliz. 223/33.

excess of zeal: by now she must have been conscious of the wisdom which long experience and mature years — not to mention exceptional ability — give to a ruler who has occupied a throne and power for thirty years. Perhaps, however, the comment came in the course of remarks on the petition about religion. Hatton had delivered a blunt message. She may have wished to wrap his reprimand in those folds of affection that miraculously preserved the love of her Commons; meaning to open the eyes of fellow-travellers to the subversive aims of their doctrinaire leaders, and wean them from bad company. But the speech is lost, speculation idle.[1]

Sixteen public bills — including the lay and clerical subsidy acts and the act of pardon — and eight private bills received the royal assent: only a moderate output and nothing of importance. Three bills seem to have been vetoed, among them the one for repeal of certain statutes, where perhaps the Commons had been too insistent on having their own way.[2] The Queen evidently had had her fill of this particular representation of Englishmen. Instead of proroguing Parliament and so keeping it on call, as policy had inclined her to do in the recent past, she dissolved it, thankful, we may assume, to be rid of these troublesome fellows, and resolved not to take another dip into her unlucky bag before necessity drove her to it.

---

[1] D'EWES, p. 459a.
[2] Cf. L.J. ii. 165. The other two were: concerning pleading in actions of trespass (ibid. p. 163); for better execution of the statute 8 Eliz. touching cloth-workers (ibid.).

PART FOUR

THE PARLIAMENT OF 1593

CHAPTER I

INTRODUCTORY

THE final instalment of the two subsidies granted in 1589 was to be paid into the Exchequer by February 12th, 1593. A week later a new Parliament met. The coincidence was not accidental. There was urgent need of money. With the assassination of Henry III of France in the summer of 1589, Elizabeth had found herself compelled to help Henry IV win his kingdom against the forces of the Catholic League, aided by the King of Spain. A new abyss opened for English treasure. An army in the Netherlands, an army in France, subsidies to its new King, and expensive naval expeditions: these made demands far beyond the revenues of the Crown, even assisted by an annual half-subsidy. The Queen had been forced to eat into her capital by selling lands.

The outlook became very grave. Philip of Spain was establishing himself on England's southern threshold and was intriguing in Scotland to secure a base to the north. The country at such a time could not afford the luxury of internal strains; and if a new harshness enters into the Queen's actions, we shall do well, in judging it, to remember that even the modern state, incomparably more stable and enlightened, is compelled to be illiberal when in mortal danger.

With the Parliament of 1593 comes a change of complexion. The previous assembly of 1589, though also a war-Parliament, had been stiffened by a national synod of Puritan ministers, meeting in London to organize and stimulate agitation in the House of Commons. In this it had been like its predecessors. But in 1593 there was no national synod. The Puritan classical movement was defunct. In the course of their hunt for Martin Marprelate, the ecclesiastical authorities had uncovered this secret ministerial organization, and, fortified by the revulsion against Marprelate excesses and by the sterner mood of wartime, had ventured to strike at its leaders. The minute-book of the Dedham *classis* records the disaster: 'The 2nd. June [1589] was our 80th. meeting', runs an entry. Then follows the business-minute, with mention of place and speakers for the next meeting. That meeting was not held. Instead, there is the note: 'Thus long continued through God's mercy this blessed meeting, and now it ended by the malice of Satan'. By October-November 1590 the great leader, Thomas Cartwright, and others had been summoned before the Ecclesiastical Commissioners, and, on refusing to take the *ex officio* oath, had been imprisoned. Unable to proceed further in the Court of High Commission, the authorities decided to transfer the cases to the Star Chamber, and prosecutions were instituted there in 1591. Cartwright was ultimately released in the Spring of 1592, after about eighteen months' imprisonment.[1]

The repellent Whitgift had triumphed; and he also triumphed against the separatists, an even more extreme set of Puritans, securing the execution of such devout if misguided men as Henry Barrow and John Penry. The way had been eased for his sombre disciplinary instincts, not merely by the tension of war, but by a change in character of the Privy Council. The Earl of Leicester had died in 1588, Sir Walter Mildmay in 1589, the Earl of Warwick and Sir Francis Walsingham in 1590: all of them Puritans and men of integrity or power. Leicester had been Cartwright's patron; and we may doubt whether, while he lived, Whitgift would have dared to strike at the Puritan leader. Nor would Walsingham and Mildmay have acquiesced in ruthless measures without vigorous protest. They would have employed every obstructive device open to them. True, Sir Francis Knollys and the incomparable Burghley were left. Both were old, Knollys especially so. The latter's radicalism and his courage persisted. He could speak his conscience, and did so. But he was rather like a privileged dodderer. Even in the congenial House of Commons he had lost his authority, while keeping his seniority. As for Burghley, though plagued by the godly importunities of Puritans, and perhaps tiring of them, his sympathies were probably still with them rather than Whitgift. But the deeper courage of the

[1] USHER, *Presbyterian Movement* (Camden Soc.), p. 74; SCOTT PEARSON, *Thomas Cartwright*, pp. 317 seqq.

martyr, or even the partisan, was not his. Expounding his principle of political conduct to his son, Robert, he explained that, when his opinion differed from the Queen's, he would not change it to please her, but as a servant he would obey her commandment.[1] Experience had reinforced a natural instinct; and that experience had been sharply repeated over the execution of Mary Queen of Scots. Age, drying up the founts of passion, could only perfect the model servant. Thus was opportunity given for Whitgift to become the Queen's 'black husband': to speak with the tempter's seductive voice and plausibility to a heart that had resented Puritanism since it forced the compromise of 1559. Elizabeth, too, was growing old: she was in her sixtieth year when this new Parliament met. Power, long enjoyed, breeds imperiousness: though in the Queen it was never entirely divorced from the milder promptings and affection of womanhood.

Life may seem a process of imperceptible change. The same is not necessarily true of human institutions. Men of like mind and experience can disappear from the scene at about the same time, and the tone of society be altered appreciably. We are at such a climacteric in 1593. Something of the old persists: that we shall see. But there is an unmistakable new look. In the nation at large it was personified in the young Earl of Essex, who already aspired to fill the vacuum left by Leicester, Hatton and Walsingham: a vacuum that would be extended when old Burghley died. Essex's adventurous spirit revelled in war; his soaring ambition aimed also at 'domestical greatness'. He was already building his clientele of men of action. He was to turn faction into a mania. His rise marks the decline of the balanced power-system of high Elizabethan days.

There was also a new look about Parliament. In 1587, when a London alderman threatened to resign because he was outvoted on an issue, Recorder Fleetwood told him that it was evident 'he was never brought up in the Parliament of England, for in the Common House there the greatest Councillor may persuade as he shall think cause; but the House will do as they shall think it good, and yet no disgrace at all'.[2] Therein lay the political wisdom and greatness of the Privy Councillors who had managed the House of Commons before 1593: Knollys, Sadler, Wilson, Hatton,

---

[1] WRIGHT, *Q. Elizabeth & her Times*, ii. 457.
[2] B.M. Lansdowne MS. 52, fols. 135 seqq.

Mildmay. Hatton was no Puritan, but he resented Whitgift's rude and contemptuous treatment of the House as much as did Mildmay. All these admirable men were now gone. Mildmay — one supposes — had set the tone of leadership in the last Parliament. It was now Vice-Chamberlain Heneage; and, as we shall see, he was not content with the tactful role described by Fleetwood. Robert Cecil, a new and young Councillor — but not yet Secretary — assisted. He was an abler and more accommodating man; but mentally he belonged to the new generation which was to emphasize the segregation of Councillors in the House. Fortescue and Wolley, other Councillors, were minor figures. As for Sir Francis Knollys, his partial eclipse from authority was made total by his intervention in support of rebel Puritans.

In the nature of things, change in the ordinary membership of the House had been cumulative; but by 1593 it was sufficiently marked to affect our story. There was Recorder Fleetwood, *sui generis*, who, for all his growing conservatism, had always been ready with his store of precedents and antiquarian lore to bolster up independence. This endearing House of Commons man had been made a Queen's Serjeant and served the last Parliament of his life as an assistant in the Upper House. The lawyer Edward Coke succeeded to his role of master *par excellence* of precedents; but unlike the warm-hearted Fleetwood, radicalism afflicted him in age, not youth. He was the Speaker this Parliament. Francis Alford was dead: an inveterate conservative, but a personality. Our former diarist, Thomas Cromwell, surely the most experienced committee-member of the whole reign, always a stout House of Commons man of radical leanings and Puritan sympathies, had ended his parliamentary career, though he was to live till 1611, burdened with the affairs of an irresponsible nephew, the latest Lord Cromwell. Sir Robert Jermyn, a resolute Puritan, no longer sat in Parliament. Sir John Higham, the same type of gentleman, intermitted from 1587 to 1604; and another of this choice group, Sir Richard Knightley, was temporarily absent, deterred, no doubt, by his trouble over the Marprelate tracts. Digges, Strickland, Topcliffe and Dr. Turner had disappeared one or two Parliaments ago. Here was a core of men who could, and probably would, have led the Parliament of 1593 to different action on several critical occasions.

Christopher Yelverton was back, golden-voiced and generously inclined, but, as Peter Wentworth declared, timid: he was on his way to royal favour. James Dalton reappeared, more deeply bitten with reaction than ever: as the renegade, taunted for his betrayal of a cause, is apt to become. Authority found in him an able champion. Sir Anthony Cope sat again, and so did Edward Lewkenor. Of their Puritanism, no doubt can be entertained, but they seem to have been curiously silent and inactive. The redoubtable Peter Wentworth was a Member; similarly James Morice and Robert Beale. But these three irrepressibles got into immediate trouble and were snuffed out. The Parliament continued without them; and — significant fact — no substitutes were forthcoming.

In a letter written to Burghley in March 1593, Robert Beale has a remark that catches attention: 'When I heard in what sort the elections of divers knights and burgesses proceeded, with no such readiness and desire as was wont to be in former times, I feared that there would have been a further backwardness than (God be thanked) hath now happened'. The evidence we possess does not help to illuminate the comment; and yet there must surely have been some basis for it. Perhaps he had in mind the destruction of organized Puritanism and the absence of its stimulus from elections. At any rate, he felt, as the historian does, that the House of Commons had lost something of its old virtue.[1]

Not that this was an undistinguished or spineless assembly. There were as great men sitting in 1593 as ever this country of ours afforded: Francis Bacon and his scarcely less able, though little-known brother, Anthony — 'a gentleman of impotent feet but a nimble head' — Sir Francis Drake, Sir Walter Raleigh, Fulk Greville, and many another who lives in our annals. Of the 462 Members, almost half were newcomers. We shall perceive the weakness of the House — if compliance be a weakness — as our story unfolds.

The new Parliament assembled on Monday, February 19th, 1593. There was plague in London and danger in crowds. The customary procession was therefore cancelled. Instead, the peers were commanded to attend the service at Westminster Abbey in the morning, where Whitgift, whose time of triumph this was, preached to a congregation shorn of state, minus robes and minus sovereign. In the afternoon the Queen came to the Parliament

[1] Lansdowne MS. 73, fol. 4b.

Chamber by barge from Somerset Place.[1] Hatton's office of Lord Chancellor was now occupied by Sir John Puckering, who had been Speaker in 1584-85 and 1586-87. He had the lesser title of Lord Keeper of the Great Seal, and in most respects was a lesser man. However, he delivered a memorable opening oration.

Praising the Queen for being 'most loth to call for the assembly of her people in Parliament', he contrasted her policy with that of predecessors, some of whom summoned Parliament yearly, and most of them frequently: a useful reminder that modern assumptions are not necessarily sound for the past. She 'hath done the same but rarely', he added, 'and only upon most just, weighty and great occasions'. 'Of her own disposition' — she wished them to know — 'she would yet still forbear, as she hath done, to draw you often together', if urgent causes did not rule otherwise. These causes were the dangers threatening the country, and the need for financial support: which he proceeded to examine.

Since the defeat of his Invincible Armada, the King of Spain 'was so far from seeing the hand of God that strake him . . . that he was thereby more furiously enraged than ever before; so as he breathed nothing but bloody revenge, vowing, as it hath been here confessed by a Jesuit, that he would spend his candle to the socket, but he would be revenged and have his will of her'. He has taken every occasion to weaken her Majesty and strengthen himself by the neighbours on every side of her. In France he fought at first with money, but of late he has made the war more open, sending thither mighty armies: twice under the Duke of Parma; once by a nephew of the Pope himself — 'who, before he was incited thereto, was contented to fight with Bulls and bolts only'; elsewhere by the Duke of Savoy; in the west by the Duke of Lorraine; and now very lately by way of Navarre, whereof he has sworn his own son to be prince. In Brittany, a place more dangerous for the invasion of England than the Low Countries have been, he already possesses a great part of the country and commands the chief ports. 'Finding that in the last fight by sea his ships were disadvantaged by the breadth of their building and high carriage of their ports and ordnances, he hath now lately both changed the form of his old shipping and built many new, after the mould and manner of the English navy.' He is consequently thought to be twice as strong today. Lastly, there were his intrigues in Scotland

[1] B.M. Additional MS. 5758, fols. 110-11.

'to make a party there ready to receive an army'. By these means he hoped to invade England by land from the north, and at the same time to assail her by sea from the south.

There were nearer, inner dangers. Not two months past, a most devilish and bloody plan had been discovered and confessed by a subject of her Majesty's to assail her person and to corrupt the people with the persuasion that she is not their lawful Queen, but 'standeth accursed and thrown out of the faith'. 'Such is the wily malice of the enemy that . . . he hath at this present lodged in our bosoms his secret intelligencers, expressly charged . . . to advertise him . . . not only of the estate in body of her Majesty and her greatest Councillors, but also of the discontentment of the Papists, of the proceedings of the Puritans and grievances of the people.'

Enjoining his audience to ponder on these things, while marvelling that the revenues of this little island must defend five countries, Puckering turned to the need for taxation. 'Her Majesty saith there was never prince more loth to have aught at the hands of her subjects than she is'. She was 'more ready to give than willing to take'. It grieved her that the subsidies did not yield what they should. To ease themselves, the better sort threw the burden on inferior subjects, whose small assessments could raise no great total. By this abuse they oppressed their neighbours and defrauded their country of essential help.

As the subsequent debates were to show, the Queen and Puckering were far from alone in recognizing this evil. It persisted nevertheless; and the yield of each subsidy continued less than the previous. Human nature could not be changed by exhortations, nor pricks of conscience and good intentions reform the behaviour of the peers and gentlemen responsible for the scandal. Puckering went on to bid his audience admire 'the high wisdom and policy of her Majesty in the conducting of these wars'. By providing that 'others should fight for us' and by joining her forces to theirs, she spared infinite treasure and effusion of blood that would otherwise have been spent had she undertaken the cause alone.

In conclusion, Puckering told them that the Queen's intention in summoning Parliament was not to spend time in devising new laws, which merely endangered quiet people and enriched the contentious. There were already so many, both for ecclesiastical and civil government, that, if time had permitted, it would have been better to abridge and clarify the old; and this it was her intention to do on another occasion. Meanwhile, she bade them eschew their customary 'vain discourses and tedious orations', savouring of ostentation. 'Misspend not your good hours upon new and curious inventions, the which, have they never so glorious a show in the first opening, yet be they but wearisome in the handling and deceivable in the winding up.' Spring approached. Their local duties and the watchfulness of the enemy, 'who sleepeth not but lieth in wait for us', required their speedy return home.

'After this speech was ended', a diarist remarks, 'the Queen's Majesty inclined herself to the speaker [and] seemed to thank him.'[1]

The Commons then withdrew to their own chamber, where Edward Coke, now the Queen's Solicitor General, was duly elected Speaker. His parliamentary experience was slight: one session only. Probably the change of atmosphere in 1593 owes something to this fact, for Coke's learning, self-confidence and domineering character rendered him insensitive to subtleties.[2]

The House met again at one o'clock on February 22nd, and after a two hours' wait escorted their Speaker-elect to the Upper House. Here Coke acquitted himself ably. 'Modest, learned, loyal and artificial', Puckering termed his disabling speech: and, except that the modesty was false, the description was apt. In the ornate oration that followed, he pulled out all his stops. Puckering replied. 'Her Majesty', said he, 'hath no delight to hear her own praises blazed before her face.' But, he added, 'you and I may speak that which both the truth of the things and the duty of our hearts do draw out of our mouth'. Speak them he did. Continuing, he delivered the Queen's own comment, in which the touch of feminism deserves notice: 'That whatsoever blessings, good fortunes, victories or prosperous events have happened in her Majesty's reign, she attributeth all to the omnipotent and miraculous goodness of our merciful God. And so much the more with humblest thanks to be acknowledged, as that He enableth the weakest sex, and makes them to admire it that ere now were wont to doubt' women's 'good success . . . And though (she saith) you may have a wiser prince — for I must use her own

---

[1] B.M. Harleian MS. 6265, fols. 111 seqq. (printed by me in *Eng. Hist. Rev.* xxxi. 128 seqq.); B.M. Cotton MS. Titus F. II, fol. 22.
[2] Cf. D'Ewes, p. 469.

ÆTATIS SVÆ 41
AN'D 1593

DI NS QVI PATIENS

SIR EDWARD COKE

words — she dare avow, you shall never have one more careful of
your safeties, nor to give more even stroke among her subjects,
without regard of person more than matter. And of such mind
she beseecheth God ever send your prince.'

Seduction gave place to discipline when Puckering came to
answer the Speaker's claim for privilege. Her gracious Majesty,
he said, is well pleased to grant your petitions, so far as they be
grantable. 'She saith there be two things in a man most behoveful
if they be well used, and most deadly if they be ill used: wit and
tongue . . . Having, therefore, especial care that that may never
hurt you which she by her grant doth yield you, she wills you
take good heed in what sort she permits it. She would be sorry
that follies past should, by new, redouble the faults; and chargeth
you, Mr. Speaker, if any shall deliver to you any bill that passeth
the reach of a subject's brain to mention, that same you receive
not but with purpose to show it where it best becometh you. Next,
if any speech undecent or matter unfit for that place be used,
remember of this lesson. Your petitions — I must use an
Exchequer term — must be ruled, and that thus: her Majesty
granteth you liberal but not licentious speech; liberty, therefore,
but with due limitation. For even as there can be no good consultation where all freedom of advice is barred, so will there be no
good conclusion where every man may speak what he listeth,
without fit observation of persons, matters, times, places and other
needful circumstances. It shall be meet therefore that each man
of you contain his speech within the bounds of loyalty and good
discretion, being assured that as the contrary is punishable in all
men, so most of all in them that take upon them to be counsellors
and procurators of the Commonwealth.

'For liberty of speech, her Majesty commandeth me to tell you
that to say yea or no to bills, God forbid that any man should be
restrained, or afraid to answer according to his best liking, with
some short declaration of his reason therein, and therein to have
a free voice — which is the very true liberty of the House: not, as
some suppose, to speak there of all causes as him listeth, and to
frame a form of religion or a state of government, as to their idle
brains shall seem meetest. She saith, no king fit for his state will
suffer such absurdities. And though she hopeth no man here
longeth so much for his ruin as that he mindeth to make such a
peril to his own safety, yet, that you may better follow what she

wisheth, she makes, of her goodness, you the partakers of her intent and meaning.' The Speaker's other petitions were then severally granted, with appropriate cautionary words.[1]

This definition of freedom of speech — with its refrain, 'You have been warned' — may not inaptly be compared with Sir Thomas More's in 1523. The latter, being, so far as we know, the first of its kind, was appropriately the longest description made by a Speaker on such an occasion. Elizabeth's was not her first: far from it. But, coming at the culmination of thirty years' trouble, when her patience was exhausted and Whitgiftian discipline her policy, it was the longest. There is nothing in the royal exposition incompatible with the pioneer request of 1523; nothing that is not expressed or implied there, though, of course, as Queen and Speaker were viewing the question from opposite angles, it is the implicit or negative side of More's petition that is made explicit by Elizabeth. Historically, the description of 1593 was irreproachable; politically, it left the Queen in the dilemma of Dame Partington, pushing away the Atlantic Ocean with her mop.

[1] Harleian MS. 6265, fols. 113 seqq.

CHAPTER II

PETER WENTWORTH AND THE SUCCESSION QUESTION

PETER WENTWORTH was a pre-meditative type of man: of slow, deliberate pace and corresponding courage. These qualities had led him into trouble at the beginning of the Parliament of 1576 and cast a gloom over that session. It happened again in 1593. But on this occasion the cause in which he played his quixotic role was the succession to the crown: a subject so notoriously taboo that it had passed out of parliamentary politics. Job Throckmorton had made reference to it in 1586-87, but even that knight-errant would have shrunk from campaigning about it.[1]

Looking back over the years, Wentworth once remarked that he had first been stirred to deal in the question in 1562, 'by God's good motion, then by sundry grave and wise men, unknown unto me, and also by lamentable messages sent unto me by men likewise unknown unto me'. Every patriotic Englishman at that time had been gravely disturbed; but since then the execution of Mary Queen of Scots had eased extreme tension. There were some — an increasing number — whose nerves were steady enough to perceive the political astuteness of the Queen and endorse her policy; but there remained very many who, like Peter Wentworth, still feared certain calamity from an unsettled succession. The older Elizabeth became, the greater was their concern. If Wentworth can be believed, Lord Burghley shared his views; and some indication of the silent support for them in the country may perhaps be gathered from a statement attributed to the Lieutenant of the Tower, who, talking to Mrs. Wentworth when her husband's activities had landed him in that place, declared that 'if the gentlemen of England were honest, there would be five hundred in prison for her husband's opinion'. Clearly, there was tinder about, and a man like Wentworth might easily set it alight. Keeping the succession uncertain, retaining it as a reward for James of Scotland, to be given or withheld according to his

[1] For most of the references to this chapter, see the second of my two articles on 'Peter Wentworth', *Eng. Hist. Rev.* xxxix. 175-205.

behaviour, and allowing time to work for his natural and peaceful inheritance of the crown: this subtle policy, so characteristic of Elizabeth with its gambling element and its aversion to action while decision was not imperative and doubts persisted, was at the very centre of the Queen's diplomacy. Her treatment of Wentworth, though distressingly severe, must be judged by his potential danger to a policy that ultimately proved of inestimable value to England.[1]

Apparently, it was in the year 1587 that Wentworth first drafted a tract, entitled *A Pithie Exhortation to her Majestie for establishing her successor to the crowne*: pithy in content, not in length. The execution of Mary Queen of Scots may have led him to think of reopening the question; but we have only to reflect that as yet neither he nor Parliament would have acquiesced in a Scottish succession, to realize how inopportune he was. Time was needed to bring about that radical change of heart; and time was what Elizabeth's policy supplied, not his. Wentworth prevailed upon an eminent Puritan minister, Dr. Thomas Sparke, to look his tract over, and this worthy subsequently said that he mollified many of its harsh phrases. Perhaps he did; perhaps its biblically inspired frankness crept back in later revisions and additions. At any rate, the final text pulled no punches.

The tract was addressed to the Queen, and its object was to urge her speedily to summon a Parliament, have all titles and claims to the succession examined there, and then forthwith, by authority of this supreme court, make known the rightful heir. Biblical, classical and historical allusions abound. 'Infinite be the stories in all chronicles', said Wentworth, after telling the tragic history of Gorboduc; and it looks as if he had read them all. The Holy Ghost, he told the Queen, calls princes 'Gods and nursing fathers and nursing mothers unto His church'. Such titles 'prove the honourableness and lawfulness of your high calling against all Anabaptistical [i.e. subversive] spirits', but they likewise 'teach you your duties', which include provision for the future. Extreme confusion and the overthrow of the Realm must result from an uncertain succession. If you would not have God regard you as 'one that had denied the faith, and so worse than an infidel', you must perform your Christian duty. Examples and quotations from the histories of Moses, David and Hezekiah,

[1] B.M. Additional MS. 24664, fol. 44b; B.M. Lansdowne MS. 79, fol. 10.

the Medes, Persians and Romans, and — not least cogent — from the actions and speeches of the Queen's father, Henry VIII, reveal the obloquy she would merit. He drew a harrowing picture of the state of England, should she die and no successor be known. Competitors and their supporters will be up in arms; common people, unacquainted with their titles, will be at their wits' end, not knowing which part to take and yet driven to take some; and soon the whole Realm will be rent into as many shivers as there be competitors. Party will consume and devour party, and the land be so weakened that it will become an easy prey to foreign enemies. The strong will be slain in the field, children and infants murdered in every town, honest matrons and maids everywhere ravished; the rich will not be able to say 'This is mine', but they, as well as the poor, will think themselves happy if they may have their lives for a prey; religion will be laid in the dust, and neither God nor man regarded.

The interests of the Queen, Wentworth wrote, equally require a settled succession, for the strength of princes and the safety of their thrones depend above all on not alienating the hearts of their subjects by unkind and merciless dealing. He drove home his point with the story of Rehoboam. 'The eyes of all England are on you', he added. Then he enumerated the arguments that might be levelled against a settlement, and answered them. The more difficult the elucidation of titles, the more dangerous would be delay; and as for danger to the Queen's person in naming a successor, even supposing such fears well grounded, yet the perils of the Realm are great and palpable, and duty is to be preferred to our own safety. Turning again to Bible stories, he reminded Elizabeth that Esther did not shrink from entering the presence of Ahasuerus to save her people.

All this was forthright enough; but in a passage near the end — which the unheroic Dr. Sparke surely cannot have seen — Wentworth ranged himself with Old Testament prophets and their Scottish imitator, John Knox, in admonitory frankness. 'True and unfeigned love doth even force us to utter unto you, our most dear and natural Sovereign, that whensoever it shall please God to touch you with the pangs of death — as die most certainly you shall, and how soon is known to none but to the Lord only — if your Majesty do not settle the succession in your lifetime (which God for His mercy's sake long prolong) we do greatly fear that your Grace shall then find such a troubled soul and conscience, yea, ten thousand Hells in your soul, even such bitter vexation of soul and heart for the perilling of the Church of God and of your natural country, as to be released thereof you would give the whole world if you had it . . . We beseech your Majesty to consider whether your noble person is like to come to that honourable burial that your honourable progenitors have had . . . We do assure ourselves that the breath shall be no sooner out of your body . . . but that all your nobility, councillors and whole people will be up in arms . . .; and then it is to be feared . . . that your noble person shall lie upon the earth unburied, as a doleful spectacle to the world . . . Again, we fear . . . that . . . you shall leave behind you such a name of infamy throughout the whole world . . . that the forethinking thereof cannot . . . but deeply grieve and wound your honourable, pitiful and tender heart.'

About three months before the Parliament of 1589, Wentworth paid a Banbury schoolmaster — a Puritan acquaintance, it seems — to make a fair copy of the tract, telling him that it was 'a supplication to be delivered by the Court of Parliament' to her Majesty. Evidently, he was intending to launch a parliamentary campaign. Perhaps he was deterred by the stringent prohibition in the Lord Chancellor's opening speech; or, more likely — for he was hardened against intimidation — he could find no fellow-Members willing to join with him. He tried to see Lord Burghley and win his support, but was denied access three or four times: which is not surprising if he stated his purpose. The Parliament ended and nothing had been done.

In the Spring of 1590 he came to London again, intent now on getting Burghley to stir the Queen to action. He seems to have opened up correspondence with a 'sharp, yet true-loving letter'. Characteristically, Burghley replied in a gentle manner; which merely evoked another letter, reproaching him for treating the writer so badly. Wentworth declared that he had shown Burghley the greatest testimony of love in prompting him to procure the high favour of his noble mistress and of the whole Realm, to win much honour, great love and a good name both now and for ever, by performing a service due from one in his place and duty. Another courteous letter, and a humble acknowledgement from Wentworth ended this chapter of the story.[1]

[1] S.P. Dom. Eliz. 232/16, 19.

Still persistent, Wentworth transferred his hopes to the young Earl of Essex. He gave his *Pithie Exhortation* to a Dr. Moffat, who was to induce the Earl to present it to the Queen. Unfortunately, Moffat sent it to a tailor's shop to be copied. Secrecy was broken, copies leaked out, and the tract came into the possession of the Privy Council. Wentworth was summoned before them in August 1591 and committed close prisoner to the Gatehouse. At that very time proceedings against Cartwright and other Puritan leaders in the Star Chamber were revealing to the authorities the organized preparation that lay behind radical agitation in Parliament, and one can see its effect in the order issued for search to be made both at Wentworth's house and at Anthony Cope's, where last he abode, for writings concerning any matter 'that hath been, or may be intended to be moved in Parliament', especially touching the establishment of the succession.[1]

Wentworth was incorrigible. Submission and apology were the essential way to pardon in those days. Instead of these, he returned to his earlier plan of using Burghley to overcome the Queen's misgivings. In later years he asserted that at his examination before the Council the Lord Treasurer had said that he had thrice read his tract and was assured that its arguments were true; but the Queen was determined that 'that question should be suppressed so long as ever she lived'. Whatever this cautious statesman said, it presumably led Wentworth once more to pin his hopes on him. From prison he sent his son with a letter, enclosing a longer and more formal one, also addressed to Burghley, which he wanted him to amend and then show to the Queen, thus raising the succession question without bearing the responsibility for doing so. He urged Burghley to be bold and of valiant courage, hoping that he would persuade the Queen to call Parliament at once and settle the problem. He anticipated that she would read his *Pithie Exhortation*, and expected her, at first, to be very offended. But, when she had patiently weighed its reasoning, 'being of that rare wisdom and deep judgment that I do hear she is of', he was assured that she would thank God for it and instantly follow its advice. He was unafraid of her displeasure, for the spirit of God in Solomon saith, 'The wounds of a lover are faithful and the kisses of an enemy are deceitful': he preferred 'to wound her Majesty faithfully, thereby seeking her

[1] Dasent, *Acts of the Privy Council*, xxi. 392-3.

preservation'. 'Perfect love hath boldness and casteth out fear.'[1]

How much the Queen herself was told of all this, it is impossible to say. Probably she saw Wentworth's *Pithie Exhortation*; perhaps she was told of the letter, though one can hardly imagine Burghley playing the role cast for him. There seems to have been a good deal of sympathy for the offender in official circles. While in the Gatehouse he wrote a short treatise answering the objection that the King of Scots would become an enemy of England if the succession were settled and proved unfavourable to him; and this treatise, so he said, was written at the instance of Councillors. He was treated with a mildness which, considering the character of the offence and his lack of repentence, is striking. He was released from the Gatehouse on November 21st, after only four months in prison, and then confined, on his own bonds, to a private house in Whitechapel. Since he later declared that he was under restraint for twenty-five weeks and five days, complete freedom must have come in February 1592.

If faith removes mountains, Peter Wentworth was of that heroic stature. He was convinced that Burghley and other Councillors sympathized with his views. Believing that the Queen had read his *Pithie Exhortation* and that her wisdom was surpassing, and knowing his own arguments to be infallible, his strong imagination — as he later confessed — led him to the conclusion that she would soon call a Parliament and allow the succession to be discussed. In the late Summer of 1592 there were at his house a certain Mr. Butler (perhaps the M.P. who failed him in 1587) and Oliver St. John, known as Black Oliver to distinguish him from two relatives who also bore this favourite family name. He talked to them along these lines. St. John, we know, talked to others. When, shortly after, a new Parliament was summoned, Wentworth took it for a sign. He travelled about the country telling friends his tale and trying to find Members of Parliament willing to co-operate with him. In a tract published in 1594 Father Parsons, the Jesuit, referred to talk in Amsterdam at this time that the Parliament would see the succession discussed; and perhaps the activity of these men explains the rumour.

Like Don Quixote, Wentworth ventured forth to make reality of his dream-world. Having learnt the art of parliamentary campaigning from his friends in the Classical Movement, he tried to

[1] WENTWORTH'S *Discourse* (1598), p. 3; S.P. Dom. Eliz. 240/21, 21[1].

be a whole puritan organization in himself. He came to town with all the paraphernalia: a speech with which he proposed to introduce the succession question in the Commons; a bill, ready drafted, with blanks to be filled in when Parliament had determined the order of succession; possibly, a petition to the Lords, seeking their co-operation; a petition from both Houses to the Queen; a thanksgiving, if she acceded to their request, and the opposite if she refused; a copy of his *Pithie Exhortation*, freshly written by the schoolmaster-scribe; and, maybe, notes of possible objections to his plans, with appropriate answers.[1]

Black Oliver St. John seems to have acted as his lieutenant. This gentleman was not a Member of Parliament: quite likely, he had failed to find a seat. All the same, he came to London for the occasion. He must have been a temerarious man to meddle in these dangerous activities as a private person. Between them, he and Wentworth managed to bring together a small company of seven, who, on Wednesday morning, February 21st, two days after the formal opening of Parliament, met at the Lincoln's Inn chambers of Humphrey Winch, Member for Bedford. They were not an impressive lot, as age and parliamentary experience went. Apart from Wentworth and Black Oliver St. John, there were Winch, a newcomer to Parliament, aged 37 or 38, Richard Stephens of the Middle Temple, Member for Newport, Cornwall, and also a newcomer to Parliament, Henry Apsley of Gray's Inn, Member for Hastings, who had sat in the Parliament of 1589 and played a prominent part in the religious agitation then, Richard Blount, son-in-law of Lord De La Warr and Member for Lymington, and Oliver St. John, Member for Bedfordshire in the last Parliament as in this, cousin to Black Oliver and brother of Lord St. John of Bletsoe, whom he succeeded in the barony in 1596. It is a fairly sound guess that they were all Puritans: certainly, Stephens and Apsley were.[2]

They spent the morning reading and discussing the papers which Wentworth pulled 'out of his bosom'. We are told that he read the speech, with which he proposed to launch the campaign in the Commons, 'very fast, for it seemed he could say it without book': a useful hint of the care with which Elizabethan Members

---

[1] The following narrative is compiled mainly from the original confessions, etc., in B.M. Harleian MS. 6846, fols. 65 seqq. (cf. *Eng. Hist. Rev.* xxxix. 187 seqq.).
[2] For Stephens, see *Hist. Mss. Com. Rep.* VI. 345-6.

prepared their set speeches. It does not surprise us to learn that
his listeners thought it too offensive. It descanted on the duty of
the Queen and of Councillors and noblemen, with many scriptural and other references; and of Wentworth's prowess in that
genre we have had some examples.

The company adjourned for dinner to Bevington's, 'a tabling
house' hard by, and afterwards spent a further two hours in discussion. Most of them were cautious, some nervous. Blount asked
Stephens if their meeting was 'within the danger of any law', and
both of these men wondered if all present were trustworthy,
whereupon they were assured that 'they were faithful gentlemen'.
Stephens was disconcerted by their youth: he had expected to
find 'more ancient gentlemen' present. Some wanted to open the
campaign with a petition to the Queen for licence to proceed,
and only to produce the bill after receiving this sanction. Wentworth replied that, being young Parliament-men, they did not
understand procedure: the House would not be possessed of the
matter and would not meddle therein without a bill. This may
have been his own notion of procedure, but it was not the Queen's.
It was novel and was obviously prompted by the knowledge that
the House would get nowhere in such matters if it had to wait for
licence to proceed. In addition to this suggestion, there was a
general desire that Wentworth should consult 'some old, discreet,
grave Parliament-men', Yelverton and Morice being mentioned,
among others; whereupon he told 'one or two long stories, how
divers old Parliament-men had failed him in former times, some
of them, having promised to second him and back him in a
motion . . ., never speaking a word therein, others, undertaking
to begin the motion, never opening their lips in the same. And
therefore (said he) I have no great hope in the great Parliament-
men'. A revealing statement; and we can only regret that no
details are given. He objected to Yelverton as too timid, but
readily agreed to consult Morice. The papers were then distributed among the three lawyers in the company, to be looked over
at their leisure, and the meeting broke up.

Next morning, Thursday, Wentworth went to see James Morice,
according to his promise. When he told him that his business
was Parliament and the succession, 'Succession!', said Morice.
'What is he that dare meddle with it?'

'Marry,' replied Wentworth, 'I mean to move it myself.'

'You, Mr. Wentworth!', exclaimed Morice, 'You should remember your late trouble about that matter.'

Wentworth asked for his counsel and left him his speech to peruse.

Next morning, he called again, dined with Morice, and had to listen to withering criticism. Morice told him that he utterly disliked his long speech, both for matter and form, and, being asked to amend it, said it passed his skill and in any case he would not busy himself therein.

Wentworth wanted to bring Stephens along, but Morice replied that he would 'neither in this case or any parliament matter confer with any man'. 'You, Mr. Wentworth,' he added, 'should beware of conferences, for, if you remember, you and others were committed to the Tower for your conference in matters of religion the last Parliament.'[1]

Turn him from his purpose, Morice could not. When Wentworth asserted that his motion would be well accepted by a great number of Members, Morice retorted, 'Never a wise man in the House will like of your motion'. And if they do, what will it avail? You will offend her Majesty and be sure of a command to surcease.

He asked about the bill, mentioned in the speech. 'It is a bill with blanks', answered Wentworth.

'With blanks!' echoed Morice. 'And when shall those blanks be filled up? . . . If we should enter into dealing with titles of the crown, we had need, I think, [of] a Parliament a whole year long.'

Wentworth persuaded him to glance at the text of the petition. 'Mr. Wentworth,' he said, 'think you that if the Lords and Commons will at any time exhibit a petition to her Majesty . . . they will use your phrases?'

There was to have been a further conference of Wentworth's group at Winch's chambers that afternoon. In the morning, Black Oliver St. John, meeting Blount, asked him to attend. He refused. On the Wednesday evening he had been at Lord De La Warr's and had told his brother-in-law, Sir Thomas West, a Member of Parliament, about their meeting. West's comments confirmed his misgivings, as also did the Lord Keeper's animadversions on freedom of speech, made on the Thursday. Whether,

---

[1] Morice clearly meant the Parliament of 1587.

if the second meeting had taken place, there would have been other defections, we do not know. Perhaps not. Perhaps, indeed, there would have been additions to the company. Somehow or other, the two knights for Worcestershire, Sir Henry Bromley, son of the former Lord Chancellor, and William Walsh, became involved. Bromley, we know, was recruited by Stephens. St. John and Wentworth cannot have been idle. But however extensive the conspiracy became, it is not likely that men of long parliamentary experience joined it.

The second meeting was not held because news had got abroad of Wentworth's intentions, and that afternoon Vice-Chamberlain Heneage summoned him to appear before a group of Privy Councillors. At first the Council clearly knew nothing about the meeting at Winch's chambers. Wentworth and Bromley, and then Stephens and Walsh were alone involved. Wentworth was sent to the Tower, the others to the Fleet prison. The Councillors treated them favourably, but her Majesty, they said, was so offended that they must needs commit them.

A fortnight later the secret of the Wednesday meeting was known to the authorities, and the episode took on a more serious complexion. A new enquiry was started, involving not only those present at Lincoln's Inn, but Dr. Thomas Sparke and others. Wentworth himself was examined two or three times. Some of the questions put to him he refused to answer; others he had to be charged on his allegiance to answer. He was asked about all his activities since the Parliament of 1589, evidently because the authorities suspected that he had conducted propaganda and organized a party in the country. Taking advantage of this range of time, he managed for a while to conceal his activities since 1592; but at length he was compelled to divulge the names of Stephens and Winch. From these men and the others, the Council discovered what had been happening. In his last examination, when asked for the draft of his speech, he replied in characteristic fashion that, as it was to have been delivered in Parliament, where speech was free, he claimed the privilege of Parliament in refusing to show it.

Wentworth was left in the Tower and Stephens, Bromley and Walsh in the Fleet, but, oddly enough, Winch, Apsley, Blount and Oliver St. John of Bedfordshire who, so far as we can tell, had committed a more serious offence than Bromley and Walsh, seem to have escaped punishment and were allowed to continue their attendance in Parliament. They were merely bound over not to leave London or Westminster without licence — a restraint apparently prolonged beyond the close of the session[1] — and to appear before the Council when summoned. Two reasons can be suggested for their lenient treatment. Their confessions suggest that they were harmless, rather timid men, misled by Wentworth's dynamic personality. The fright they had received was enough to keep them silent. But the Council, and perhaps even the Queen herself, must surely have reflected that if Members of Parliament were to be imprisoned or sequestered on a wholesale scale — and, as we shall see, these men were not the sole offenders this session — then the House of Commons would be shocked into revolt. No such cautionary counsels applied in the case of Black Oliver St. John. We do not know what happened to him, but he can hardly have escaped imprisonment. As his later career showed, he was made of stern stuff.

Bromley was released in late April, shortly after the end of the Parliament. There was no release for Wentworth; and in letters of his to the Council we follow, with emotion, the sad close of an exemplary life. His spirit remained unbroken and superb, though he was an old man and in wretched health. He was utterly unrepentant. The first of his extant letters, written on November 6th, 1593, begins: 'I do perceive that no submission will be accepted unless I acknowledge myself to commit a fault'. Far from doing so, he embarked on a long and earnest justification of his actions, full of biblical quotations and allusions. The peril to the Church of God, the sacred person of their noble Queen, and this her famous Realm and people of England could not, he wrote, be avoided by any other means than the settlement of the succession. How else could he have behaved, 'the Lord opening a clear view thereof to mine eyes, and I being a Parliament man?' 'I do hear that her Majesty conceiveth that I have an opinion of my own wit.' God sometimes will show wisdom by the simple; 'and, my Lords, I presume to have so much understanding as to judge between an apparent good and an apparent evil. Children for sport may use this accustomed passtime, to cry "A new king, a new [king]", and no inconvenience to arise thereof; but when the whole realm shall proclaim sundry kings in all the shires thereof, with sword and

[1] Cf. BIRCH, *Memoirs of Queen Elizabeth*, i. 96.

shield, that will prove a woeful and fearful tragedy.' 'I protest before God, if her Highness would make me a Duke and give me twenty thousand pounds a year of her best land, to have my consent to forbear the settling of the succession for the space of one quarter of a year longer than it might conveniently be effected . . . I would deny and defy that honour and inheritance as bastardly, poisonful and misbegotten honour.' His 'humble and earnest suit' was that 'for pity's sake', the Council would be a mean unto her Majesty for his liberty.[1]

What could the Queen do? Release him and let him sow discord in the country? She could not surrender her judgment to his. She could not jeopardize her delicately balanced policy.

His temerity and obstinacy were well illustrated when, in 1594, the famous Jesuit, Father Parsons, under the pseudonym of Doleman, published his *Conference about the Next Succession to the Crown of England*. It was an important and disturbing book, repudiating the doctrine of divine hereditary right, placing election alongside birth as a way to the succession, and by implication arguing that Parliament could take away the King of Scots' right to the English throne: a seductive and dangerous thesis. At the request of friends, Wentworth wrote an answer, entitled *A Discourse containing the Author's opinion of the true and lawful successor to her Majesty*, thus, for the first time, departing from his prudent policy of not meddling with actual titles to the throne. He pronounced for the right of James. In common with all or most English Protestants, he had long been opposed to the Scottish claim; and his conversion, made possible by the execution of Mary Queen of Scots, had probably been slow and only recent. It was now complete, and he found himself in the strange position of criticizing Doleman for over-exalting Parliament.

Parliament, he wrote, 'is most sacred, most ample and large, and hath prerogatives and preeminences far above any court whatsoever which is established by God under the heavens.' Yet its authority is not unlimited. It 'is straitly stinted and defined with the limits and meres of justice and equity, and is appointed by God, as the power next to himself, to reform and redress wrongs and outrages which cannot be holpen by any other means, and by good and wholesome laws to procure the peace and wealth of the realm'. Parliament is 'the court of most pure and exquisite

---

[1] Additional MS. 24664, fols. 43-8.

judgment'. If by presumption of its power it do injury to any man or transgress the bounds of right, this transgression is accounted of before God and the iniquity is the iniquity of the whole land.

Restating his views in the language of political theory, his argument amounted to this: Parliament was not sovereign, according to modern, Austinian ideas. It had a sphere of power within which it was 'absolute', in the sense that there was no superior authority to overrule it; but within that sphere it operated subject to the fundamental principles of God's law and natural law — principles, that is to say, of justice and equity. Wentworth — and his contemporaries also — would, within another sphere of power, have said the same of the Crown and its prerogative. By including the doctrine of divine hereditary right in his fundamental principles, he made it one of the limitations on Parliament's power. But — and here the Puritan spoke — the right was conditional. 'A Prince which hath the right (as we speak) of God, he is the ordinance, not of any man, but of God, appointed and substituted by God Himself, as His deputy, for the maintenance of His truth and to minister justice according to the good and wholesome laws of that land.' To maintain God's truth and observe the laws of England: these — and not parliamentary election — were the conditions that would validate James of Scotland's succession. Kingship was a combination of hereditary right and contract. And since Wentworth was by now assured of James VI's protestantism, he could content himself on both counts. Be sure, he would have been as pragmatical as Parsons and would have found a way to exclude James, if this had not been so.

Wentworth's *Discourse*, along with his *Pithie Exhortation*, was published by a friend in 1598, after his death: in order that 'he who hath spoken in the Parliament with so great regard and good liking of all the hearers should now, as it were with his own mouth, speak to all the subjects of England'. By writing the *Discourse*, Wentworth risked aggravating his offence exceedingly: it was a statutory crime. But there is no evidence to suggest that the authorities heard of his new defiance. He remained a prisoner, with the liberty of the Tower: that is to say, with as much freedom and comfort as was compatible with restraint there. His wife was allowed to keep him company.

His second surviving petition to the Council is dated August 10th, 1595. The implication behind it — and perhaps behind the previous one of November 1593 — is that he could have had his freedom at any time, on condition of apology and a pledge of silence. 'Shall I now', he wrote, 'be forced, my Lords, to confess these to be faults, or else to end my days in miserable imprisonment? . . . I dare not confess these to be faults, for fear of deserved shame and peril unanswerable.' 'The case is very hard with us poor Parliament-men', he once wrote, depicting the tragedy of his life, 'when we deserve to hang in Hell, by the justice of God, if we neglect His service or the service of our Prince or State; . . . and may neither serve God or Prince or State truly nor faithfully . . . but are sure of displeasure and punishment therefor.'[1]

The third petition was written in September 1595. Wentworth's attitude was not changed. In November of that year, the Lieutenant of the Tower, Sir Michael Blount, brother to the Blount present at the Lincoln's Inn meeting in 1593, was accused of planning to hold the Tower at Elizabeth's death, in favour of the Suffolk claimant to the throne. Queen and Council were naturally alarmed, and the Lieutenant was promptly deprived of office and imprisoned in the Tower. Though Wentworth no longer belonged to his faction, it appeared that the two of them had discussed the succession question. The episode may have stayed any tendency to show him mercy. Certainly it emphasized his capacity to make trouble, if freed; and this impression must have been strengthened by the discovery in the Summer of 1596 that he still possessed a copy of his *Pithie Exhortation* and had permitted another copy to be made of it for a bookbinder.[2]

Elizabeth Walsingham, Wentworth's wife, died in the Tower in July 1596: 'my chiefest comfort in this life, even the best wife that ever poor gentleman enjoyed', as the forlorn prisoner told the Lords of the Council. He wrote them another petition on January 16th, 1597, when he had been a prisoner for just on four years and was seventy-two years of age. He was still indomitable. 'If ever man', he wrote, 'did suffer for a good and important cause, it is poor Peter Wentworth'. His petition was a reiteration of the *Pithie Exhortation* rather than a confession of fault: which latter, he declared, would be to 'give her Highness a most detestable Judas-kiss'. In the exalted mood of the martyr, he echoed the

---

[1] Additional MS. 24664, fols. 48b-50; Harleian MS. 1877, fol. 56b.
[2] Additional MS. 24664, fols. 50b-51; *Eng. Hist. Rev.* xxxix. 198-9, 202; *H.M.C. Hatfield MSS.* v. 475-6; *Cal. S.P. Dom. 1595-97*, pp. 137, 160.

biblical words of Joseph: 'God did send me hither of His good purpose — I do verily persuade myself — to be a continual remembrance of your Honours to seek, crave and earnestly to persuade her Majesty of pity to preserve God's holy Church, her own sacred person, and also this her whole and worthy Commonwealth of England'.[1]

In July 1597 negotiations were afoot to release him on the pledge of sureties. The intention was to let him go home to Lillingstone Lovell and confine him to the house. But he shrank from the memories of his dearly loved wife that would be revived there, and asked instead to go to Lord St. John's at Bletsoe. The Countess of Warwick was interesting herself in his release, and so was Sir Robert Cecil. On July 15th Wentworth wrote to the latter: 'As the hope that is deferred is the fainting of the heart. . . when the desire cometh, as Solomon saith, it is a tree of life'. He sent Cecil the names of those with whom he wished to stay: the Earl of Kent, Lord St. John of Bletsoe. Also of relatives and friends whom he wished to see: among the latter, his neighbours and parliamentary friends, Sir William Lane, Sir Anthony Cope, and Mr. Jerome Farmer. 'I hope', he ends, 'that I shall have this liberty with her Majesty's favour, the which I do most chiefly desire.' A fortnight later he had to send Cecil a reminder. He asked to see the conditions of his release, 'for otherwise I may not, with honesty, entreat any sureties to enter into bonds for me'. Pleading for speed, he referred to his 'oftener than weekly sickness', which, for want of air, exercise and liberty had afflicted him for the last three months. 'Some compassion, I trust, will be carried toward me, in regard of my old years, being above seventy-three'.

What went wrong; whether he refused the conditions of release when shown them, whether his illness took a critical turn that forbade removal, or whether mercy was slow and forgetful, we do not know. Some three months later, he was dead, still a prisoner in the Tower of London.[2]

Though pathetically at fault, Peter Wentworth was one of the choice, representative figures of his time. As in the Earl of Essex, so in him, the spirit of the age burnt with such intensity as to be insufferable and consume itself. The Elizabethan era was great because it could produce such men, produce them in abundance.

---

[1] Essex Record Office MS. D/DBa. 27.
[2] *Hatfield MSS.* vii. 286, 303, 324.

He died, unaware of his place in the splendid annals of his beloved country. He wrote his own epitaph, 'The causes of my long imprisonment': 'a truth plainly and truly delivered, albeit rudely'. The verse, alas, is doggerel, the gloom unrelieved save by devotion to his God and Queen and country:[1]

> Sith I have said and done my best,
> Meekly, with prayer, God grant me rest.

[1] B.M. Egerton MS. 3139B.

CHAPTER III

JAMES MORICE AND ANGLICAN DISCIPLINE

THIS Parliament made a dilatory start. Opened on Monday, February 19th, the Speaker was not presented till Thursday, and then, on royal instructions, both Houses adjourned until the Saturday, probably because the government was not ready with its programme and the Queen did not wish to encourage free-lance enterprise in the Commons. Saturday came, but Speaker Coke was absent. The Clerk read the Litany and Prayers, and then a message arrived that the Speaker 'had been this last night and also was this present forenoon so extremely pained with a wind in his stomach and looseness of body that he could not as yet, without his further great peril and danger, adventure into the air': a human glimpse of the redoubtable Edward Coke. 'Being very sorry for Mr. Speaker his illness', the House rose. Serious business was therefore not begun until Monday, February 26th, by which time Peter Wentworth's escapade had become known to the authorities.[1]

An anonymous diarist noted Wentworth's fate in his journal, and presumably it was generally known among Members. In such an atmosphere it must have required unusual courage to launch another campaign on a forbidden topic. The brave man was James Morice, Attorney of the Court of Wards. Wentworth had consulted him about his succession campaign; and the astringent quality of the discussion between these two earnest Puritans may have owed something to Morice's secret reflection that his own plans would be endangered by Wentworth's.

Morice intended to launch a decisive attack on the legality of proceedings in the Court of High Commission. He and Robert Beale had in recent years been the two most active lawyers focusing the agitation of moderate Puritans on constitutional issues, and this Parliament was to witness the culmination of their campaign; just as the Parliament of 1587 had seen the culmination of the extremist, Presbyterian campaign. True, there is no suggestion in Morice's own account of events that others were

[1] D'EWES, p. 470.

involved in his plans; nor can we suspect contact with any organization of Puritan ministers. We also recall his warning to Wentworth against private conferences in Parliament matters. Perhaps he did act alone, relying — as he knew he could — on support from the body of the House of Commons. But it is hard to believe that he and Beale, if no one else, were not hand in glove; and, as we shall see, Beale also ran into trouble this Parliament, evidently over the same subject.

Monday, February 26th, the first full day of business, was too heavily occupied with government matters to allow Morice the opportunity he sought; but the following morning, after two unimportant bills had been read and the House was full, he addressed the assembly. 'My religion towards God' — he began — 'my allegiance to the Queen's Majesty, the oath which I have so often taken to assist and defend the jurisdictions and authorities of the Crown of this Realm, and the love of my country move and constrain me to declare and recommend to the consideration of this High Court of Parliament certain matters of very great weight and importance.' The matters were three: the *ex officio* oath — 'an ungodly and intolerable inquisition'; the articles imposed by Whitgift on the clergy — 'a lawless subscription'; and the oath of obedience to all ecclesiastical laws and episcopal orders exacted from excommunicated persons before absolution. Each of these practices he described in turn, denouncing them as contrary to law and common justice and a dishonour to the Queen's regality. 'Where', he asked, 'is now become the Great Charter of England, obtained by many difficulties, confirmed by sundry Acts of Parliament? . . . What may be said in defence of these matters, I know not; but it is now high time' for the bishops 'to declare to the world by what authority they do these things.'

Morice then reviewed the grievances drawn up by the House of Commons in 1585, and the curt, offensive answers of the bishops. 'These extorted oaths and examinations', justified in general terms by the bishops, 'are ungodly and unjust, invented and brought in first for none other purpose but to maintain a Romish hierarchy'. He developed the argument that they were illegal, then, in an eloquent, memorable passage, analysed the constitution of England, 'exquisitely planted and established in great wisdom'. 'Behold with us the sovereign authority of one, an absolute Prince, great in majesty, ruling and reigning, yet guided and directed by principles and precepts of reason, which we term the law: no Spartan king, or Venetian duke, but free from account and coercion of any, either equal or superior, yet firmly bound to the Commonwealth by the faithful oath of a Christian prince; bearing alone the sharp sword of justice and correction, yet tempered with mercy and compassion; requiring tax and tribute of the people, yet not causeless, nor without common assent. We, again, the subjects of this kingdom, are born and brought up in due obedience, but far from servitude and bondage; subject to lawful authority and commandment, but freed from licentious will and tyranny; enjoying by limits of law and justice our lives, lands, goods and liberties in great peace and security. This our happy and blessed estate, if we may continue the same, dearly purchased ... by our ancestors, yea, even with the effusion of their blood ... And shall we, as a degenerate offspring, by negligence and security suffer the loss of a precious patrimony; yield our bodies to be burned, our consciences to be ransacked, and our inheritance to be disposed at the pleasure of our prelates; and not so much as once open our mouths to the contrary? ... If these things move us not, at the least let the regard of our posterity, whom we suffer to fall into extreme thraldom.'[1]

For this speech and his earnest enunciation of the great principles underlying the English Common Law, Morice deserves place on Liberty's long and honoured roll. Though he was blind to the technical justification for his opponents' case, while Puritan sympathies led him to ignore the problem of discipline, he was surely right in thinking Whitgift a sinister figure, whose practices were a menace to the emergent liberalism of English life. Morice concluded his speech by announcing that he had drawn up two bills, couched as petitions: the one against unlawful oaths, inquisitions, and subscriptions; the other against unlawful imprisonment and restraint of liberty. He delivered them to the Speaker, asking that the first be read immediately, and the other at the good pleasure of the House.

The first bill opened with a long preamble, describing the procedure by *ex officio* oath in the High Commission and other ecclesiastical courts, and emphasizing its essential injustice and

---

[1] Camb. Univ. Lib. MS. Mm. 1. 51, pp. 105 seqq.; St. Paul's Cathedral Add. MS. VII. 6 (37), (38); D'EWES, p. 474. My account of the subsequent debate is constructed from these sources, and B.M. Cotton MS. Titus F. II, fols. 31 seqq.

violation of the secular law. The enacting clause provided that if the Commissioners or any ecclesiastical person in future offered 'any such or like kind of general oath', or punished anyone for refusing such an oath, or offered any oath contrary to the laws, statutes or liberties of this Realm, then the offender should incur the penalties of praemunire — the ancient defence of the State against the Church. The second half of the bill dealt with Whitgift's notorious articles of subscription, administered to the clergy since 1583. Again there was a descriptive preamble, citing the famous clause thirty-nine of Magna Carta against depriving any freeman of his freehold except by lawful judgment of his peers or the law of the land. The operative section forbade the imposition of any such subscription on pain of praemunire. Had the bill passed, the Church would have been helpless against Puritanism.

After Morice had sat down, James Dalton rose to oppose the motion, 'with much earnestness'. 'It is hard for me', he said, 'upon a sudden to answer a long-premeditated speech.' The bill 'pretendeth great things': that their laws were being overthrown and all their liberties violated. It made a mountain out of a molehill. Ecclesiastical government had always been distinct from temporal. The practices attacked were neither unlawful nor prejudicial to her Majesty's regality. 'With vehemence' he 'fell to inveigh against Puritans and the Church of Middelburg in the Low Country'. Morice's purpose, he averred, was merely 'the maintaining of Puritans in their impure opinions and breach of all good orders'. Says our anonymous diarist, whose bias is easily perceived: 'The reasons which he gave were few or none; only, his great mislike was that, having received so strait commandment from her Majesty not to meddle with things concerning reformation in the church and state of this Realm', the bill, in his opinion, ought to be suppressed.

Dalton — who, as a young man, had been the hero of the radical clique in the House — was on this occasion subjected to vicious barracking. 'It was strange and shameful', wrote one on his side, 'to see how a number of the House, without all modesty or discretion, coughed and hawked' — 'spat', says Morice — 'of purpose to put him out.'

Sir John Wolley, a Privy Councillor, hastened to his assistance. Morice, he said, being a student of the common law of the Realm, could have no understanding of the civil laws. As for the controversy in the Church, which he had blamed on the bishops, 'it might very well be returned upon himself and such as he is, that have been the special occasions of all the late contentions'. Wolley repeated the warning against disobeying the Queen's commandment and urged that the bill be suppressed.

After Wolley came an eminent civilian lawyer, Dr. William Lewin, Member for Rochester, protégé of Bancroft and one of the ecclesiastical commissioners against whose practices the bill was directed. He likened the politic to the natural body: both were desirous of change. This overthrow of bishops had long been sought. In shooting at their jurisdiction, their critics aimed at their places. He then discoursed on forms of government. Monarchy was the best, and bishops an integral part of it. Turning to Morice's speech, he answered 'every part' of it, justifying ecclesiastical procedure as both reasonable and lawful. Subscription was also practised at Geneva. The bill, he concluded, should first be considered by the bishops and judges before being read.

The mounting attack was too much for old Sir Francis Knollys. Throwing off his responsibilities as the senior Privy Councillor in the House, he rose in defence. Morice, he declared, was not to be reproved for his good zeal and meaning. Dealing with Lewin's opening argument, he asserted that the bill did not seek to overthrow a member of the State, but to reform abuses and restrain prelates. He cited the Act for the submission of the clergy, made in 1534, when he himself was a Member of Parliament: If bishops 'meddle against the law, they should incur a praemunire'. 'Looking up to Dr. Lewin' — who presumably sat on one of the back benches — he exclaimed, 'Whatsoever your laws, civil or canon, be, if they be contrary [to] or against the laws of the Realm, they must stoop and submit themselves.' The bill was good, and fit to be read, he concluded.[1]

Knollys, incidentally, made the fundamental issue clear in a letter that he wrote to Burghley the following day. Sending him one of those historical 'collections' — disjected and misinterpreted precedents, with which Puritan lawyers briefed themselves and their supporters in their fight against the Church — he denounced Dalton and the civil lawyers. 'These civilians and other confeder-

---

[1] The anonymous diary differs from Morice and Whitgift's reporter in placing Knollys's speech before Lewin's, but clearly errs in this. Cf. also, *Informations or a protestation offered to the Parliament* . . . (1608), with its appended speech by Knollys.

ates ... would fain have a kind of monarchy in the ... clergy government, as is in the temporalty; the which clergy government they would have to be exempted from the temporal government', save that they speak not against the royal supremacy. In a crude sort of way it was a sound diagnosis, except for attributing innovation to the Church and not to its critics. We stand at a point in history where the English Reformation, with its implicit trend towards the sovereignty of the State over the Church, was working itself out. The historical order of separate spheres of power — of divided sovereignty — was under attack; and in the nature of things, as Elizabeth perceived, the Leviathan State, after destroying the Church as an independent power, was certain to crash on and destroy the last sphere of rival authority, the royal prerogative. 'No bishop, no king', said James I: he merely turned an Elizabethan thought into an epigram. Knollys ended his letter by assuring Burghley that Morice had spoken modestly, wisely, warily and truly about the abuses in Church government.[1]

After Knollys had finished his speech, 'one, Mr. Stephens', spoke. If this was Richard Stephens, then he cannot as yet have been sent to the Fleet for his association with Wentworth, but, knowing he was in trouble, he proved liver-hearted. 'It seemed', says a recorder, 'he was somewhat affected to the bill, yet he wished her Majesty's pleasure were first known.' Probably he was the 'unknown and obscure' person 'from the upper end of the House', who, according to our robust Puritan diarist, 'did speak also against the bill' — that is, against reading it.

The next speaker, Henry Finch, Member for Canterbury, had neither cause nor inclination to be timid. 'It is and hath been always', he began, 'the manner of this House to allow a mixture in speaking, and after the grave, honourable and wisest to hear the meanest also. For myself, I am but young' — he was thirty-five — 'yet will show unto you matter which is old, in answer to them that did speak last. The ancient charter of this Realm saith, *Nullus liber homo imprisonetur, etc.*, which is flatly violated by the bishops' jurisdiction.' 'These matters ... were some of the quarrels between King Henry II and Thomas Becket, as Mr. Foxe reporteth in *Acts and Monuments*.' Finch 'peremptorily vouched' that her Majesty through the Lord Keeper had not prohibited any

[1] B.M. Lansdowne MS. 73, fol. 109 (printed in Ellis, *Original Letters*, III. iv. 111-12).

speech or meddling with a mere renovation, a removal of abuses
grown through the corruption of bishops and their officers, with
which he was better acquainted than any in the House. And so, in
vigorous vein, he continued. He was scornful of the argument
from former usage, and told of a retort made by a gentleman in
the House of Commons in 1529 when the bishops were justifying
the legality of testamentary fees merely because they had long
been paid: 'Thieves on Shooter's Hill used to take purses there;
ergo it was lawful'. The bill, he concluded, was 'very worthy and
fit to be read'. Apparently, an Oliver St. John followed Finch, and
if — as seems likely — he was Wentworth's cousin and friend, he
no doubt was for the bill.

Robert Cecil then intervened to calm down the House. Expressing his diffidence at speaking, he criticized the barracking of
Dalton and deplored the contention between Lewin and Finch.
Morice, he said, was learned and wise, and one whom he loved;
but he could not support his bill in face of the Queen's express
command. She was concerned about the state of the Church,
and before the summoning of Parliament had ordered the Archbishops to inform her about divers matters. He wanted the Queen
to be consulted first and the bill stayed till the next day.

In spite of this balm, the House called for a reading, showing
clearly where its sympathy lay. Speaker Coke was forced to rise.
Reckoning the number of leaves to the bill, he said it was long
and he could not immediately expound its contents to the House,
as was his duty. He asked leave to consider it, promising to keep
it secret, and made a tentative suggestion for a committee to
determine whether it was fit to be read: a suggestion to which the
House would not agree, as they refused to agree to his conferring
with Privy Councillors. Morice proposed that the second and
shorter bill be read. 'A great many' still clamoured for the main
bill. In the end, time supplied the answer. It was noon and too
late to do anything. The House rose.

Whitgift's reaction was prompt: though, as we shall see, not as
prompt as the Queen's. One of his adherents in the Lower House
wrote out an account of the debate, at the foot of which the archbishop jotted down in pencil the draft of an appeal to the Queen.
Next day, he sent the report of the debate, along with his letter,
to Elizabeth. 'It is meet', he wrote, 'that your Majesty should
understand that the chief thing which moveth Mr. Morice is our

proceeding against Cartwright and others, who seek to bring in a
new kind of ecclesiastical government, like unto that in Scotland,
and do, as far as they dare, impugn your Majesty's authority in
causes ecclesiastical . . . In the end, your Majesty will find that
those which now impugn the ecclesiastical jurisdiction [will]
endeavour also to impair the temporal and to bring even kings
and princes under their censure.' How right, yet how impolitic
this proud prelate was![1]

Whitgift's appeal was not needed. Elizabeth had already acted.
Within a couple of hours of the debate ending — before 2 p.m.
on the Tuesday — the Speaker had been sent for to the Court,
where the Queen herself gave him a special commandment to
deliver to the House. Next morning, February 28th, at the end
of government business, he delivered the message, first reminding
the House of yesterday's proceedings and then telling them of his
summons to Court and audience. 'Who is so impudent', he mused,
'whom the presence of such a majesty would not appal?' He was
comforted, he explained, when some of the Councillors of the
House came into the room, and when the Queen, 'in her most
gracious wisdom', knowing his promise to the House, did not
press him to deliver up Morice's bill, but merely asked about its
purport.

The message she committed to him consisted of three points.
'First, she remembered unto me the chief cause of the assembling
of this present Parliament: which was not to make any new laws or
to spend any time about other matters, but only to treat and devise
of all the good ways and means that might be invented for the
safety of her person and defence of the Realm. And as she had
the authority to summon the Parliament and to continue the same
at her good pleasure and to dissolve it when she thought good, so
had she likewise power to appoint unto them . . . what causes they
were to treat of, and meant, when those causes were dispatched,
to dissolve the meeting and send them home to their countries, as
now it was most requisite. Secondly, she rehearsed her commandment, delivered by the mouth of the Lord Keeper, that they should
intermeddle neither with making any new laws — for now there
was no time for it — nor with any innovation of state or government, but only with the main cause for which they were specially
assembled. And therefore she marvelled that any of that House

[1] St. Paul's Add. MS. VII. 6 (37), (38); B.M. Additional MS. 28571, fol. 172.

would presume, contrary to her express pleasure and command-ment, so openly delivered, to attempt the contrary. Thirdly, she signified her singular love and good affection to the House, for that she understood of their willingness and readiness to use their best endeavours ... for her safety and defence of her Realm; for the which she would in good will answer them with all correspond-ency. And therefore [she] desired them that they would continue in their good purpose ... ; commanding expressly that they should not intermeddle at all with any other matter of state or touching causes ecclesiastical, and charging me upon my allegiance that if any bill should be preferred touching those two points, I should not suffer it to be read.'[1]

The same morning that Coke reported this message, Morice appeared before the Lords of the Privy Council in the Council Chamber. Five were present: the Lord Keeper, Burghley, the Lord Admiral, Essex and Buckhurst. The Lord Keeper told Morice that he 'was a gentleman whose good fortune he had always wished'. But he had now greatly hindered himself, incurring her Majesty's high displeasure for dealing in matters of state, contrary to her express commandment. Her Majesty's order was that he 'should be sharply chidden, yea, and com-mitted also'. 'Yea', interposed the more friendly and merciful Burghley, 'to some Councillor's house.' The Lord Keeper pro-ceeded with the reprimand, 'growing by length of speech into some warmness'. Burghley followed, obviously well-disposed to the culprit and disliking the business. The bills, he said, contain good matter: 'your fault is only in form'. After criticizing Morice's action, he turned to Buckhurst. 'My Lord,' he said, 'her Majesty commanded you also to chide him; but I think there is enough said.' Morice was allowed to defend himself, which he did stoutly. 'Some little submission, Mr. Morice', said Buckhurst, 'would do well.' For the third time, Burghley declared the fault or error to be one of form. This nettled the Lord Keeper, who added, 'And somewhat in matter'.

That afternoon, Morice surrendered himself to Sir John Fortescue at his house in the Old Wardrobe, where he was honour-ably received and indulgently treated. From this mild confine-ment, he proceeded to write impenitent letters to Burghley and the Earl of Essex, who had also, apparently, shown sympathy to

[1] St. Paul's Add. MS. VII. 6 (39); B.M. Cotton MS. Titus F. II, fols. 36-7.

Whitgift's victim. He expected early release, but was disappointed. In another letter to Burghley, on March 13th, he wrote: 'Many knights and burgesses have offered me to move the Lower House to be suitors for my delivery and restitution'. He had refused their offer. On March 17th he was examined about his connection with Peter Wentworth's escapade; and he tells us that the Queen had his deposition read to her. Someone seems to have informed Elizabeth that he had dealt with others about the succession question, after his interview with Wentworth. He wrote in much concern to Burghley refuting the charge. Possibly, the Whitgift party were doing their best to alarm the Queen with exaggerated stories of Puritan conspiracy; and Morice may have endured a longer spell of confinement in consequence. When he heard that Sir Henry Bromley — one of the imprisoned Wentworth group — had been released, but there was no such news about himself, he grew alarmed. Later that day, however, he was summoned before the Lord Keeper and Burghley — the latter in bed with gout — and there told 'that her Majesty's pleasure was, I should be delivered, thinking me, notwithstanding anything past, to be both an honest man and good subject. Nevertheless, her Majesty would have me to be admonished of two things; the first was, that if aught were amiss in the Church or Commonwealth, I should not straightway make it known to the common sort, but declare it to her Majesty; the next was, that when any men should come unto me in any such cause as Peter Wentworth did, I should disclose the matter to her Majesty or some of her Privy Council.' Burghley reinforced the admonition by reminding Morice that he, like they, was of the Queen's counsel. It was their duty to complain only to the Queen. 'If it please her to reform it, it was well: if not, we were to pray to God to move her heart thereunto, and so to leave the matter to God and her Majesty.' In this advice, Burghley disclosed his political creed. Constitutionally it was faultless; though it makes nonsense of the legend that Elizabeth's England was 'Cecil's Commonwealth'.

Morice was forthwith released. His restraint, he says, lasted 'eight weeks and odd days'; which dates this final interview on the last day or two of April. He still remained an avowed enemy of the Whitgiftian system. But it was his last Parliament. He died in 1597.[1]

[1] Camb. Univ. Lib. MS. Mm. 1. 51, fols. 105-34.

There is a mystery surrounding Morice's brother-in-arms, Robert Beale, Clerk of the Council. A letter of his to Burghley, dated March 17th, reveals that the Queen, through this statesman, had ordered him to forbear coming 'to the Court and Parliament'. He was then at his home and had been 'daily and hourly' expecting a summons to appear before the Council. The last reference to him in our accounts of the Parliament is on March 5th, and it seems likely that he received the Queen's order on or about the 12th of that month. We have no evidence that he reappeared in Parliament: presumably he did not. One seeks an explanation of the Queen's action, for, though it was legitimate, it has the look of a sinister precedent. In his letter Beale refers to offence given over the subsidy: about which we shall hear later. But he was surely right in surmising that the principal cause of his restraint was the assumption that he was 'a plotter of a new ecclesiastical government'.

Now there exists an undated paper by Whitgift, itemising charges against Beale, which must — there can be little doubt — have been written some time after the Parliament of 1593. It refers to the fact that 'before the last Parliament' he wrote a book against oaths ministered in the Court of High Commission, that this was printed abroad 'a little before that Parliament' and copies brought to England in a Scottish ship. Beale may or may not have been responsible for the publication of his tract; but the coincidence with Parliament and with Morice's two bills certainly suggests that the latter's action, despite the innocence which he himself imparts to it, was the crucial move in an organized campaign. Certainly, a government, now aware of the tactics of the Classical Movement, was entitled to think so; and this alone would explain and condone the action against Beale. But Whitgift goes on: 'In the Lower House of that Parliament he openly spoke of matters concerning ecclesiastical jurisdiction, etc., contrary to her Majesty's express pleasure ... For the which he was also at that Parliament time committed.' If Whitgift was right — and it must be presumed that he was — then our sources strangely omit any such speech, either when Morice made his motion, or afterwards. It looks as if Beale was duly summoned before the Council, examined, and committed, probably to a Councillor's house like Morice. The protestations of innocence in his letter to Burghley need not confuse us. His impenitence and pugnacity were, however, genuine and remained so.[1]

Though the next episode has no connection with affairs of the Church, there is point in telling it here. It rounds off the tale of royal discipline. The victim on this occasion was Burghley's nephew, Sir Edward Hoby, that hot-tempered, radical young gentleman. At a committee meeting in early March he insulted Sir Thomas Heneage. We know no details, but it is not surprising that the two men irritated one another. An offence of this sort against a Councillor might have landed a person in prison at any time. Heneage — not a great or magnanimous parliamentary leader — probably complained to Elizabeth, and she either had Hoby imprisoned or confined him in private custody. He was only released a few days before the end of the Parliament; and on the closing day, not only the Lord Keeper but the Queen herself, in a speech she made, referred to the incident: 'a notable public disgrace', as Anthony Bacon termed it. Said the Lord Keeper: Her Majesty 'misliked greatly that, this Parliament, such irreverence was showed towards Privy Councillors'. They were not to be accounted 'common knights and burgesses of the House'. The latter were counsellors merely during Parliament; the former 'are standing counsellors and for their wisdom and great service are called to the Council of State'. This doctrine, though sound enough, was not one that Heneage's predecessors had stressed in earlier Parliaments. The change of emphasis, as we have already noticed, marks a decline from high Elizabethan days.[2]

In the course of this Parliament, the Queen imprisoned or sequestered seven Members: action unprecedented in scale during her reign. It was crude, but not unconstitutional. Perhaps her father's temperament was asserting itself in her: certainly, the Court atmosphere was changing, and Whitgift's noxious influence was too apparent. An old and gouty Burghley could not arrest time's mutation.

As we reflect on the past, we recall the fiery protests against Strickland's sequestration in 1571: they had astonished, alarmed, and defeated the Council. We also recall the less dramatic but nevertheless persistent intervention of Members on behalf of their

---

[1] Lansdowne MS. 73, fols. 4-13; STRYPE, *Whitgift*, i. 401 (wrongly assigned to 1585).
[2] Lansdowne MS. 72, fol. 222; BIRCH, *Memoirs of Elizabeth*, i. 96; HYLAND, *A Century of Persecution*, p. 230; Cotton MS. Titus F. II, fols. 97-8.

imprisoned colleagues in the unpropitious circumstances of 1587. By 1593, with the great age moving into decline, the spirit had weakened. On this occasion, we are told, some of Morice's friends offered to raise his case in the House, and he declined their aid. Surely, it was not Morice's wishes, it was the principle that mattered. Earlier assemblies would have been set aflame. True, intervention was attempted. Significantly, it came from a Member who had sat in every Parliament since 1563: Robert Wroth, knight for Middlesex, a wealthy gentleman, and formerly a Marian exile; a Puritan in his sympathies. On March 10th he moved that since some constituencies might complain at a tax of so many subsidies, to which their knights and burgesses had not assented, being absent at the granting of them; and since an instrument, wanting some strings, cannot give its perfect sound; therefore, they might all be humble and earnest suitors to her Majesty that she would be pleased to set at liberty those Members who were restrained.

All the Privy Councillors present, Sir John Wolley, Sir John Fortescue, Sir Robert Cecil and Sir Francis Knollys, along with Sir Henry Knyvet, opposed the motion. Her Majesty, they argued, had committed these Members 'for causes best known to herself', which 'may be high and dangerous'. 'The House must not call the Queen to account for what she doth of her royal authority.' She 'liketh no such questions, neither doth it become the House to search into such matters'. 'For us to press her' would merely 'hinder them whose good we seek'. Which of the speakers said what, we are not told; but perhaps it was Sir Francis Knollys, who, letting the wish father the thought, added that 'it is not to be doubted but her Majesty of her gracious disposition will shortly' yield what we ask for them, 'and will like the better to have it left to herself than sought by us'. 'Hereupon', notes our diarist, 'the motion ceased from further speech.'[1]

Those last words are the measure of this Parliament: 'The motion ceased from further speech'. Though subsequent days and weeks revealed the falsity of the hope held out by Councillors, no one, so far as we know, ventured to echo Wroth's lonely voice.

---

[1] This is a conflated account from the anonymous diary (Cotton, Titus F. II, fol. 57) and from Roger Twysden's Journal (B.M. Stowe MS. 359, fol. 206b), who was probably quoting from his father's diary of the Parliament, now lost.

CHAPTER IV

CATHOLICS AND SECTARIES

THE activities of Peter Wentworth and James Morice were diversions from the main business of this session. In summoning Parliament the Queen had intended to concentrate attention and time on the two problems presented by the menacing war situation. The first of these was internal security; and that, owing to the nature of the conflict, was primarily a matter of religious conformity. In spite of the penal legislation of 1581, Jesuit and seminary missionaries remained at work, secretly strengthening the faith of Catholics and making new converts, especially among women. In the government's opinion the time had come for another twist of severity.

Two bills were prepared by the judges. One started its course in the Upper House on February 24th, the other in the Lower House on the 26th. In the form in which they ultimately emerged, they became notorious statutes; and though their story will lead us into considerable detail, it is well worth telling.

The original title of the bill introduced into the House of Commons was 'An Act for the reducing of disloyal subjects to their due obedience'. 'Many unnatural and evil-affected persons . . .', declared the preamble, 'do not cease, under pretence and colour of conscience and religion, daily to seduce and withdraw the Queen's Majesty's good and faithful subjects from their natural and bounden duty of allegiance, and thereby to stir up sedition and rebellion . . . to the great peril of her Majesty's most royal person . . . and subversion of the happy state of this Commonwealth.' They endeavour to allure subjects to adhere secretly to her Majesty's most capital enemies, and by entertaining and relieving of Jesuits and massing priests, and by refusing to come to church, manifest their submission to the usurped power and authority of the bishop of Rome, who has denounced her Majesty to be deprived of her government and her subjects to be discharged of their obedience to her. Previous laws — the preamble concluded — have not provided sufficient remedy to prevent their 'malicious and devilish purposes'. In view of the subsequent history of the bill, the concentration of purpose against Catholics, and Catholics only, should be noted.

The bill contained fifteen clauses. Whereas the penal Act of 1581 had inflicted on recusants — those convicted for violating the Act of Uniformity by not attending church — a uniform fine of £20 per month, in this new bill the penalty varied with the wealth of offenders. It came near to expropriation. Such persons were to forfeit to the Queen all goods and chattels and two-thirds of the profits of their lands; recusant wives were to lose their dowers or jointures; anyone marrying a recusant heiress lost two-thirds of the inheritance; and all recusants were disabled from purchasing, selling or leasing lands. They were harsh penalties. And there were more of them. As contemporary Catholic narratives show, at the heart of the problem was the need to restrain the gentry from harbouring Catholics in their homes. The bill inflicted a fine of £10 a month on anyone keeping a recusant, guest or servant, in his house; and the clause was deliberately left vague and wide to entrap husbands with recusant wives. Another provision was one which Parliament had failed to secure in 1581: the exclusion of Catholics from all offices and the learned professions. Finally, to prevent the contamination of a new generation, children were to be taken from recusant parents at the age of seven, and brought up, at the parents' expense, under official supervision.[1]

As we reflect on these proposals and on the subordinate measure — a 'five-mile' Act — concurrently begun in the Lords, they assume for us contemporary as well as historical interest, for they serve as a case-study in the ideological state. Catholics were to be treated as an alien pest in society; immobilized, rendered impotent by virtual expropriation and exclusion from all influential vocations, and eradicated in a single generation: though it must be added that Tudor laws were often intended to be held *in terrorem* over offenders, and were neither expected to be, nor capable of being, rigidly enforced. In 1581 a fanatical Parliament had wanted such a policy: now the initiative came from the government. We need not assume that the Queen knew what her Councillors were proposing. It is likely she did not.

---

[1] The bill itself is in House of Lords Papers, 1592-93, fols. 1-15 (cf. *Hist. MSS. Com. Rep.* III. 7a); a summary of its provisions is in the anonymous diary (B.M. Cotton MS. Titus F. II, fols. 25-6).

282 THE PARLIAMENT OF 1593

The debate on the bill, which took place at its second reading on February 28th, revealed a very different House of Commons from the passionate assembly of 1581. The first speaker was Francis Craddock, Recorder of Stafford and Member for that borough: a townsman by birth. 'There is no man', said he, 'so irreligious towards God, so unloyal to her Majesty, so careless of the common state but thinketh the bill good and the law very necessary.' However, Craddock wanted every part scrutinized. He thought the clause imposing a fine for housing a recusant dangerously general, and questioned the wisdom of depriving recusants of all their goods: 'we shall leave them no means of living'. John Hele, another Recorder-Member — this time of Exeter — followed, pointing out more flaws. These advocates of moderation were refuted by Edward Phelips, a lawyer who was to have a distinguished career.

Then came the authentic Puritan voice of the past: from Henry Finch. He had perceived that though the preamble spoke only of Catholics, the clauses of the bill might catch Protestants. 'We have two kinds of recusants', he said. The one — Catholics — 'quite opposite to us and our religion, denying the fundamental points of our faith and profession: touching these, although some gentlemen have spoken for some qualification and consideration of them, yet I for my part could be content that the law might run in all rigorous sort against them.' The second sort — and here he was referring to separatists or sectaries known as Barrowists and Brownists, or, as we might say, Congregationalists — 'openly pretend to be of our religion, but do neither frequent our churches nor sermons, nor communicate with us. These, although I do abhor [them] as greatly as I do the other sort, yet because they carry the name of our brethren and are enemies to the other kind, I could wish' that the law did not run as heavily against them.

Then he turned to a further point, of great moment. He was thinking of Puritans. 'I know divers godly and zealous poor men, desirous to hear the word preached and to have the sacraments rightly administered', who have incapable or negligent or non-resident ministers in their parish — 'of all which sorts the Church of England is too full' — and consequently resort to some godly preacher in a neighbouring parish. 'I have known' such zealous people 'cited and excommunicated by the bishop's officers and handled in more rigorous manner than any recusant Papist'. He wished to have a proviso inserted in the bill exempting such honest, godly men, 'lest it be wrested against them, as other statutes have heretofore been, which have been made especially against the recusant Papist'.

Another Puritan, Nathaniel Bacon, one of the knights for Norfolk — a wholly different type from his half-brother, the famous Francis — seized the occasion to express his dislike of bishops and their officials. He wanted them excluded from the functions allotted them in two of the clauses. 'They ought rather to attend their vocation and calling and to discharge the same, as it were to be wished they would do, rather than to have such trouble laid upon them, whereby they may pretend colour to be negligent in doing their duty.' He also accused bishops' chancellors of being 'so much affected to the Canon Law that some are infected with Popish religion'.

It is a sign of the co-ordination and direction of conservative opinion — the emergence, in fact, of a parliamentary party — that Whitgift's agent in the House of Commons sent him a résumé of these two radical speeches, as a couple of days before he had sent an account of the debate on James Morice's motion. It was a flagrant breach of the secrecy of debate; a symptom of the new repressive atmosphere of these years.

Other Members spoke. Finch and Nathaniel Bacon excepted, the old fanatical note seems to have been absent. The bill might have been a normal one and their purpose to expose its weaknesses, rather than an anti-Catholic measure which in the past would have excited blind fear and hatred. Clearly, it went as far as most speakers wanted, and further than many wished: a strange metamorphosis of the Elizabethan House of Commons. A Mr. Wroth — who must surely have been the obscure Member for Liverpool and not the Puritan Member for Middlesex — spotted that a husband would be fined for housing a recusant wife, and wished this altered. In the end, the House appointed a large committee, and then, on a division, insisted that it should meet in their Chamber, where, presumably, very many other Members turned up to speak and listen.[1]

The bill came back to the House on March 12th, 'altered in every or most parts thereof': so much so that it was received as a

[1] Anonymous diary; St. Paul's Cathedral Add. MS. VII. 6 (39).

new bill, to which a first reading was given. The alterations reflected the two lines of criticism in the debate. Those who thought the measure too harsh scored notably. For example, the provision about forfeiting all goods and chattels was — in the words of our diarist — 'altogether omitted, being too hard'. Elsewhere, there was a scaling down of penalties; and, as Mr. Wroth wished, men were not to be fined for housing their recusant wives, while other modifications of this clause added further safeguards. Also, children were to be taken from their parents at eight instead of seven years of age. All these changes indicate the new spirit in the House of Commons, rendering it more tolerant towards Catholics than the government wanted to be.

But the old vigilance and sympathy with Puritanism, though strangely muted, remained. Despite its preamble, the Council's bill would have caught sectaries, and even Puritans, in its mesh: possibly it was intended to do so — to catch sectaries, at least. The committee removed the danger by restricting the provisions to '*Popish* recusants'.[1]

Another debate took place when the new measure was read a second time on March 13th; and now the forces of conservatism marshalled themselves to try and undo this crucial radical amendment. First in the attack was a Mr. Sandys: probably Edwin, the Archbishop's son and a pupil of Hooker's. He urged that the bill should remain as originally planned, against recusants generally, and not be confined to Popish recusants. He thought it 'justice' to include Barrowists and Brownists. Sandys was answered by Mr. Lewis, a newcomer, Recorder and Member for King's Lynn, who declared that the purpose of the measure was to include only Catholics. At this juncture, Speaker Coke intervened to clarify the debate.   If the preamble and the body of the bill were to be compatible, then — he pointed out — Popish recusants only could be included, for both title and preamble ran only against such as were enemies to the State, being adherents to the Pope. The House might, if it wished, frame another bill against sectaries, but not include them in this.

Thereupon, Dalton rose. True to his latter-day role, he demanded the inclusion of Brownists and wanted the preamble altered by substituting the dangerously broad term 'disobedient'

---

[1] The new bill is in House of Lords Papers, 1592-93. The changes are noted (not always accurately) by our diarist (Cotton MS. Titus F. II, fol. 26b).

for 'disloyal' subjects. He was supported by the ecclesiastical lawyer, Dr. Lewin. Says our Puritan diarist, Lewin 'made a long speech to little purpose'. No doubt it was long. It was not purposeless. His object was to destroy sectaries, either by this or another bill. Presumably, our diarist has left us the right flavour of the debate. If so, it is surprising that such advocates of Whitgift's policy were not castigated by their opponents. Perhaps the fate of the intrepid ones — of Wentworth, Morice and Beale — explains the silence of the radicals; perhaps Speaker Coke helped to keep them down; or several causes may have combined to produce an unrepresentative effect. In the end, the bill was committed.

It looks as if the committee met the next day, and produced a head-on collision between the two parties. This would explain why on March 15th the whole House was again asked to decide whether the bill should retain the words 'Popish recusants' or be extended to recusants in general. 'After many words', notes our diarist, 'the voice of the House was to have Popish recusants only': from which we may conclude that though the conservatives might dominate a debate, the silent rank and file remained radical. The bill was sent back to the committee — which, incidentally, was also charged with the Lords' bill against recusants—and they were ordered to meet in the Chamber itself. The scene next day, when they met, may well have resembled a Stuart committee of the whole House.[1]

The amendments made in committee — probably of little substance — were read and agreed to on March 17th. And then the bill stuck. It was allowed to sleep. An anti-Catholic bill abandoned! The explanation may be twofold. Anthony Bacon, brother of Francis, told a Catholic correspondent that many disliked its rigours, that he did not think it would pass unless they were abated, and that he and Francis would do their best in opposition. Anthony Bacon: a man who had lived on the continent so long and mixed so intimately with Catholics that his devout mother, daughter of the Marian exile, Sir Anthony Cooke, a learned and a great lady, feared for his soul. And his brother, Francis: wisdom's child, but lacking in virility, emotionally cold, the antithesis of the religious *dévot*. Also, there were the Whitgiftians — Dalton, Lewin and the rest — purposeful, and seemingly organized. They had been obstructive in committee,

[1] Cotton MS. Titus F. II, fols. 58-9, 62; D'EWES, pp. 500-1.

ignoring the will of the majority of the House. Reflecting their master's mind, they thought the virtue had gone out of the bill by confining it to Popish recusants. How the scene has changed! What a contrast with the days of Thomas Norton, even with the temper of the previous Parliament of 1589! Puritanism had lost its capacity for leadership.[1]

Whether the Queen herself had any part in the bill's fate, it is impossible to say. There is no need to invoke her intervention; but we can be reasonably sure that if she had wanted the measure, Sir Thomas Heneage, the effective leader of the House, would have received instructions to promote its third reading. Court policy, as the next stage in our strange story indicates, was similar to that of Dalton and Lewin: it was intensively set against sectaries. Whitgift was in the ascendant.

The bill fell asleep on March 17th. On the 30th of that month, during a conference between the two Houses on another matter, Burghley referred to the measure. He had heard that it 'had no proceeding', and announced that the Lords had thought among themselves of a general bill to the same purpose, including in its scope all who refused to come to church or persuaded men not to come. They did not — he evasively added — offer this 'as a thing they had agreed upon in any bill', but wanted to know if it would be acceptable to the Lower House. In other words, having failed to persuade the Commons to couple Protestant sectaries with Catholics in the derelict measure, authority proposed to secure this object by a Lords' bill. Such effrontery would have set any earlier House of Commons ablaze. Heneage, true to character, pressed the House to return a favourable answer, and Sir Robert Cecil urged the same. But prudence and propriety, if not courage, prevailed. They decided that it was not fit to commit themselves in advance. Some ventured to speak of privilege. The House returned answer that if the Lords sent down such a bill, they would consider it.[2]

Burghley had not been frank. The government had in fact started its substitute bill three days before. It was drafted by the judges, and — we are told and can believe — passed the Upper House 'by means of the bishops', who in number were a solid third of the attendant peers. It was with the Commons by March

---

[1] BIRCH, *Memoirs of Elizabeth*, i. 94; *Cal. S.P. Dom. 1591-94*, p. 341.
[2] Cotton MS. Titus F. II, fol. 80.

31st. Unfortunately, the original text has not survived and our evidence about it is not clear. It bore the unwieldy title, 'An Act for explanation of a branch of a statute made in the twenty-third year of the Queen's Majesty's reign, entitled "An Act to retain the Queen's Majesty's subjects in their due obedience", with some additions to the same'.

The Act referred to in this cumbersome title was the notorious anti-Catholic Act of 1581, and the branch mentioned had made it treason for anyone to withdraw subjects from their natural obedience, the same penalty being applied to their converts. The new bill 'explained' this provision by extending its operation to seditious sectaries. Consequently, leading separatists, presumably along with their active followers, were now to be condemned as traitors.

In addition to the core of principal offenders, there were the rank and file to be dealt with. 'Obstinate recusants' epitomizes the longer description of them in the bill. If by printing, writing or speech they persuaded anyone to deny the Queen's power in ecclesiastical causes, or 'to that end' persuaded anyone to be absent from church or to attend unlawful assemblies, conventicles or meetings, or were present themselves at any such assemblies, then they were to be imprisoned and, if at the end of three months they had not conformed, were to be banished. Another provision — taken over from the bill that foundered — imposed a fine of £10 a month on anyone keeping an obstinate recusant in his house, after due warning; but a proviso was added, which — in appearance at any rate — excepted near relatives. The wording of the bill was loose: deliberately so, one suspects. It would undoubtedly have trapped Puritans as well as separatists.[1]

It was a severe measure. What is more, it symbolized a new era. The Queen herself had coupled Protestant nonconformity with Catholicism as a menace to the State. Whitgift's behaviour and speech went further. Earnest Protestants believed that he and other bishops hated the former more than the latter. Perhaps they did, in a human sort of way that implies no leanings towards Catholicism. Nor must we forget that sectaries were associated in the minds of many with Anabaptists, vulgarly supposed to be subverters of the social order. Puritans had no sympathy with these Protestant extremists: 'I do abhor them as greatly as I do

[1] *L.J.* ii. 182, 184; *Cal. S.P. Dom. 1591-94*, p. 341; D'EWES, p. 513.

the other sort', Henry Finch had said. But the great distinction in Puritan minds — as clear as that between Christ and Antichrist — was between Protestant and Catholic. It was this distinction, hitherto the sign and inspiration of Elizabethan patriotism, that Whitgift and those responsible for the bill were destroying. Though Burghley sponsored the measure, he cannot have been happy about it. He seems at this time to have been outcountenanced in Court and Council by Whitgift.

The bill was given its first reading in the Commons on Monday, April 2nd. There was no debate. Next morning, 'very late in the day and after eleven o'clock', it was offered for the second reading, doubtless on instructions from Heneage, who was attempting, by this manœuvre, to force it through the House with as little debate as possible. The Puritan Robert Wroth at once protested. 'The day', he said, 'was spent, it was a bill of great importance and would require much speaking to.' But the official and Whitgift group pressed hard, remaining in their seats when 'many of the House rose and would not hear it read'. Anxious, no doubt, to help them, the Speaker put the question whether it should be read. 'It was denied by a No!'

The second reading and debate therefore took place next day, April 4th, virtually the whole morning being spent on it. The speakers included Heneage, Robert Cecil, Sandys and Lewin on the official and conservative side; on the radical side, the faithful Finch and Nicholas Fuller, the latter being a new Member, a lawyer, and an intrepid Puritan, who had been Cartwright's counsel in his Star Chamber trial, and was to die in prison in the next reign. Fuller denounced the bill as 'dangerous to good subjects' and needless for sectaries. Though entitled an explanation of the 1581 statute, it 'makes schisms to be equal with seditions and treasons, which is against the equity of the former law'. Whoever writes or speaks in these matters of controversy — he warned the House — is within the danger of this law.

Sir Walter Raleigh contributed a liberal-minded, independent speech. He 'counted the Brownists, in his conscience, worthy to be rooted out of any commonwealth. But', he added, 'what danger may grow to ourselves, if this law pass, it were fit we considered. It is to be feared that men not guilty might be included in it. The law is very hard that taketh life or sendeth into banishment, where men's intentions shall be judged by a jury and they shall be judges what another meant.' On the other hand, a law that is against a fact is just: punish the fact as severely as you will. Then, with a practical touch, he asked: 'If two thousand or three thousand Brownists meet at the sea' — to abjure the realm and go into banishment — 'at whose charge shall they be transported, or whither will you send them? I am sorry for it: I am afraid there be ten thousand or twelve thousand of them in England. When they be gone, who shall maintain their wives and children?'

Henry Finch — who emerges (at any rate in our admirable diary) as the chief Puritan spokesman after the suppression of Wentworth and other stalwarts — tore the bill to pieces. 'It pretendeth a punishment only of Brownists and such sectaries', but throughout there is nothing strictly confined to them. If we want to make a law against such people, let us set down some note as to who they are. The bill is directed against failure to come to church, or speaking against the government established: this is not descriptive simply of Brownists. It is entitled 'an explanation' of the statute of 1581; but it is not that, and yet, being so entitled, traps people in the penalty of treason. The Act of 1581 was only for those of the Romish religion: to make it include all other opinions is to make an addition to it, but no explanation. The clause about speaking against any of the laws established is very dangerous. Who can be secure from this? It will not be safe to talk to one's dearest friend. 'Though a man speak but against non-residency, or excommunication as it is used, or any other abuse in the church, he incurs the danger of this law. The clause against conventicles is very dangerous, for the conference of any persons together, being any number, the prayers and holy exercises in any place not allowable already by the laws, is an assembly against the law.' 'Whosoever repaireth not to his own proper parish' is a recusant within the terms of this bill.

Be it added, that from what we know of the administration of the law by Elizabethan judges, and their subtlety in framing bills, we cannot think Finch ultra-cautious.

Our Puritan diarist selected only these three hostile speeches for notice. The bill, he tells us, 'was much in debate, and so long till we were weary of it'. Some wanted it committed, some wished to continue the debate at another sitting, others feared that if the question were now put the bill would be 'dashed'. Eventually, it was committed.

'A great committee' — including, in all likelihood, a lot of supernumeraries — met the next day between 2 and 3 p.m. They sat, doing nothing, until about 5 p.m., for Sir John Fortescue had taken custody of thè bill and he and Sir Robert Cecil were detained at Court by the Queen: possibly a legitimate excuse, possibly another government manœuvre to cut short discussion. After they arrived, says our diarist, 'we fell to the bill presently. Upon a motion of Mr Fuller's the whole committee assented to the striking out of the title and the whole preamble. No man spake for it. So off went the head of it at one blow. When we came to the bill many faults were found in the penning of it, and divers mischiefs . . . which might entrap the best subjects.' After much time spent over the wording, it was thought preposterous not to consider first what type of person the measure was to affect; and because they thought Barrowists and Brownists were intended, they wanted some description of them, in order that they alone should be involved. Someone produced a book containing twelve articles of the Brownist creed, and for a long time the committee's mind ran on setting these down and letting the bill remain as it was, but only against persons holding all these opinions. On further reflection, however, it was thought that the name of twelve articles would be odious. In the end, they agreed that 'whosoever, being an obstinate recusant, should hold that we had no church, that we had no true sacraments, nor no true ministry' — salient beliefs of Barrowists and Brownists, but not of Puritans — and should print or speak to this effect, and persuade men to these opinions, or be at conventicles where these opinions were maintained, 'this man solely to be within the law'. The penalty for a first offence was to be three months' imprisonment; for the second, loss of an ear; and for the third, either to abjure the realm or suffer as a felon — leaving undecided which it was to be.

The committee sat till 8 p.m.: for its members, a twelve-hour day. Ultimately, they instructed Mr. Brograve, an eminent lawyer and Attorney General of the Duchy of Lancaster, to draft a new bill in accordance with these amendments.[1]

They had played havoc with the original bill, drawn most of its teeth. Even to run into danger of their new, milder penalties required such an accumulation of offensive actions that no innocent or merely indiscreet person could be entrapped, and

[1] D'EWES, pp. 513, 517; Cotton MS. Titus F. II, fols. 88b-90, 92-3.

certainly no Puritan. The Whitgift party had been defeated. Its reaction was sinister, if contemporary gossip be reliable. Next morning, 'early and secretly', the two leading sectaries, Barrow and Greenwood, who had been condemned to death for sedition, were taken out and hanged. They had been tried under an anti-Catholic Act of 1581, made proof, as the Commons of that Parliament thought, from use against loyal Protestants by a qualifying phrase, which the judges subsequently ignored. These two men had been twice reprieved: the second occasion being only a week before, at the instance of Burghley. Burghley, says a letter-writer, 'spoke sharply to the Archbishop of Canterbury, who was very peremptory, and also to the Bishop of Worcester, and used some speech to the Queen, but was not seconded by any.' 'The executions', adds this writer — and circumstances seem to lend credence to his statement — 'proceeded through malice of the bishops to the Lower House.' A few weeks later, the youthful, ardent, misguided John Penry was also put to death.[1]

Through their instrument, the domineering Sir Thomas Heneage, the Whitgiftian party now set about jockeying the House of Commons. Parliament was near its end. If the Lords' bill were dropped and a new one started in its place, as the committee had decided at their meeting, the odds were against getting it through its many stages in time. Accordingly, the morning after the meeting Heneage misreported their proceedings to the House, declaring that they 'could not agree upon the bill, but rather had rejected it'. He went on to announce that the Lords were offended, and urged Members, as 'a thing safest for us and fittest', to seek a conference with the Upper House. He was handling a body of men more malleable than in the past, and surely knew it. 'Divers' opposed his motion, and it was 'with very great difficulty' that he got his way. But get it he did.

At the conference, the Lords were all compliance, though the judges, who had drafted the bill, wanted to stand by it. In fact, the only way to get any measure through Parliament at this late hour was to acquiesce in the Commons' wishes and let them be embodied as amendments in the existing bill. When the bill came up for the report stage and third reading, on April 7th, 'the alterations were so many that Mr. Brograve was fain to draw it into a

[1] S.P. Dom. Eliz. 244/124 (*Cal. S.P. Dom.*, *1591-94*, pp. 341-2); F. J. POWICKE, *Henry Barrow*, p. 79.

new bill'. The sponsors of the measure, with time running against them, had to resist this. They had to resist again when Puritan critics, led by Fuller and Finch, wanted to recommit it. Privy Councillors 'would in no wise consent', unless — as Sir Robert Cecil suggested — the committee 'might go up presently into the Serjeant's Room and despatch it while the House sat'. Cecil thereupon had the doors shut, locking Members in the Chamber, while the committee and any critics went upstairs to add more amendments. Meanwhile, those in the House 'passed away the time reasonably pleasantly in arguing to a merry bill of the brewers'.

Back came the committee with another string of amendments. The critics seem to have been given fair indulgence, except that they could not get one dangerous phrase altered, to minimize the risk to Puritans. The bill now passed, with none speaking directly against it. 'We were content', wrote a Member, 'to yield to anything, so we might rise, for it was past three ere this was concluded and ended. I assure you, Sir, a great many of us caught such a faintness there with so long fasting, having neither meat in our bellies nor wit in our heads, that we shall not (I doubt me) be able to make a wise speech there while we live.'

'The proceeding of this bill', wrote our diarist, 'was in a strange course, and I think extraordinary: therefore I will note it.' He then narrated its history. Our letter-writer was equally amazed. The bill, he wrote, 'passed the House, not as a new bill, but still as the bill from the Lords. But how it can be, I know not, for now it hath a new title, a new preamble, and almost a new body; and yet it must be the old bill still. All this is for the speedy passage of it.'[1]

By some authority or legerdemain — as mystifying, questionable and irregular to our minds as the course of procedure to our diarist and letter-writer — the much-altered parchment bill, which ought in its flagrant and unique untidiness to have remained the official record of the Act, was subsequently written out anew. At Westminster today there awaits the expectant historian a chaste parchment, whose virginal purity is a fraud. In consequence, we can share neither the knowledge nor astonishment of our commentators. However, if a schedule of amendments,

---

[1] D'EWES, pp. 519, 520; Cotton MS. Titus F. II, fols. 90-1, 92-3; HYLAND, *A Century of Persecution*, pp. 229-30.

still among the House of Lords' papers, represents the whole
handiwork of the Commons — and perhaps it does — then the
alterations were not as extensive as we might have expected,
though in places they were undoubtedly vital.

In the title, the odious reference to the Act of 1581 was cut out
and the cumbrous title reduced to 'An Act to retain the Queen's
subjects in obedience'. Apparently, what the Commons mystify-
ingly referred to as the 'preamble' contained the 'explanation' of
the Act of 1581 by which its treason clause was extended to
seditious sectaries. This was eliminated. 'Put out all the preamble . . .' runs the instruction in the schedule of amendments.
Most of the other, verbal excisions and additions might be
briefly described as directing the penalties more precisely at
sectaries and diverting them from Puritans. Our diarist — over-
optimistic, we fear, since he did not make allowance for the
capacity of Elizabethan judges to drive a coach-and-six through
any statute — throws light on the point. 'The bill', he wrote, 'is
intended against Brownists only, but yet the Privy Councillors
would not have it only bear the badge of them, but go generally
against recusants, as it is.' The diarist explains the Commons'
intentions. 'Whosoever shall speak against pluralities, non-
residence, excommunication as it is used, and such other abuses
in the Church' — in short, a good Puritan — this man was not
meant to be endangered by the branch about infringing or denying her Majesty's authority in causes ecclesiastical. 'By the word
"conventicles" ', he adds, 'no meetings for conscience or other
divine uses' — Puritan gatherings — 'are understood', unless
'there be conference about some things forbidden in this Act.' He
tells us that 'the reach of this word, "conventicles", was much
feared'.

Our diarist has a puzzling comment on the clause imposing a
£10 fine for harbouring recusants. As we read the statute today,
the proviso to this clause appears to exempt a householder from
any fine for keeping a wife or certain other relatives in his house.
The diarist, however, believed that husbands were in fact trapped
by the statute. Whether right or wrong, what he has to say is so
instructive that it is worth recounting.

He tells us that there were many 'who had special eye to both
the statutes of recusants, that no such thing might be inserted
which might wind them within such a penance'. In other words,

there were Members with recusant wives: a remark that helps to explain the new parliamentary outlook this session. The judges, says our diarist, were discontented when the Commons deleted wives from the earlier, abortive bill against Catholics; but, being told that if the same clause were inserted in another bill, it would certainly pass unespied, Judge Anderson put it in this bill against sectaries. Unless the whole story is a mare's nest, we must assume that, in adding the proviso, Anderson intended to lull both Lords and Commons into a false sense of security, knowing that he and his fellow-judges would put another construction on its meaning. The diarist states that, to ensure the success of the trick, 'Mr. Serjeant Harris and Mr. Attorney Brograve' — two Members likely to be on the alert — 'were charmed by some great men that they should not discover it'. He tells us that the clause 'passed the Lords, never espied. In like sort, when it came into the Lower House, though all the rest of the bill was almost clean altered, yet this part . . . was never excepted against'.

At their conference with the Lords, Burghley, through a mis-understanding, nearly gave the game away by expostulating too warmly about 'how pernicious the women recusants were grown'; though he quickly changed his tactics when he realized that all was well. Suspicions were aroused, but 'few found' the trap. However, when the bill returned to the Upper House some peers, now aware of the danger, wanted to avert it. Whitgift and Burghley 'stood stiffly' for the wording, and so the bill passed, 'infolding recusants within a greater penalty than they were aware of, and more than the House knew of, except some few'.

After Parliament had ended, adds our diarist, doubt being raised, the judges all met, and all, except Justice Walmesley, decided that a husband by this statute must pay for his wife's recusancy. Surely, a very odd tale. But then, the whole history of this bill is strange. Its life, incidentally, was limited to the end of the next session of Parliament: a Commons' precaution. They would have liked the limit to be the Queen's life: as though they hoped for an end of the Whitgiftian regime when Elizabeth died. But the Lords of the Council objected. 'Her death', they said, 'should not be mentioned'.[1]

The second of the two anti-Catholic bills with which the

---

[1] House of Lords Papers, March-April, 1593, fols. 9-11; Cotton MS. Titus F. II, fols. 93-5; *Statutes of the Realm*, IV. ii. 841-3.

government started the session had an easy, though not uneventful, passage. It was introduced into the Lords on February 24th, the first day of business, and was devised as a complement to the bill launched at the same time in the Lower House. Its purpose was to immobilize Catholics. By its main clause obstinate recusants were ordered to remain within five miles of their homes, on pain of forfeiting all goods and chattels and all income from land. A second clause raised this penalty to felony — that is, death — for an offender who had insufficient land, etc. to maintain himself. Another clause dealt with a recurrent problem facing the authorities when they arrested persons suspected of being Jesuits, seminary priests or 'massing' priests. Any such person who refused to answer directly and truly whether the suspicion was correct, or, after confession, refused to say where and by whom he was made priest and where he had lived during the last two years, was to be guilty of felony. In what appears to have been a preliminary draft that passed through Burghley's hands, there were two other penal clauses, omitted when the bill was finally framed.[1]

This fearful measure — ruthless against suspected Jesuits — was given a second reading on February 28th and presumably committed. Alas! not a word survives to tell us what happened at this, or indeed at any other domestic committee of the Lords, though the Earl of Essex's man of affairs, Richard Broughton, pays tribute to the assiduity with which his master discharged his parliamentary duties this session. 'Every forenoon', he wrote, 'between seven and eight his Lordship is in the Higher Parliament House; and in the afternoons, upon committees, for the better penning and amendment of matter in bills of importance, both his Lordship, and sometimes myself, are busied.'[2]

The committee so amended the government's measure that a new bill had to be drawn: a much longer bill, with significant modifications in the penalties. The main five-mile clause remained unaltered in scope and penalty, but the clause about poor offenders, besides defining the degree of poverty, reduced the penalty from felony to banishment. More striking still, the clause dealing with suspected Jesuits and priests in the new bill not only reduced the test questions to the one about identity, but substituted imprison-

---

[1] *L.J.* ii. 170-1. The text of the bill is in House of Lords Papers (supplementary), 1576-93, fols. 119-28. The Burghley draft is S.P. Dom. Eliz. 244/108.
[2] Bagot MSS. in the William Salt Society MSS. (cf. *Hist. MSS. Com. Rep.* IV. 335). Mr. John Cooper of Oxford kindly sent me a transcript of this.

ment for felony as the penalty. Here, then, were the Lords, like
the Commons, being more lenient to Catholics than the judges
and Privy Councillors, framers of this legislation. What a contrast with the situation in 1581, when the only lenient agent in
government and Parliament was the Queen! The leadership in
both Houses must have become less fanatically disposed. And
there was another striking similarity between the two Houses. In
this bill, as first presented to the Lords, though the preamble
referred to Catholics only, the relevant enacting clauses spoke
simply of recusancy, an offence of which Protestants were also
guilty. The Lords, like the Commons, introduced into their new
bill (in body and title) the limiting term '*Popish* recusant'. In
both Houses the leadership may have been conservative and
Whitgiftian, but Puritan sympathies still commanded a numerical
majority.[1]

The new bill had an easy passage through Parliament. The
only change of any substance made by the Commons was to
exempt wives from banishment. It led to a procedural difficulty,
but that, though pedantically argued, was readily settled.[2]

With this bill, the anti-Catholic legislation of Elizabeth's reign
had at last reached its limit. Hitherto the passion and fanaticism
of Members of Parliament had urged the government to new
extremes. Now, however, their full force was spent. This is
evident in the remarkable modifications of the government's
original plan. That plan had envisaged two drastic laws, directed
avowedly against the rank and file of Catholics. In framing them,
Council and judges had blurred the distinction previously maintained between being and becoming a Catholic, between 'old'
and 'new' Catholics: a not unreasonable change of policy, since
there no longer remained much justification for the distinction.
This was the thirty-fifth year of the reign. A generation had
passed; and as neither contemporary thought nor domestic and
foreign politics permitted a theory of religious toleration, the case
for being gentle to a mere remnant of Marian Catholics cannot
have seemed a strong one. Certainly, the government thought not.
That the Queen shared her statesmen's views, we may doubt.

Two anti-Catholic bills. Surely the supreme interest of their
story is that one was transformed into an Act against Protestant

---

[1] *Statutes of the Realm*, IV. ii. 843-7 (an act against popish recusants).
[2] *L.J.* ii. 174-88; D'EWES, pp. 501-19; Cotton MS. Titus F. II, fols. 79-80.

sectaries. And it was the severer of the two laws. Obstinate sectaries were liable to banishment: only poverty-stricken Catholics could suffer this penalty. A proviso specifically excepted 'Popish recusants' from banishment under the Act against sectaries. We can only conclude that those responsible for this astonishing bias would sooner eject troublesome Protestants from the community than Catholics. To describe it as a revolution in parliamentary policy is no exaggeration; and undoubtedly its inspiration came from the Whitgift party, whom Puritans repeatedly accused of preferring Catholics to 'good' Protestants.

Fanaticism, we might reflect, lacks enduring qualities. Its achievements may be great, but it does not last. The dynamic of Elizabethan England was weakening and the period entering its silver age: the Queen herself in her sixtieth year, a generation rising that had not known exile or reaction under Mary Tudor or shared the elation and purpose of November 1558. Old Sir Francis Knollys, protesting against his impotence, longing to be un-Councilled in order that he might testify to the truth within him, is a symbol of this moment. So, too, is Peter Wentworth, immured in the Tower. So, in a sense, is our former diarist, Thomas Cromwell, withdrawn from the parliamentary stage, on which he had been so competent an actor. And many more. For what remained to them of life, they had memories to feast on. But their day was yesterday. The present and the future belonged to others.

CHAPTER V

TROUBLE OVER THE SUBSIDY

THE second reason for summoning Parliament had been the need for money. The appeal was made at the earliest opportunity, on February 26th. In the past the government had been able to rely on the eloquent and popular Chancellor of the Exchequer, Sir Walter Mildmay, as its principal, if not sole speaker. He was dead, and we note that his successor as Chancellor, Sir John Fortescue, came only third in the chorus of orators needed to fill his place. Sir Robert Cecil spoke first, then Sir John Wolley, the Latin Secretary, then Fortescue, and after him Sir Edward Stafford and Francis Bacon.[1]

Cecil's speech opened with a pleasant but artificial show of modesty, after which he analysed the dangers in which the country stood, supplying a historical setting and praise of the Queen, in Mildmay's vein though less elegant. He stressed the danger from the presence of Spanish forces in the ports of Brittany and the threat to England's trade with La Rochelle and Bordeaux; the attempts of Philip II by pressure in Germany and Poland to hinder our trade in those parts, and his intrigues with Scottish noblemen in the business known as 'the Spanish blanks' — a recent sensation that drew attention once more to the possibility of Scotland becoming a springboard for attack on England. With the Spanish King's malice thus daily increasing, and the number of English Papists daily growing, or, at least, becoming more manifest, it behoved them, said Cecil, to consult how to withstand such imminent dangers.

Wolley's speech followed the same lines. He added an injunction to end the Parliament as soon as possible, since the season of the year approached when many knights and burgesses needed to be at home; also, 'the sickness' was in London, and some Members were unaware whether they were lodging in houses infected by it.

As became his office, Fortescue focused attention on finance. 'The burden of four kingdoms', he said, 'hath rested upon her

---

[1] The following narrative, except where stated, is compiled from the anonymous diary (Cotton MS. Titus F. II, fols. 20 seqq.) and D'EWES, pp. 471 seqq.

Majesty': France, England, Ireland and Scotland. 'How could the French King, at his first coming to the crown, have held out against these Leaguers, had not her Majesty assisted him with her men and money, which hath cost her above £100,000?' The Low Countries, since the Queen undertook their defence, had cost £150,000 yearly. 'When her Majesty came to the crown she found it four millions indebted; her navy . . . she found greatly decayed. Yet all this hath she discharged, and, thanks be to God, is nothing indebted. And now she is able to match on sea any Prince in Europe; which the Spaniards found when they came to invade us . . . She hath with her ships compassed the world, whereby this land is made famous throughout all places. She found all iron pieces in her navy: now hath she furnished them with artillery of brass, so that one of her ships is not a subject's but rather a petty king's wealth.'

After this matter-of-fact but impressive survey, he turned, no less cogently, to the Queen's economy in private expense. 'In building she hath consumed little or nothing; in her pleasures, not much. As for her apparel, it is royal and prince-like, beseeming her calling, but not sumptuous nor excessive. The charges of her house small, yea, never less in any king's time: which she meaneth to look better unto. And shortly, by God's grace, she will free her subjects from that trouble which hath come by the means of purveyors.' He trusted that 'every good subject would assist her Majesty with his purse, seeing it concerned his own good and the preservation of his estate . . . As for these subsidies which are granted nowadays to her Majesty, they are less by half they were in the time of her father, King Henry VIII. And although her Majesty had borrowed money of her subjects, besides her subsidies, yet had she truly repaid it and answered everyone fully.'

As for Francis Bacon's speech, it can hardly have been made under commission, for after remarking that the assembling of all Parliaments had hitherto been for laws and money, 'the one being the sinews of peace, the other of war', he confessed his ignorance of the latter and embarked on a historical disquisition about the codifying of law. Unless our diarist misrepresents him, he was as irrelevant as old Recorder Fleetwood, without the latter's humour or sense of timing. It looks as if he were showing off.

The House appointed an extraordinary committee of about 150

Members, which met the following day and, having agreed to repeat the exceptional grant of two subsidies made in the last Parliament, reported back to the House through Sir John Fortescue on February 28th. A debate followed. Nathaniel Bacon put in a reminder that some of the committee wanted a statement in the preamble showing the necessity that moved them to give a double subsidy: evidently — and in view of later events, we should note it — they thought they were being excessively liberal. Another Member, Sir Henry Knyvet, approving of the grant, 'withal desired these three things. First, that it might be lawful for every subject to annoy the King of Spain . . . Secondly, that weak forces might not be sent to encounter him, but a royal army. Thirdly, that we should not wrestle with him upon our own ground, but abroad.' He also wanted the Queen's debts called in and other steps taken to increase her revenues. It rejoiced his heart that by the bill against Catholics, then before the House, they were going to mulct these recusants: little did he imagine that the bill would ultimately emerge as a measure against Protestants!

Serjeant Harris, a Devon lawyer, contributed a robust speech. He agreed to the exceptional tax, Parliaments being nowadays seldom, whereas by a statute of 4 Edward III they might be called every year. 'But one thing', said he, 'is needful to be spoken of, and now is the time to speak of it . . . The subsidies are granted to maintain the wars; but whether it be a war or no war yet, we know not. And the things which we take from the Spaniards is doubted by many not to be lawful prize.' He wanted it set down in the subsidy bill that the money was granted 'to maintain a war, repulsive and defensive, against the Spaniards, and the same to be a lawful war'. The ground for his complaint was that both Elizabeth and Philip II were fighting without a formal declaration of war: a lawless state into which — as we, better than Elizabethans, understand — the 'cold war' of ideological conflict tends to drift. Harris's speech brought Sir Walter Raleigh to his feet in support. He knew many troubled in conscience about the legality of spoiling Spaniards. He also knew that if open war were declared, 'there would be more voluntary hands ready to fight' than the Queen would need to send to sea. The debate ended with the appointment of a committee to draw the articles and preamble of the bill.

So far everything had gone smoothly. There seems no reason to doubt that the Privy Councillors in the House, including Robert Cecil and the Chancellor of the Exchequer, were satisfied and that a double subsidy was as much as they had asked for. Next day, March 1st, came a premonition of trouble. The Commons received a message from the Lords, reminding them of the Lord Keeper's opening speech, with its charge about 'consultation and provision of treasure' to meet the dangers of the Realm. Their Lordships — ran the message — had expected to hear from the Commons ere this. They now asked for a conference.

Unfortunately, the Lords Journals tell us nothing; but it seems from the text of his speech which we possess, written in his own hand, that Lord Burghley had been addressing the Upper House: 'an old man, beside his years decayed in his spirits', imparting to them 'his knowledge of the dangers and peril imminent'. In content, the speech was not unlike the relevant section of the Lord Keeper's opening oration or Sir Robert Cecil's speech for supply, but oratorical skill was lacking. Perhaps speeches in the Upper House, then as now, avoided artifice: they were made to a small, aristocratic company. In any case, Burghley was no stylist. He spoke of the continuous and deadly malice of the King of Spain, the Bishop of Rome, and their confederates; of Philip II's unexampled might since he usurped the kingdom of Portugal and with it the East Indies. The emperor Charles V and the French kings, Francis II and Henry II, had fought their wars 'to be revenged of supposed injuries', and then made peace without upsetting the balance of power. But now Philip II's intention was to conquer all France, England and Ireland. 'He hath invaded Brittany, taken the ports, builded his fortresses, carried in his armies . . . He is become as a frontier enemy to all the west part of England', threatens the southern counties, and is a dangerous neighbour to the Channel Isles, 'never conquered in the greatest wars with France'. Not content with Brittany, he has bribed factious noblemen and disposed his forces in various towns and quarters of France to conquer the kingdom. His son-in-law, the Duke of Savoy, has invaded the country through Provence and Dauphiné, and the Duke of Lorraine through Burgundy and Champagne. The Pope is so addicted to him, that 'he that never was wont to send . . . out of Italy but bulls with lead and parchment, did now levy and send an army into France'.

The danger to France, he went on to say, draws England to like peril. The Spanish King will not rest on the disgrace of the Armada. In the last two years he has built a great number of new ships, and, 'finding by experience his monstrous great ships not meet for our narrow seas', has moulded them on English lines. 'He and the Pope ply themselves to win a party in England to be ready to second his invasion. I am sorry and loth to relate how far they have prevailed therein.' To clinch his argument about imminent danger, he then gave details of Spanish intrigues in Scotland: the affair of 'the Spanish blanks'. He told of Philip's offer to send an army of 25,000 men to the west of Scotland this next summer and pay the wages of 10,000 Scots. Of this combined force, 5,000 were to remain in Scotland, overruling the King and changing the religion, while the rest were to invade England.[1]

Burghley concluded his speech by asking the Lords for a committee; and it was presumably in committee that the proposal was made to seek a conference with the Commons.

The conference took place in the afternoon of March 1st, with Burghley as spokesman. He told them that the double subsidy of the last Parliament had yielded only £280,000, and yet, since it was granted, the Queen had spent in her defensive wars £1,030,000 of her own treasure and been driven to sell some of her lands. Weighing the need for greater and more speedy supply, their Lordships, he announced, 'do negatively affirm' that they will in no wise assent to any Act for less than three subsidies. And not only that. The customary rate of payment was half a subsidy each year, commencing about six months after the passing of the subsidy Act. The Lords now insisted on two payments per annum, to begin shortly after Easter and be completed in three years: a formidable prospect to tax-shy subjects. Also, the assessments must be improved. Burghley complained that subsidies were for the most part imposed upon poorer subjects: hence the small yield. He knew one wealthy shire where no one was assessed in the last subsidy at above £80 annual value of land, while in London, where was the greatest part of the riches of the Realm, no one was assessed at above £200, merely four or five even at that figure, and only eight above £100. He 'insisted' on further conference between the two Houses and that the Commons be urged to yield a greater supply.

[1] B.M. Lansdowne MS. 104, fols. 78-9, 81-2 (undated).

It was an ultimatum, and it was astonishing; for if anything had become clearly established by Elizabeth's reign it was the prescriptive right of the Commons to initiate taxation. If we had been able to suggest that the Commons had overruled their Councillor-leaders in proposing no more than a double subsidy, the action of the Lords might have seemed reasonable and justified. But we can almost certainly eliminate any such conjecture. In all probability, what happened was that Councillors had gone ahead without consulting the Queen, and on hearing that no more was suggested than a repetition of the hopelessly inadequate grant of 1589, she revolted. Indubitably she was right. Burghley was presumably commanded to take action. Whether the tactics were devised by the Queen — which seems most likely; or by Burghley — in which case his statesmanship faltered; they were ill-conceived. They were in keeping with the tactless, not to say ruthless handling of this Parliament that we have already had occasion to notice.

It fell to Sir Robert Cecil to report to the House of Commons the following day. Francis Bacon had been thinking overnight of the situation, and, in an ill moment for his own fortunes, had decided to give an independent and popular lead to the House. He rose after Cecil had spoken, proposed that they should yield to the demand for three subsidies, but opposed joining with the Lords in the granting of it. They should stand upon their privilege of being first to make offer of a subsidy. The greater burden was theirs; the thanks also should be theirs. He cited a precedent of Henry VIII's reign, and drew out of his bosom an answer to be made to the Lords. The matter was referred to a committee.

That afternoon the committee met in the House itself: a growing habit this session. They spent a long time discussing what their commission was: whether to agree on three subsidies and report that to the Lords, or merely to frame an answer according to Bacon's motion, refusing to mention or discuss the size of the subsidy. Sir William More spoke first: entirely for yielding three subsidies. In comparison with Henry VIII, Edward VI, or Mary, there was, he declared, much greater justification for aiding Queen Elizabeth. Sir Henry Unton, who had been English ambassador in France, was critical of the speedy and extra-ordinary rate of payment that the Lords were demanding. We must have regard for those we represent and for their estates, he said. Sir George Cary, Governor of the Isle of Wight and a relative of the Queen, answered him. He thought that their constituents would better thank them for taking their money than for abandoning them to the spoil of the enemy. Stressing the imminence of danger, he told that the Spaniards, apart from bribing the Scots, had already sent 70,000 pistols of fair gold into England to corrupt the nobility. The Queen, he added, was determined to dispatch Sir Francis Drake to sea to encounter them with a great navy. Her infinite expenses must be met.

Raleigh spoke in favour of the increased tax, 'not only, as he protested, to please the Queen, to whom he was infinitely bound above his desert, but for the necessity of what he saw and knew'. The King of Spain, he declared, 'possessed all the rich parts of the world'. On every side, by his activities and his bribes, 'he had beleaguered us': in Denmark, in the Low Countries and Norway, in France and in Scotland. Turning to Ireland, he spoke from his own knowledge: 'the people are so addicted to Papistry that they are ready to join with any foreign forces . . .; I think there are not six gentlemen of that country of our religion'. Raleigh expected an invasion of England that summer, with Plymouth, or other havens, as the Spaniard's objective. 'We must then have no ships riding at anchor . . .: all will be little enough to withstand him.' The way to defeat the Spaniard was 'to send a royal army and supplant him in Brittany and possess ourselves there'; also to send a strong navy to sea to intercept his ships, coming with riches from all places. This we could do royally.

Obviously, there was no inclination to jib at the demand for heavier taxation, but over other points there was confusion and divergence of opinion. The committee had to meet again, very early next morning, before the House assembled; and when, later, Sir Robert Cecil reported to the whole assembly, he could only record their differences and give a majority decision in favour of further conference with the Lords. Our diarist notes that several Members then spoke, some for the conference, because the Lords 'did expect it', some against, as being a breach of privilege. Among the opponents was that stalwart parliamentarian, Robert Wroth. The decisive speech, however, was Robert Beale's. Naturally, he thought as Wroth and others of the opposition, but his distinctive contribution was to produce the infallible Elizabethan charm — a precedent. He cited an occasion in Henry IV's reign which, according to his description, offered an exact parallel. The Commons had then refused to confer with the Lords, on the ground that it would be a breach of privilege, and the King himself had supported them.

Beale's precedent was like the touch of a holy relic. Speaker Coke — that worshipper of precedents — felt its miraculous efficacy and 'was much satisfied'. So, of course, were the majority of Members: it was what they wanted. Privy Councillors and courtiers fought back: a forlorn hope in face of mystical power. Robert Cecil made an urgent, persuasive speech. Sir William Brounker of Wiltshire supported him. The question for or against conferring with the Lords was put to the House. The scene seems to have been exciting and rowdy, and the question had to be put a second time and then proceeded to a division. The 'Ayes' went out of the Chamber: usually a disadvantage, though on this occasion, with Councillors and courtiers in imposing respectability leading the way, it cannot have operated thus. The official party lost: 128 to 217 states the Clerk's Journal, 124 to 310 says our diarist. If the diarist be correct — which seems unlikely — the attendance was remarkably high.

An impressive delegation was then sent to the Upper House to convey, in a most placatory way, their refusal. They returned with a friendly but critical answer. The Lords asked that the precedent — Beale's precedent — be sent them; and this request in turn had to be put to the Commons. The answer was a clear 'No'.

It appeared a decisive, a dramatic defeat for authority. But authority had other resources. What they were became apparent at the next sitting, on Monday, March 5th. Beale rose to make a personal explanation. He had mistaken the question before the House on Saturday. The Lords had merely wanted a conference, not confirmation of their decision. His precedent was therefore not applicable, and he now urged the House to grant the conference. It requires no great effort to imagine what had been happening in Court circles, where Beale was an official, that week-end.

Heneage, the disciplinarian, was in his place to hear Beale's explanation. He promptly propounded anew the question defeated on Saturday, referring to the existence of precedents in its favour. Sir John Wolley followed: another Privy Councillor.

Fortunately, there were still courageous men left. Sir Henry Knyvet, of the old breed, 'moved for the freedom of the House: that it might be concluded amongst us a matter answerable at the bar for any man to report anything of men's speeches, or matter done in this House'. Sir Henry Unton again ranged himself with the critics and independents. He rehearsed the proceedings of the House and defended them. Then he complained that the names of those who had spoken against the subsidy had been reported to the Queen. Finally, he moved that they should confer with the Lords, but not be directed by them. He also desired that the Speaker be sent to the Queen and report the truth about their proceedings.

Knyvet's and Unton's speeches and another that had preceded them brought Cecil to his feet, in the tartest of moods. The first speaker had evidently suggested that the Queen herself was behind the demand for three subsidies. He was surely right, but Cecil roundly asserted that she 'never demanded three, nor yet one'. Knyvet he answered by conceding that the counsels of the House should be kept secret and nothing reported prejudicially; but he would not allow that this principle barred the Queen from being told of their proceedings. When he came to Unton's speech, it seems from our diarist's summary as if he injected a caustic venom into his remarks: probably because Unton belonged to the Earl of Essex's faction. It was news indeed, he said, 'that men's names were given up to the Queen . . . I heard it not before'.

By chance we are able, on this occasion, to measure Cecil's veracity. A couple of relevant letters survive, from Essex to Unton. Essex was trying to obtain some office for his friend, but found the Queen prejudiced against him by reports of his speeches. 'She startles at your name, chargeth you with popularity, and hath every particular of your speeches in Parliament . . . , as the anatomy, the pots and pans, and such like.' Apparently, Unton at some time replied in kind to Cecil's vindictive attack on him. 'She stands much upon the bitter speech against Sir Robert Cecil', Essex reported.[1]

After Cecil's outburst, Sir Walter Raleigh intervened to restore harmony. He suggested that the whole trouble had arisen through a misunderstanding. Nothing more was asked for than a general

[1] *H.M.C. Hatfield MSS.* iv. 68-9, 452-3. The letters clearly fit this juncture, and the month, 'October', given to the first in the *Calendar*, must be wrong.

SIR HENRY UNTON

conference with the Lords, without naming a subsidy. The Speaker seized on this as a promising formula, repeated it, put it as a motion and received a unanimous 'Aye'.

Next day, before they went to the conference, there was another flare-up. Heneage asked for instructions for their delegates, and, in the opinion of Oliver St. John, tried to extend the limits already decided upon. St. John criticized Heneage and was then taken to task by Cecil, who, still petulant, demanded that the House clear Heneage of the accusation and call St. John to answer for it. Wolley obediently seconded Cecil, but Heneage put a stop to the folly. Raleigh made a good speech, as did Unton, and then Fulk Greville, Sidney's friend, who, for all his distinction, seems to have been a reticent Member of Parliament, attempted to remove two scruples from Members' minds. On the subject of precedents, he took the sane view that, though valuable, they were not eternal and could be overruled by necessity. As regards the poverty of the country — on which more had evidently been said than is recorded — he doubted it. 'Our sumptuousness in apparel, plate and all things else argueth our riches; and the dearth of everything amongst us showeth plenty of money.' True, the poor were grieved by being overcharged in the subsidies: this must be helped by increasing our own burden. 'Otherwise, the weak feet will complain of too heavy a body.' If the multitude of Parliaments in former times be remembered, many subsidies now in one Parliament will not seem burdensome. Some Member had complained of the Queen's order against making new laws. 'Since the Queen', Greville commented, 'is not bound by our Acts, the more laws we make the less liberty we leave ourselves.' 'And now', he concluded, 'one word for myself: if my speech hath offended, excuse me; I will not often trouble you hereafter.' An attractive, mellow speech.

Speaker Coke, becoming impatient of the time consumed over misunderstandings, now rose to announce that in future, if anyone mistook the point at issue in matter or bill, he would interrupt to tell him so. As for the present question: if there was to be a general conference, their delegates must clearly be told what to confer upon.

The conference took place in the afternoon of March 6th, and Burghley — 'as noble, wise, grave a counsellor as any was in Europe' — expounded the dangers confronting the country. The

Lords were disappointed that the Commons were not ready with a decision about the tax, but agreed to a later meeting on this point. Reporting back to the House next day, Heneage urged them to act quickly and go to work heartily.

A debate followed about the nature of the tax, initiated by Sir Thomas Cecil, who proposed three subsidies, to be paid in four years — not in three, as the Lords had earlier demanded, but were now probably prepared to ameliorate. He suggested that the tax be levied only on men assessed at £10 and upwards. Sir Henry Knyvet, ever the critic, stressed the poverty of the country, due, he said, to the excess of imports over exports. He proposed that a survey be made of all men's lands and goods and a proportion levied, yielding the Queen £100,000 yearly, to maintain the wars: a capital levy. Sir Francis Hastings had another plan: three subsidies, the first confined to lands valued £5 and upwards, with goods proportionately, the second starting at £12, the third a normal subsidy. Sir Walter Raleigh contributed his views. The number of beggars, by which some Members judged the country poverty-stricken, was, he declared, due partly to the return of maimed soldiers who did not go back to their home-towns, and partly to the policy of clothiers who took the spinning of their wool into their own hands and caused unemployment through engrossing so many trades. He was opposed to Knyvet's survey of men's wealth. 'Many', he said, 'were now esteemed richer than they were. If their lands and wealth were surveyed, they would be found beggars; and so their credit, which is now their wealth, would be nothing worth.' He spoke of seizures at sea from west-countrymen, amounting to £44,000 since the Parliament began, and of Newcastle colliers afraid to put to sea. 'This is certain: the longer we defer aid, the less able we shall be to yield aid; and in the end, the greater aid will be required of us.' Raleigh was for granting three subsidies, exempting persons assessed under £3 and adding their contributions to those assessed at £10 and over. He also wanted speedy payments. The last suggestion was opposed by Unton, who was for the old terms of payment.

Others spoke: Sir Edward Stafford; Dr. James, a physician and follower of the Earl of Essex; Sir Francis Drake, who tried to stir Members by describing the King of Spain's strength and his cruelty; and Serjeant Harris, who was against excusing £3 men, 'for then', he said, 'every man will labour his friends to be set under £3'. Sir Robert Cecil tried to stop the flood of speeches by moving for a committee, but the Chancellor of the Exchequer felt impelled to utter a realistic warning that 'men of £3 goods' constituted half the payers of a subsidy, and to exempt them was impracticable. Heneage then wound up the debate, in happy humour. 'He never saw the House so willingly to yield all needful aid as now it did.' As for the miscellany of new-fangled suggestions, he advised against them. The Queen, he knew, disliked them and had said 'that she loved not such fineness of device and novel inventions, but liked rather to have the ancient usages offered'. After this, the House referred the matter to a committee, deliberately leaving its terms of reference general.

The committee met that afternoon. If our weary Councillors thought that Members would now abandon talk for decision, they sadly underestimated the interest of men in their own purses. There was 'great debate' how the subsidies could possibly be levied in shorter time than usual. Necessity was opposed to poverty, and 'all the afternoon, until seven of the clock at night, was spent and nothing concluded'. When the leaders tried to narrow the issue to paying three subsidies in four years or alternatively in three, the majority wanted to substitute six years. They had to adjourn until the next morning.

Next morning, March 8th, they were at it again. Our diarist records eleven speeches, and there were probably more. The resumed debate started promisingly, and Privy Councillors must surely have thought that, having got their grumbles off their chests in a long day's dispute, a night's sleep had brought the critics round to sense and sensibility. They were shocked — as we know the Queen was — when one of their own Court circle rallied the rebels and plunged the question back into uncertainty. The culprit was no other than Francis Bacon, committing, for so astute a person, a strange blunder. If he foresaw its repercussions, then he was a courageous man: but perhaps he had merely become intoxicated by popularity — an unaccustomed experience for him. The Queen was so incensed that he had to withdraw from the Court; and, as the office of Attorney General, to which he aspired, was about to become vacant, he was made to feel her anger in the ruin of his prospects: prospects, be it added, that had little substance in any case.[1]

---

[1] Cf. SPEDDING, *Letters & Life of Bacon*, i. 231 seqq.

In his speech, Bacon accepted a tax of three subsidies, but opposed payment in less than six years: that is to say, he wanted the old rate of payment of half a subsidy each year. To do more, he argued, was impossible. The poor man's rent will not yield it. The gentlemen must sell their plate and farmers their brass pots. We are here to search the wounds of the Realm, not to skin them over. We must not persuade ourselves that their wealth is more than it is. We shall breed discontent in the people; and, when in jeopardy, her Majesty's safety must rest more in the love of her people than their wealth. By putting two normal payments into one we make it a double subsidy. Other princes will expect the like, and thus we shall impose on ourselves and our posterity an ill precedent. 'In histories it is to be observed that of all nations the English care not to be subject, base and taxable.' Should a financial crisis come, he suggested that it could be met by a levy or imposition.

If we are to judge by our diarist's selection of speeches, Bacon found no support: an anti-climax and a disconcerting experience for a man in his position. Heneage emphasized that time was the essence of the situation: 'in two years our dangers will be over'. Raleigh assessed the present threat to the country as greater than in the Armada year of 1588. Cecil refuted each of Bacon's arguments. As regards the ill precedent, 'We have no reason', he declared, 'to prejudice the best Queen or King that ever came, for fear of a worse King than ever was.' 'Her Majesty', he added, 'will never accept anything that is given her unwillingly.' In the Parliament of 1584-85 she refused a benevolence offered to her, because, having no need of it, she would not charge her people.

In the end, the committee agreed to three subsidies: 'gladly and cheerfully' as to the amount. The first was to be levied in one payment in the first year, the second similarly a year later, and the third in two payments in the third and fourth years. They then returned (very late) to the House, where Heneage described his report as a majority decision. There was another debate, probably over the dates of payment: 'many long and grave speeches and arguments'. Wearied in turn, our diarist did not report them. The House at length confirmed the Committee's decision, and that afternoon a delegation reported to the Lords. It was led by Cecil, taking Heneage's place, who, as the Clerk noted, 'was then at that very instant very sharply grieved and pained

with his infirmity of the gout'. Who knows? the gout — Burghley's
as well as Heneage's — may have had something to do with the
initial conciliar blunder that started all this fuss. We are told
that, 'being brought in betwixt two of his men, when he was so
troubled with the gout that he could neither go nor stand', Heneage once said: 'Mr Speaker, I am fitter to cry than to speak'.[1]

The following morning, after prayers, Sir John Hart, Alderman
and Member for London, rose to refute the calumnies against
citizens uttered earlier by Burghley and Cecil. He had examined
the City subsidy book and found that at the last assessment 544
persons were rated at £50 and upwards, 148 in the £100 range,
32 in the £200 range, 17 at £300 or more, and 4 at £400 or more.
Hart's figures certainly gave the lie to Burghley's; but when we
consider the immense fortunes of many merchants, their distance
from reality still remains startling.[2]

Later that morning, Robert Cecil reported on their conference
with the Lords. All had been bliss, and Lord Burghley, as spokesman for the Lords, had been singularly gracious. 'Now this is my
motion', concluded Robert Cecil: 'that we rid our hands of this
great cause' and hasten to dispatch other business. How well one
understands the mixture of fatigue and relief. The House seems to
have been in the same mood. Mr. Stevenson of Boston got up to
comment on an item of business linked to the burden of subsidies.
'I protest', he began, 'I no more meant to speak in this matter than
I did to bid you all to breakfast.' 'At this', says our diarist, 'there
was a general laughing.' Then Mr. Stevenson announced that the
themes of his speech would be two: 'The nature of man'; 'The
benefit of repose'. But this most appropriate curtain to a wearing
play was never lowered. Our diarist tells us, 'he followed neither'
theme.

Alas! the play was not, as Robert Cecil fondly hoped, over.
Elizabethan subsidy bills carried important preambles of a
propagandist character, expounding the reasons for the grant,
extolling their Queen's qualities, and voicing the boundless affection and loyalty of her subjects. The preamble of 1589 had been a
notable patriotic utterance. This one, as ultimately worded, was
to be still finer. But in its draft form, submitted to the House by

[1] Lansdowne MS. 88, fol. 189.
[2] I cite the figures from the anonymous diary as they present a reasonable grada-
tion. Those in D'EWES, p. 496, from the Clerk's rough notes, vary in giving 80 at
£300.

the Chancellor of the Exchequer on March 13th, it aroused criticism. Mr. Broughton, the Earl of Essex's man, objected to the phrase, 'prostrating ourselves, our lives and lands at her Majesty's feet'. Heneage was alarmed at the disturbing effect of the words, 'persuaded no remedy, how extraordinary soever, can be proportionable to the dangers that are imminent'. Others objected to other phrases. The preamble had to go back to the committee for amendment. The House — spendthrift of time, and ready to welcome any excuse for holding up the money bill and prolonging Parliament — wanted the revision done at leisure. Obedient to the Queen, Heneage was for speed. He brazenly asserted that it was usual on such occasions to send the committee immediately to the Upper Chamber to make the amendments; and Speaker Coke supported the manœuvre by propounding the question in such a form that Members were beguiled into submitting to government tactics. The committee went upstairs and came back with a noble passage of English prose, which, if books were interminable, it would be a pleasure to quote.

The rest was plain sailing, and our story can end. Sir Henry Unton, Francis Bacon, and possibly others, felt the Queen's displeasure for impeding and endangering the passage of the bill. There was every excuse for Elizabeth's anger. She was desperately in need of money. If the dangers to the Realm had developed as they were expected to do, making the year 1593 more fateful for England than 1588, the financial problem might have wrecked defence. She knew herself to be the most provident of sovereigns, spending little on herself and painfully careful of the burden on her people. It was perhaps pardonable — certainly it was human — that ordinary folk, reared on the obsolete doctrine that the King should live of his own, thought more of protecting their purses than the Realm. But that her own servants and courtiers should be remiss was not merely a failure of patriotism: it was a lapse in personal loyalty. She was hurt as a woman as well as a sovereign.

CHAPTER VI

END OF THE SESSION

SOME interesting speeches and a great deal of time were devoted to a privilege case in this Parliament. The Member concerned was Thomas Fitzherbert, representing the borough of Newcastle-under-Lyme. He had been outlawed after twenty-two judgments against him for debt and had been arrested on the morning of his election, whether before or after the election is not clear, but certainly before the return reached the sheriff. The debts involved £1400 to the Queen, and a total of £4000 to others. No pity need be wasted on the man. He seems to have been party to a particularly unsavoury pact with the brutal priest-hunter, Richard Topcliffe, who, as we shall see, stood by him on this occasion.[1] The odds are that he sought election for the express purpose of eluding arrest. If so, his case was a glaring example of the abuse to which the privilege of freedom from arrest was increasingly subject. In granting the Speaker's claim of this privilege, the Queen had usually appended a warning; and at the beginning of the Parliament — as we learn from a remark by Speaker Coke — she had ordered the Lord Steward, when administering the oath to Members, to command anyone outlawed for debt to forbear attendance in the House until he had compounded with his creditors. The chronicler, William Harrison, noted that 'more than a hundred of the Lower House' stood outlawed: an exaggeration, no doubt, but the number was presumably exceptional.[2] It is a pity we have no further details about this interesting exercise of royal power. It was a valiant but fruitless effort to stay a scandal. The House itself was so sensitive about matters of privilege that effective action could not be expected from that quarter.

When Parliament met, Fitzherbert was in the custody of the sheriff of Staffordshire, his cousin (and enemy) William Bassett. He was still in alliance with Topcliffe, and it was apparently this busy agent who brought his case before the committee of privileges.

---

[1] Cf. JESSOPP, *One Generation of a Norfolk House*, pp. 97-8. Mr. R. C. Gabriel kindly called my attention to the Chancery bill and depositions concerning this pact (P.R.O. C.2 Eliz. F 9/63; C. 24/247).

[2] *Description of England*, ed. Furnival (New Shakespeare Soc.), p. lx.

The committee seems to have been divided in its judgment, a majority, including the *rapporteur*, Serjeant Yelverton, being opposed to the claim, on this, among other grounds — that the writs enjoined the election of a 'fit' man (*idoneus*) and an outlaw could not be so described. Fitzherbert was therefore ineligible. It was a doctrine with which the Queen would have been whole-heartedly in sympathy, but it can hardly be said to have been established by precedent or free from undesirable repercussions. When the committee made its report on March 1st, one of its members, the irascible Sir Edward Hoby, challenged the doctrine. A party outlawed is not out of his wits, he said. Being capable, he is *idoneus*. An outlaw in a personal, as distinct from a criminal, case can be an attorney or executor: then why not a burgess of Parliament? Hoby was for granting Fitzherbert the privilege.

Here was the sort of non-stop topic, with its dependence on uncertain precedent and equally uncertain prejudice, that ap-pealed to the many lawyers, not to mention radicals, in the Elizabethan House of Commons. They settled themselves for an interminable debate, and when a message from the Upper House diverted them from the subject for that day, they resumed im-mediately after prayers the next morning. Our diarist was bored. Of Mr. George More, who reopened the debate, he says: 'He gave not one speech that was not spoken of the day before; and he was against Fitzherbert. After him spake Sir Henry Knyvet to the same question, but never a new reason.' Knyvet, if devoid of new reasons, at any rate had something to say about his audience that is worth reporting. He 'took exception that the privileges and ancient grants of the House were not observed, and that men were not patient to hear' those 'that did speak and pleased them not'. Possibly there had been some barracking. On this or another occasion, Knyvet apologetically remarked, 'I mean not to be long.' 'You shall please the House the better', noted a Member who jotted down this and other snippets.[1]

Our diarist's patience was certainly being tried. 'Mr. Tasburgh, Mr. Stevenson, Mr. Bowser [? Bourchier], Mr. Sandes, Mr. Dalton', he continued, 'did speak, all to the same matter, but not a word more than was spoken before.' Then came someone whom he treated with more respect. This speaker pointed out that if they declared Fitzherbert ineligible because of his outlawry, then

---

[1] B.M. Lansdowne MS. 73, fol. 132.

the statute prescribing the qualification of resident burgess would disable most of the House. If, on the other hand, Fitzherbert's election were good, 'though the Common Law do disable the party, yet the privilege of this House, being urged, it prevaileth over the law'.

That Edward Coke would remain dumb, as became his office of Speaker, while others spoke on the law and its antiquities, was hardly to be expected. He intervened in the debate, asking to be heard: 'not that I have any voice or assent to give — though I am of the House — but because I am a servant to the House' and wish to inform it of my knowledge. 'It hath been my manner, since my first practice, to observe strange learnings', especially concerning the law, such as the privilege of this House. Two questions he said, were at issue: whether Fitzherbert was a Member of the House; and if he was, should he be privileged? He reminded them of the procedure involved. A writ of privilege must go from the body of the House, made out by the Speaker and sent into Chancery, and then the Lord Keeper must issue the writ. 'For my own part, my hand shall not sign it unless my heart assent unto it, and though we do make such a writ, if it be not warrantable by law and the proceeding of this House, the Lord Keeper will and must refuse to allow it.'

Coke proceeded to examine the pros and cons of the case. Evidently someone had cited in argument the Queen's command against admitting outlawed Members to their seats. 'I obey unto any commandment of her Majesty's', said Coke; but she 'sent no such commandment to the House'. On the question of Fitzherbert's membership, he was emphatic. The test was the election return. If a person be returned, whether outlawed, attainted, excommunicated or unlawfully elected, 'out of all doubt this man is a lawful burgess . . . If we shall examine elections, we shall then dissolve all Parliaments and call in question all former laws made, by reason there were not lawful lawmakers. If it appeareth once unto us of record that such a man is burgess, we must believe the record.' It was better constitutional doctrine than that advanced by the Commons in the Norfolk election case of 1586 or practised by Jacobean Parliaments.

Coke then declared that for his part he would allow privilege for every member of the House during the sitting of Parliament or proceeding to or from it, or even (it seems) while awaiting the

meeting of Parliament. However, he barred Fitzherbert because
the sheriff, at the time of the arrest, had not yet received the
election return and therefore had no official knowledge that he
was a Member of Parliament. Finally, Coke suggested that they
should bring the sheriff and Fitzherbert before the House by
means of a writ of *habeas corpus*, issuing out of the Chancery: a
curious innovation. The House succumbed to his learning and
followed his lead.

It would be wearisome to pursue the case in all its detail. It
cropped up on two further days before, on March 17th, the sheriff,
William Bassett, and the notorious Richard Topcliffe, acting on
Fitzherbert's behalf, appeared at the bar of the House. Topcliffe
was no longer a Member of Parliament, but he evidently remembered how in 1587 he had been able to stampede the assembly
with his alarmist stories about Catholics. He tried the same trick
now, accusing the sheriff of being a receiver of priests and having
intelligence with Catholic refugees. The magic, however, did not
work: another sign that times had changed. He spoke of 'ancient
cause of malice' between Fitzherbert and his cousin, Bassett. He
feared that if Fitzherbert continued prisoner in this man's house,
he would come to harm. He told 'what traitors and bad people
resorted now of late to Bassett's house'. Without any apparent
objection from Members, Speaker Coke stopped his game: 'Of
these things', says our diarist, 'the Speaker would not give him
hearing'.

The case dragged on. Thrice it interrupted proceedings before,
on April 3rd, a messenger from Chancery brought them the
record of the actions for debt against Fitzherbert. Being called to
the bar of the House, the messenger was appointed to read the
documents, but, since he did not read 'as a clerk', the Clerk of the
House was instructed to read them instead. One wonders what
reading 'as a clerk' meant. Was it an esoteric science, or mere
clarity and audibility?

In the debate that followed, the big guns fired. There were
Dalton, Brograve, Serjeant Harris, Francis Bacon; and finally, a
major allocution from Speaker Coke, to his summary of which
our diarist devoted five pages. True, Coke asked leave to speak;
true, as the diarist noted, 'the House willingly granted' it, 'for
they desired it — at least, I did': but how in keeping with later
form the young Coke ran! He explained that he had been re-

searching into the history of privilege ever since the Parliament began, his guiding principle being, '*quod non lego, non credo*', what I do not read, I do not believe. He had read [and therefore believed] 'a precedent . . . of a Parliament holden before the Conquest by Edward, the son of Ethelred (for there were Parliaments before the Conquest)'. And so his lecture on parliamentary antiquities proceeded, to the edification and great satisfaction of his audience. Whether, in the end, they were much clearer in mind about the case at issue may be doubted.

The House found itself in a dilemma. Had Fitzherbert been in a London prison, no doubt they would have sent their Serjeant with his mace to bring him and the gaoler before them, as they had done in the case of Arthur Hall's servant in 1576: though even then they would have feared to release him, since the debts were so large and the Queen a party. Since their Member was in the custody of the sheriff of Staffordshire, they had, on Coke's suggestion, secured a *habeas corpus*, returnable in Chancery; and they were perplexed as to what to do next. They would have to operate through Chancery, the most conservative of courts. Would it obey them if they wanted to release Fitzherbert? Brograve had spoken grandly: 'This court' — that is, the House of Commons — 'for the dignity and highness of it, hath privileges as all other courts have; and as it is above all other courts, so hath it privileges above any court; and as it hath privilege and jurisdiction, so hath it also coercion and compulsion, otherwise the jurisdiction in a court is nothing'. But even Brograve did not see the way out, and urged them to consult the judges. Coke, with the aid of his pre-Conquest precedent, explained that originally Parliament was one House, and that in consequence any writ, returnable in Parliament, was returnable in the House of Lords, where alone error could be reversed. They were inescapably tied to Chancery — the secretariate of Parliament — and to the procedure he had suggested. What neither he nor the rest of them would realize — such was their non-evolutionary, legalistic approach to history — was that their theory about the House of Commons being a court in itself was yesterday's child, still adolescent. Coke, like Brograve, was for consulting the judges, though, as he reminded the House, time was the essence of a judge's office and the Parliament was drawing to an end.

Fortunately for them — since we cannot doubt what the judges

would have said — sheriff Bassett now had Fitzherbert in London,
and the House decided first to hear the prisoner's evidence. On
April 5th, as our diarist succinctly reports, 'Fitzherbert was heard
and the matter received judgment'. He was denied privilege on
three grounds, the third being that he was arrested neither while
Parliament was sitting nor in going to or returning from it. It was
a prudent decision, but what a time had been spent in arriving
at it![1]

There was a bill this session which, had it become a statute,
would have made Fitzherbert's case the last of its kind. It was
'against persons outlawed and such as will not pay their debts and
duties', and one of its provisions disabled anyone outlawed from
being a sheriff or a knight or burgess of Parliament. If, as seems
probable, it was a government bill, prompted by an evil grown to
scandalous proportions, then the decision to introduce it first into
the Lords was a symptom, either of the new authoritarian mood in
this Parliament or of conspicuous lack of imagination. To attempt
to legislate by a Lords' bill about qualifications for parliamentary
elections was not unlike dictating the character of the money bill
from the Higher House. The bill had a speedy passage in the
Lords. By an appropriate coincidence, it was given a first reading
in the Commons on March 17th, just before an episode in the
Fitzherbert case. So far as we know — and it is all we know —
the bill did not reappear. The silence is eloquent.[2]

In another case, the hand of authority revealed itself. This was
over a bill to prohibit the transporting of iron ordnance, delivered
by a private Member to the Speaker in the hope of having it read.
Our diarist tells us that Sir John Fortescue at once showed the
Speaker 'a letter from the Queen, forbidding any such bill to be
read'; and that was the end of the matter. It is the crudity of
method, not the principle, that attracts attention.[3]

There were occasions when the Commons displayed a vigilant
spirit. One such was when a Lords' bill came before them, concerning the counterfeiting of Privy Councillors' (and certain other
officials') hands. By its provisions, those accused were to appear
before the Privy Council, and were saddled with the onus of
proving the hand in question to be genuine. If found guilty, they

[1] The narrative is compiled from the anonymous diary; D'EWES, pp. 479-518
passim; S.P. Dom. Eliz. 244/124.
[2] *L.J.* ii. 176-8; B.M. Cotton MS. Titus F. II, fol. 63.
[3] Cotton MS. Titus, F. II, fol. 62b.

could be set on the pillory and suffer any other corporal punishment, short of death. When committed by the Commons, the bill was unanimously pronounced 'very dangerous . . . and not fit . . . to pass this House'; but out of deference to the Lords, instead of being instantly suppressed it was delivered back into the House and there, a fortnight later, given a formal third reading and, on the question, 'dashed with a flat No.'[1]

There was another Lords' bill, which some of the House at first suspected to have a hidden purpose of benefiting bishops. It was a bill confirming Henry VIII's acquisition and disposal of monastic lands. The House approached it warily, but in committee it was found to be nothing short of a blessing. When returned to the assembly, Members resisted every attempt to limit its virtues by personal provisoes. One, put forward by a courtier, found strong backing from other courtiers in the House and from the Speaker, and was pressed to the question three times and the House divided on it; but it was rejected. Without proviso or alteration, 'even as it came from the Lords . . ., it passed with a very frank and full Aye'. 'It was counted the most beneficial bill that came from this Parliament into the House', says our diarist, 'and a bill of that price, as it alone was worth our three subsidies.' The diarist must surely have held monastic lands, perhaps by insecure title.[2]

Parliament ended on April 10th, the Tuesday before Easter. That afternoon the Commons sat idly in their chamber, awaiting the coming of the Queen, who did not arrive until between five and six o'clock. Speaker Coke's oration — as our diarist summarizes it — was perfectly in character. He began: 'This High Court of Parliament (most high and mighty Prince) is the greatest and most ancient court within your realm. For, before the Conquest, in the Heptarchy of the West Saxons, we read of a Parliament holden . . . Parliament was summoned by the noble Queen Ine by these words: "I, Ine, Queen of the West Saxons, have called all my fatherhood, aldermen, and wisest commons, with the godly men of my kingdom, to consult of great and weighty matters." Which words do plainly set out the parts of this High Court, still observed to this day. For in Ine is your Majesty's most royal person represented; the fatherhood in ancient time were those

---

[1] D'Ewes, pp. 503-4, 513; Cotton MS. Titus F. II, fols. 65, 83b.
[2] Cotton MS. Titus F. II, fols. 91b, 95.

whom we now call bishops ...; by aldermen are meant your noblemen ... ; by wisest commons is signified your knights and burgesses ... ; by godliest men is meant your Convocation House.' And so this strange lesson continued. From historical he turned to poetic imagination, in an analogy with the 'sweet Commonwealth of the little bees', which he pursued with the same thoroughness and adorned with Virgilian quotations. One half suspects that he had composed his masterpiece for an earlier start to the ceremony, and in the fading light began to sense that brevity would have better pleased the Queen, for, with an apology — 'I fear to be long' — he turned abruptly to business, mentioning among the bills passed, two in particular, the one about monastic lands, the other against recusants and sectaries. A pleasing, if artificial, plea for the Queen's gracious pardon of his ignorance and insufficiency brought the speech to an end.

The Lord Keeper, in his reply, seems to have spent some time, as custom demanded, pursuing the themes developed by the Speaker, and then came to the Queen's particular instructions. Our diarist reports him as saying: 'Her Majesty did graciously accept our service and devoirs this Parliament, commending us that had employed the time so well and spent it in necessary affairs, save only that in some things we had spent more time than needed'. After a rebuke for those who had shown irreverence to Privy Councillors, the speech dealt with the money bill. The Queen had heard that some men, 'forgetting the urgent necessity of this time and dangers that are imminent', had seemed to think too much of the burden on their constituents. 'This their doing, her Majesty imputeth more to their simplicity than any other ill meaning.' Interposing an injunction from the Queen not to alarm her people with reports of great danger to the country, but to encourage them to boldness against the enemy; also a charge to see to the musters and provision of armour; the Lord Keeper resumed his comments on the money bill, for which, he said, her Majesty 'in all kindness most graciously thanketh her subjects'. 'Except it were freely and willingly given, she did not accept it ... If the coffers of her treasure were not empty, or if the revenue of her crown, or her princely ornaments would suffice to supply her want and the charges of her realm — in the word of a Prince she doth pronounce it — she would not now have charged her subjects nor accepted this, though they gave it her.'

'After some time of intermission', says our diarist — perhaps the candles were being lit — 'the Queen herself used a most princely speech to the House ... Ill fortune was, I stood so as I could not hear but little of it.' She spoke, notes another diarist, Roger Wilbraham — who, though not a Member, had evidently found a place for himself in the audience — 'in golden words'. In spite of his remark, the parliamentary diarist managed to hear, or at any rate, report much of the speech, and Wilbraham entered a brief summary in his *Journal*. There can be no doubt, however, that, despite the difficult, involved structure of the sentences, our text must come from Stow's *Annals*. It looks as if the Queen prepared a written text of the speech, of which the chronicler secured a copy. But, if we may judge from some sentences in our diarist's report, then in all probability she did not read her manuscript, but spoke freely, attaining, let us hope, at least a fraction of the diarist's greater clarity. Stow prints the speech as follows:

Elizabeth's first theme was the money bill. 'My Lords, and you my Commons of the Lower House, were it not that I know no speeches presented by any other, nor words delivered by any substitute, can be so deeply imprinted into your minds, as spoken by herself — whose order and direction was but followed and delivered by the Lord Keeper — I could be content to spare speech, whom silence better pleaseth than to speak. And, because much hath been spoken, much less shall I now need to speak of mine own indisposition of nature and small desire, in private respect, to be enriched by you present; which words shall not witness but deeds, by your former experience having expended what I have received to the preservation and defence of yourselves.

'And thus much I dare assure you: that the care which you have taken for myself, yourselves, and the commonweal — that you do it for a Prince that neither careth for any particular, no, nor for life, but so to live that you may flourish. For before God and in my conscience I protest — whereunto many that know me can witness — that the great expense of my time, the labour of my studies, and the travail of my thoughts chiefly tendeth to God's service and the government of you, to live in a flourishing and happy estate. God forbid you should know any change thereof. Many wiser princes than myself you have had, but, one only excepted [i.e. her father] — whom in the duty of a child I must regard, and to whom I must acknowledge myself far shallow — I may truly say, none whose love and care can be greater, or whose desire can be more to fathom deeper for prevention of danger to come, or resisting of dangers if attempted towards you, shall ever be found to exceed myself. In love, I say, towards you, and care over you.'

Having made this moving declaration of affection and dedication, with its interesting — for we may take it as sincere — reference to Henry VIII, Elizabeth spoke the inspired language of a supreme leader, evoking and personifying the heroic spirit of a great people: 'golden words', indeed, to her audience; passages that bear comparison with her immortal speech at Tilbury. Let us remember that she had reason to anticipate, in the coming months, as crucial a test of the nation's valour as in 1588.

'You have heard, in the beginning of this Parliament, some doubt of danger: more than I would have you to fear. Doubt only should be, if not prevented; and fear, if not provided for. For mine own part, I protest I never feared, and what fear was, my heart never knew. For I knew that my cause was ever just; and it standeth upon a sure foundation — that I should not fail, God assisting the quarrel of the righteous and such as are but to defend. Glad might that king, my greatest enemy, be to have the like advantage against me: if, in truth, for his own actions he might truly so say. For in ambition of glory I have never sought to enlarge the territories of my land, nor thereby to advance you. If I have used my forces to keep the enemy far from you, I have thereby thought your safety the greater, and your danger the less. If you suppose I have done it in fear of the enemy, or in doubt of his revenge — I know his power is not to prevail nor his force to fear me, having so mighty a protector on my side.

'I would not have you returning into the country to strike a fear into the minds of any of my people; as some, upon the arrival of the late navy [the Armada], dwelling in a maritime shire, fled for fear farther into the middle of the land; but if I had been by him, surely I would have taught him to have showed so base and cowardly a courage. For even our enemies hold our nature resolute and valiant: which, though they will not outwardly show, they inwardly know. And whensoever the malice of our enemies shall cause them to make any attempt against us, I doubt not but we shall have the greater glory, God fighting for those which truly serve Him, with the justness of their quarrel. Only, let them [i.e. the English people] know to be wary and not to be found sleeping. So shall they show their own valour and frustrate the hopes of the enemies. And thus far let me charge you that be Lieutenants and you that in shires have the leading of the most choice and serviceable men under your bands, that you see them sufficiently exercised and trained, so oft as need shall require; that the wants of any of them be supplied by others, to be placed in their rooms; and that all decays of armour be presently repaired and made sufficient. The enemy, finding your care such, and so great to provide for him, will with the less courage think of your disturbance.'

As she had begun, so she ended, on the theme of the subsidy bill. It was exceptional in amount: it had caused much concern in the Commons. 'To conclude', she said: 'that I may show my thankful mind. In my conscience, never having been willing to draw from you but what you should contentedly give, and that for yourselves; and having my head, by years and experience, better stayed, whatsoever any shall suppose to the contrary; then this[1] you may easily believe — that I will [not] enter into any idle expense. Now must I give you all as great thanks as ever prince gave to loving subjects, assuring you that my care for you hath, and shall, exceed all my other cares of worldly causes, whatsoever.'

Need we wonder that patriotism and romance flourished in this reign? Or that Parliaments bent to the Queen's will?

When Elizabeth had ended her speech, the royal assent was given to twenty-seven bills and the veto applied to one.[2] That only one was vetoed — a bill of no particular consequence — was symbolic of authority's sterner hand and the Commons' greater compliance in this Parliament. Parliament was then dissolved. It was about 8 p.m.: an exceptionally late hour.[3]

---

[1] Stow reads, 'that'.
[2] A bill repealing 23 Eliz. cap. 7 (cf. *L.J.* ii. 183).
[3] Cotton MS. Titus F. II, fols. 95-9; 'Journal of Sir Roger Wilbraham', pp. 3-4 (*Camden Miscellany*, vol. x).

PART FIVE

THE PARLIAMENT OF 1597-98

CHAPTER I

INTRODUCTORY

THE final payment of the three subsidies granted in the Parliament of 1593 was due in February 1597. No long interval could be allowed before obtaining authority for further taxation. The war against Spain was again active, and a new naval expedition was planned for the summer of 1597. So desperate was the need for money that the government had to have recourse to a forced loan: a doubtful expedient in the gloomy mood then pervading the nation, and one which met with considerable opposition in many parts of the country. The summoning of a Parliament inevitably followed in the autumn. The writs went out at the end of August and the date of assembly was fixed for October 24th.

Rather more than half those elected were newcomers to Parliament. There was nothing abnormal in this; but successive change was telling. Another batch of 'old Parliament-men' vanished from the scene, and, coupled with other factors — some operative in 1593 — this resulted in a transformation in the character of the House of Commons, so that in retrospect the previous Parliament of 1593 appears as the hinge between old and new.

Sir Francis Knollys was now dead: in his eighties, and with about sixty years of parliamentary experience, broken by Marian exile. Latterly he had watched the destruction of the Puritan party, by Queen and Archbishop, with constant distress and a sense of impotence. Writing to Burghley in May 1591 about the proceedings against Cartwright and others in the Star Chamber, he had explained the strait he had been in when asked his opinion by the Lord Chancellor: 'It is a deadly grief unto me to offend her Majesty, especially publicly'. He asked Burghley to show the

Queen his letter, in order that 'her Majesty may give me leave to speak mine own conscience freely': alternatively, 'my desire is, that to avoid her Majesty's offence, with the offence of my conscience also, . . . it will please her Majesty to make me a private man, that I may so be silent and avoid her Majesty's offence'. 'I do marvel', he commented, nine months later, 'how her Majesty can be persuaded that she is in as much danger of such as are called Puritans, as she is of the Papists.' Such sentiment was out of date by 1597. The struggle was over: Elizabethan Puritanism, of the heroic, revolutionary kind, was destroyed.[1]

Another official, whom authority seems to have disciplined at long last, was Robert Beale. He was alive and active in 1597 but inexplicably absent from Parliament, after an unbroken membership since 1576. Could testimony be more eloquent to the passing of an era? His absence cannot have been accidental. Had his brother in arms, James Morice, lived, he too would presumably have retired from the parliamentary scene. Peter Wentworth was dead; the Puritan lawyer, Nicholas Fuller, intermitted until hope dawned again with the accession of James I; and of the remnant of courageous radicals, still defiant in 1593, Henry Finch alone reappeared, to pipe a modified melody and evoke but a slender chorus.

Other conspicuous men of the past were absent or dead. That formidable champion of conservatism, James Dalton, did not reappear. Why, we do not know: perhaps age and health explain. Though a turncoat in politics, we cannot deny him the respectful Elizabethan salutation of 'old Parliament-man'. Sir Henry Unton was dead: no more disconcerting speeches from him. Among Privy Councillors, Sir Thomas Heneage and Sir John Wolley were dead. Sir Robert Cecil took Heneage's place as government leader of the House, while Sir John Fortescue, Chancellor of the Exchequer, came to the fore, through age and experience, not ability. The senior Privy Councillor, by virtue of his office of Comptroller of the Household, was Sir William Knollys; son of Sir Francis, but a lesser personality than his father. Francis Bacon, now in his fifth Parliament, was an outstanding Member: never diffident, usually oracular, a government-man, repenting his indiscretions of 1593.

The newcomers were not a striking lot, but they included Hay-

[1] B.M. Lansdowne MSS. 68, fol. 190; 66, fol. 150.

ward Townshend, a Shropshire youth of twenty, Member for Bishop's Castle, who in the last Parliament of the reign was to keep a remarkably full and deservedly famous diary, and for this Parliament exercised a prentice hand, writing a fragmentary journal or scrapbook. Perhaps the most significant feature of this private diary is its omissions: above all, its lack of interest in Church questions and in the relations of Crown and Parliament. How different from the anonymous diarists of 1571, 1586-87, and 1593; from Thomas Cromwell and William Fitzwilliam! Youth is scarcely the answer. Youth responds to enthusiasm, and, if Townshend's scrapbook had been written twenty or thirty years earlier, it would have been as Puritan and radical and, within its limits, as informative as any of the others. He was of his generation. Alas, he fails us; and so do other sources.

When the Parliament met, on October 24th, 1597, there was a new Lord Keeper, Sir Thomas Egerton, a very able lawyer, who had been Solicitor General, Attorney General, and Master of the Rolls, and now was to prove a great head of the Chancery. He made the opening speech. 'I must confess truly', he began, 'that the royal presence of her Majesty, the view of your Lordships and this honourable assembly, together with the consideration of the weightiness of the service and my own weakness do much appal me and cause me to fear.' After this agreeable show of modesty, he expounded the causes for summoning Parliament, the first and fundamental of which was the Queen's care to preserve the Kingdom in peace and safety from all foreign attempts. This she had performed, by the space of many years, to the great and inestimable benefit of her subjects, so that 'the simplest amongst them could not but see, and the wisest but admire, their happiness therein; the whole Realm enjoying peace in all security, wherein our neighbour countries have been torn in pieces and tormented continually with cruel and bloody wars. This her Majesty is pleased to ascribe to the mighty power and infinite mercy of the Almighty.' 'Upon the knees of our hearts', we should 'acknowledge no less unto His holy name, who, of His infinite goodness still preserves her Highness.' May He 'send her many years over us all in happiness to reign'.

A review of the laws of the country was his first specific recommendation; and yet, before and above this, provision against the malice and force of their enemies. 'Wars heretofore were wont to

be made, either of ambition to enlarge dominions, or of revenge
to quit injuries. But this against us is not so. In this the holy
religion of God is sought to be rooted out, the whole Realm to be
subdued, and the precious life of her excellent Majesty to be
taken away.' 'Her Majesty hath not spared to disburse a mass of
treasure and to sell her land for maintenance of her armies by sea
and land.' Faced still with infinite charge, she nevertheless hears
of nothing more unwillingly than aids and subsidies from her
people. Taxation, he pointed out, is nothing like so great now as
in former times. Under Edward III and the two preceding and
three succeeding kings, 'the payments of the Commons did far
exceed any that have been since her Majesty's reign . . .; but
never [was] cause so great to employ great sums of money as
now'. Anyone, Egerton commented, who will not be forward to
contribute, cannot be well advised. 'He that would seek to lay up
treasure and so enrich himself, should be like to him that would
busy himself to beautify his house when the city where he dwelleth
were on fire, or to deck up his cabin when the ship wherein he
saileth were ready to drown, so as perish he must of necessity,
either with it or for it . . . To give is to give to ourselves.'[1]

The speech ended, and back in their own House, the Commons
had to listen to Sir William Knollys practising, for the first time,
his duty of nominating a Speaker. His nominee thought he spoke
'very wisely and very briefly'; but then, this gentleman, too,
though wise was not brief. Judging from Townshend's report,
Knollys was as platitudinous and long-winded as his father. When,
for dramatic effect, he paused before naming his candidate, 'the
House hawked and spat'. His official nominee was Serjeant
Christopher Yelverton: 'Yelverton the poet', as he had appeared
thirty years before in the 'choir' of radicals. Now prosperous,
respectable, mellow and cautious, he still remained — if we may
judge from his orations which have come down to us among his
own manuscripts — an endearing man, though in Peter Wentworth's eyes too timorous.

Yelverton's two 'disabling' speeches were delightful exercises.
In the one to the Commons, he contrasted the training of a
lawyer with the skill demanded of a Speaker: In the law courts, he
said, 'sound and naked reason is but sought to be delivered; and
here, reason must be clothed with elegant speeches. Demosthenes,

the flower of all Greece and the prince of all orators, trembled as often as he began to speak in public assemblies, especially if Phocion were in presence. How much more then will my fear deject me, that am to speak, not so much in the assembly of many Phocions, as in the presence of her most excellent Majesty'; I, who 'was never trained up in this art nor professed not this skill, but am a man only attired with vulgar ornaments'. Then came a sentence that may be the confession of one whose radical indiscretions of the past lingered as a sore memory: 'I have now of some long time endeavoured to embrace a low life and as it were divorced myself from intermeddling with high matters of Parliament'. In his speech before the Queen, he explained: 'I never inured my tongue with the sweet speech of persuading rhetoric, nor never sought to attire my naked phrase with elegancy . . . If I should particularly descend into all my defects and severally make an anatomy of all my wants, I should do justice to myself in deciphering myself, but wrong to your Majesty in being too tedious'.

His main oration, delivered in the Upper House, was a surpassing lecture in political philosophy, based on Aristotle, illustrated by classical and biblical examples, and applied to Queen Elizabeth and her England. 'What is in the power of God to give, either more gracious or more glorious to a country, than a Prince that is good?' With this question he ended the preamble, and then, in magistral phrases, opened his main theme. 'At the beginning — though nature abhorred solitaryness as a consuming enemy to the happiness of life, and embraced society as a most blessed and unspeakable comfort for the preservation thereof, as well for the better attaining by discourse to reason, as for the better procuring by mutual conference of delight — yet there were but private, small, and domestical governments. Men ruled but their own slender families, dispersed into several remote habitations.' In equally choice language, he explained how 'the little seeds of private families brought forth at first but mean villages, then grew to strong and stately cities, and after aspired to famous and most flourishing commonwealths'.

Of all forms of government — he continued — a kingdom is the best. It is 'freest from ambition, safest from dissension, and least suspected of corruption. And the blessed and heavenly government of God over all His angels and creatures is not called an aristocracy or democracy, but a kingdom or a monarchy'. Turning to consider the sources of strength in a state; 'religion and justice', he declared, 'are the two only golden and glorious pillars that do uphold a throne. Without them no commonwealth can long endure, and with them little commonwealths be greatly enlarged and great commonwealths in glory continued . . . If the excellency of man's restless brain could [in itself] have promised security unto princes, Caesar, Pompey, and many others that brought into the Capitol victories, no less renowned for justice than famous for felicity, had still triumphed . . . But man's vain, presuming wit and high conceited reason is stained with the perpetual blemish of disgrace in the successive ruin of the famous succeeding monarchies. For the Persians destroyed the Assyrians, the Grecians the Persians, the Romans the Grecians; and now the Turk hath much depressed the glory of the Roman Empire . . . There is no State, how great or glorious soever, without God, but hath his certain and determined period'.

The foundation of all government is true religion, and its preservation, as the common voice of all philosophers testifies, rests in the rewarding of virtue and the punishment of vice; not forgetting virtue in the meanest, nor favouring offences in the greatest. In his sustained stress on the latter, Yelverton may have had in mind Elizabeth's treatment of Mary Queen of Scots: certainly he was echoing the past, where his rare spirit happily belonged. 'God's most equal and unchangeable laws, unto which kings should conform themselves, do, in cases, admit no dispensations. The father shall not pity his idolatrous son . . . but his own hand shall wound him. Even so, your Majesty's immoderate pity and never-satisfied mercy is, by your Highness's favour, to retire and give place when either the majesty of God shall receive dishonour, your sacred person danger, or this most noble realm ruin.'

From general reflections to panegyric was a natural transition. 'Even in the very first entry into your Kingdom, though you found foreign nations mighty and puissant in protecting the Romish, falsely pretended Catholic religion, and your own Realm possessed thereby with many perils, yet the very first care you took — like to Numa Pompilius, the second king after Romulus — was for the true service and divine worship of God. This blessing and this benefit alone, if it were not accompanied — as it is — with infinite others, doth as far overreach all the riches and treasures of the world, as the sun doth surpass the shadow and the soul doth exceed the body. It was reputed a very difficult matter for Numa to reduce the Romans from war to peace, from the fury of arms to the fear of religion; but it was more than one of Hercules' labours for your Majesty to plant religion and to root up superstition: it was so deeply and so monstrously seated and so Hydra-like increased, and was so guarded with force and so armed with power. And besides, as all great alterations in commonweals are dangerous, so is there no alteration so perilous as that of religion. But, although all the world, in effect, did therefore abandon your Majesty and . . . become your enemies, labouring to rear up accursed Jericho and to restore confused Babel, yet, because no worldly danger hath daunted your Majesty's earnest profession . . . the Lord hath thrust their own swords into their own sides.

'You behold other kingdoms distracted into factions, distressed with wars, swarming with rebellions, and imbrued with blood. Yours — almost only yours — remaineth calm without tempest and quiet without dissension, notwithstanding all the desperate and devilish devices of the Romish crew and Jesuits, whose unnatural affections, bloody hands, and most cruel hearts do too, too evidently bewray their irreligion . . . But God, the most mighty and all-sufficient God, in whose zeal you do so constantly persevere . . . maugre all their despites, doth — and long and long may he — preserve you.'[1]

Yelverton — he was in his sixties — had rivalled, and in elegance and sweetness of language surpassed, the great panegyrists of the past, Mildmay and Hatton. To his younger listeners, his 'many well-couched sentences, somewhat imitating but bettering Euphues', sounded old-fashioned. The diarist, Roger Wilbraham, who heard and reported his closing oration this Parliament, while himself appreciative of its qualities — for he was a connoisseur in such matters — commented that it was 'thought too full of flattery, too curious and tedious'. But to the Queen, the music of his prose, intoned by an orator, was charming, and the sentiment congenial: they reflected the England she had so carefully nurtured. She went out of her way to express approval.[2]

---

[1] B.M. Additional MS. 48109 (Yelverton 121). There are copies of these speeches in the Ellesmere (Lord Keeper Egerton's) MSS. in the Huntington Library, U.S.A. Other passages are quoted in my *Elizabethan House of Commons*.

[2] *Camden Miscellany*, x. 10-12.

Yelverton ended his speech with the customary petition for privileges, not baldly stated, but succinctly reasoned. Alas! we have no account of the Lord Keeper's reply, other than the entry in the *Lords Journals* that her Majesty 'did yield her gracious assent, with admonition that the said liberties and privileges should be discreetly and wisely used, as was meet'. It may well be that the Queen, knowing she need no longer fear organized Puritan agitation, confined her strictures on freedom of speech to generalities: as she apparently did in the next and last Parliament of the reign. If so, then the counter-definition of the privilege that she had propounded in 1593 may be regarded as the end of a chapter: another sign that the high Elizabethan period was past. Townshend's silence can imply as much: or it may, with equal significance, reflect the indifference of the new generation to words that would have angered and so caught the attention of a Fitzwilliam.

On instructions from the Queen, the Lord Keeper adjourned the Parliament for nine days. News had just come that a Spanish armada — which, as it happened, was caught by gales and driven back to Spain — was approaching England. The government needed to be free of parliamentary business while taking urgent steps to meet the threatened invasion.

In the previous August, Sir Thomas Egerton had written to Sir Robert Cecil about the forthcoming Parliament: 'Here is like to be new Lord Keeper, new Speaker, new Clerk, and all of us newly to learn our duties'. The new Clerk of the Parliaments, officiating in the Lords, was Thomas Smith, Clerk of the Privy Council, who had been one of the Earl of Essex's secretaries and secured his parliamentary clerkship through his master's unscrupulous pressure. His predecessor, John Mason, had been notoriously negligent, not least in the keeping of the Lords' Journals. When, this session, a committee, under Burghley's chairmanship, searched the Journals in connection with a question of precedence, they must have been shocked at their state; and in consequence an order was made that they were to be perused each Parliament by a group of peers. What with this order and with the proverbial efficiency of a new broom, we are now able for the first time to learn something about the actual working of the Upper House.[1]

---

[1] *H.M.C. Hatfield MSS.* vii. 359; *L.J.* ii. 195.

Procedure in the Upper House is seen to be very similar to that in the Lower, though rather more flexible. Most bills, for example, were committed on their second reading, but apparently committal arose solely out of a desire for detailed scrutiny and was not so near to a formal procedural stage as it was in the Commons. Some ten or twelve members usually constituted a committee, though the number might fall to three, or, on an important bill, rise to thirty-one out of the thirty-six peers present that day. It looks as if the tendency towards very large committees, approaching committees of the whole House on signal occasions, which we know to have been a new feature in the House of Commons at this time, was also present in the Lords. Judges and other legal assistants were invariably appointed to attend the meetings, imparting to the work both a professional competence and an official conservatism that strengthened the role of the Upper House as the bulwark of the Crown. A large committee might have the assistance of all three chief justices, a fourth judge, the Attorney General and a serjeant-at-law. The senior peer in precedence seems to have chaired the committee and reported its findings: 'the first of the committees', he was termed. Whitgift had this role whenever he sat on a committee. He was significantly active, but, as might be expected, Burghley — despite his age — was the most active, sitting on half, and those the most important, committees. During the pre-Christmas sittings, the Earl of Essex was absent, sulking at home on a plea of sickness because his rival, Lord Admiral Howard, had been made an earl and took precedence of him. When this petulant child got his way and was made Earl Marshal, thus resuming senior place, his illness vanished and in January he returned to Parliament. He was immediately added to the two most important committees and took an active part in this onerous, but important business. The amount of work falling on the House of Lords and its leading members is impressive: the pity is that no diary exists, and virtually no speeches, to put flesh and blood on the skeleton supplied by the official Journal.

We see the Lords, like the Commons, exercising discipline over the attendance of their members. Early in the session, Burghley moved that those who were absent without proxies, or had begun and then ceased attendance, should be admonished; and thereafter came a number of requests to be excused attendance, usually on the ground of illness. Again like the Commons, the

Lords protected their privilege of freedom from arrest and molesta-
tion, for themselves and their servants. They used a serjeant-at-
arms to bring offenders before them, and committed the guilty to
prison. It is all very similar to the House of Commons; but there
is a pervading sense of the dignity and decorum of peers of the
realm, greater expedition, as one might expect of a very small
assembly, and — not least notable — limitations imposed by
having to play second fiddle to the Commons.

CHAPTER II

SOCIAL AND ECONOMIC
LEGISLATION

SINCE the dissolution of the 1593 Parliament, the domestic annals of England had been weighted with misfortune. Even during the meeting of that Parliament there was concern about the plague in London. It proved a grievous visitation all that year. Stow, the Chronicler, tells that of 17,893 deaths within the City and its liberties between December 1592 and December 1593, 10,675 were due to the plague, among the victims being the Lord Mayor and three aldermen. Bartholomew Fair had to be cancelled and, in Michaelmas Term, the law courts sat at St. Albans instead of Westminster, a serious monetary loss to Londoners and a nuisance to lawyers. The following year, 1594, was the first of five continuous years of dearth. Great storms of wind in March were followed by torrential rains in May, June and July: 'as if the four ends of Heaven had conspired to turn the province of the Earth upside down'. There was a fair harvest in August, but destructive rain in September; and the price of grain soared. Dearth continued in 1595; in London there were food riots.

> A colder time in world was never seen;
> The skies do lour, the sun and moon wax dim,
> Summer scarce known but that the leaves are green.

A similar tale came with 1596. 'This year', wrote Stow, 'like as in the month of August, so in September, October and November fell great rains, whereupon high waters overflowing the low grounds, wheat and other grains grew to great price.' Summing up, a preacher exclaimed: 'One year there hath been hunger; the second there was a dearth; and a third there was great cleanness of teeth . . . Our summers are no summers; our harvests are no harvests; our seed-times are no seed-times . . . Scant any day hath been seen that it hath not rained upon us.'[1]

Though the government attempted to relieve the situation by

---

[1] STOW's *Annals*; STRYPE, *Annals*, iv. 294; E. P. CHEYNEY, *History of England* . . . ii. 3 seqq.

foreign buying, the grain market was not then a flexible, international one: indeed, within England itself it was local rather than national. Crop failure therefore meant starvation for the poor. The strain reached breaking point in one county — Oxfordshire — in the autumn of 1596, when some exasperated, foolhardy men planned a rising. They talked of spoiling the gentry, cutting their throats, and marching on London, there to make common cause with the prentices, who had demonstrated their rebellious mood the year before. There were food riots elsewhere in this and other years.[1]

Discontent also manifested itself over the constant impressment of men for war-service overseas; and doubtless it was this which led Burghley, in August 1596, to note that, since 1589, 17,800 men had been pressed for foreign parts and 3,293 for Ireland. Whatever their accuracy, the figures in themselves convey only a dim impression of the burdens of war. The levying of men imposed financial charges on the country and was often accompanied by bribery and corruption. Then, in addition to exceptionally heavy national taxation, there was the increasing burden of ship money, against which the Lord Mayor and Aldermen of London were protesting in 1596. Compared with our own times, the nation in general was only lightly touched by it all; but that thought is no guide to the discontent aroused. Apparently, there were some lawyers arguing that it was unconstitutional to levy men for foreign service against their will. In 1596, some such talk led an elderly Essex gentleman, Sir John Smith — a writer on military matters, with a longish entry in our *Dictionary of National Biography* — to commit a dangerous indiscretion. Smith was a feckless man at all times, and on this occasion was additionally stupefied by drink. At the musters, he told the men that 'there was a press out for a thousand men' and that lawyers held it to be illegal. 'My masters', he announced, 'if you will go with me, you shall not go out of the land.' Fortunately for Smith his drunken invitation proved a damp squib: as did the meeting on Enslow Heath on the night of November 25th, when the Oxfordshire ringleaders hoped to start their *jacquerie*. But such incidents, in the prevailing economic distress of the people, were most alarming to the goverment and to the ruling class, the gentry.[2]

[1] *Cal. S.P. Dom. 1595-97*, pp. 316-20; *H.M.C. Hatfield MSS.* vii. 49-50.
[2] *Hatfield MSS.* vi. 534-6; *Cal. S.P. Dom. 1595-97*, pp. 235 seqq., 275.

At the time of the previous Parliament, in 1593, grain had been cheap and plentiful: too plentiful. The problem had then been how to avoid a surplus, and the government had consequently repealed the main clause of an Act of 1563 forbidding the conversion of land from tillage to pasture. There seems to have been a difference of opinion about the extent to which the new freedom was exploited. However, conversion to pasture could involve depopulation in rural areas, and any such change was bound to strike public imagination during these exceptional years. Combined with industrial unemployment, it was a factor in the great increase of vagrancy and vagabondage. There were gloomy prophets who, like Malthus in the years of distress following the Napoleonic wars, regarded the country as over-populated.

By the time the 1597 Parliament met, the multiplicity of ills was such as to make a general overhaul of economic and social legislation seem imperative. In earlier assemblies the initiative would probably have been taken by the government; if for no other reason, then because the unofficial leadership in the House of Commons was so absorbed with religious causes that there was little energy for other matters. But now, with the eclipse of Puritanism, a vacuum existed, into which rushed concern for the economic disorders of the day. There could be no more striking indication of the passing of an era than the change of interest which is forced upon this narrative of ours. The main Acts of the Parliament of 1597 — the first five chapters of the Statute — were economic and social ones. They were not government bills, but were framed in committees of the House of Commons. Being, in the Queen's phrase, 'Commonwealth matters', the initiative of the House was in accord with her definition of their privilege of freedom of speech. But one cannot help wondering at such a recession of government leadership. Certainly, as we reflect on this Parliament, it marks, in a strange new way, a significant advance in that 'winning of the initiative' by the House of Commons, which was to be the outstanding theme of Jacobean Parliaments, and in course of time was to effect a constitutional revolution.

It was Francis Bacon who, on November 5th, the first day of business, initiated the main legislative work of the session with a motion against enclosures and the depopulation of towns and houses of husbandry, and for the maintenance of tillage. He had,

he said, perused the preambles of former statutes on the subject —
'medicines of our understanding' — and had drafted two bills,
'not drawn with a polite pen, but with a polished heart, free from
affection and affectation'. 'Lords that have enclosed great
grounds and pulled down even whole towns and converted them
to sheep pastures' might be harmed by the bills, but it is praise-
worthy, he remarked, to revive 'motheaten laws' if they bring
forth good. Enclosures cause depopulation, and that in turn
produces idleness, decay of tillage, decrease in charity, charge in
maintaining the poor, and finally the impoverishment of the
Realm. 'I would be sorry to see within this kingdom, the piece
of Ovid's verse prove true: *Iam seges est ubi Troia fuit*' — crops grow
where Troy once stood; and 'in England, instead of a whole town
full of people, nought but green fields, a shepherd and his dog.
The eye of experience is the sure eye; but the eye of wisdom is the
quick-sighted eye'. By experience we daily see that no one regards
as shameful what is profitable to himself; 'and therefore there is
almost no conscience in destroying the savour of our life — bread,
I mean'. Bacon concluded by urging the House to read his two
bills, as 'laws tending to God's honour, the renown of her Majesty,
the fame of this Parliament, and the everlasting good of this
Kingdom'.[1]

Though an independent Member, Bacon stood in close relationship with the government, and it may well be that there was
official inspiration behind his initiative. But the limits of that
inspiration were revealed when the Chancellor of the Exchequer,
Sir John Fortescue, spoke. His opinion, we are told, was very
similar, but instead of backing the motion for a present reading
of the bills — which he surely would have done if the Council had
commissioned them — he moved for a committee to consider the
subject. The House responded by appointing a large committee,
consisting of all Councillor-Members, all county and city representatives, and others chosen individually. This done, Mr. Finch,
the Puritan lawyer, rose to broaden the scope of their inquest with
a speech on the 'horrible abuses of idle and vagrant persons,
greatly offensive both to God and the world', and 'the miserable
estate of the godly and honest sort of the poor subjects of this

---

[1] Townshend's Journal, printed by A. F. Pollard in *Inst. Hist. Research Bulletin*,
xiii. 10 (note that I occasionally take a variant reading from the Cotton MS. copy of the
Journal); D'EWES, pp. 551-2.

Realm': in brief, vagrancy and poverty. These two subjects were also referred to the grand committee.

The committee met that afternoon. No account survives of its proceedings, but it is not surprising to learn that Bacon's two subjects, affecting the economic interests of many Members, monopolized attention, to the exclusion of vagrancy and poverty. How long they sat, how often they met, we do not know; but they set up a sub-committee to prepare bills on tillage and depopulation, and on November 14th Bacon asked the House to assign another meeting of the full committee, to report progress. The meeting was fixed for the following afternoon, in the Commons' Chamber: an indication, perhaps, that many supernumeraries were expected to attend. By November 21st the committee had its main bill, on tillage, ready.[1]

Broadly, the bill enacted that land converted to pasture since the accession of the Queen, after twelve years in tillage, should be restored to tillage, and such conversions prohibited for the future.[2] Referring back to this bill in 1601, Robert Cecil spoke of the 'great arguments' and 'deliberate disputation' it provoked. Much, no doubt, had already been said in committee, but the second reading, on November 26th, led to a crucial debate. We have two speeches, written for that occasion and presumably delivered: one — anonymous — for the bill, the other against. The contrast is sharp. The former speaker, in his fervent idealism, might be a protagonist of the welfare state; the latter, in his cool rationalism, a disciple of Adam Smith. Though, as we shall see, the House could applaud idealism and act realistically, the former evidently voiced the sentiment of the assembly: so much so that his opponent — in a rejected draft of his speech — felt impelled to write, 'I have therefore thought it necessary first, by way of protestation, to declare myself to be a religious Christian to my God, a true lover of my country, and charitably affected to the poor'. Such, one concludes, was the surge of emotion that gave this bill its momentum: not unlike the emotion that had formerly been the ally of Puritanism.

Our anonymous speaker was probably a lawyer, certainly a man of culture and literary taste. He began by referring to Bacon's initial speech: 'the first motion that sounded in this place',

[1] D'EWES, pp. 552-60.
[2] B.M. Lansdowne MS. 83, fols. 199b-206. This appears to be Henry Jackman's copy of the bill, bought for the debate from the Clerk.

a lamentation for the poor, deprived of their living by the conversion of tillage into pasture. The motion, he commented, had gratified the affections of the House, won general applause, and caused them all to resolve on immediate and effective remedy. The only remedy was the utter suppression of enclosures. They 'spring from a bad root, spread unto worse mischiefs, and strive against the best rules of religion, policy and humanity'. Dilating upon this theme, he spoke of the 'swelling pride' and 'deceitful covetousness' of enclosers. God's initial purpose was 'to have the earth fruitful, joined with the cross and correction of labour'. But then came 'the law of property, whereby men could say, "This is mine" '. Supplanting the love of our neighbour, it introduced a threefold love — of money, of pleasure, and of ourselves — causing men to engross the whole commodity of the earth to themselves. Since pasture is maintained with less charge and returns more gain than tillage, 'therefore of gentlemen they will become graziers, factors for the butchers; and because tillage in their own hands yields more private profit than dispersed into the hands of many, of gentlemen they will become ploughmen, grinders of the poor, whereby, if not the heart of Cain, they yet strive to bring the punishment of Cain upon their younger and weaker brethren, to make them vagabonds and runagates upon the earth'.

Solomon had said that the honour of a prince rested in the multitude of his subjects, and his strength in the field that was tilled. Nothing poisons the mind of man so soon as idleness, and nothing drives this sin so far to flight as husbandry. 'It grew in proverb among the Romans that the husbandman was seldom or never seen either traitorous or contentious.' None 'pass their days with fewer cares, nor run their race with fuller strength, fitter to do her Majesty service upon some small training, than is the husbandman: whereupon Socrates was wont to say that the plough was the seed of soldiers.' Tillage has these two benefits. Its fruit is bread; and 'no realm, rich or populous in itself, can either long have joy in the streets or continuance in the State, where there groweth cleanness of teeth through scarcity of bread'. Secondly, it returns its 'profit even to the Prince and is without limitation, breaking forth as the sun from whose beams every particular person receiveth comfort'. Though 'we live not in a savage land, where wolves can devour sheep', shall we be known to live 'in a more brutish land, where sheep shall devour men?'

After this preamble, the speaker turned to comment on the provisions of the bill, which he considered 'too weak for the disease'. Certain he praised. For example: though some Members were concerned that innocent purchasers of enclosed land would be compelled to revert to tillage, he thought it wise not to limit the bill to the original offenders. He cited the Common Law on nuisance, and warned the House that if 'the ruder sort' of people became privy to the strength and liberty it allowed them, they would be as unbridled and untamed beasts. Among the points that he criticized was the penalty of 10s. an acre yearly for land not returned to tillage. 'The ears of our great sheepmasters', he declared, 'do hang at the doors of this House; and myself have heard, since this matter grew in question . . . that some, enquiring and understanding the truth of the penalty, have prepared themselves to adventure 10s. upon the certainty of the gain of 30s. at the least.' Our speaker also wanted to place a stint on the amount of converted land left in the hands of present owners. Redistribution of land in the interest of the poor was his object.

'The eyes of the poor', he exclaimed by way of peroration, 'are upon this Parliament, and sad for the want they yet suffer . . . This place is an epitome of the whole Realm . . . We sit now in judgment over ourselves . . . As this bill entered at first with a short prayer, "God speed the plough", so I wish it may end with such success as the plough may speed the poor.' It was a speech — so have the hands of the clock turned — that has a more congenial ring today than in the intervening centuries.[1]

Our other speech was written by Henry Jackman, a London cloth-merchant, aged forty-six, son of a London alderman and educated at Magdalen College, Oxford, and the Inns of Court. He sat for Wiltshire boroughs in the four Parliaments from 1589 to 1601. Probably he had business dealings with the wool-growers of that county; certainly, his genealogical tree was linked with Wiltshire gentlemen and on at least two occasions he must have owed his parliamentary seat to the nomination of relatives. His interests were associated with sheep, not grain. But we have already met him as the courageous author of a speech against the double subsidy of 1589, and he seems to have been an independent type of man, resistant to mass emotion.

---

[1] Hatfield MS. 176, fols. 11-13 (cf. *Cal.* vii. 541-3). The manuscript gives no clue to the author. I am not inclined to think that he was Robert Cecil.

He was conscious that his was a discordant voice. 'I am not ignorant', he began, 'how difficult and how dangerous a thing it is for any one man . . . as it were to profess that he only is to be heard.' The Speaker, however, would have petitioned for freedom of speech in vain if they themselves subsequently became votaries of silence and, by smothering their conceits, declared themselves unworthy of the honour of this place and unprofitable servants of their constituencies. 'My purpose', he announced, 'is to speak against the body of this bill; not only to tick it on the finger, or to touch it on the toe, but to stick at the very head and heart thereof.' Although previous speakers had done their utmost to persuade Members that the bill could not be impugned without suspicion of impiety, cruelty and partiality — as though opponents 'went about wholly to take the use of the plough from the bowels of the earth, or the nourishment of bread from the bellies of the poor' — nevertheless he would endeavour to prove, first that it was utterly weak and incapable of remedying the present disease of dearth, and secondly that in many ways it was mischievous and inconvenient.

Briefly, Jackman's argument was that the dearth of grain was not due to decay of tillage, but to the inscrutable and unavoidable will of God: that is, to the weather. He asked Members to recall the period of plenty which had led to the statutory relaxation of 1593. He was convinced that everyone, from his own experience and observation, would acknowledge that 'the plough hath in these latter years of dearth been put both into more and better land than in those former years of plenty'. The want of tilled land could therefore not be the cause of dearth. In confirmation of his argument he cited two comments made in this Parliament: the one about a neighbouring kingdom, almost wholly given to tillage, yet reported to have suffered greater famine than England in this time of distress; the other about a county on the Welsh border, dependent on the plough, yet forced to pay a great price for corn this last year. He also cited a precedent from Henry III's reign, when the whole land lay in open fields, subject only to the hand of the husbandman, yet in one year corn rose in price from 2s. to 24s.

The text of Jackman's speech breaks off at this point, but preliminary notes indicate his second line of argument. It was economic realism. The price and rent of pasture-land would rise with the diminution of area; there would be a dearth of cattle of all sorts, but especially of sheep, which would cause a decline in the cloth industry and so increase the number of beggars. In tillage, the first year of conversion would create great dearth because of the extra seed required. The following year grain would be plentiful and cheap, and farmers would be unable to pay their rents because of the low price. 'Men', he declared — in this proclaiming his social philosophy — 'are not to be compelled by penalties, but allured by profit, to any good exercise.'[1]

It is interesting to note that in 1601, when the Act came before the Commons for renewal, a strong opposition employed the same line of argument. Sir Walter Raleigh — that great individualist — was then hostile. The best course, he declared, is to set corn at liberty 'and leave every man free, which is the desire of a true Englishman'. Sir Robert Cecil, on the other hand, joined Bacon in being the champion — impatient and truculent — of the measure. 'Whosoever doth not maintain the plough, destroys the kingdom', he asserted. There can be no doubt that his view, and the government's view, was the same in 1597.[2]

In the absence of any adequate record, we can only guess at the trend of the second-reading debate in 1597. There were critics, we know; but, with a background of prolonged economic distress and social unrest, most of them probably paid lip homage to the doctrine of the welfare state — or, to use their phrase, 'the common weal' — and set about undermining the bill by other means. Jackman certainly expected to be regarded as something of a leper. He probably was. He would not have been in the different circumstances of 1601.

The bill was committed and re-emerged as a new bill: seemingly a stiffer one, with its penalty doubled, in response to the enthusiasts. But its operation — which was general throughout the kingdom in the first version — was now limited to only twenty-three counties. The critics appear to have got their way by extolling the medicine for others and excusing themselves from taking it. At the third reading, Serjeant Harris, a prominent lawyer and powerful House of Commons man, made a speech. 'The fairest day', he declared, 'hath a cloud to shadow it. Yea, even in the face of Venus there was a mole or a wart, and a spot in

---

[1] Lansdowne MSS. 105, fols. 201-3; 83, fol. 198.
[2] TOWNSHEND, *Historical Collections*, pp. 299-300.

the neck of Helen. So, in every bill, though never so well looked into, yet there is somewhat unprovided for, and in it some scruple which a reader of an Inn of Court can find out. And, for my part, as the bill did stand, I was utterly against it; yet, considering the proviso to be added, I am of Saul become Paul and [am] like Ovid's fair dame who came and said, *Cupido super omnia vincit*' — love conquers all. 'And therefore I think it now fit to pass.' The proviso which converted the Serjeant from Saul into Paul was the one limiting the bill to half the counties of England and Wales. Harris was a Devon man — so was Sir Walter Raleigh — and Devon was exempt. Shropshire had a narrow escape. After successfully emulating Serjeant Harris, its Members were confounded by one of their number, Robert Berry, a Ludlow townsman and Member for that borough, who, at the third reading, moved that Shropshire should be reincluded in the bill. Sir Thomas Coningsby, one of the knights for Herefordshire, came to the rescue, declaring that Shropshire was wholly given over to woodland, oxen and dairies. To include it in the bill would breed a greater scarcity among the people there than the present scarcity of corn. On one fair-day in that county there was more than £10,000 worth of cheese and butter sold. He hoped 'that as Herefordshire and the other countries adjoining were the barns for the corn, so this shire might and would be the dairy-house to the whole Realm'. Coningsby's speech saved Shropshire. Townshend — a Shropshire man — tells us that Berry's motion 'was utterly disliked by all the burgesses of that country and the knights of that shire, and he greatly frowned at for it'.[1]

There had been some amendments to the bill at its second reading; there were 'many arguments' at the third. Bacon spoke for his bedraggled offspring at the second reading, saying that he was as glad to be discharged of it 'as an ass, when he hath laid down his pack'. The bill, he added, 'was like the cock, which, though it do no good in punishing offenders past, yet it cuts short the like offence to come'.[2]

As Bacon's comment suggests, official circles were disgusted at the severe territorial limits set to the bill. We learn that when they were first proposed — probably on November 26th — Robert Cecil, 'in a grave and wise speech', tried to prevent the omission

---

[1] *I.H.R. Bulletin*, xii. 15-16.
[2] Ibid. pp. 13-14.

of Northumberland, Cumberland and Westmorland, arguing that of all counties these were in most need of reform — not so much to produce food as to maintain men, on whom the defence of the border depended. Writing to encourage him in his stand, the Dean of Durham declared that in these counties whole villages had been dispeopled by landowners. Cumberland and Westmorland remained out of the bill, but Northumberland was got in by a late amendment, probably made by the House of Lords, which also added the county of Pembroke. That was evidently as far as the government dared go in asserting its will against the Commons. Be it added, there was never any question of omitting Durham: this county had no Members to speak for it.[1]

We might feel inclined to be cynical about the homage of these Elizabethan legislators to the common weal. They had tempered idealism with realism. But when they came to the second of their social-economic bills — the one concerned with depopulation — not a single friendly voice seems to have been raised in defence of landlords who had destroyed farm houses in the process of enclosing their estates. Indeed, in their eagerness to deal with this evil, they appear to have outrun the intentions of the government and the prudence of the House of Lords.

The title of the bill — 'for the increase of people for the service and defence of the Realm' — proclaimed their patriotic purpose. At the second reading, the Clerk tells us, there were 'many speeches, all tending to' its 'good liking and furtherance'. The general call was probably for more severity. At any rate, their first bill — framed by Francis Bacon on instructions from the grand committee — was committed and re-emerged as a new measure. This in turn provoked so much discussion at its third reading that it was decided, after a division on the point, to continue the debate next day. Of the 'many arguments', some, we are told, were for the bill, some against, though 'only to some parts or branches'. In the end it passed. The critics belonged to two camps: some, objecting to the 'strictness and impossibility' of its provisions; others — displaying 'heat and animosity' — who wanted it 'violently penned'. Sir Anthony Cope, who may be assumed to represent the Puritan point of view, was one of the latter. He failed to catch the Speaker's eye, and therefore wrote to Lord Burghley in the hope — quite misplaced — that Burghley

[1] *Cal. S.P. Dom. 1595-97*, pp. 542-3.

would 'better' the measure, now in the Upper House, with additional provisions for the victims of depopulation.[1]

In the Lords, an impressive committee, of almost all the attendant peers, with five legal assistants, considered the bill. They set out their criticisms in the form of thirty-one objections, and to these, after a conference between the two Houses, the Commons duly made their answers. Neither party was satisfied and yet both wanted legislation. Consequently, at another conference the Lords announced their intention of drafting a new bill, and in order to avoid further disagreement they sent down a summary of their proposals. The wiser men in the Commons disliked the procedure, but the House, being curious, had the summary read and then returned it privately and without comment to the Lords. The rest of the story need not detain us. Serjeant Harris found a glaring flaw in one of the clauses, which was amended; other changes were made; the bill duly passed. The new title which the Lords had given it reflected their less exalted mood: 'An Act against the decaying of towns and houses of husbandry'.[2]

The enacting clauses of the Act began with a definition of a 'house of husbandry': a house with twenty acres of land, occupied or let to farm over a period of three years since the beginning of the reign. They were to continue in that state 'for ever'. The Commons, in their bill, had ordered the rebuilding of all such houses that had been allowed to fall into decay, if the land was still owned by the original offender; and the rebuilding of 'the greater part', if in the possession of an heir or purchaser. They also ordered the restoration of the whole land formerly attached to the house, if the decay had occurred within the last seven years; and of twenty acres, if longer decayed. The House of Lords evidently thought that the Commons had let zeal swamp discretion. In their bill, they drew a justifiable distinction between the original offenders and their heirs on the one hand, and purchasers of the land on the other. The former were to rebuild half the number of houses decayed for more than seven years, attaching forty acres of land to each, and all houses decayed within seven years, attaching forty or twenty acres, according to the size of the former holding. Purchasers, however, had to rebuild only a quarter of the number. The Lords also modified the rate of replacement and reduced one of

[1] D'Ewes, pp. 562-74; Lansdowne MS. 83, fol. 195; *Hatfield MSS.* xiv. 27-8, 37-8.
[2] *L.J.* ii. 212 seqq.; D'Ewes, pp. 578-93; *I.H.R. Bulletin*, xii. 17-18, 21-2.

the penalties. Be it added that Sir Anthony Cope, far from regarding the rate specified by the Commons as excessive, had thought it far too slow, and had wanted to supplement it with a weekly monetary levy, to be devoted to the relief of the poor.[1]

Dry as these details may seem, they deserve reflection, for the House of Commons was predominantly a body of landed gentry, and yet we find them running ahead of the House of Lords — where Burghley and other Councillors dominated opinion — in the interests of the defenceless, small farmer.

Let us recall that when the grand committee had first been set up to consider tillage and depopulation, it had also been charged — following a motion by Henry Finch — with the problems of vagrancy and poverty. Six days later, Sir Francis Hastings — like Finch, a keen Puritan — told the House that the committee had devoted its whole time to the two former subjects and done nothing about rogues and the poor. Consequently, some Members had been informally at work and had framed 'two or three bills' on the neglected topics, which he asked the House to receive. It looks as if a group of Puritans — who, in the nature of their faith, were acutely sensitive about the welfare of society and now lacked the old outlet for their energy — had made the problem of poverty their concern.

By cutting out the orderly, if dilatory procedure of an initiating committee, these earnest and impatient men — with the hearty concurrence, we must assume, of a majority of Members — loosed a flood of reforming zeal on the House and recreated, in the secular sphere, something of that surgent independence which had formerly been evoked by religion. 'A feast of charity', Bacon called it.[2] No less than fifteen bills on poverty and vagrancy were introduced and given at least two readings: a prodigal use of precious time. Who drafted them we do not know, and their titles are the only clue to their contents. Some clearly covered the same ground; others reflected pet nostrums. There was a bill to relieve the poor out of impropriations and other church livings — a radical Puritan notion; another for 'petite forfeitures' to go to the relief of the poor. The House was converted into an exploratory committee and must have spent two field-days, plus odd

---

[1] *Statutes of the Realm*, IV. ii. 891-2; S.P. Dom. Eliz. 265/59 (a breviate of the Commons' bill, with critical notes); Hatfield MS. 141/193 (*Cal.* vii. 546), criticisms by the Lords; the original Act at Westminster; Lansdowne MS. 83, fol. 195.

[2] TOWNSHEND, *Historical Collections*, p. 290.

occasions, on the subject. The great day was November 22nd, when eleven of these bills were given their second reading. Three were rejected, including the one for raiding impropriations and church livings, which stimulated a debate and a division, the voting being 117 for and 146 against the measure — most interesting figures, especially if we bear in mind that the sponsors of a bill were usually handicapped by the process of dividing. The rest of the bills were sent to a grand committee; and, as the same body of men had already been charged with three other bills on the subject, a single committee now found itself with eleven bills to scrutinize: surely a most remarkable and probably unprecedented occurrence. Its chairman was Sir Robert Wroth, and the Member who subsequently delivered at least one of its reports to the House was Henry Finch: Puritans, both.

Out of the grand committee and its eleven bills came two of the three great Acts of this Parliament: 'for the relief of the poor', and 'for punishment of rogues, vagabonds and sturdy beggars'. The third Act — 'for erecting of hospitals or abiding and working houses for the poor' — had got an earlier start, with a different committee. They are famous Acts, especially the one for the relief of the poor, which remained the basis of our English poor law down to our own day. This particular bill, once it emerged from the grand committee, seems to have had an easy passage; and the same is true of the bill for erecting hospitals and working houses for the poor.

It is quite a different story with the vagrancy bill. In committee, after the second reading, it received many amendments and considerable additions: so much so that the House would not let the subsequent debate be curtailed — as Speaker and Councillors probably wished — by dealing with them towards the end of a sitting. However, the amended bill had a safe passage.

In the Lords the reception was critical. The second-reading debate revealed a desire for amendments, obviously expected to cause trouble below. Unfortunately, we remain ignorant of the issues: whether the Commons, in this Act — which strikes us today as brutal and uncivilized — wished to continue, or perhaps extend, the extreme severity of earlier legislation, while the Lords insisted on modifying it; or whether the conflict of opinion was over such details as the categories of persons deemed to be rogues and vagabonds. At any rate, the Lords amended the bill and the

Commons, when it returned to them, set up a committee, held a conference with the Upper House, and, after a third-reading debate, with 'sundry speeches' for and against, finally rejected the bill, on a division, by 106 to 66 votes. The procedural escape from such a deadlock was for the Lords to frame a new bill, which they did. Presumably a compromise, it passed both Houses with little or no trouble.[1]

Behind the dry facts of all this legislation — as the two surviving speeches on the tillage bill indicate — there was an interesting divergence of social philosophies. Unfortunately, without the debates we are unable to follow the conflict; but there exists a document which will serve to get our story into focus. It is entitled 'Notes for the Parliament' and is a diagnosis of the ills of society, written at the beginning of the Parliament. In all probability the author was Robert Cecil, and the Notes may have been his brief for a speech made, or intended to have been made, on the first day of business, November 5th.[2]

His chief concern was the high price of corn, and in his opening paragraphs he mentioned two of its consequences: the inability of many to 'keep hospitality' — that is, to observe the social obligation of maintaining open house; and 'the lamentable cry of the poor, who are like to perish'. The prominence given to hospitality may seem curious, but it was in accord with the social philosophy of the author. Twice during the session an attempt was made to include a bill on the subject in the programme of reform, and twice it was defeated at the second reading. One presumes that the sponsors — Cecil, perhaps, being one — were anxious, in the words of Henry Jackman, to compel the gentry by penalties to a good exercise, while the majority of the House rebelled against any such encroachment of the law on their private lives.

Cecil went on to consider the cause of excessive prices, arguing that it must be scarcity, or ingrossing and forestalling — that is, cornering commodities — or else superfluous consumption. By general report, he added, it was the second rather than the first; and he therefore proceeded to urge control of these offenders, whom he described as 'odious to the Commonwealth'. In fact, the first bill read in this Parliament was one against forestallers,

---

[1] D'EWES, passim; *L.J.* ii. 203-20.
[2] Hatfield MS. 56/83 (*Cal.* vii. 497-8). The Manuscript is in the hand of a secretary of Cecil's.

regrators and ingrossers. We may probably assume that it was a
government bill, or, at least, one with official blessing; but though
ingrossers were deemed authentic 'caterpillars of the Commonwealth' and can have had few friends in Parliament — one
Member actually moved that their offence be made a felony —
nevertheless the bill foundered. We cannot be certain why. It
was twice committed in the Commons — which suggests much
criticism; and on the second occasion the committee took out the
provisions affecting 'corn, grain and other victuals' — presumably,
the guts of the measure — making a separate bill of them, which
seems to have lapsed after a first reading. The debilitated old bill
went on, reached the Lords, was there amended, and, after an
indecently long interval, was dashed by the Commons, who dis-
approved of the amendments. The readiest explanation of this
strange history would be that the Lords — perhaps under Burghley's leadership — had tried to restore its original virtue. Here,
again, it looks as if the Commons were rebelling, not against the
purpose of the measure, but against the excessive regimentation
that would be incidentally imposed on inoffensive subjects. At
any rate, this was the second bill, favoured in 'Notes for the Parliament', to meet defeat in the Lower House.[1]

In his memorandum, Cecil next returned to the question of
scarcity — the first of his three possible causes of high prices. This
led him to the central and less controversial themes of tillage,
depopulation, and rogues and idle persons, where his proposals
are in too general terms to differentiate him from others in the
House. In a pious reflection on enclosures, he noted that 'these
last few wet years', many sheep, kept on lands formerly used for
tillage, had died, thus manifesting the displeasure of Almighty
God.

Superfluous consumption was his next theme. Too much was
spent in ale and tippling houses, the bread was too fine in quality,
the beer too strong, and there were far too many of these houses.
It was 'most necessary', he declared, to abridge their number,
and have coarser bread and smaller drink. Victuals would be
increased if ale houses were closed one day a week. All, in fact,
that emerged from this line of thought was a discretionary Act
to restrain the excessive making of malt.

At some stage or other in the many debates and many discus-

[1] D'Ewes, passim; *L.J.* ii. passim; *I.H.R. Bulletin*, xii. 14.

sions in committee, Robert Cecil presumably preached his gospel of regimentation, and no doubt a section of the House agreed wholeheartedly with him. A paternal State and an ordered economy, dedicated to the common weal, were natural concomitants of personal monarchy. But the age was also one of individual initiative and acquisitive instincts. Henry Jackman's remark — 'Men are not to be compelled by penalties, but allured by profit, to any good exercise' — and Sir Walter Raleigh's cry in 1601 — 'Leave every man free' — were in fundamental opposition to the mentality of 'Notes for the Parliament'. We can glimpse enough of this Parliament to know that in losing the debates we have lost a story of topical interest for our own day.

CHAPTER III

MONOPOLIES, RELIGION, THE SUBSIDY

IT was inevitable, as the ills of society were probed in debate, that attention should be directed to monopolies. Away back in 1571, when the practice was in its infancy and abuses already evident, that attractive parliamentarian, Robert Bell, had brought the wrath of authority down on his head by denouncing them in the House of Commons. Since then, and particularly in latter years as the lethargy of age stole into politics and corruption luxuriated, they had become a scandal.

Monopolies or licences were privileges granted by the Queen's letters patent to one or more individuals. They were of various kinds. In their original, inoffensive form they were like the patents of more modern times, used to protect inventions or new processes, etc. But from new manufactures they were extended to old — to the making of salt, starch, paper, and in time a host of other commodities — either creating a monopoly for the patentee or compelling tradesmen to pay him for authority to continue in their established livelihoods. In addition there were licences to export goods, otherwise barred from export by statute — a defensible device if used (as, of course, it was not) merely to temper the rigidity of the law; licences, also, to dispense (at a price) with penalties incurred by the breach of penal laws; licences, indeed, to exercise many of those residuary rights and powers left to the Crown by the constitution. The practice could not be controlled by statute, since the Crown, by what was known as a *non obstante* clause in letters patent, could dispense with a penal statute: after all, in so doing it was merely forgoing a penalty due to itself. Nor could the courts of Common Law give redress to victims, since these courts could not proceed with cases concerning the prerogative without the Crown's consent, while patentees had recourse to the Privy Council and the Star Chamber, whose duty it was to defend and enforce the royal prerogative.[1]

The system was logical; indeed, defensible provided it was not

[1] Cf. W. H. PRICE, *English Patents of Monopoly*; E. P. CHEYNEY, *Hist. of England*, ii. 285 seqq.

abused. But both Court life and politics under personal monarchy revolved round royal grants and favours: organized mendicancy, quite unabashed in Elizabethans, and progressively unscrupulous. Officials, for the most part, were paid static and often grossly inadequate fees, which the Queen was expected to supplement by rewards and favours; and in time of continuous inflation the importunity of such men, and their ingenuity in devising new favours, naturally increased. It was inevitable: the Crown did not have the monetary resources to pay its servants properly. Courtiers were the chief beneficiaries of these licences, and they exercised their powers through agents, who descended like harpies or black-mailers on their victims throughout the country. In the 1590s they became as obnoxious as purveyors had been before Burghley's reforms, or as informers continued to be, who, like them, battened on the penal laws. Once more we are witnessing the decline of the Elizabethan age. But the story, prolonged into the early decades of the next century, carries a moral of permanent significance. These were inherent weaknesses in a political and social system, attracting exploitation until corruption sapped the system's vitality and it collapsed.[1]

Appropriately, it was on the same day as the second-reading debate on the bill against forestallers, regrators and ingrossers — those other monopolists — that a motion was made 'touching sundry enormities growing by patents of privilege and monopolies'. We know nothing more, except that Robert Cecil spoke and no action was taken. Doubtless he frowned on the motion: it threatened both the prerogative and the interests of officials and courtiers. The next day a Mr. Wingfield — probably Robert, Cecil's cousin and Burghley's nominee for the borough of Stam-ford — renewed the motion. This time the Solicitor General seems to have defended the prerogative; but the Puritan, Nathaniel Bacon, seconded Wingfield, while Sir Francis Hastings moved for a fact-finding committee, preparatory to seeking ways of redress. Probably other government speakers backed up the Solicitor General, and the Speaker also may have taken his cue from the front bench: at any rate, the motion was talked out and the House rose. At the next sitting — but only at the end of it, which sug-gests a hostile manoeuvre — the House returned to the subject and began to nominate a committee, whereupon Cecil intervened,

[1] Cf. my Raleigh Lecture, *The Elizabethan Political Scene.*

still obstructive, urging postponement on the plea that the hour was late and they would need to define the committee's functions. The following day — again, be it noted, at the end of the morning — a Member reopened the matter. There were sundry speeches. The Court group must once more have been stalling. But the House now insisted on implementing its former resolution. It appointed a very large committee, to meet in the House the following Tuesday afternoon.

Obscurity dogs us in this story. Perhaps the committee held its meeting on the Tuesday and adjourned to the following day. At any rate, on the Wednesday morning Sir John Fortescue tried to get the meeting for that afternoon postponed because he and Cecil had to be at Court. The House went to a vote on the request and refused it, evidently impatient, at long last, of persistent delaying tactics. Nevertheless, three weeks pass before we hear of the matter again, when, on December 8th, Sir Thomas Cecil moved that a petition be drafted and presented to the Queen: another interesting example of family independence. Francis Bacon spoke; and, though unrecorded, we cannot doubt that he talked of the prerogative and opposed his relative. A debate ensued. The Clerk merely notes, 'Sundry motions and speeches', leaving us to guess at the conflict of views. In the end, the House adopted Sir Thomas Cecil's motion, reinforced the old committee, and charged it to prepare a petition, to be delivered to the Queen by the mouth of their Speaker. It had all been very mild and proper, not to say supine: in striking contrast to the great days of Norton, Fleetwood, the Wentworths, and those other sturdy fighters.

The purpose of Robert Cecil and the Court party in delaying any action by the Commons now became apparent. It was to gain time for the Queen herself to do something about their grievances, without ostensible coercion. Between December 8th and 14th the petition had become 'humble thanks to be yielded unto her Majesty by Mr. Speaker . . . for her Highness's most gracious care and favour in the repressing of' the abuses connected with patents of privilege. It looks as if Elizabeth had issued instructions to her Councillors to scrutinize existing grants and not to use prerogative machinery to prevent patentees from being sued in the Common Law courts. This last was the crucial point: to submit patents of monopoly to the test of the Common Law. It meant a weakening of the prerogative and cannot have been palatable; but needs (or, at any rate, discretion) must, in face of the mounting and justifiable indignation of Parliament.[1]

The address of humble thanks, framed by the committee and approved by the House, was ready for an expected dissolution before Christmas, but Parliament was merely adjourned over the holiday and it was not until February 9th that the Speaker delivered the address in the course of his closing oration. 'It hath pleased your Highness' — declared the Commons, with flattering prevarication — 'even now of late and before we had any thought of it' to command 'reformation in your courts of justice of the strange and exceeding abuses of the patents of privilege, commonly called monopolies, practised both contrary to your Majesty's most princely meaning and to the too, too much grievance of your people.' Having expressed their thanks, the Commons took care to let her know their complaints. Her gracious clemency, they declared, was never more generally abused. No doubt she had been informed that these patents were necessary and profitable for her subjects, whereas, on the contrary, they prove to be so prejudicial that they impoverish the people and debar them from the lawful use of their trades. Patents had been issued on the pretence of having many political laws, passed for the good of the people, better executed; but they had been used to hinder reform, thus exchanging public good for private gain. They beseeched the Queen, with her 'sacred eyes of pity and compassion', to behold their calamities and vouchsafe relief, persevering in her most royal and gracious course.[2]

The Lord Keeper, Egerton, referred to the address in his reply to the Speaker's oration. 'Her Majesty', he said, 'hoped that her dutiful and loving subjects would not take away her prerogative — which is the chiefest flower in her garland and the principal and head pearl in her crown and diadem — but that they will rather leave that to her disposition. And, as her Majesty hath proceeded to trial of' these patents 'already, so she promiseth to continue, and . . . they shall all be examined to abide the trial and true touchstone of the law.'[3]

It had been an amicable and statesmanlike handling of a threatening situation, leaving the royal prerogative unharmed by

[1] D'Ewes, pp. 554-5, 558, 570, 573.
[2] B.M. Additional MS. 48109 (Yelverton, 121).
[3] I.H.R. Bulletin, xii. 25.

Parliament. But the promised reforms, though begun, were not sustained. The times were not good; discipline and probity were deteriorating; and what with the death of Burghley, the demoralizing and fatal rivalry of Essex and Robert Cecil, and old age creeping on the Queen, the good intentions of 1597 remained unredeemed when Parliament next met in 1601. In due course we shall witness the pent-up anger of the Commons.

The Church also excited criticism in 1597-98: not premeditated and planned, as in the past, but starting in a casual way. It seems to have begun with a motion about abuses connected with marriage licences. These licences dispensed with the delay and publicity involved in publishing bans before marriage. As an extraordinary procedure they met a legitimate need, as, indeed, they do today; but in the hands of careless or corrupt officials and with the assistance of unscrupulous priests they had became part and parcel of a notorious social evil: the abduction of heiresses. The previous summer a west-country heiress had been stolen from her parents by a Dorset gentleman and married in this way. The case was brought up in Parliament and probably started the whole business. Many Members had similar stories to tell, and it was a staid trio of gentlemen who next day revived the motion. On the initiative of Sir Thomas Cecil the House appointed a committee to draft a bill on the subject, thus poaching — perhaps thoughtlessly — on the royal prerogative.[1]

Once started on ecclesiastical abuses, there was no telling where the Commons would stop. This was shown when a Member rose, after the committee had been appointed, and talked about probate of wills. It became still clearer, a few days later, when a preliminary report from the committee disclosed that they had decided nothing, because some of their company — the Puritan group undoubtedly — had tried to extend their terms of reference to cover other grievances. The moment was a critical one. There was a long debate in prospect in which the Court and Church party would have been struggling with anti-clericalism and Puritanism. However, Sir John Fortescue immediately rose to announce that the Queen had sent for him and Cecil yesterday and told them that she 'had been informed of the horrible and great incestuous marriages discovered in this House'. Intending to see due punishment and redress, she had commanded them to

[1] *I.H.R. Bulletin*, xii. 12; DASENT, *Acts of the Privy Council*, xxvii. 201-3; D'EWES, p. 555.

collect information from the House, whereupon she would herself take action. The Queen's informant was probably Archbishop Whitgift, who had his minions in the House to give him instant warning of any anti-clerical agitation. Fearing and detesting Parliament even more than his royal mistress, it had become his habit to pass these warnings on to her with impressive celerity and emphasis, knowing that he could count on her support.

The Queen's tactics were once more subtle and prudent. Instead of forbidding the House to proceed with a bill, as she had cause and right to do, she was inviting them to produce evidence, on which she herself would act, as Supreme Governor of the Church. Thus their grievance could be remedied while the prerogative remained inviolate.

There was a debate following Fortescue's announcement, with 'sundry speeches, tending to sundry courses'. The Clerk tells us that most of the House liked and approved the Queen's message. They ordered their committee to meet again to carry out her wishes: which they did, delivering their evidence to Fortescue a week later, probably in the form of a document we possess, entitled 'A note of divers incestuous and unlawful marriages'.[1]

So far, so good. But a section of the committee had already started trouble by demanding a roving commission on ecclesiastical abuses, and had clearly been vocal in the debate on the Queen's message. They got their way. The House set up a new committee to 'receive informations of the grievances touching ecclesiastical causes this day moved'. In membership it overlapped the other committee, but seems to have been weighted with Puritan sympathisers and certainly was inadequately restrained by authority. The initiative was probably seized by the intrepid Henry Finch, and it may well be that he and fellow-enthusiasts forced so many meetings that staider members tired, leaving them as a rump, going their own sweet way.

On November 22nd, instructed, presumably, by the rump, Finch produced in the House a bill of his own drafting on marriage licences. It was a tacit defiance of the Queen's message, and the House ought to have frowned on the irregularity. Instead, it received the bill. Six days later another anti-clerical bill appeared: how, we are not told. It was 'against excessive fees and exactions in ecclesiastical courts', apparently a drastic and quite unreason-

[1] D'Ewes, pp. 555-6, 560; Strype, *Whitgift*, ii. 378-80.

able measure, which caused alarm in orthodox circles. One angry critic, perhaps hoping to scare high authority, described it as 'a device of some such as seek to overthrow the ecclesiastical government and to erect the presbytery and new platform of popular government'. Five days later the authentic Puritan banner was indeed raised when Mr. Finch made a speech in the House about the Act of Uniformity and the Articles Act of 1571, at the close of which he introduced a bill to qualify these two Acts in favour of Puritan ministers. Other grievances and other ecclesiastical bills were brought before the Commons. It looks as if Finch and his rump were at the centre of the attack; but it was evidently not a premeditated and planned campaign, and except for Finch's second bill, was anti-clerical rather than Puritan.[1]

We are unable to say how the agitation was stopped or what happened to the bills. On the whole it seems best to assume that while Finch and his friends could procure a fleeting majority in the House, they could not command sustained enthusiasm; and that, in consequence, Privy Councillors and Speaker were able to suppress their bills and motions without the intervention of the Queen. Perhaps it was a vague and muddled recollection of this Parliament which led Serjeant Harris in 1601, in a somewhat similar situation, to speak of 'a custom which we have ever observed, viz. to meddle with no matter which toucheth her Majesty's prerogative'. He was unwittingly acknowledging the triumph of Whitgift. But both Archbishop and Queen showed their healthy respect for parliamentary agitation by passing through the Convocation of 1597 a series of 'constitutions' dealing with certain of the grievances: the correct constitutional procedure, preserving the Crown in Convocation as a distinct sphere of power from the Crown in Parliament.[2]

The better discipline of this Parliament, evident in their treatment of secular and ecclesiastical grievances, is also apparent in the story of the subsidy bill. The Chancellor of the Exchequer, Sir John Fortescue — deemed worthy of the initiative, now that the memory of Mildmay's oratory was fading — opened the subject on November 15th. Recalling the Lord Keeper's initial speech, he expounded the great and excessive charges sustained

---

[1] D'EWES, pp. 561, 565, 567; STRYPE, *Whitgift*, ii. 374-8; Inner Temple, Petyt MS. 538/54, fols. 58-61; B.M. Lansdowne MS. 439, fol. 232.
[2] TOWNSHEND, *Historical Collections*, p. 219 (Harris's further comment does not seem to fit the 1597 Parliament); STRYPE, *Whitgift*, ii. 383-4.

by the Queen in defence of the Realm, amounting to more than treble the value of the three subsidies granted in 1593. More was now needed: 'some mass of treasure ... against the forces and invasions of the King of Spain'. Moving for a committee, he left particulars of Spanish designs to be described by Mr. Secretary. Robert Cecil then rose to review the past and present purposes, practices and attempts of Philip II: a speech, it seems, in the Mildmay tradition, described by the Clerk as 'a large discourse, most excellently delivered by him'. The morning was already far spent, but there were two further speeches, by Sir Edward Hoby and Francis Bacon. 'It hath been always used, and the mixture of this House doth so require it', declared Bacon, 'that in causes of this nature there be some speech and opinion, as well from persons of generality as by persons of authority.' An interesting gloss, but in fact the custom was far from old. It looks as if Hoby stole a march on his rival, and took 'so much time' for his own speech that Bacon was left with a hungry, impatient audience.

We have Bacon's own version of his speech, perhaps — if we may hazard a guess — written out afterwards to show to the Queen, for both author and sovereign must have remembered the tactless, obstructive role he played over the subsidy of 1593. After an opening paragraph, the text continues: 'I will not enter, Mr. Speaker, into a laudative speech of the high and singular benefits which by her Majesty's most politic and happy government we receive ...; partly because no breath of man can set them forth worthily, and partly because I know her Majesty in her magnanimity doth bestow her benefits ... not looking for anything again ... but love and loyalty ... Neither will I make any observations upon her Majesty's manner of expending and issuing treasure, being not upon excessive and exorbitant donatives, nor upon sumptuous and unnecessary triumphs, buildings, or like magnificence, but upon the preservation, protection and honour of the Realm ... Sure I am that the treasure that cometh from you to her Majesty is but as a vapour which riseth from the earth and gathereth into a cloud and stayeth not there long, but upon the same earth it falleth again. And what if some drops of this do fall upon France or Flanders? It is like a sweet odour of honour and reputation to our nation throughout the world.'

Since the last Parliament, Bacon declared, there had been four events which increased the danger of the Realm. The King of

France had turned Catholic, thus bringing him nearer to peace with Spain — a prophetic comment. Secondly, Spain had captured Calais, thus 'knocking at our doors'. Thirdly, 'that ulcer of Ireland ... hath run on and raged more', which cannot but attract the ambition of Spain: another prophetic reflection. 'And lastly, it is famous now and so will be many ages hence', how we have braved him by the 'two sea-journeys' — Cadiz and the Islands Voyage; and he 'must needs take flames of revenge upon so mighty disgraces'. Bacon then reminded the House how forward and affectionate men were at the time of the last Parliament to have 'an invasive war', and how they described a defensive war as 'like eating and consuming interest'. They had got what they desired. The Cadiz expedition 'ravished a strong and famous port in the lap and bosom' of Spain, brought the Spaniards 'to such despair as they fired themselves and their Indian fleet in sacrifice, as a good odour and incense unto God', and 'the next news we heard of was of nothing but protesting of bills and breaking credit'.

'To conclude, Mr. Speaker ... I doubt not but every man will consent that our gift must bear these two marks and badges: the one of the danger of the Realm, by so great a proportion since the last Parliament increased; the other, of the satisfaction we receive in having obtained our so earnest and ardent desire of an invasive war.' The Queen, if she saw the speech, must have been pleased with it, and a preceding speaker — Hoby perhaps — nettled by its supercilious allusions to his remarks.[1]

At the conclusion of these speeches, the Commons appointed a great committee, to meet in the House, with invitation to anyone else to attend: as near to a Committee of the whole House as the Elizabethan Parliament could reach.

In 1589 the Commons had been afraid of a double subsidy setting a precedent for the future; in 1593 they had been similarly afraid of a treble subsidy; but now the committee accepted, probably without a qualm, the necessity for another treble subsidy. It is not surprising. A Spanish armada had been on England's threshold only a few weeks ago. However, in 1593 the burden had been eased a little by spreading the payment of the third subsidy over a fourth year. Now, the three were to be col-

---

[1] D'EWES, p. 557; B.M. Harleian MS. 6842, fols. 131-2 (printed Spedding's *Bacon*, ii. 85-9). Townshend (*I.H.R. Bulletin*, xii. 12) mixes Bacon's speech with previous ones.

lected in three years. This aroused criticism when the committee reported back to the House, and Robert Cecil came to the Chancellor's assistance with 'very many forcible reasons and causes of very great importance'.

One of Burghley's dependants, John Hare, Member for Horsham and Clerk of the Court of Wards, was among the critics and incurred Robert Cecil's anger. Hare wrote him an apologetic letter: 'I grieve that by my late speech in Parliament you have conceived mislike of me. I beseech you, out of your love for the Nether House, that I may not be misconceived and so misjudged. There are some of that House who, out of old ill-affection to me, will be glad to blow this coal, besides other great personages at Court . . . Your Honour seemeth persuaded that I did deny that any aid at all should be given to her Majesty. This thing was far from my thought.' Hare then explained what had happened. Sir Edward Hoby, pursuing his role of unofficial champion of a liberal grant, had in reply to various criticisms roundly declared that three subsidies, far from being too much, were too little, and that they should either contribute an annual payment to the Queen during her lifetime — a revolutionary proposal, conceding the principle, still many decades from recognition, that taxation must be an ordinary instead of an extraordinary source of Crown revenue — or alternatively, grant at least four subsidies, to fall most heavily on the gentry. These drastic proposals brought Hare to his feet. Reading between the lines of his letter, we can see that he stressed the danger of discontent among the people, oppressed with many other payments and charges in their localities; and urged consideration for the gentry, who were burdened with hospitality, the cost of which was heavier because the nobility were neglecting their duty in all counties. Recalling the *contretemps* over the 1593 subsidy, he proposed that they should hold up any decision until they had conferred with the House of Lords.

Cecil had obviously regarded this as an obstructive, wrecking speech, provoking delay and discord where speed and harmony were most advisable. Certainly, it was inept. As for the letter: it gives us a glimpse of the silent forces of coercion operating in an Elizabethan Parliament.[1]

At the end of the debate, the committee's recommendations were agreed to, and the bill passed through all its stages, 'well

[1] D'EWES, p. 559; *H.M.C. Hatfield MSS.* vii. 489.

liked of'. Robert Cecil worked as a happy stylist, composing the address to the Queen which was to be its preamble: a lengthy, eloquent, loyal and patriotic expression of all that was best in Queen Elizabeth's England, that land — as it declared — which 'is become sithence your Majesty's most happy days, both a port and haven of refuge for distressed states and kingdoms, and a rock and bulwark of opposition against the tyrannies and ambitious attempts of mighty and usurping potentates'. Still under the illusion — how natural, but how pathetic, we in our time can testify — that the good old days of light taxation might return, they put in a *caveat* that this which they had done 'upon so extraordinary and urgent necessity to so good and gracious a Princess' should not be drawn into a precedent.[1]

By odd chance, we have a copy of the speech made by Bishop Westphaling of Hereford at the passing of the bill in the House of Lords. It is like the man: sound and sober, without a smile. While approving of the grant, he referred in a vague, allusive way to some scheme whereby a financial Heaven could be made to descend on the country, reducing the Prince's need of taxation, increasing the subjects' ability to pay it, ridding society of discontent, begging, bribery and other ills; and that, 'not for a few years, or some one Prince's time, but for many hundred years, and as I may say, for ever'. One can only guess that his magic was deflation; but to read such penetration into utterance as obscure as the Delphic oracle and turn the bishop into both an economist and a woolly dreamer, is perhaps an error. Truth to tell, his speech is not worth quoting.[2]

---

[1] D'EWES, pp. 560, 569-73; *Hatfield MSS.* vii. 535-6; *Statutes of the Realm*, IV. ii. 937-8.
[2] Additional MS. 11055, fols. 7-8.

CHAPTER IV

END OF THE SESSION

THE trouble in describing so ill-reported a Parliament as this of 1597-98 is to be reasonably assured that we have got the general interpretation, the atmosphere right. Was it quite as amenable as we might think? Townshend, for example, in a passing allusion, mentions those 'in the rebellious corner in the right hand of the House': furthest away from the Speaker. They were trying to silence Burghley's secretary, Michael Hicks, on a point of order connected with a bill in which his master was possibly interested; and another undignified scene afterwards developed as to whether the Ayes or the Noes should be subjected to the disadvantage of going out of the House for the division. Who knows? an interesting and significant story might lie behind the episode.[1] Or again: we learn that on November 21st Henry Bourchier, a dependant of the Earl of Essex, complained about a Member revealing the proceedings of the House to outsiders; whereupon Sir Edward Hoby, a former victim of such tale-telling, moved that the matter be examined and the culprit named. We would fain know whether there was little or much in this, and what happened. Or once more: there were two bills for the draining of fenlands which passed both Houses and, two days before the end of the session, merely required approval of amendments made in the Upper House. The Commons were dealing with one of them when Sir John Fortescue entered the Chamber and told Speaker and assembly that the Queen had commanded him to notify them of her 'express pleasure' that neither bill should 'be any more read in this House'. For the moment, that was that. But next day, Robert Wingfield 'moved for the ordinary proceeding of this House, in the usual course of Parliament, to be permitted'. It seems to have been no more than a protest from one who was interested in the bills, as his cousin, Sir Thomas Cecil, was. No action resulted. Presumably, the Queen had decided to veto the bills — doubtless for good reasons —

---

[1] *Inst. Hist. Research Bulletin*, xii. 20. The bill may have been one to explain the Act of 5 Eliz. for maintenance of the navy (cf. D'EWES, p. 589).

and wished to save any waste of the precious last few hours of the Parliament. Wingfield's motion, which in any case could have had no effect on the royal veto, seems to indicate that this sort of intervention by the sovereign, unexceptionable in earlier and more flexible days, was becoming politically inexpedient. We might regard the incident as another of those minor signposts on the road to restricted monarchy.[1]

Both Houses expected the session to finish before Christmas. Indeed, on December 17th the Speaker informed Members that Parliament was near its end. But the Queen changed her mind. The session was adjourned from December 20th till January 11th and finally closed on February 9th, 1598. In the morning of that day there was business to transact, and the Commons had to distribute the usual levy for charitable purposes. It was after 3 p.m. when the Queen came to Parliament and about 4 p.m. before proceedings started.[2]

Speaker Yelverton's oration on this occasion was a perfect set piece: so knit that quotation spoils it; so artificial to modern ear and mind that its luscious verbiage would be as indigestible as its length; so ethereal and courtier-like in argument that one risks banality in epitomizing it. It opened in sonorous tones, befitting so mellifluous an orator: 'If that Commonwealth (most sacred and most renowned Queen) was reputed in the world to be the best framed and the most likely to flourish in felicity, where the subjects had their freedom of discourse and their liberty of liking in establishing the laws that should govern them; then must your Majesty's mighty and most famous realm of England, by this your most gracious benignity, acknowledge itself the most happy of all the nations under heaven, that possesseth this favour in more frank and flowing manner than any kingdom doth besides. Singular was the commendation of Solon that set laws among the Athenians; passing was the praise of Lycurgus that planted laws among the Lacaedemonians; and highly was Plato extolled that devised laws for the Magnesians: but neither yet could the inconveniences of the state be so providently foreseen, nor the reason of laws be so deeply searched into . . . as when the people themselves be agents in the framing of them.' With appropriate

---

[1] D'EWES, pp. 560, 594-5 (and cf. pp. 564, 567). Cf. TOWNSHEND, *Historical Collections*, p. 288.

[2] D'EWES, pp. 574, 595; *I.H.R. Bulletin*, xii. 22-4.

classical allusions he discoursed on law-making, before asking the Queen for her royal assent to their bills. Typical of his style was the conceit in which he wrapped the nature of that assent: 'The picture of Pygmalion, though by art it were never so curious and exquisite, and that in all the lineaments, almost, it had overcome nature and enticed the artizan himself, through the fineness of the features, to be fondly enamoured with his own creature, yet had it not the delight of life until Jupiter, assuming some pity of his woeful state and travail, inspired breath into it.'

His praise of the Queen appropriately stressed her learning and wisdom: her 'profound knowledge of the learned tongues' and her 'perfect skill of so many other several languages', in this surpassing all kings and most other people. 'Wisdom excelleth both strength and riches.' Presenting the subsidy bill — 'passed, as I certainly persuade myself, without the thought of a No, but passed, I do undoubtedly know, without the word of a No' — he commented on its need and justification. A wise and religious prince, he said, should not go to war, except as constrained to it. But 'all the world knoweth how much your Majesty hath been unjustly provoked to war, and how loth the sweet mildness of your princely nature hath been to entertain it'. 'The pride of Rome and the ambition of Spain have been the two whirlwinds of all the mischiefs in Christendom.'

In accordance with his instructions from the House, Yelverton inserted into his speech the Commons' address on the subject of monopolies, and then went on to ask indulgence for any offence that Members might have given during the session. 'We esteem nothing more dear nor more tender in our affections than the uncontrolled liberty your Highness hath vouchsafed your subjects in the free debating of the matters of this great council . . . When nothing is done with purpose of opposition, but with mind only of declaration of the true state of the causes that be treated (as I dare protest, in all their behalfs, it only was . . .) then may it both the better be excused and by your Majesty the sooner pardoned. Let me therefore . . . most humbly beseech your Majesty that this instant may raze the remembrance of all the errors that by them all have been committed; and that you will vouchsafe to receive them all into the centre of your gracious favour, howsoever, in the severity of your judgment, some perhaps heretofore have been omitted.' A plea for his own pardon followed.

The speech closed with an eloquent tribute to the Queen: 'It is a wonder to other countries, amid the tempestuous storms they be tossed with, to behold the calm and halcyon days of England, that possesseth a princess in whom dwelleth such undaunted courage without all dismay of any womanish fear, such singular wisdom without insolency, and such sincere justice without rigour. If Plato now had lived, he should not only have seen the mind of a philosopher in the majesty of a queen — which he only wished; but the perfection of a Christian in a princely virgin — which he could not have imagined.

'But into what an amazed labyrinth or endless sea do I run, if I do but sparingly prosecute either the glory of your virtues in yourself, or the greatness of your benefits to the Commonwealth? I can neither recount the one, they be so rare; nor rehearse the other, they be so many: for we be not more bound to your Majesty for reducing again the golden world of Saturn, than for restoring again the peace and flourishing prosperity of Solomon. But I fear, with grief and sorrow of soul I fear, that, as it was said of Hannibal, "The glory and skill of war amongst them of Carthage, after so long and so secure a repose from it, began and ended in his excellency"; so I fear, I do wonderfully fear, it will hereafter be said of you, "The honour and happiness of peace amongst us of England, after so many and so great interruptions of it, began and ended in your Majesty." '[1]

'After which speech ended', notes our diarist, 'the Queen called Sir Thomas Egerton, Lord Keeper; to whom, kneeling down before her, she spake in private. And so, after, he went unto a place like a desk, made even with the cloth of estate on the right side, and there made an answer to the Speaker's speech.'[2]

Her Majesty, Egerton said, had given him express charge to reprove the negligence of Justices of Peace and Assize in not providing for the poor, in not dealing with forestallers, regrators and ingrossers, and in not punishing sturdy vagabonds, who, in some commonwealths, would be put to death. 'Justices of Peace were like dogs in the Capitol, that, being set to bark at rebels, set themselves to annoy the good subjects ... Their greediness was the grievance of the people.' Voicing the Queen's thankful acceptance of the subsidy, he testified of his own knowledge that her Majesty

---

[1] B.M. Additional MS. 48109 (Yelverton, 121).
[2] *I.H.R. Bulletin*, xii. 24.

never desired her people's money. He transmitted the Queen's message about monopolies, touched on other points, and then told the Speaker that her Majesty 'saith you have so learnedly and so eloquently defended yourself now, and painfully behaved yourself heretofore, that your labour deserveth double hire and thanks'. Citing 'some sentences of Jerome, &c., of the blessings of a just prince', he 'prayed for her sententiously and briefly, and craved pardon for himself'.[1]

Then followed the ceremony of the royal assent. Forty-three bills were passed, twelve vetoed. None of the vetoed bills was of particular significance, and the notoriety that this Parliament has acquired in our history — with its legend of forty-eight bills quashed — is pure fiction.[2]

Apparently, Elizabeth had intended to speak herself, on the social and public duties of the gentry and of justices, enjoining them to return home and keep hospitality for the relief of the poor, instead of dwelling 'like battelers in London'. 'Each should guard his own quarter, look to musters and armour for provisions, [and] not upon any event shun from his own house for fear'; this, should an invasion occur, as it nearly did in October. 'As preparation was wisdom, so her heart feared nothing, but [she was] assured of victory by God's hand.' However, the speech was not made. Time did not permit. It must have been nearer seven than six o'clock by the time Yelverton and Egerton had concluded their orations and the titles of fifty-five bills had been read, with their appropriate French responses. Parliament was dissolved, and the themes of the Queen's intended speech were declared to the assembled justices and others in the Star Chamber some six weeks later by the Lord Keeper, at the great end-of-term congregation: the close of the London season.[3]

[1] Wilbraham's Journal, *Camden Miscellany*, x. 12; *I.H.R. Bulletin*, xii. 24-5.
[2] B.M. Lansdowne MS. 83, fols. 207-8 (cf. my notes in *Eng. Hist. Rev.* xxxiv. 586-8, xxxvi. 480).
[3] Wilbraham's Journal, *Camden Miscellany*, x. 12-13.

CHAPTER I

INTRODUCTORY

Between the dissolution of the Parliament of 1597-98 and the summoning of Elizabeth's last Parliament there were two domestic events of surpassing significance. The one was the death of Lord Burghley in August 1598, almost forty years since the beginning of the reign. Though we are granted few glimpses of this great statesman's part in parliamentary debates and committee-discussions, no one had been more assiduous in attendance, no one worked as he did in supervising, directing and controlling business. His mind and hand are seen in scores of draft bills and papers; and, whether in the Commons or the Lords, he was and remained the supreme manager. Even in 1597-98, old and perceptibly near his end, he was the dominant member of the whole Parliament. To assess the influence of such a man in the evolution of an institution is not easy, but his calm, moderating temper, even his unheroic nature, combined with utter devotion and a phenomenal capacity for work, were the ideal complement and foil to his sovereign's genius. The successful emergence of the House of Commons through adolescence to maturity needed Burghley's liberal outlook and restraint as well as the ebullience and romantic inspiration of Queen Elizabeth. That neither Queen nor Commons, each highly strung, made shipwreck of their relations, surely owed much to the perfect servant. No one replaced, or could replace, him.

The other event was the rebellion of the Earl of Essex in February 1601: climax of a struggle for power which had disordered and partially paralyzed the Court since Burghley's death. The execution of Essex expelled a fatal poison from the Commonwealth, but it shadowed the land and shook the old unity of spirit and purpose. Robert Cecil was left supreme. It was an uneasy supremacy, quite unlike his father's. There was a lack of cohesion on the front bench of the 1601 Parliament: the aftermath of faction, not the tradition of independence developed in the high Elizabethan period, which departed with that admirable generation of Councillors. Sir William Knollys was uncle to the dead Essex, and, though no upholder of his follies, can hardly have welcomed Cecil's leadership. They clashed in the House of Commons. Raleigh, who had run with Cecil in the anti-Essex pack, had expected to be a Privy Councillor in the new power-grouping. Passed over in the summer of 1601, he wrote to a friend: 'I am left out till the Parliament, they tell me'. Parliament came, and no reward. He too clashed with Cecil in the Commons. Perhaps it is this lack of cohesion that explains why, as in 1597-98 — when the lethargy of old Burghley weakened government direction — the initiative in the Commons was left strikingly to the House itself. If so, then we must ascribe to mere circumstance the final spurt in a long and vitally important development.[1]

Had it not been for the Essex Rebellion, Parliament would probably have been summoned for the beginning of 1601, when in fact it was expected. The last payment of the treble subsidy granted in 1597-98 had been due in October 1600; and be it added, despite everyone's good intentions and the knowledge that tax assessments were scandalously low, the yield repeated the pattern of the reign, with each subsidy producing less than the previous one. Money was more desperately needed than ever. Essex had spent lavishly and failed lamentably to crush rebellion in Ireland; and now Spain had landed a substantial army there, converting the country into a major seat of war and expense. The financial burden was becoming too much even for the prudential management of Queen Elizabeth, and the Tudor state was moving inexorably into bankruptcy. Only the crisis of domestic rebellion could have stayed the calling of Parliament until October 1601. As it was, the Queen had to insist on a short session in order that its first subsidy might be collected without delay.

Parliament was summoned to meet on October 27th. It is symptomatic of the climatic change since 1593 that, whereas the Puritans had once been active in elections, securing that core of determined Members who could set the tone of a Parliament,

---

[1] P.R.O. State Papers, 9/55/10.

SIR WALTER RALEIGH

now there was a new policy, arising out of the faction rivalry of
Essex and Cecil. This was to canalize nominations into politi-
cians' hands; and it was more marked in 1601 than in 1597. Robert
Cecil secured the nomination to at least fourteen, possibly twenty,
possibly more, borough seats. Six of his secretaries and gentlemen-
servants sat in the House. The Lord Keeper had four there
(including the poet, John Donne), and the Lord Treasurer three.
There were very many others, tied by office or service to the
government: more in number, it seems, than in any earlier Parliament. There was also a small but closely knit party of eleven
ecclesiastical officials, ready to repel attack on the Church. Archbishop Whitgift probably nominated half-a-dozen of the Members
of the Parliament and was very much alive to the need for apologists and supporters in the House of Commons. The desire to get
hold of seats for motives no longer confined to the simple and
innocuous one of patronage seems to have extended even to Sir
Walter Raleigh. 'I pray you', he wrote to Sir John Gilbert, 'get
some burgesses if you can, and desire C[hristopher] Harris to
write in my name for as many as he can procure.' All this was not
incompatible with a remarkable show of independence in Parliament. But, combined with the disappearance of organized
Puritanism and the temperament of a new generation, not to
mention the more tolerant policy of the government towards
Catholics, it explains the predominantly secular interest of the
1601 Parliament, which in this and other respects repeated the
character of the previous one.[1]

The proceedings of the new Parliament were reported at
remarkable length by Hayward Townshend, the young lawyer
who had kept a scrapbook in 1597-98. On this occasion he
assiduously wrote a diary during the actual sittings of the House.
He was not the only Member to do so. There once existed a second
diary, kept by William Twysden, which seems to have been a
worthy rival. It has disappeared, and only one or two titbits and an
indication of its length survive to measure our loss.[2] Townshend's
diary has been in print since the seventeenth century. By this very
fact, it has given a false notoriety to the Parliament and distorted
the general picture of the reign.

---

[1] MARGARET K. MORT, 'Personnel of the House of Commons in 1601' (London
Univ. M.A. thesis); State Papers, 9/55/10.
[2] Cf. B.M. Stowe MS. 359, fols. 274-301.

Townshend tells us that on the first day of Parliament many of the Commons, through the blunder of an official, were excluded from the House of Lords, and did not hear Lord Keeper Egerton's oration: an unfortunate beginning. Possibly, Townshend himself was among the disgruntled victims. At any rate, all we get from him is the gist of Egerton's opening speech as Robert Cecil later reported it to the Commons: dull reading. Apparently, the Lord Keeper began with the Queen's desire to dissolve Parliament before Christmas. He then explained the necessity they stood in, and the means to prevent it; the former being the war with Spain, and the latter, treasure. For their work this session he advised the revision of existing laws and the making of no new ones. After that, he expanded on the themes of war and treasure, urging them to be both provident and confident: provident because the enemy was provident, and confident because 'God hath ever, and I hope ever will bless the Queen with successful fortune'. Alluding to the desperate devices employed by the late King Philip II, he remarked: 'I have seen her Majesty wear at her girdle the price of her blood; I mean jewels which have been given to her physicians to have done that unto her which, I hope, God will ever keep from her'.[1]

After returning to their House, the Commons, on the initiative of Sir William Knollys, Comptroller of the Household, elected John Croke, Recorder of London, as their Speaker. When first named, 'Mr. Croke put off his hat, with a kind of strange admiration' — rehearsed, maybe, like his speech — and then, with becoming modesty and appropriate felicity, went through the accustomed drill of a 'disabling speech': 'I find nothing in myself but fear and trembling and quailing under so great a burthen; my heart with amazedness to say unto myself, "Who am I that should go on such a service?" . . . I am plain bred, of a weak understanding and judgment for so great a work, of frail memory. Neither nature hath given nor art hath added unto me those furnitures which might enable me . . . I have been brought up in the plain study and learning and profession of the law . . . I am of a slow and unready speech'. They elected him unanimously.[2]

On October 30th Croke was presented to the Queen, and, after another studiously prepared disabling speech, followed by royal

---

[1] TOWNSHEND, *Historical Collections*, pp. 182-3.
[2] Ibid. p. 174; All Souls Coll. Oxf. MS. 180, fol. 96.

confirmation of his election, delivered his ornate oration. 'Enjoying you,' he told the Queen, 'we enjoy all . . . God hath placed
you by Himself, and, therefore, let the hand of who will, fight
against you, they have not prevailed, they shall not prevail. The
name of the mighty God hath been still your tower.' Thankfulness for what they owed to the Queen was his first theme; and
his Anglican orthodoxy reflected the new tone of these latter
years. She had defended them in true religion, rooting out superstition and sects and schisms of giddy-headed sectaries. She had
maintained them with all clemency and justice in most inward
and comfortable peace, when all their neighbour-countries had
been infested with bloody wars and massacres, blood streaming in
their streets with civil dissensions and foreign invaders. 'Every
one of us sit in safety, in peace and quietness under our own roof,
enjoying comfort of conscience by true religion, and, with our
wives and children, reposing ourselves under the fruition of these
inward and outward blessings, that never people under Heaven
enjoyed greater.' To bring them to such happiness the Queen had
exposed her own sacred and royal person to peril. If not duly
thankful, they might justly fear that God would take these blessings from them and give them to a nation that will produce better
fruit. The sentiment deserves our thought, for one is apt to
forget how precious the immunity from fighting on English soil
must have seemed to neighbours of France and the Netherlands,
and Ireland also.

Croke proceeded to denounce their adversaries: 'that Man of
Sin and Belial or Beast of Rome — for so he is truly called' — who
sent Jesuits, 'or rather Jebusites and priests of Baal', to seduce the
people, 'having holiness in their mouths but wickedness in their
hearts'. Of 'that man of sin and his instruments', he said: 'like the
crawling pieces of a snake cut in sunder, they seek to join together
and become a new snake'. He spoke next of Spain, 'bewitched
with that cup of the whore of Babylon, the firebrand of dissension
through all the parts of Christendom, a nation sometime of
honourable report, but of late years irreligious and intolerable,
swelling to that height of pride that it can neither abide an equal
nor endure a superior'. 'We your people', he assured Elizabeth,
'under the conduct and protection of you, our most gracious
Gideon and the anointed Queen of God after His own heart, will
lay life and living at the stake and all that under God and you we

enjoy, for the safety of your Majesty, defence of our religion and safeguard of our country, the common parent of us all, wherein no man's particular can stand when the public shall be infected.' Genuine and noble sentiment no doubt: yet subsidies continued to yield less and less.[1]

The Speaker closed with his customary petitions for parliamentary privileges, phrasing the most important in these words: 'To permit unto us that freedom of speech in debating of important causes as may be comely and convenient'. In his reply — Townshend is now our authority — the Lord Keeper answered this crucial petition as follows: 'For freedom of speech, her Majesty willingly consenteth thereunto, with this caution: that the time be not spent in idle and vain matters, painting the same out with froth and volubility of words. And her Majesty commandeth that you suffer not any speeches made for contention or contradiction sake, maintained only by tempest of words, whereby the speakers may seem to gain some reputed credit by emboldening themselves to contradiction, and by troubling the House on purpose, with long and vain orations, to hinder the proceedings in matters of greater and more weighty importance'.

We should ponder this reply. There is no indication that the Queen was moderating her right and desire to define the nature of the privilege or relax her discipline of Parliament. Indeed, the Lord Keeper spoke at some length on the privilege of freedom from arrest. Her Majesty, he said, 'ever intendeth to preserve the liberties of the House, and granteth freedom to the meanest follower of the meanest Member of this House. But her Majesty's pleasure is, you shall maintain and keep with you no notorious person, either for life or behaviour: as desperate debtors, who never come abroad, fearing her laws, but at these times; pettifoggers and vipers of the Commonwealth, prowling and common solicitors that set dissension between man and man; and men of like condition to these'. Moreover, the Queen had an injunction for the Speaker: 'She willeth you to have an especial eye and regard not to make new and idle laws and trouble the House with them, but rather look to the abridging and repealing of divers obsolete and superfluous statutes; as also, first to take in hand matters of greatest moment and consequence'.[2]

---

[1] Huntington Library, U.S.A., Ellesmere MS. 2587.
[2] TOWNSHEND, pp. 177-8 (here and elsewhere I have adopted better readings from the text in Stowe MS. 362, fols. 56 seqq.).

No: Queen Elizabeth was not relaxing her discipline. And yet, in granting freedom of speech she made no explicit reference to the Church or the prerogative. The contrast with 1593, and with earlier Parliaments back to 1571 when definition was first forced upon her, is striking. We can only conclude that she anticipated no serious difficulty over the prerogative and was confident that the danger to the Church was past. She believed, as we also sense, that the House of Commons had changed. Volubility, waste and misdirection of time, these were the abuses she expected. Whether she was right or wrong we shall be able to judge later on. Certainly she would have been surprised at the reputation that this Parliament has secured in our history books.

As the Queen passed through the throng of Commons on her way out of the Upper Chamber, she was silent and aloof, depressed there is reason to think, in health and spirit. Few greeted her. Returning to their own House, the Commons were addressed by the Speaker, who repeated her injunction against wasting time in 'frivolous, vain and unnecessary motions'; and then, assuming that the Lord Keeper's adjournment of Parliament for six days applied to both Houses, he omitted the formal reading of a bill. Later that day he was put right on the matter of the adjournment and the House did in fact meet next morning. Many, however, misled by the same error, were then absent, including our diarist. With extraordinary tactlessness, Privy Councillors moved that the absentees be fined. The fine was remitted; but what a series of minor blunders and irritants with which to start a Parliament![1]

[1] D'EWES, pp. 621-2; TOWNSHEND, p. 179; Stowe MS. 359, fol. 275b.

CHAPTER II

MONOPOLIES

WHILE approximately half the Members of this Parliament were newcomers, some 157 of the remainder had sat in 1597-98 and returned with lively memories of the proceedings in that Parliament and of the promise extracted from the Queen to deal with the abuse of monopolies. In the interval she had not altogether ignored her promise. If Francis Bacon can be believed, fifteen or sixteen patents had been repealed on her express command and others exposed to the test of the law in the Court of Common Pleas and the Exchequer. But the pressure of suitors for privileges continued unabated, and the tone of government in these years was not healthy. The sense of restraint, on which public morality depends, was weakening, while the need for money, from whatever source it could be got, was desperate. More new patents seem to have been created than were rescinded. Conscious of what might happen when Parliament met, the Lord Treasurer and Robert Cecil had investigated the problem in the Spring of 1601 and found monopolies very great in number and odious in character. They reported to the Queen, who appointed a commission of four Councillors along with the Lord Chief Justice, instructing them to take action. August came, they had done nothing: though in fairness it should be added that the aftermath of the Essex Rebellion was not conducive to administrative efficiency. At the beginning of that month, the Lord Treasurer wrote to Cecil to remind him of the situation and urge action before Parliament met: 'the sooner we begin, the better'. Again, nothing seems to have been done.[1]

They had been warned, and ought not to have been surprised at what followed in Parliament. The matter was first raised on November 4th when a Member, in 'a very long and good speech', referred to three of last Parliament's bills, including the one on monopolies, and moved that they be reintroduced and read. The Speaker probably averted trouble. A fortnight passed before this lone reforming voice stirred an echo. Then, on November 18th,

---

[1] TOWNSHEND, *Historical Collections*, pp. 232, 238-9; *H.M.C. Hatfield MSS.* xi. 324-5.

a Staffordshire lawyer, a newcomer, revived the subject in a temperate speech, offering a bill with 'a very long title'. Immediately, another lawyer, Mr. Lawrence Hyde rose: 'I would, Mr. Speaker, only move you to have an Act read, containing but twelve lines. It is an exposition of the Common Law touching these kinds of patents, commonly called monopolies'. By proceeding to the reading of another bill, the Speaker hoped once more to stifle the attack; but while they were choosing the committee for this bill, the Lord Keeper's secretary, Gregory Downall, a courageous, not to say rash, gentleman, tried to have Mr. Hyde's bill read. The Speaker interrupted him. He promised to let him speak later; but Cecil whispered in his ear, and in due course he rose, ending the sitting without honouring his promise. Furious at the slight, Downall threatened to complain at the next sitting of the House. It was clear that Chair and Front Bench were determined, if possible, to suppress the subject.[1]

So far the House had shown nothing of its old capacity for opposition. But it was warming up. Two days later there was a clash with the Speaker. He gave the Clerk a bill to read. The House cried out for another: one officially frowned on. 'Some said "Yea", some said "No"; and a great noise there was'. Like an inspired tactician, Mr. Hyde rose: 'To end this controversy', he declared, 'because the time is very short, I would move the House to have a very short bill read, entitled, "An Act for explanation of the Common Law in certain cases of Letters Patent". And all the House cried "I, I, I" '. The monopolies agitation was safely launched.

Mr. Hyde's bill was read, and some enthusiasts wanted it ingrossed at once. In the debate that followed, Mr. Spicer, a Warwick townsman, set the tone in a speech laden with Latin phrases. This, he declared, may be said to be a free assembly and therefore I hope there is free thought and speech. The bill 'may touch the prerogative royal, which, as I learnt the last Parliament, is so transcendent that the eye of the subject may not aspire thereunto . . . I speak not, Mr. Speaker, either repining at her Majesty's prerogative or misliking the reasons of her grants, but out of grief of heart to see the town wherein I serve pestered and continually vexed with the substitutes or vicegerents of these

[1] The following narrative, except where indicated, is constructed from Townshend's diary in *Historical Collections*, with an occasional better reading from Stowe MS. 362, fols. 56-261.

monopolitans'. He gave an account of one 'substitute' or deputy, an obstinate recusant, who had been abusing his powers at Warwick.

Francis Bacon now rose and, after a disdainful allusion to the previous speech, proceeded to defend the prerogative. 'For my own part, I ever allowed of it; and it is such as I hope I shall never see discussed. The Queen, as she is our sovereign, hath both an enlarging and restraining liberty of her prerogative: that is, she hath power by her patents to set at liberty things restrained by statute-law or otherwise, and by her prerogative she may restrain things that are at liberty.' After informing the House of the remedies already effected, he posed the issue that was to trouble this Parliament, as it had done the last; namely, whether they should proceed by way of a bill, thus threatening to limit the prerogative by statute — constitutional violence; or by way of petition, leaving the remedy to be made by the Queen. 'The use hath been ever by petition to humble ourselves unto her Majesty and by petition desire to have our grievances redressed, especially when the remedy toucheth so nigh in point of prerogative. All cannot be done at once, neither was it possible since the last Parliament to repeal all.' Warning them to be careful, he called them to witness that he had discharged his duty to the Queen.

Dr. Bennett, Chancellor in the Diocese of York and Member for the city of York, followed. 'He that will go about to debate her Majesty's prerogative royal', he began, 'had need walk warily.' In the name of his constituency he attacked the monopoly of salt, 'which would walk in the forerank' of abuses. He mentioned other monopolies, including cards, whereat, says our diarist, 'Sir Walter Raleigh blushed', for it was his. Dr. Bennett was for proceeding with the bill, 'mannerly and handsomely'. Such a speech from such a man was disquieting. It was followed by one from the author of the bill, who presented the House with what it loved — a precedent, as old as Edward III's reign. 'Mr. Speaker', he affirmed, 'as I think it no derogation to the omnipotency of God to say He can do ill, so I think it no derogation to the majesty or person of the Queen to say the like.' Both his theology and his political theory must have given many the shudders.

The tide was now running hard and Serjeant Harris, a prerogative man, tried to direct it by assuming that the House wanted the bill to be in the nature of a petition. 'It must then begin with more humility', he added. His manœuvre was seen by Henry Montague — a Northamptonshire gentleman, one of three brothers in the House — who reminded Members that last Parliament they proceeded by way of petition, 'which had no successful effect'. The next two speakers backed up Montague. Francis Moore, a Berkshire lawyer and Member for Reading, was forthright. 'I cannot utter with my tongue or conceive with my heart the great grievances that the town and country for which I serve suffer by some of these monopolies. It bringeth the general profit into a private hand; and the end of all is beggary and bondage to the subject . . . What purpose is it to do anything by Act of Parliament when the Queen will undo the same by her prerogative? Out of the spirit of humility, Mr. Speaker, I do speak it: there is no act of hers that hath been or is more derogatory to her own majesty or more odious to the subject or more dangerous to the Commonwealth than the granting of these monopolies.' Richard Martin, a London lawyer, a wit and a spirited speaker, was even more outspoken. He called monopolists 'these bloodsuckers of the Commonwealth'.

A moderate voice was now heard: from Sir George More of Loseley. He was for proceeding with all humbleness by petition and not bill. Likening the Queen, the patentee, and the subject to head, hand, and foot, he put their case thus: 'the head gives power to the hand, the hand oppresseth the foot, the foot riseth against the head'. 'We know the power of her Majesty cannot be restrained by any Act. Why, therefore, should we thus talk? Admit we should make this statute with a *non obstante* [a clause barring the Crown's right to grant exceptions] yet the Queen may grant a patent with a *non obstante* to cross this *non obstante*.' Robert Wingfield spoke: a man we have already met, who, in spite of his Cecilian connections, was an independent, and, as he confessed, had fallen foul of the prerogative in the last Parliament. He reminded them of the Queen's answer through the Lord Keeper in 1598: 'That she would take care of these monopolies and our griefs should be redressed. If not, she would give us free liberty to proceed in making a law the next Parliament.' 'The wound, Mr. Speaker,' continued Wingfield, 'is still bleeding . . . It was my hap, the last Parliament, to encounter with the word prerogative. But, as then, so now, I do it with all humility.' He was indifferent whether they proceeded by bill or petition.

Sir Walter Raleigh then rose, stung by a reference to tin in Mr. Martin's speech. He spoke so sharply that a 'great silence' fell on the House, only broken by Sir Francis Hastings, who implicitly rebuked him and asked for freedom of speech and tolerance for all. Thereupon, discussion was resumed and Gregory Downall intervened to remind them that petitions had got them nowhere last Parliament. The cries against monopolies, he declared, were never greater or more vehement.

The tone of the debate, if earnest and critical, had on the whole been restrained, and certainly fell short of the passionate, rebellious mood when religion was the issue in earlier Parliaments. The House finished by appointing a very large committee to meet in the Chamber next day, after dinner.

At their meeting, many supernumeraries were probably present. Our diarist, for example, was there, and, though not a member, spoke. Sir Edward Stanhope, a Yorkshire gentleman of eminence and a Councillor in the North, must have stirred the committee by his attack on the salt monopoly and his figures showing the immense rise it had caused in the price of the commodity. He calculated that its abolition might save the ports of Lynn, Boston and Hull £3000 a year. Francis Bacon followed with a vigorous, withering attack on Mr. Hyde's bill, which he described as very injurious and ridiculous. He was not against action: who could be? But he wanted them to petition the Queen. The Solicitor General tried to assuage tempers by telling them that the Queen, in her provident care, had instructed the Attorney General and himself, at the beginning of Hilary Term last, to take speedy action; but the Essex Rebellion had interfered and there had since been no leisure. His excuse was wrecked by Sir Robert Wroth, who pertinently asked, 'Why not before?' 'There was time enough ever since the last Parliament. I speak it, and I speak it boldly: these patents are worse than ever they were'. Why dilly-dally with the slow legal process of *quo warranto*, when the patents could be simply revoked? He read out a list of patents. 'Is not bread there?' interjected the young lawyer, William Hakewill. ' "Bread?" quoth one; "Bread?" quoth another. "This voice seems strange", quoth a third. "No", quoth Mr. Hakewill, "but if order be not taken for these, bread will be there before the next Parliament." '

The diarist, Hayward Townshend, now intervened to try and

bring the committee by way of compromise to a resolution. He proposed that they should send their Speaker to the Queen, humbly requesting two things: the repeal of all monopolies grievous to the subject, and permission to make an Act of Parliament withdrawing such patents from the protection of the prerogative, thus leaving their validity to be tested at the Common Law. The mood of the assembly had evidently become dangerous, for Bacon rose to support Townshend's motion, though he cannot have liked its second string. He made a long speech, concluding with commendation of 'the wise and discreet speech made by the young gentleman, even the youngest of this assembly'. '*Ex ore infantium et lactantium*', he added: 'out of the mouth of babes and sucklings'. Townshend, no doubt, was flattered, but the committee broke up without any decision.

By now, the agitation, begun in a casual way, without any signs of organized preparation, had become consolidated and had probably acquired unofficial management, busy with propaganda both in the House and in the City without. At the next sitting of the full assembly, on Monday, November 23rd, Townshend records that a gentleman, sitting by him, showed him a paper containing the discommodities of divers monopolies: clearly a propaganda sheet, drawn up in imitation of the argumentative briefs circulated by parties interested in private bills. Later that morning, probably through a concerted move, the monopolies bill was again read. There was another debate. Townshend records one speech (by Mr. Spicer) in favour of a petition, another (by the poet, John Davies) advocating the bill. And then Secretary Cecil made an impatient, hectoring, ill-tempered speech. It was a case of a leader, handicapped physically in stature and shape, and not quite sure of himself. Not surprisingly, 'Monsieur de Bossu', who could be afraid that a young lady would shrink from his love because of his deformity,[1] became strident at times in asserting his authority in Parliament; though his ability and capacity were superb and he had the art to be most winning.

Cecil told them that had it not been for the confusion of their committee he would not have spoken. They had failed to deal with the question before them. 'If every man should take leave to speak for the common subject, I am afraid, in these vast

[1] Cf. his letter – of great psychological interest – in B.M. Lansdowne MS. 101, fol. 127.

powers of our minds, we should dispute the project and reformation quite out of doors.' Two things were at issue: the Prince's
power and the freedom of Englishmen. He respected the latter,
but was a servant of the Queen and would wish his tongue cut out
rather than speak or consent to anything abridging her prerogative. He quoted Bracton: 'Let no one dare to dispute our prerogative'. The mere rumour that the House called her Majesty's
prerogative in question would lead to popular disorder.[1] 'For
my own part, I like not these courses . . . And you, Mr. Speaker,
should perform the charge her Majesty gave unto you at the
beginning of this Parliament, not to receive bills of this nature.'
'I had rather', he went on, 'all the patents were burnt than her
Majesty should lose the hearts of so many subjects, as is pretended
she will.' He then showed that he was not a friend of burdensome monopolies, and moved for a commitment, not of the bill
but of their mode of procedure.

It needed courage to defy Cecil in his schoolmasterly mood, but
Henry Montague rose to the occasion.[2] 'Mr. Speaker', he began,
'I am loth to speak what I know lest perhaps I should displease.'
The House had been drawn from the real question, which was
the content of their bill or petition. It did not touch the prerogative, 'because there is no rule of prerogative but the laws of the
land'. The judges had pronounced 'that law and prerogative are
one and the same thing; that a grant to the hurt of the subject is
void; that in a penal law the Queen may dispense with the penalty
but not alter the law, which cannot be but by Act of Parliament'.
The solution of their problem was simple: deny patentees any
remedy against infringement of their patents except that which
the laws of the Realm gave them.[3] The impulsive Richard
Martin backed up this rebel, and the House loudly applauded the
two of them. A committee was set up to meet that afternoon, its
terms of reference drawn from Cecil's speech — out of deference —
and from Montague's — out of conviction.

Townshend, the diarist, again attended the committee-meeting
and notes that a gentleman showed him a list of monopolies with
the names of their holders: another instance of propaganda at
work. The proceedings started with an extravagant proposal by

---

[1] This point is from B.M. Stowe MS. 359, fol. 284b.

[2] I identify him as Henry, who was one of the committee (cf. the manuscript
D'Ewes Journals in B.M. Harleian MS. 75, fol. 234b).

[3] This from Stowe MS. 359, fols. 284-5.

the poet, John Davies: they should 'do generously and bravely like Parliament-men', send for the patent-holders, cancel their patents before their faces, arraign them at the bar, and send them to the Tower. The whole company laughed; but Richard Martin, the lawyer — who, incidentally, had had a cudgel broken over his head by Davies four to five years before — restored sobriety with a long and moderate speech, ending with an apology for his poetic friend, whose zeal, as he put it, had misled his reason. Martin, and presumably most of the Members, were now reconciled to petitioning the Queen, and the suggestion was made that they should compile a list of the most grievous monopolies to present to her, if needed. One suspects that this was a diversionary move from the government side, for Cecil was ready with a paper containing a list of all the patents granted since 1574. The reading of it started the company off again, and while they were arguing Sir Edward Hoby left the Chamber. Outside the door — notes Twysden — he 'found a multitude of people . . . who said they were Commonwealth men and desired' the House 'to take compassion of their griefs, they being spoiled, imprisoned and robbed by monopolists'. Turning back, Hoby informed the committee and was told to bid them depart. Sir William Knollys also went out to appease them. 'In the meantime', adds Twysden, 'Mr. Secretary Cecil rose in a great passion and said, "What meaneth this? Shall we suffer it?"' No one supported him and the committee soon broke up. Cecil, however, managed to get them to agree that the leading demonstrators should be reported to the House next day. So far as we know, it was mere face-saving: nothing was done.[1]

Twysden tells us that the episode 'was thought only a device and no such thing indeed': presumably a courtier's trick to discredit extremists. The odds, however, are that the opposition, now well organized, had taken their cue from earlier Puritan tactics and marshalled their supporters in the City to crowd the Parliament Lobby and stairs. Cecil's anger and alarm were justified. The precedent was significant, perhaps sinister.

Next morning there was trouble in the House. 'Some private murmur' was circulating. Perhaps opposition leaders had been led by Cecil's mood to think that Parliament would be prematurely dissolved. At any rate, when the Speaker ordered the

[1] Also see ibid. fol. 285.

Clerk to read the subsidy bill 'the House cried it away and called for the report of the monopolies; and so the subsidy was deferred'. The classical strategy of linking redress of grievances with supply — irresistible against a poverty-stricken government — had been openly adopted. [1]

In the debate that followed, Herbert Croft, Member for Herefordshire, criticized yesterday's committee — in effect, Cecil and the government party — for departing from their instructions. This brought Cecil to his feet, who, we are told, 'spoke with great heat':[2] 'The duty I owe and the zeal to extinguish monopolies makes me to speak now and to satisfy their opinions that think there shall be no redress of these monopolies'. He admonished them: 'Order is attended with these two handmaids — gravity and zeal, but zeal with discretion. I have been, though unworthy, a Member of this House in six or seven Parliaments, yet never did I see the House in so great confusion. I believe there was never in any Parliament a more tender point handled than the liberty of the subject and the prerogative royal of the Prince. What an indignity then is it to the Prince, and injury to the subject, that when any is discussing this point he should be cried and coughed down? This is more fit for a grammar school than a Court of Parliament.' Cecil went on to describe the divergent proposals made in committee, pouring ridicule on some of them. He bade the House wait until the committee had come to a decision.

The committee met again that afternoon, November 24th. For reasons which they did not divulge, the Privy-Councillor Members did not arrive until about 5 o'clock; but the sitting ended with the committee ready to report to the House. [3]

The moment had come for the Queen to act, and her sense of timing, if deliberate, was superb. She had sent for the Speaker while the committee deliberated: that explained why the Privy Councillors were late. Next morning, 'every man marvelling why the Speaker stood up', he made his report. Considering how the House had deferred the reading of the subsidy bill, we must acknowledge that the first part of Elizabeth's message was masterly diplomacy: she thanked them in effulgent terms for their 'speedy resolution in making so hasty and free a subsidy'. Neither tongue nor heart, declared the Speaker, could express or conceive the zeal of her affection in speaking of their loyalty. 'It pleased her

---

[1] Stowe MS. 359, fol. 285b.   [2] Ibid. fol. 286.   [3] Ibid.

Majesty to say unto me that if she had a hundred tongues she could not express our hearty good wills; and further she said, that as she had ever held our good most dear, so the last day of our or her life should witness it; and that the least of her subjects was not grieved and herself not touched.' Partly through her Councillors and partly by petitions delivered to her, both going to her Chapel and also walking abroad — an interesting pointer to the publicity given to this parliamentary agitation — 'she understood that divers patents . . . were grievous to her subjects and that the substitutes of the patentees had used great oppression'. She had 'never assented to grant anything that was *malum in se*', and would take present order for reformation of anything evil. 'I cannot express unto you', continued the Speaker, 'the apparent indignation of her Majesty towards these abuses. She said her kingly prerogative (for so she termed it) was tender, and therefore desireth us not to speak or doubt of her careful reformation.' She explained the reason for the delay, now, however, promising that some monopolies 'should be presently repealed, some suspended, and none put in execution but such as should first have a trial according to the law for the good of her people'. 'God make us thankful', concluded the Speaker, 'and send her long to reign amongst us.'

At the invitation of the Speaker and the instance of his colleagues, Cecil rose to confirm the message. It was a happy occasion. With inspired statesmanship, the Queen had decided to concede the Commons all they could desire, and that instantly. Cecil was to expound her policy, and — able and seductive speaker that he was, when spiritually at ease — his mind soared to the magnanimity of the concession. It was a long and thrilling speech, dissolving all the ill temper of the last three weeks. After telling them of the drastic action to be taken, he continued: 'You will perhaps judge this to be a tale to serve the time. But I would have all men know thus much: that it is no jesting with a Court of Parliament, neither dares any man — for mine own part, I dare not — so much abuse all the subjects of this Kingdom in a matter of this consequence and importance'. He then announced that there was to be a Proclamation throughout the Realm, and he itemized the monopolies to be revoked. 'Every man shall have salt as cheap as he can buy it or make it.' For those with cold stomachs, there would be the same benefit for *aqua vitae*; for weak stomachs, vinegar and alegar. 'Train-oil shall go the same way; oil of blubber shall march in equal rank.' The sowing of woad, restrained by proclamation, would be free, though the Queen prayed 'that when she cometh on progress to see you in your countries, she be not driven out of your towns' by the stench. Starch, too, was doomed, and those who wished could 'go sprucely in their ruffs'. As fetter after fetter was thus lightheartedly cast off, Members' hearts must have leapt with joy and gratitude. Nor can they have begrudged a parenthetic remark, that 'the Queen means not to be swept out of her prerogative'. Cecil hastily added: 'I say it shall be suspended if the law doth not warrant it'.

As though Councillors had kept their mistress in the dark — or more likely, because he needed an excuse to condemn organized propaganda — Cecil professed himself troubled as to how the Queen had learnt of their grievances. 'I fear we are not secret among ourselves. Then must I needs give you this for a future caution: that whatsoever is subject to a public exposition cannot be good. Why! Parliament-matters are ordinarily talked of in the streets. I have heard myself, being in my coach, these words spoken aloud: "God prosper those that further the overthrow of these monopolies. God send the prerogative touch not our liberty".' 'The time', he added, 'was never more apt to disorder.' He thought that those responsible for the publicity 'would be glad that all sovereignty were converted into popularity . . . The world is apt to slander most especially the ministers of government'. Cecil had some excuse for his fears. It was less than a year since the Earl of Essex, after courting the London populace, had made his bid for their support in rebellion. And the people still mourned their dead hero, loathed the name of Cecil. It was a world of shadows, even for Gloriana.

Cecil then made a handsome apology for yesterday's speech, in which he had likened the House to a grammar school. He reminded them that Demosthenes had been even ruder to the Athenians. 'If any man in this House', he concluded, 'speak wisely, we do him great wrong to interrupt him. If foolishly, let us hear him out: we shall have the more cause to tax him.'

It was a brilliant speech, in excellent taste and most artfully framed. It brought the critics to their feet in rapturous loyalty. 'If a sentence of everlasting happiness had been pronounced unto me', declared the rebellious Mr. Wingfield, 'it could not have made me show more outward joy than now I do'. 'And here, as I think', noted our diarist, 'he wept.' They were an emotional lot, these Elizabethan gentlemen. The Queen knew it and fostered it.

The House decided to send their Speaker to the Queen, accompanied by about a dozen Members, to express their most humble and hearty thanks. But next day Cecil brought a message from her: 'You can give me no more thanks for that which I have promised, than I can and will give you . . . for that which you have already performed'. Its meaning, like the words of the Delphic oracle, was not clear.[1] Some thought her thanks were for the subsidy; and indeed — probably shamefacedly — they gave the subsidy bill its first reading that morning. Cecil went on to say that the Queen would not grant them audience until she had fulfilled her promise by issuing the proclamation. 'At that time she will be well pleased to receive your loves with thanks and return unto you her best favours.'

Another day passed; the opposition grew restless. On November 27th, Mr. Downall, the Lord Keeper's undisciplined secretary, voiced their fears. He moved two motions: 'first, that that gracious message which had been sent from her Majesty might be written in the books of record of this House, being worthy to be written in gold'; and secondly — here was the rub — that Councillors would move her to speed, lest delay alter her intention. John Davies, our impulsive poet, rose, but Cecil intervened, and, 'with a sad, settled countenance',[2] both reproached and appeased them. 'It is no matter of toy for a prince to notify in public a matter of this weight. Though the idol of a monopoly be a great monster, yet after two or three days I doubt not but you shall see him dismembered.' He told them that the Queen had yesterday given order for the proclamation to be drafted, and that he, Cecil, had had it with him in the House that morning. A few more speeches restored their former bliss, and the Speaker closed the sitting with a prayerful encomium of the Queen, to which the whole House responded 'Amen'.

Next morning, Saturday, November 28th, the proclamation was in print, a copy in every man's hands: a skilful touch. It did all that could be seriously desired: declared void the principal patents complained of in Parliament; authorized anyone grieved or wronged by other patents to seek ordinary remedy by the

---

[1] Cf. Stowe MS. 359, fol. 287.   [2] Ibid. fol. 288.

laws of the Realm; and — the crucial point — rescinded, and for the future forbade, all letters of assistance from the Privy Council in support of patentees. As promised, it set people free to sow woad, with a proviso to save London and the royal palaces from its offensive smell. There was a clause warning subjects of the power and validity of the prerogative royal and the severe punishment awaiting offenders. It saved the principle from the wreck of the substance.[1]

That morning, Cecil announced that on Monday afternoon the Queen would receive their deputation — 'a convenient number of forty, fifty, or a hundred, they shall all be welcome'. The House proceeded to name them, but anon 'the lower end of the House' — the small fry — cried 'All, All, All'. On the Monday morning, November 30th, Sir William Knollys brought word that the Queen was pleased to hear the acceptable news that they all wanted to see and thank her. Her only reason for suggesting a stint had been the size of the audience room. But she was glad there was such sympathy betwixt her and them and was well pleased that they should all come, without restraint or limit. It is rather an anticlimax to be told that the number who did attend was some seven or eight score.

The audience took place in the Council Chamber at Whitehall at about 3 p.m. on November 30th. Speaker Croke was but meanly endowed with eloquence, yet his heart spoke the abundant gratitude of the Commons: 'They come not as one of ten to give thanks, and the rest to depart unthankful; but they come, all in all, and these for all, to be thankful . . . for gracious favours bestowed of your gracious mere motion and of late published by your Majesty's most royal proclamation'. For this and for all else, 'they give glory first unto God, that hath in mercy towards them placed so gracious and benign a prince over them, praying to the same God to grant them continuance of your so blessed and happy government over them, even to the end of the world'.[2]

'Mr. Speaker', began Elizabeth, in reply, 'We have heard your declaration and perceive your care of our estate, by falling into a consideration of a grateful acknowledgement of such benefits as you have received; and that your coming is to present thanks to us, which I accept with no less joy than your loves can have desire to offer such a present.

---

[1] PRICE, *English Patents of Monopoly*, pp. 156-9.   [2] Harleian MS. 787, fol. 127.

'I do assure you there is no prince that loves his subjects better, or whose love can countervail our love. There is no jewel, be it of never so rich a price, which I set before this jewel: I mean your love. For I do esteem it more than any treasure or riches; for that we know how to prize, but love and thanks I count unvaluable. And, though God hath raised me high, yet this I count the glory of my crown, that I have reigned with your loves. This makes me that I do not so much rejoice that God hath made me to be a Queen, as to be a Queen over so thankful a people. Therefore, I have cause to wish nothing more than to content the subject; and that is a duty which I owe. Neither do I desire to live longer days than I may see your prosperity; and that is my only desire. And as I am that person that still yet under God hath delivered you, so I trust, by the almighty power of God, that I shall be His instrument to preserve you from every peril, dishonour, shame, tyranny and oppression; partly by means of your intended helps [the subsidies they were granting] which we take very acceptably, because it manifesteth the largeness of your good loves and loyalties unto your sovereign.

'Of myself I must say this: I never was any greedy, scraping grasper, nor a strait, fast-holding Prince, nor yet a waster. My heart was never set on any worldly goods, but only for my subjects' good. What you bestow on me, I will not hoard it up, but receive it to bestow on you again. Yea, mine own properties I account yours, to be expended for your good; and your eyes shall see the bestowing of all for your good. Therefore, render unto them, I beseech you, Mr. Speaker, such thanks as you imagine my heart yieldeth, but my tongue cannot express.'

Hitherto, the Commons had been kneeling, but now her Majesty said: 'Mr. Speaker, I would wish you and the rest to stand up, for I shall yet trouble you with longer speech'. Thereupon they all stood up, and she continued:

'Mr. Speaker, you give me thanks, but I doubt me I have a greater cause to give you thanks than you me, and I charge you to thank them of the Lower House from me. For, had I not received a knowledge from you, I might have fallen into the lapse of an error, only for lack of true information.

'Since I was Queen, yet did I never put my pen to any grant but that, upon pretext and semblance made unto me, it was both good and beneficial to the subject in general, though a private profit to some of my ancient servants who had deserved well at my hands. But the contrary being found by experience, I am exceedingly beholding to such subjects as would move the same at the first. And I am not so simple to suppose, but that there be some of the Lower House whom these grievances never touched: and for them, I think they spake out of zeal to their countries, and not out of spleen or malevolent affection as being parties grieved; and I take it exceeding gratefully from them, because it gives us to know that no respects or interest had moved them, other than the minds they have to suffer no diminution of our honour and our subjects' love unto us. The zeal of which affection, tending to ease my people and knit their hearts unto me, I embrace with a princely care, for above all earthly treasure I esteem my people's love, more than which I desire not to merit.

'That my grants should be grievous to my people and oppressions privileged under colour of our patents, our kingly dignity shall not suffer it. Yea, when I heard it, I could give no rest unto my thoughts until I had reformed it. Shall they, think you, escape unpunished that have thus oppressed you, and have been respectless of their duty, and regardless of our honour? No, I assure you, Mr. Speaker, were it not more for conscience' sake than for any glory or increase of love that I desire, these errors, troubles, vexations and oppressions, done by these varlets and lewd persons, not worthy the name of subjects, should not escape without condign punishment. But I perceive they dealt with me like physicians who, ministering a drug, make it more acceptable by giving it a good aromatical savour, or when they give pills do gild them all over.

'I have ever used to set the Last-Judgment Day before mine eyes, and so to rule as I shall be judged to answer before a higher Judge, to whose judgment seat I do appeal, that never thought was cherished in my heart that tended not unto my people's good. And now, if my kingly bounties have been abused, and my grants turned to the hurt of my people, contrary to my will and meaning, and if any in authority under me have neglected or perverted what I have committed to them, I hope God will not lay their culps and offences to my charge; who, though there were danger in repealing our grants, yet what danger would I not rather incur for your good, than I would suffer them still to continue?

'I know the title of a King is a glorious title; but assure yourself that the shining glory of princely authority hath not so dazzled the eyes of our understanding, but that we well know and remember that we also are to yield an account of our actions before the great Judge. To be a King and wear a crown is a thing more glorious to them that see it, than it is pleasant to them that bear it. For myself, I was never so much enticed with the glorious name of a King or royal authority of a Queen, as delighted that God hath made me His instrument to maintain His truth and glory, and to defend this Kingdom (as I said) from peril, dishonour, tyranny and oppression.

'There will never Queen sit in my seat with more zeal to my country, care for my subjects, and that will sooner with willingness venture her life for your good and safety, than myself. For it is my desire to live nor reign no longer than my life and reign shall be for your good. And though you have had and may have many princes more mighty and wise sitting in this seat, yet you never had nor shall have any that will be more careful and loving.

'Shall I ascribe anything to myself and my sexly weakness? I were not worthy to live then; and, of all, most unworthy of the mercies I have had from God, who hath given me a heart that yet never feared any foreign or home enemy. And I speak it to give God the praise, as a testimony before you, and not to attribute anything to myself. For I, oh Lord! what am I, whom practices and perils past should not fear? Or what can I do? ["These words", says our diarist, "she spake with a great emphasis"]. That I should speak for any glory, God forbid.

'This, Mr. Speaker, I pray you deliver unto the House, to whom heartily recommend me. And so I commit you all to your best fortunes and further counsels. And I pray you, Mr. Comptroller, Mr. Secretary, and you of my Council, that before these gentlemen go into their countries, you bring them all to kiss my hand.'[1]

This mellow speech, spoken in the Queen's sixty-ninth year and the forty-fourth of her reign, and surely inspired as much by the heart as the head, was to become known to posterity as 'The Golden Speech of Queen Elizabeth', being printed time and again

---

[1] TOWNSHEND, *Historical Collections*, pp. 263-6. My text is from the manuscript version in Stowe MS. 362, fols. 169-72, with an occasional reading from the printed text.

in the course of the seventeenth and eighteenth centuries, at crises in the nation's history. Curiously enough, the Queen very nearly deprived herself of this posthumous tribute to her fame, for she was responsible — or so we may confidently conjecture — for a version of it put out by the royal printer in 1601. And that version deservedly sank from memory under the leaden weight of its euphuistic artifice and obscurity.

The story is an interesting one, and concerns us intimately in the choice of our text. From a private letter of December 13th we learn that the Queen's 'gallant speech' was not to be had at any ordinary or tavern in London — a remark suggestive of how previous speeches got into circulation — but that the Queen herself had given a copy to Henry Savile, Provost of Eton. However, next day she sent a groom to his house forbidding him to show it to anyone and on no account to copy it.[1] Presumably, she had by then decided to have the speech printed and wanted to titivate the text. Later that month it appeared in print,[2] purporting, however, to be 'taken verbatim in writing by A.B. as near as he could possibly set it down'. As in 1586 when printing her speeches about Mary Queen of Scots, so now, the Queen, with commendable propriety, did not wish to assume responsibility for a propagandist tract; equally, she would permit no text other than her own to be made public. On this occasion, however, either 'A.B.' must have been pure fiction, or — if the only M.P. with these initials, Anthony Blagrave, did in fact report her speech — Elizabeth must have discarded his text when revising it. That the printed text of 1601 is entirely the Queen's composition, and that it cannot be a recension of a 'verbatim' report, no one need doubt.[3]

Four versions of the speech survive.[4] Evidently, Elizabeth spoke freely, without reading. In all probability, she had prepared a draft beforehand, to shape her thoughts; and we may guess that this was the text she gave to Savile and that it approximated to the short 1601 printed version. Alternatively, it is just

---

[1] *Beaumont Papers*, ed. W. D. Macray (Roxburghe Club), p. 10 (checked with the original MS.).

[2] Carleton to Chamberlain, December 29th, S.P. Dom. Eliz. 283/48.

[3] The printed tract is in S.P. Dom. Eliz. 282/67; a manuscript copy in Lansdowne MS. 94, fol. 123.

[4] The 1601 printed text; the later printed text, included in the *Harleian Miscellany* and *Somers Tracts*; Townshend's, in *Historical Collections*; and an anonymous report by someone present, in Harleian MS. 787, fols. 127-8.

possible that she spoke altogether extempore, without troubling to write a preliminary draft. In that case, there may really have been a 'verbatim' report by A.B., and it may have been the version known as 'The Golden Speech', rediscovered and printed after Elizabeth's death, and possibly derived from Henry Savile's copy. Townshend also reported the speech, in almost the same words. His is the version quoted above, and it is probably the nearest we can get to this historic occasion, without risking the dubious experiment of a conflated text.

Another reporter adds agreeably to the scene by referring to the many 'gestures of honourable and princely demeanour' used by the Queen: 'As when the Speaker spake any effectual or moving speech from the Commons to her Majesty, she rose up and bowed herself. As also, in her own speech, when the Commons, apprehending any extraordinary words of favour from her, did any reverence to her Majesty, she likewise rose up and bowed herself.' An 'etc.' leaves the rest to our imagination. A treasured memory it must have been for those seven or eight score gentlemen, who were soon to have another sovereign and look back nostalgically to the spacious days of Gloriana.[1]

[1] Harleian MS. 787, fol. 128b.

CHAPTER III

RELIGION

As we begin our account of the religious issue in this Parliament, we need to recall the past. In 1584-85 both Houses of Parliament had poured their blessings on a bill for the stricter observance of the Sabbath, and the Queen had been compelled to use her veto. Later, in 1589, there was the same enthusiasm in the House of Commons for a bill against pluralities, and on this occasion the Queen had intervened to stop its progress in the Upper House. Bills on the same two subjects were before the House of Commons in 1601. Nothing could illustrate the changed mood of a new generation more convincingly than the story of their vicissitudes.

Who was responsible for the latest attempt at reform, we do not know. Our diarist notes that the pluralities bill was drawn by Robert Eyre of Lincoln's Inn, who was not a Member of Parliament, and the odds are that the initiative came from outside: probably, as Anglican apologists hinted, from adherents of the old Puritan Movement. Indeed, there was another bill, whose title might have come straight out of early Puritan manifestoes: a bill for 'the putting down and abolishing of certain idle courts, kept every three weeks by archdeacons and their officials and commissaries and registers'. These were the courts that touched every Tom, Dick and Harry in the land, and that their betters resented when summoned before them. To mangle the archdeacon's authority was to strike at the root of ecclesiastical discipline. Our diarist notes the reading of this impudent bill on November 16th, but it can have received no substantial support in the House, for we hear no more of it. Authority evidently found no difficulty in putting it to sleep.[1]

The main effort to deal with religious shortcomings started in the first few days of the session, with a bill for the better keeping of the Sabbath. Its contents we do not know. It may simply have followed the lines of the one vetoed by the Queen in 1585, or may, in addition, have incorporated provisions to enforce attendance at church. It got through its committee stage without

[1] TOWNSHEND, *Historical Collections*, p. 217.

serious challenge; perhaps, also, without enthusiasm. Our diarist was not much interested, and all he records is an amusing sally, during the third-reading debate, from a young lawyer, Edward Glascock, of Gray's Inn; one in whom wit and cynicism exceeded discretion. There was a clause declaring all contracts made on a Sunday in fairs or markets utterly void, and the goods forfeit to the Queen's use. 'If a man', asked Glascock, 'take a wife on the Sunday in a fair or open market', would this be void, 'and she and the goods forfeited to the Queen's use? for this is a contract'. All the House laughed. The bill was sent back to the committee. Surely, not as a result of Glascock's quibble; but if there were provisions about attendance at church, then we might guess that the opposition had marshalled itself, and the House wanted the bill divided into two.[1]

At any rate, two bills were subsequently brought into the House, one of which was entitled, 'An Act prohibiting fairs and markets to be holden on the Sunday'. That, and that alone — without the other sabbatarian frills of 1584-85 — is what it did; enjoining that fairs and markets, held by charter or prescription on a Sunday should be transferred to the Monday. The penalties were a £10 fine for each offence and forfeiture of the goods. This new bill — probably adopting the wording of the original one — showed an emphatic preference for the word 'Sabbath': a clue to the 'precise' mentality of the author. But, when it in turn was sent to a committee, 'Sabbath' was everywhere deleted and 'Sunday' substituted: a significant sign. Another interesting change in committee was the addition of a proviso exempting the annual free fair at Great Yarmouth from the ban imposed by the bill. The 'burgesses of Yarmouth' — *eo nomine* — had been placed on that committee, and these influential gentlemen had evidently persuaded their fellow-Members that godliness was not good for Yarmouth. A strange new wind to be blowing in the Elizabethan House of Commons!

The bill duly passed the House on December 11th: our diarist remained so little interested that we can say no more. In the Lords, it was read twice and committed: then, oblivion. Either the old virtue had gone out of the Upper House, or the Queen stopped further progress: perhaps the latter, perhaps both.[2]

[1] Ibid. pp. 185, 189, 194; D'EWES, pp. 624, 626, 628.
[2] S.P. Dom. Eliz. 283/12; TOWNSHEND, pp. 227, 285, 313; D'EWES, pp. 643, 668; *L.J.* ii. 248, 251.

The other of our two bills aroused much discussion and has quite a history. Its title was, 'against wilful absence from divine service upon the Sunday': a cause which, in earlier years, when patriotism and religious zeal were synonymous, would have been assured of overwhelming support. That, indeed, is why its story is so well worth telling. It was brought into the House on November 13th by Sir Robert Wroth, the last of the Marian exiles there; a gentleman now sixty-one years old, who had sat in every Parliament since 1563. And its other chief supporter was Sir Francis Hastings, a slightly younger man, who had been taught by that famous Puritan don, Dr. Laurence Humphrey of Magdalen College, Oxford. Hastings had missed only one Parliament since 1571, and, like Wroth, preserved the qualities of the past.

The purpose of the bill, as our diarist phrased it, was the better gathering of the shilling fine imposed by the Act of Uniformity for absence from church. Although, since the severe anti-Catholic Act of 1581, wealthy and persistent recusants were liable to the swingeing penalty of a monthly levy of £20, the shilling fine still remained the appropriate instrument for dealing with poor or intermittent offenders. Under the Act of Uniformity, churchwardens had been saddled with the task of levying it. If, however, they failed in their duty, or if offenders refused to pay, the only method of enforcement, other than by ecclesiastical discipline, was indictment before the justices of assize: a process, as the authors of our bill stated, much too cumbersome for the nature of the offence and the penalty.

Although, from time to time, in their visitation articles, bishops and archdeacons enquired whether churchwardens were carrying out their duty, while, in this very year, 1601, Bancroft included such a question in his articles for the London diocese, quoting the relevant section of the Act of Uniformity,[1] it seems clear, from the debates on our bill, that by 1601 the shilling fine had fallen into general disuse. This is not surprising. It needed a very different mood from that of late-Elizabethan years — a mood of national alarm or of aggressive religious ardour — to keep churchwardens up to the mark in a most invidious duty. If they could not be relied upon, the obvious remedy was to call in the Justice of the Peace, an official whom the Puritans were always trying to

---

[1] *Eng. Hist. Rev.* xxxiii. 517-28; W. P. M. KENNEDY, *Elizabethan Episcopal Administration* (Alcuin Club), passim and iii. 335.

intrude into the machinery of church discipline. Consequently, the authors of our bill, attributing the non-enforcement of the fine to the 'chargeful and long' process of indictment at the assizes, repealed this provision of the Act of Uniformity, substituting presentment before the Justices of the Peace in their Quarter Sessions, or, alternatively, the evidence of witnesses before two or three Justices out of session, who, on conviction, were to use the churchwardens to levy the fine.[1]

The bill also dealt with a problem that had troubled Burghley and others in the past: women offenders. It laid down that every husband was to pay for a wife's absence from church, every master for a servant's. Our diarist tells us, incidentally, that a clause, limiting its duration to the Queen's reign, was 'greatly whispered at and observed in the House'. Everyone was conscious of Time's approaching stroke and uncertain of the shape of things to come.[2]

The bill caused much dispute at its second reading on November 18th; and at this stage criticism was centred on its most vulnerable provision — the one concerning wives and servants, which was generally disliked, presumably because many Members, in these degenerate days, feared that they or their friends would be caught. Said Anthony Dyott, Recorder of Tamworth, 'Every man can tame a shrew but he that hath her'. Perhaps, he added, she will not come to church: that is no reason why the husband should be punished. The bill was committed.

Returning it after amendment, Sir Francis Darcy, one of the Earl of Essex's knights, but now a dependant of Cecil's, spoke on behalf of the committee: 'Mr. Speaker, methought I heard a strange voice at the committing of this bill. I hope, after these amendments, it will have better success in the passage than that voice did presage, but more especially of us who are the mouths of the most grave and religious commons of this realm. By this bill every husband must pay for the wilful absence of his wife, children above twelve years of age, and servants.'

In the 1580s such an appeal would have found instant response in most hearts, but now it failed to quieten the critics. Sir Edward Hoby, alluding to the anti-Catholic statute of 1581, which imposed a penalty of £20 a month on recusants, wondered whether there was a secret purpose, by implication from this new bill, to

[1] S.P. Dom. Eliz. 283/16. This is the text of the later bill, but I assume that in these items it was the same as the first.
[2] TOWNSHEND, p. 210.

extend that ruinous fine to wives. Sir George More of Loseley reassured him, while Francis Moore, the distinguished lawyer, explained that it was intended to deal with negligent, though well-addicted subjects, not with ill-affected Catholics, adding: 'For my own part, I do so much desire the furtherance and good success of this bill, or any of the like nature, that he that doth not the like, I would he had neither heart to think nor tongue to speak'. Neither speech carried conviction. Richard Martin, our lawyer acquaintance, desired a plain answer as to whether anyone paying £20 a month under the Act of 1581 would now also have to pay 1s. 0d. a week. To this Sir William Wray, a Lord Chief Justice's son, answered that the committee's intention was not to impose a double penalty on wealthy Catholics, but merely to fine poor offenders.

Dr. Bennett, the Yorkshire ecclesiastical Chancellor, sensing that the bill was in danger, rose, reluctantly, to add his persuasion. The bill, he declared, merely gave life to the Act of Uniformity, which, because of its cumbersome procedure, 'never almost' had execution. 'A law without execution is like a bell without a clapper.' 'There are, Mr. Speaker,' he added, 'in the county in which I am, at the least twelve or thirteen hundred recusants, most of which this law . . . would constrain to come to the church: I mean only those of the poorer sort . . . Punishment will make them do that by constraint which they ought to do in regard of religion.' A west-country sea-captain then posed a question that must have worried Members, and two further critics implanted more doubts. One of these — also a west-countryman — started a promising line of attack by criticizing the bill for saddling Justices of the Peace with imposing the fines. 'They have already enough to do; and, therefore, no reason they should meddle in ecclesiastical causes.' He objected to giving them such power over their neighbours. The second critic feared that churchwardens might succumb to bribery and corruption. What, he asked, if they secretly keep a list, and instead of gathering a shilling for the poor, perhaps take fourpence for themselves and dispense with the rest?

There was 'long dispute', and in the end a division. It went against the bill by three votes — 140 to 137; a comment on the poorish attendance, but also on the lack of religious ardour.[1]

---

[1] TOWNSHEND, pp. 224, 227-9.

The bill had been dashed. That should have ended the matter for this Parliament; but through the pertinacity of devout men and the indulgence — one must suppose — of the Speaker, Members were given another chance when, a week later, Sir Francis Hastings introduced a new bill. This, he explained, met four objections taken to the old one: the husband would not pay for his wife, nor the father for the son, nor the master for his servant, while recusants paying the £20 penalty of the Act of 1581 would be exempt from its operation. 'He that seeketh to please all', he declared, 'shall please none; and he that seeketh to please all in God's cause shall not please a good conscience.' He went on to say that he knew some parishes where half the people were perverted by Jesuits and seminarists: the poorer and meaner sort of people, whom a shilling tax, if levied, would more pinch than any law yet devised. His bill was given a first reading.

The issue had now become very simple: whether the House — rid of its fear about wives and servants — wanted to impart new vitality to the shilling fine and thus make use of the one device capable, through its relative moderation, of getting the maximum number of people to church on Sunday. In high-Elizabethan days there would have been no doubt whatever of the answer. But now there were critics, and they were quite unabashed. At the second-reading debate on December 2nd, they sought for a new focus of attack and found it in the use of Justices of the Peace to enforce the fine.

It so happened that the day before, in a bill against swearing, the young Mr. Glascock had delivered a violent attack on Justices. Probably he thought to establish a reputation as a wit in a major, well-prepared speech. 'We use so much lenity in our law', he declared, 'that as good make no law. For we give a penalty, and to be taken upon conviction before a Justice of Peace. Here's wise stuff! First, mark what a Justice of Peace is, and we shall easily find a gap in our law. A Justice of Peace is a living creature that for half-a-dozen of chickens will dispense with a whole dozen of penal statutes . . . These be the Basket-Justices, of whom the tale may be verified of a Justice that I know, to whom one of his poor neighbours said, "Sir, I am very highly rated in the subsidy-book. I beseech you to help me". To whom he answered, "I know you not". "Not me, Sir?" quoth the countryman, "Why, your worship had my team and my oxen such a day, and I have been ever at your worship's service." "Have you so?'' quoth the Justice. "I never remember I had any such matter; no, not a sheep's tail.'' So, unless you offer sacrifices to these idol-justices of sheep and oxen, they know you not. If a warrant come from the Lords of the Council to levy 100 men, he will levy 200; and what with chopping in and crossing out he'll gain £100 by the bargain. Nay, if he be to send forth a warrant upon a man's request . . . he will write you a warrant himself, and you must put 2s. in his pocket as his clerk's fee, when — God knows — he keeps none but two or three hinds for his better maintenance. Why! we have had here five bills: of swearing, going to church, good ale, drunkenness, etc. This is as good to them as if you had given them a subsidy and two fifteenths.'[1]

Glascock's speech was surely in mind when Mr. Roger Owen, a Shropshire lawyer, son of a judge, and also a young man — younger than Glascock — got up to attack Sir Francis Hastings's bill. He criticized it on two grounds, one being its use of Justices of the Peace. 'They already are loaden with a number of penal statutes; yea, a whole alphabet.' A Justice's house will be like a Quarter Sessions with the multitude of these complaints. Owen also thought the bill an infringement of Magna Carta, since, instead of trial *per pares*, its procedure involved two witnesses before a Justice. 'Therefore', he concluded, 'for my part, away with the bill.'

Sir Francis Hastings rose angrily: the anger of age for flippant, irresponsible youth. 'I never in my life heard Justices of Peace taxed before in this sort.' For aught I know, they are 'men of quality, honesty, experience and justice'. He asked Owen two questions: whether he wanted any penalty at all inflicted on absentees from church; and whether this bill or the Act of Uniformity offered the easier way. 'If he deny the first, I know his scope; if the second, no man but himself will deny it; and to speak so in both is neither gravely, religiously, nor rightly spoken . . . For God's, the Queen's, and our country's sake', I beseech that the bill may be committed.

There were staid men anxious to support Sir Francis. Sir Carew Reynolds, another of the Earl of Essex's knights, but a royal official, ten years older than Owen and a Member of the 1593 Parliament, when godliness still prevailed, expounded the purposes

[1] TOWNSHEND, pp. 267-8.

for which the Sabbath was ordained: among others, 'to meditate on the omnipotency of God'. He reminded Members of the strict character of both law and practice in Scotland, and recalled visitations of divine wrath in France and in England on those who profaned that day. Sir George More, a man close on fifty who had sat in Parliament since 1584, employed an anatomical argument. The tongue, he asserted, 'is tied deep in the stomach with certain strings which reach to the heart . . . This I know to be true because I find it in the Word of Truth: "Out of the abundance of the heart, the mouth speaketh" '. Suggesting that Owen's attack on Justices proceeded from the corruption of his heart, he left him to Solomon and to silence and went on, with fitting gravity, to argue the case for compelling attendance at church. 'Amongst many laws which we have, we have none for constraint of God's service', since the Act of Uniformity is not enforced.

Then rose another critic of Justices: John Bond, also a west-countryman; a classical scholar, once a schoolmaster, but turned from that drudgery to be a physician. Appropriately, he pointed his argument with Latin quotations. 'Who, almost, are not grieved at the luxuriant authority of Justices of Peace?' he asked. Magistrates are men, 'and men have always attending on them two ministers, *libido et iracundia*' — desire and passion. 'Men of this nature do subjugate the freeborn subject.' He went on: 'The poor commonalty, whose strength and quietness is the strength and quietness of us all, he only shall be punished, he vexed, for will any think that a Justice of Peace will contest with as good a man as himself? No; this age is too wise.' Asking whether it stood with policy, when they were imposing exception-ally heavy taxation, to bring this greater fear on the poorer sort, he continued: 'In the gracious speech [that on monopolies] which her Majesty lately delivered unto us, she used this phrase — "That she desired to be beloved of her subjects". It was a wise speech of a wise Prince'.

Sir William Knollys, the Comptroller, intervened, with the stern mien of authority. Expressing his sorrow that, after forty-three years under her Majesty's happy government, they should now dispute, or even commit, such a bill, he exclaimed: 'I wonder that any voice durst be so bold or desperate to cry "Away with this bill" '. As for accusing Justices of the Peace — ministers to her Majesty, without whom the Commonwealth cannot be — 'if this boldness go on, they will accuse judges, and lastly the seat of Justice itself . . . When her Majesty shall have understanding hereof, it will be no contentment unto her and a scandal unto us all'.

The wretched Glascock, who had begun all the mud-slinging, rose to make an apology; but such was his incorrigible facility of wit and phrase that he heaped Ossa upon Pelion. 'Mr. Glascock', interrupted the Speaker, 'you speak from the matter and purpose, and this that you have spoken you must justify.'

Members were becoming uneasy. They wanted to commit the bill and hush the matter up. Sir Robert Wroth made a personal attack on Glascock and moved that he should answer for his words at the bar; but 'all cried, "No, No, No!"' Another Member repeated Wroth's motion. It was diverted and the bill at last committed.

Then, once more, the storm broke, on Bond as well as Glascock. 'What shall be done against these two general slanderers of Justices of the Peace?' demanded one Member. Another wanted both culprits set at the bar. Glascock injected a word of explanation, mercifully brief. Thereupon Sir Francis Hastings returned to the attack, fearful, he declared, of the scandal being blazed abroad. He concentrated on Bond: 'He that sits over against me (pointing at Mr. Bond) is my countryman'. 'The speech', he concluded, 'was insolent . . . I wish it might be answered there (pointing to the bar).' But the House, notes our diarist, 'said "No, No, No!"' Bond tried to appease his critics; Mr. Martin, the lawyer, lent him countenance by wishing perdition on oppressors of the people; and then the House turned to other business.[1]

It was Sir Francis Hastings who, on December 5th, reported the committee's doings. Their amendments reflected the criticisms made in the House and reduced the innovations to the barest possible. In fact, all the bill now proposed to do was merely to add to the Act of Uniformity a process before the Justices of the Peace in their Quarter Sessions for absence from church on Sundays, even omitting the Holy Days included in the 1559 Act.[2] It was a very pale reflection of the original measure. Nevertheless, ominous doubts and opposition showed themselves.[3]

---

[1] TOWNSHEND, pp. 254, 273-8.
[2] So I read the amendments in the text of the bill, S.P. Dom. Eliz. 283/16.
[3] D'EWES, p. 668; TOWNSHEND, p. 287; S.P. Dom. Eliz. 283/2.

The third reading took place in the afternoon of December 12th and provoked a debate that occupied almost all that sitting. Mr. Bond had recovered his self-confidence, probably because he had been assured of substantial support. He smote the bill with classical learning, practical argument, and open scorn. It was 'altogether needless', he declared. Every evil in a state does not call for a law: indeed, Aristotle and Demosthenes both condemned legal innovation. The bill would be an infamy to our ministers, for 'our adversaries may say, "This is the fruit of your labour, to have preached away your audience out of the church" '. Among practical objections, he instanced the breach of unity and peace in a parish if the churchwardens delated some offenders and not others; also the cumbersome and costly nature of the procedure. 'So', he concluded, 'because this bill is slanderous to the clergy, scandalous to the state, repugnant to charity, and *crambe recocta* [a stale rehash], I humbly pray it may receive the like entertainment the former bill had, namely, to be rejected.' It was a studied, venomous speech, meant to kill.

Sir Francis Hastings denounced Bond as a man 'far from religion'. Two days before, in a speech on another bill, this young reprobate had justified himself against insinuations by Hastings, saying, 'I am a Devonshire man, and I speak plainly from the heart of him that hates Popery and defies Puritanism'.[1] Hastings now denied that he had called him a Papist, adding that if not a Papist, Bond was certainly not a Puritan, for of the four sorts of Puritans — according to the division he had learnt from his Oxford tutor, Dr. Humphrey — one was a Catholic, the second a Papist, the third a Brownist; and 'the fourth and last sort are your evangelical Puritans, who rely wholly upon the scriptures as upon a sure ground. And of these, I would we had many more than we now have'. Evangelical Puritans! Bond was far indeed from that exalted state. And so were very many of this unfanatical House. Sir Francis must have thought nostalgically of Parliaments a decade and more ago, when Mildmay and Sir Francis Knollys sat on the front bench and Thomas Norton and Peter Wentworth spoke for the opposition.

More Members joined in the debate: 'Mr. Glascock, Mr. Spicer, and divers others'. The two named we can count with the

---

[1] TOWNSHEND, p. 306.

opposition. Townshend does not record their speeches: 'It grew very dark', he says; 'I could not write them'.

At length, the bill was put to the question, and the voices were so equal that the majority could not be discerned. Thereupon, Sir Robert Wroth tried to save the measure by producing a proviso, already ingrossed on parchment, which made a last concession, exempting anyone who attended church eight times in the year and said divine service twice every Sunday and Holy Day in his house, with his whole family. The proviso, Townshend tells us, was utterly misliked, but at the division a number of opponents voted for it, in order to ensure that the bill would afterwards be rejected. The proviso was carried by 126 to 85.

Once again the bill came to the question, and the opposition renewed the debate. Sir Walter Raleigh made one of those fresh, unconventional speeches of his, which reveal the rational bent of his mind and the individualism of his nature. He showed, says Townshend, 'that all the churchwardens of every shire must come to the [Quarter] Sessions to give information to the grand jury. Say, then, there be 120 parishes in a shire: there must now come extraordinarily 240 churchwardens. And say but two in a parish offend in a quarter of a year: that makes 480 persons, with the offenders, to appear. What great multitudes this will bring together; what quarrelling and danger may happen, besides giving authority to a mean churchwarden!' The newly added proviso, he pointed out, was 'a plain toleration from coming to church'. The parson would be unable to constrain any if they had service at home. What a new, a cold, albeit a bracing world of thought we enter with such a speech!

Raleigh also was a Devonshire man; and we are reminded of an earlier occasion this session, when our diarist tells us that 'the Devonshire men made a faction' against a bill and overthrew it.[1]

The bill had now come to issue. Thrice the question for passing was put. No majority could be discerned, and they proceeded to a division. The 'Ayes' went forth and numbered 105. The 'Noes' sat: they were 106. The bill was lost by one vote. Sir Edward Hoby, an 'Aye', tried to claim that the Speaker was entitled to vote. Raleigh and the Speaker himself denied that. Thereupon, Robert Bowyer, the Lord Treasurer's secretary, revealed that

[1] TOWNSHEND, p. 298.

one Member, who had wanted to vote for the bill, had been pulled back and kept in his seat by another (Matthew Dale). Cecil demanded that the offender be named, but Raleigh exclaimed: 'Why! If it please you, it is a small matter to pull one by the sleeve, for so have I done myself oftentimes'.

Raleigh's shocking frankness caused 'a great loud speech and stir'. Then, 'after some silence', Sir William Knollys, senior Councillor, rose. 'We have often been troubled by physicians (meaning Mr. Bond), and they have been spoken against. He [Bond] troubled us with Aristotle and other books. If he had stayed there, it had been well. But I think we had need of physicians to stay our heads and cool our heats and humours, not fitting a Court of Parliament; for it is a most intolerable disorder.' Knollys condemned the voting incident. 'And for the other gentleman (meaning Sir Walter Raleigh) that said he had often done the like, I think he may be ashamed of it.' Then he suggested that Dale should answer for his offence at the bar, but he so phrased his words that the House thought he meant Raleigh.

Robert Cecil now spoke. 'Little do you know how for disorder the Parliament is taxed: I am sorry I cannot say slandered. I had hoped, as this Parliament began gravely and with judgment, so we should have ended modestly and at least with discretion. I protest, I have a libel in my pocket against the proceedings of this Parliament.' He condemned Mr. Dale's offence, and hoped that a man, 'whose voice may be drawn either forwards or backwards by the sleeve, like a dog in a string', would never again be a member of the House. The offence, however, was not so great as to demand an answer at the bar; 'neither' — he added, here becoming openly rude to his colleague, Knollys — 'do I know why any of this House should speak so imperiously as to have a gentleman of his place and quality (pointing at Sir Walter Raleigh) called to the bar.' The voting, Cecil concluded, was 106 to 105; 'and though I am sorry to say it, yet I must needs confess, lost it is, and farewell it.' 'So,' adds our diarist, Townshend, 'the House rose, confusedly, it being after six a clock.'

Townshend tells us that, as one Member was forcibly kept in his seat at the division, so another was forcibly dragged out. The majority, therefore, was correct. It was a Saturday afternoon when this notable sitting occurred. Next day, Sunday, Townshend made an entry in his diary that has an artistic appropriateness: 'This day a great eclipse about noon; the sun was thus darkened':[1]

The bill against pluralities — the strange history of which we must now relate — was described as a bill for redressing certain inconveniences in Henry VIII's pluralities statute of 1529, and was given a first reading on November 12th. Suggestive of Puritan authorship, it seems to have been even more drastic than the one passed by the Commons in 1589, for whereas that measure permitted existing pluralists to continue in their benefices, this apparently allowed no exception, temporary or otherwise, to the principle of one benefice, one minister — if the benefice was worth £8 or upwards in the Queen's books. It achieved its purpose by repealing those provisoes in the Henrician statute that allowed dispensations in the interests of the Crown, the Church, the nobility and learning. The bill can hardly be said to have acquired further justification since 1589, especially as Queen and Convocation, in the Canons of 1597, had recently legislated on the subject. In fact, it was visionary, impracticable and irresponsible in its rigidity, while the attempt to discipline the Church through parliamentary legislation violated both prerogative and constitution, though the form it assumed of amending a previous statute was a clever camouflage of that fact.[2]

When the bill came before the Commons for its second reading on November 16th, the wisdom of Whitgift and others in using their borough patronage to secure a solid, if small Church party in the House manifested itself. Dr. Daniel Dunne, a civilian lawyer, Dean of Arches, and an episcopal nominee for the borough of Taunton, opened the attack and was followed by Dr. Thomas Crompton, another civilian, also an ecclesiastical official, and also an episcopal nominee — for the borough of Whitchurch. Crompton seems to have regarded the bill as an exhibition of anti-clerical prejudice. Let the laity, he retorted, be first deprived of

---

[1] TOWNSHEND pp. 218, 317-22. The drawing is from the text in B.M. Harleian MS. 2283.

[2] The contents of the bill can be inferred from various attacks on it, especially in St. Paul's Cathedral Add. MS. vii. 26.

plurality of offices and then deal with clerical pluralism. The laity had taken impropriations from the spirituality; marriage was now permitted to the clergy and hospitality demanded from them. In these circumstances, one benefice of small size was insufficient.

To this assault, Sir George More replied by praising the bill as 'tending to a good and religious end . . . Such is the iniquity of this age that for want of a good law of this nature many souls do not only languish, but perish everlastingly, for want of spiritual food.' He asked for a committal. A Mr. Locke, supporting Sir George, told Dr. Crompton that it was for the Church to set an example: 'If they begin first, we shall follow in avoiding of pluralities.'

From this dangerous class recrimination another civilian lawyer and ecclesiastical official, Dr. Francis James, tried to steer the debate by arguing that it was poverty, rather than pluralities, that brought corruption into the Church. If ministers were deprived of a competent living, there would be less, not more preaching, for 'the best wits' will refuse to study divinity. He cited, as defenders of pluralities had done in 1589, the number of parish churches in England and the small proportion — 600 out of 8,800 odd — which afforded a competent living.

Dr. Crompton had riled Members with his attack on the laity. A Common Lawyer, Mr. David Waterhouse, an official in the Queen's Bench, reverting to that speech, pointed out that by the Common Law an officer forfeited his office for non-attendance. So it should be with ministers. He ended with 'this caution . . . That commonly the most ignorant divines of this land are double-beneficed'.

Serjeant Harris now spoke, introducing his favourite line of argument into the opposition. 'If we proceed to determine of this bill, Mr. Speaker, we shall not only infringe a custom which we have ever observed, namely, to meddle with no matter which toucheth her Majesty's prerogative, but also procure her great displeasure. Admit we should determine this matter; yet her Majesty may grant toleration with a *non obstante*.' He reminded them of the bill's fate before, and of the Queen's warning through the Lord Keeper not to meddle in cases of this nature, so nearly touching her prerogative.

The debate continued. 'An old Doctor of the Civil Law spake, but because he was too long and spake too low, the House hawked and spat and kept a great coil [rumpus] to make him make an end.' It is possible that a document we possess is his brief for the speech. If so, we may attribute the barracking to his arrogance, as well as the other faults. Arrogance like the following: 'the barbarous author of this bill'; 'if such fellows . . .'; 'such an absurd, unreasonable and irreligious bill'; 'neither let the author escape censure, that thus audaciously propoundeth matters prejudicial to her Majesty's prerogative'.[1]

Sir Francis Hastings, always magnanimous on such occasions, rose to rebuke his colleagues: 'My Masters, I utterly mislike this strange kind of course in the House. It is the ancient usage that every man here should speak his conscience, and that both freely and with attention; yea, though he speak never so absurdly'. This said, he proceeded, 'out of the conscience of a Christian, loyalty of a subject, and heart of an Englishman', to answer the Doctor's speech. 'If then, by the distributing and severing of benefices to divers learned men, the Word may be the better distributed unto the people and preached (as, God be thanked, it hath been these forty-three years under her Majesty's happy government, the period of whose days I beseech the Almighty may be prolonged) I see no reason, Mr. Speaker, why we should doubt of the goodness of this bill, or make any question of the committing thereof.'

The perky Mr. Roger Owen — anti-clerical, not puritan — then made a fighting speech against the Doctors. He answered one who had cited the authority of a Canon 'under the great seal of England': 'I say, under favour, that they of the clergy, and not we of the laity, are bound thereby'.

After this, the Speaker put the question for commitment, and the bill was referred to a huge committee, consisting of all Privy Councillors, all the learned counsel, and about fifty others.[2]

Several features emerge from this debate: the marshalled strength and truculence of the ecclesiastical opposition; the utter silence — at least in our diarist's report — of Privy Councillors; and the anti-clerical, rather than puritan mentality of the bill's supporters. The first is confirmed by the number of papers that have come down to us, setting out detailed criticism of the bill: briefs for speeches and propaganda. The Church party, under

---

[1] St. Paul's Add. MS. vii. 26.
[2] TOWNSHEND, pp. 209, 218-20; D'EWES, p. 641 (for committee list, see Harleian MS. 75, fol. 222, Stowe MS. 359, fol. 282).

Whitgift's leadership, appears to have organized itself for the contest as efficiently as Puritans once did for their battles.[1]

But Whitgift did not confine himself to party action in Parliament. He called on the Queen for assistance, as he had done in the past. We have a draft of his letter, dated November 19th: 'There is a bill read in the Nether House of Parliament, tending . . . to the undoing of the best learned ministers in this Church of England, and . . . to the derogating of your Majesty's prerogative and power in causes ecclesiastical . . . It goeth to my very heart to think that in this time, when there is least cause and wherein there are more learned men placed in the Church . . . than in any time past, or in any other particular Church known to us, such attempt should be made.' It had so worried the hearts of the better sort of clergy, added Whitgift, that he would have been sorry to have lived to see it, if he had not been assured of the Queen's dislike of such great innovations, and her goodness to her poor clergy. He reminded her that, whereas it was now in her power through the Court of Faculties to regulate pluralities as she saw cause, 'if this bill should pass you shall abridge yourself of that authority and power'. 'The King of Kings bless and preserve your Majesty long and long, to the benefit of His Church and to the comfort of all . . . faithful and loving subjects.' He sent the Queen 'some few notes of [the] absurdities of the bill', and also, it seems, a petition from Convocation against it.[2]

In the Commons, the bill came back from its committee, replaced by a new one. Fortunately, we have its text, and now at last are on firm ground in measuring the shift of sentiment between past and present. In 1589 — as initially in this Parliament — the plan had been to strip Henry VIII's pluralities Act of its provisoes and compel the clergy to conform to the main clause of that Act, which forbade licences for more than one benefice, if the living already held was valued at £8 and over. In 1589 the Commons had been overwhelmingly in favour of this restriction. Now, however, in their new bill, the committee — an exceptionally large one — had raised the limit from £8 to £20

---

[1] I believe that the following papers are concerned with this bill: St. Paul's Add. MS. iv. 138 (also in S.P. Dom. Eliz. 223/15); St. Paul's Add. MS. vii. 8 (29), (33); ibid. vii. 26, 27; B.M. Lansdowne MS. 42, fol. 211 (printed under wrong date in Strype, *Whitgift*, i. 380-1); ibid. 396, fols. 57, 66 (and Inner Temple, Petyt MS. 538/52, fols. 31b, 36b-37); B.M. Additional MS. 32092, fol. 98; B.M. Cotton MS. Cleopatra F. II, fol. 24b (printed Strype, *Whitgift*, i. 533-4).

[2] St. Paul's Add. MS. vii. 8 (33); S.P. Dom. Eliz. 223/15.

(indeed, to 40 marks in the case of a vicarage). Not only that. They left the provisoes of the Henrician Act — which it had been the main purpose of the authors of the original bill to repeal — unrepealed and still operative. Had it been passed, this bill — though still carrying the title, 'against pluralities' — would actually have increased, not abolished pluralities. What a tribute to the Whitgiftian phalanx in House and committee! What a comment on the decline of Puritanism! Sir Francis Hastings, Sir George More, Sir Anthony Cope, Humphrey Winch were on the committee. What did these puritan-minded Members say? Alas, our diarist was not interested.[1]

The new bill was given a first reading on November 23rd. After that, we hear no more of it. No longer anybody's friend, there is just a possibility that the House allowed it to fall into 'an everlasting sleep'. But, remembering Whitgift's letter to the Queen and her usual reaction, the more likely explanation is that she intervened to stop its further progress, either by open message or private order to the Speaker. For, though the new bill turned the tables on the radicals, Elizabeth could not afford to let her prerogative be regulated by Act of Parliament. From the silence of our diarist we can at least infer that her prohibition, if used and known, caused no protest. Gone, indeed, were those heroic days through which we have accompanied our Elizabethan House of Commons.[2]

[1] S.P. Dom. Eliz. 282/59.   [2] TOWNSHEND, p. 243; D'EWES, p. 650.

CHAPTER IV

THE SUBSIDY AND OTHER TOPICS

In his opening speech to this Parliament the Lord Keeper had dwelt on the financial burdens of the Queen and her urgent need of money, particularly to resist the Spaniards in Ireland. Reporting the speech to the Commons, on November 3rd, Sir Robert Cecil added his own reflections, thus, in effect, making a speech for supply, similar to those that Sir Walter Mildmay had made in the past. The King of Spain, he said, 'hath put an army into Ireland of four thousand soldiers, under the conduct of a valiant and hardy captain who chooseth, rather than to return to his own country without any famous enterprise, to live and die in this service. These four thousand are three parts natural Spaniards, and of his best expert soldiers except them of the Low Countries.' Cecil emphasized the seriousness of the situation. In the Low Countries, should Ostend fall, English trade would be quite dissolved. In Ireland, the intention is 'to tear her Majesty's subjects from her, for I may say she hath no Catholic obedient subjects there', since she stands excommunicated by force of two Papal bulls. 'We have there an army, and nothing but an army; fed, even, out of England.' The Queen, said Cecil, 'selleth her land to defend us. She supporteth all her neighbour princes to gain their amity and establish our long peace: not these five, or seven, or ten years, but forty-three years, for all our prosperities. I hope I shall not see her funeral, upon which may be written, *Hic solum restat victrix orientis*; and I pray God I may not. What we freely give unto her, s' ᵎ living bestows it to our good, and dying doubtless will leave ᵎ for our profit.'[1]

Later that morninᵎ, an impressive committee was set up to consider 'the greateᵎ ᵎ matters' to be handled this Parliament: in effect, to consider supply. It met at 2 p.m. on Saturday, November 7th. Our diarist was present, among the supernumeraries — so many of them that the company, as Cecil later reported, was 'little inferior' to the whole House.

We may pause awhile to recapture the scene. Entering the

[1] TOWNSHEND, *Historical Collections*, pp. 183-5.

Chamber — presumably, a little late — Sir Edward Hoby found a great crowd, and looked round for a seat for himself. Sir Walter Raleigh beckoned him to come 'near the Chair', but when he arrived, there was no room. We can imagine his embarrassment. In the sulks, he retreated and sat by the door: no fit place for one of his station. Later, when Raleigh was speaking — sitting, as was customary at committees — Hoby vented his spleen by crying out twice or thrice, 'Stand up!': or, as Townshend reports the incident, 'Speak out! You should speak standing, that the House might hear you.' 'Sir Walter Raleigh', says Twysden, 'brake off his speech and, with a countenance full of disdain,' muttered: 'It is said to the contrary, I would have beleft you better in a forenoon.'

It looks as if Hoby continued being a nuisance, for Cecil afterwards interrupted his own speech to say: 'If any that sit next the door be desirous to sit next the Chair to give his opinion, I will not only give him my place but thank him to take my charge. We that sit here (for my part) take your favours out of courtesy, not out of duty.' In the end, Hoby recovered himself, asked pardon, and added that he was indeed unable to hear.[1]

We have had occasion, already, to comment on the lack of official initiative in this Parliament. It is noticeable at our committee, and it was deliberate. From Twysden's lost diary, we learn that when the committee met, they 'sat silent a good while', and 'one . . . said softly to the Council, that he thought they did expect some direction from them': that is to say, the company awaited their lead. 'Have they not tongues as well as ears?' came the answer.[2]

It was the unbashful free-lance, Sir Walter Raleigh, who broke silence, reminding Members that at the last Parliament three subsidies had been granted, 'upon fear that the Spaniards were coming'. Now they were come; and the Queen had sold her jewels and her land, 'sparing even out of her own purse and apparel for our sakes'. Great loans from her subjects remained unpaid. He wished that they might not do less than they had done before and that also they might contribute bountifully to her Majesty's necessities, according to their estates. In other words, he was suggesting three subsidies, supplemented by a

[1] B.M. Stowe MS. 359, fols. 278b, 279; TOWNSHEND, pp. 198-9.
[2] Stowe MS. 359, fol. 278b.

SIR EDWARD HOBY

benevolence, hoping, no doubt — as Members had hoped in
1589 when one subsidy became two, and in 1593 when two became
three — to avoid a harmful precedent for future taxation. And
though in the end, under conciliar and other guidance, the committee decided against innovation, acquiescing in both the name
and form of a subsidy for the additional grant, rather than a
benevolence, Cecil, when reporting its conclusions to the full
House at the next sitting, distinguished the extra subsidy from the
others. It was referred to as the 'fourth subsidy', though it was to
be levied first: at one payment, in the following February. 'The
first three subsidies' were to follow, each paid in two instalments
a year, commencing in June 1602. Be it added that this illogical
distinction, useful enough in debate, was not incorporated in the
ultimate wording of the Act.

Raleigh had started one contentious argument. The next
speaker introduced another. He was William Wiseman, an
Essex lawyer, who described himself as 'a rural and country man',
out of his own element. He wanted to ease an exceptional burden
of taxation on smaller men by reducing the subsidy from 4s. to
2s. 8d. in the pound on lands assessed at or under £3. Sir George
More agreed with him. Sir Robert Wroth — a generous, public-
spirited man — went further, suggesting that the special subsidy
fall only on four-pound lands and over, while Sir Francis Hastings,
after advancing a new suggestion, finally adopted the same proposal. Sir Francis remarked that 'he knew some poor people pawn
their pots and pans to pay the subsidy'. After two other Members
had spoken along similar lines, Raleigh seems to have intervened
to stem the flow of novelties with some practical reflections.

This was the moment that Robert Cecil chose to make his
speech: very different from the days of Mildmay and Hatton,
when government leaders took their place at the head and not in
the middle of the column. The Spaniards, said Cecil, were en-
trenched in Ireland: 'it is time to open our coffers'. The Queen
needed £300,000 before Easter, and it was simply a question as
to how this should be raised. Even if the Spaniard were expelled
from Ireland at less charge, was anyone so foolish as to think that
would be the end of the danger? 'If we had been of that mind
when he had that great overthrow of his Invincible Navy in anno
1588, we had been destined to perdition.' Cecil contrasted the
yield of the last subsidy with the far greater expenditure incurred

by the Queen. 'Thus', he went on, 'we refer the matter to your judicial consideration.' Though our diarist reports him as declining to give a lead to the committee — 'the wisdom of the land' — another account of the proceedings suggests that he resisted Raleigh and the rest, advocating a speedy, whole subsidy on conventional lines: which in fact was ultimately agreed to.

Playing second fiddle on what should have been his special occasion as Chancellor of the Exchequer, Sir John Fortescue, that mediocre man, followed. He asked for a grant of four subsidies, pointing his speech with a story about the Grand Turk, who when he conquered Constantinople, 'found therein three hundred millions of gold. Which, being told him: "If they", said he, "had bestowed but three millions in defence of their city, I could never have gotten it" '.

In spite of these two official speeches, the desire to ease the small man and raise more money from the wealthy persisted. Raleigh, for example, spoke again, and now wanted to spare the three-pound man, while others suggested that 'four-pound men should give double, and the rest, upward, should be higher cessed'. The Comptroller, Sir William Knollys, and Secretary Herbert were used to resist these aberrations. Herbert commented that if the meaner taxpayers were spared, two-thirds of the contribution would be lost. It was an effective criticism, but a damning reflection on the prevalent system of taxation, with its scandalous assessments. Of course, the 'three-pound men' included many who were under-assessed, but it was the rich who got off lightly and the poor who were squeezed — 'almost *secundum sanguinem*', as Cecil put it. The committee sat for four hours.

At the next meeting of the House, Cecil, in a happy speech, reported the committee's proceedings, as also their differences, not over the size of the grant, but over its form and incidence. He was glad that three-pound men were not to be exempted. 'Neither pots nor pans, nor dish nor spoon, should be spared when danger is at our elbows . . . I do wish the King of Spain might know how willing we are to sell all in defence of God's religion, our Prince and country. I have read, when Hannibal resolved to sack Rome, he . . . never feared or doubted of his enterprise till word was brought him that the maidens, ladies and women of Rome sold their ear-rings, jewels, and all their necessaries to maintain wars against him.'

The resolutions were then put to the House, 'and all said "Yea",
and not one "No" '. Sir Robert Wroth wanted the fourth, the
additional subsidy made into a separate bill, with an appropriate
preamble, to prevent it becoming a precedent. His motion was
resisted. Others gave voice to their fear that now the subsidy
was granted — 'the Alpha and Omega of this Parliament' — the
session might be ended before their bills were passed. Bringing
the talk back into focus, Francis Bacon repeated 'the sum of what
was done yesterday', commending the decision to tax the poor as
well as the rich, for 'it was *dulcis tractus pari iugo*' — a pleasant
course to go in equal yoke. His false and priggish sentiment
stung Sir Walter Raleigh. 'And for the motion that was last
made, *dulcis tractus pari iugo*: call you this *par iugum* [an equal yoke],'
Raleigh scornfully asked, 'when a poor man pays as much as the
rich?' Peradventure his estate is no better, or but little better,
than he is assessed at, while our estates are £30 or £40 in the
Queen's books — not the hundredth part of our wealth. 'It is
neither *dulcis* nor *par*.' As a verbal portrait in miniature of two
supremely famous men, how revealing this incident is!

Raleigh seems to have dealt as witheringly with Cecil's smug
argument about the moral effect on the Spaniard of knowing that
Englishmen sold their pots and pans to pay the subsidy. The
latter rose to answer 'the gentleman on my left hand'. After
correcting Raleigh's interpretation of his speech, Cecil declared
that he did not believe anyone would have to sell his pots and
pans. Thereupon, 'all the House cried, "No, No, No"; as much
as to say, no man did so'.

The debate straggled on. Sir Arthur Gorges — Gentleman
Pensioner, man of action, poet, friend of Spenser and Raleigh —
suggested that Justices of the Peace should be assessed at £20 of
land: the statutory qualification needed for that office. Few, he
remarked, are assessed at above £8 or £10. Our diarist tells us
that Mr. Secretary Cecil noted this 'in his tables', but we can be
confident that the note had no effect: such anomalies were bed-
ded deep in the social and administrative structure of Elizabethan
England.

And now came an intervention from a die-hard, prerogative
man, Serjeant Hele. 'Mr. Speaker', he said, 'I marvel much
that the House will stand upon granting of a subsidy, or the time
of payment, when all we have is her Majesty's, and she may law-

fully, at her pleasure, take it from us. Yea, she hath as much right
to all our lands and goods as to any revenue of the Crown.' It
was too much for the House. They all 'hemmed and laughed and
talked'. 'Well!', said Hele, 'all your hemming shall not put me
out of countenance.' The Speaker intervened to rebuke Members,
and the doughty Serjeant proceeded; but 'when he had spoken
a little while, the House hemmed again, and he sat down'. Hele
had cited precedents to prove his obnoxious theory, and now Sidney Montague of the Middle Temple rose to refute them. 'If all the
preambles of the subsidies were looked upon', said Montague, 'he
should find that it was of free gift; and although her Majesty
requireth this at our hand, yet it is in us to give, not in her to exact
of duty. And for the precedents, there be none such.'

This aftermath of debate, at the fag-end of the morning, had
broken out, irregularly, in the course of appointing committee-
members. To stop the flow and release Members for dinner, the
Speaker hastily nominated the rest of the committee himself.[1]

As already noted, the House held up the reading of the subsidy
bill to ensure time for their agitation over monopolies. It finally
passed on December 5th, when 'all cried "Aye, Aye, Aye", and
not one "No" '; and, as a further token of unanimity, they decided
to carry the bill up to the Lords, 'with all the House and not by
the Privy Council alone, for the more honour thereof': another
tribute to Queen Elizabeth's Golden Speech.[2]

In the early days of the session, perhaps because concerted
leadership of the old type — official and unofficial — was lacking,
Members seem to have been susceptible to snap judgments and
irresponsible action. On November 4th, for example, a bill to
prevent bishops from leasing their lands in remainder till within
three years of a former lease expiring — a salutary measure, it
might be thought — came up for a second reading. Apparently,
it had been one of the anti-clerical bills of 1597-98. Mr. John
Boys, Member for Canterbury, steward to the Archbishop and himself 'farmer to a bishop' — avowedly an interested party — rose to
oppose it. He demonstrated that it would impoverish bishops:
but then, that was its obvious purpose. Under the influence of
this one man's speech, the House permitted the question for committal to be put immediately; 'and all said "No", not one "Yea" '.

---

[1] TOWNSHEND, pp. 197-200, 202-5; Hatfield MS. 89, fols. 82-3 (*Cal.* xi. 484-5).
[2] TOWNSHEND, pp. 286-7.

The bill was thus summarily rejected. In times past, it would have evoked stout backing from puritan and anti-clerical speakers.

The same day, a bill was read 'touching sowing of hemp'. Sir Walter Raleigh, whose championship of individual freedom blows as a refreshing breeze through so much paternalistic regulation, spoke against it. 'For my part', he said, 'I do not like this constraining of men to manure or use their grounds at our wills; but rather, let every man use his ground to that which it is most fit for, and therein use his own discretion.' He proceeded to illustrate the stupid and harmful consequences of rigidity. Thereupon, 'all the House bade "Away with the bill!"' The government, however, appears to have wanted it, and therefore it was twice put to the question and to a division. In spite of a speech from the Comptroller, it was 'absolutely rejected'.

Next day, Francis Bacon, officious as ever, animadverted on such incidents. 'We have turned out divers bills without disputation; and for a House of gravity and wisdom, as this is, to bandy bills like balls and to be silent, as if nobody were of counsel with the Commonwealth, is unfitting.'[1]

The same youthlike trait is perceptible in the handling of the many privilege cases this session. Members waxed indignant, they sent for culprits; then they proved surprisingly and pleasingly lenient when the sinner turned out to be 'a poor simple fellow'. Said one disciplinarian: 'Some we pardon out of discretion, some out of commiseration. I think — set all Parliaments together, they will not match this Parliament with numbers of offences of this nature; and only our impunity is the cause.' The burgess for Beaumaris related that his servant had been arrested at Shrewsbury, on the way up to Westminster, and that serjeant, bailiff, and creditor had refused to respect his privilege. 'Methinks this action is very scandalous to the whole House', declared a Member: 'whereupon all the House cried, "To the Tower, to the Tower with them! Send for them, send for them!"' Accordingly, the Serjeant of the House was instructed to go to Shrewsbury and arrest the culprits. A week later, nothing had happened, because no one would pay the Serjeant's expenses. Nothing did happen.[2]

There were two bills this session that had caused trouble with the Queen in the past. One was for the reformation of abuses concerning process and pleadings in the Exchequer. It was our

[1] Ibid. pp. 186-90.   [2] Ibid. pp. 229, 256-7.

old friend of 1571 and 1589, adapted to take cognizance of the
reforms ordered by the Queen in 1589, which, evidently, had not
achieved their purpose. In 1589 Peter Osborne had been a Remem-
brancer of the Exchequer, in charge of the Department concerned.
He had been a Member of Parliament and had given his blessing
to the Commons' attempt at reform. His son, John, now held the
office, and he was also a Member of Parliament, though whether
his blessing was forthcoming we are not precisely told.[1]

At its second reading on November 9th, the bill was committed
to all Privy Councillors, all the Queen's learned counsel, and
others of the House. Here was no irresponsibility; and the committee framed a new bill, with a new title mentioning the Queen's
orders of 1589. Moreover, it was Francis Bacon who reported
to the House on November 18th: in Baconian phrases recorded by
our diarist. After saying that Mr. Osborne appeared before the
committee, he went on: Though they 'have reformed some part,
yet they have not so nearly eyed every particular as if they would
pare to the quick an office of her Majesty's gift and patronage . . .
I will not tell you what we have taken away, either in *quo titulo*
or Chequer language, but according to the poet, who saith, *Mitte
id quod scio, dic quod rogo* — I will omit that which you have known
and tell you that you know not'. He then described the substance
of the bill. 'Her Majesty's learned counsel', he added, 'were there
in sentinel to see that her Majesty's right might not be suppressed.' With a final touch of bombast, 'he called aloud to the
Serjeant of the House and delivered him the bill, to be delivered
to the Speaker'.[2]

The letter-writer, John Chamberlain, wrote a prescient sentence
in a letter to Dudley Carleton on November 14th: 'The Parliament handles no high matters, only they have had a cast at
Osborne's office, to correct and amend it at least; but there is no
great hope of success'.[3]

The House was keen and urgent. Bacon, in contrast, seems to
have developed cold feet: perhaps there had been rumblings at
Court. At the second reading, when it was urged that counsel
for Mr. Osborne's clerk should be heard at the bar, Bacon
favoured the suggestion, being opposed to haste. In contrast,
Mr. Martin, the outspoken lawyer, made a vigorous speech for

---

[1] See above, p. 208.   [2] D'EWES, pp. 631, 642; TOWNSHEND, pp. 201, 223.
[3] *Letters of John Chamberlain*, ed. N. E. McClure, i. 135.

immediate commitment; and the House backed him. 'To the question for commitment', they cried. It was committed, and learned counsel were referred to the committee. Ultimately, the bill passed both Houses.[1]

Here, then, was a measure — touching the prerogative, it is true, but sponsored by that champion of prerogative, Francis Bacon, and vetted by Privy Councillors, the Queen's learned counsel, and the judges in the Upper House, all intent on safeguarding the Crown's rights. If substance alone mattered, the Queen could safely grant her royal assent. She vetoed the bill, giving a final demonstration of her inflexible adherence to principle.

The other threat to the prerogative came in a bill prohibiting the transportation of iron ordnance by way of merchandise. Since ordnance could only be exported under royal licence, it was, in effect, a measure to prohibit a particular monopoly; and to proceed with it, after the Queen's proclamation and her Golden Speech was, to say the least, ungracious, however acutely the Commons felt about the grievance. Even the impetuous Sir Edward Hoby thought so, when, on December 8th, the Member for Colchester secured a second reading for the bill. 'This bill', said Hoby, 'is an excellent bill, the matter foul, the request and remedy good and honest; but this is not our means of redress. Her Majesty, in the late Proclamation, took notice thereof, and no doubt but she will redress it. And for us now to enter again, bringing in or allowing bills against monopolies, it is to refuse her Majesty's gracious favour and cleave to our own affections. I think, therefore, if we will deal herein, by petition will be our only course. This is a matter of prerogative, and this no place to dispute it.'

Dispute it the Commons certainly did. They were given an authoritative lead by the next speaker, Thomas Fettyplace, a London ironmonger and M.P. for the City. He declared that the Queen received £3,000 a year in customs from the export of iron ordnance. Mentioning the four sizes exported — a falcon, a minion, a saker, and a demi-culverin — he exposed the fraud of sending abroad falcons of the weight of minions (and so on), there to be rebored to the greater size. Their export had grown so common, that foreigners refused to carry English merchandise, unless their ships were ballasted with ordnance. As he built up his

---

[1] TOWNSHEND, pp. 237, 247, 269, 323; D'EWES, pp. 647, 684-5; *L.J.* ii. 254, 256.

damning, expert case, the House must have been roused to anger. 'If the Queen', he declared, 'would but forbid the transportation of ordnance for seven years . . . we might have' the Spaniard 'where we would . . . They have so many iron ordnance in Spain out of England.' He was for proceeding by way of petition rather than bill, 'because we have already found it successful'.

Sir Walter Raleigh made a characteristic speech: 'I am sure heretofore one ship of her Majesty's was able to beat twenty [another reading gives a hundred!] Spaniards; but now, by reason of our own ordnance, we are hardly matched one to one'. He was for petitioning, 'lest we be cut off from our desires, either by the Upper House' — the loss of the bill there — 'or before, by the short and sudden ending of the Parliament'. How realistically his mind worked!

And now came a discordant note from 'Mr. Cary' (probably George Carew), who said: 'We take it for a use in the House that when any great or weighty matter or bill is here handled, we straight say, it toucheth the prerogative and must not be meddled withal . . . Mr. Speaker, *Qui vadit plane, vadit sane* [the plain way is the right way]. Let us lay down our griefs in the preamble of our bill, and make it by way of petition, and I doubt not but her Majesty, being truly informed of it, will give her royal assent.' In other words, the language of the bill was to be petitionary; the form an Act of Parliament. From the Queen's point of view, it was the sin against the Crown.

Secretary Herbert spoke. The making of armaments, he said, was a regality, and no one could either cast or transport ordnance without licence. It stood perhaps with the policy of former times to permit export, but now, no doubt, it is very hurtful and pernicious to the State. He conceded that it should be stopped, but would agree only to a petition. William Hakewill, the young lawyer, tried to counter the effect of Herbert's speech, and particularly an argument of his (not recorded by our diarist) that export to our friends and allies must continue. 'Our ordnance — this precious jewel of our Realm, worth even all that we have — is as familiarly sold in the country of our confederates as anything within this land.'

Two elder statesmen, Sir Francis Hastings and Sir George More, tried to wean the House from its desire for a bill, reminding them of the Queen's recent magnanimity. 'How swiftly and sweetly her Majesty apprehended our late grief'; 'The late experience of her Majesty's love and clemency towards us and of her care over us striketh such an awful regard into my heart...' But Mr. Lawrence Hyde, the Member who had been so importunate over monopolies, resisted the seduction, and provoked Sir William Knollys to speak *ex cathedra*. 'Her self and her prerogative', Knollys said, 'will not be forced. And I do not hold this course by way of bill to stand either with respect or duty.' In the end, the conservatives let the bill be committed, hoping to get their way in committee.

They hoped for a petition, but it was a new bill that came back to the House on December 10th; and it was read then after a disorderly scene in which the assembly refused to let the Speaker have a principal government measure read, clamouring for the ordnance bill instead. The Speaker's right to order the business of the House came in dispute. Sir William Knollys tried the heavy hand once more, but Cecil — an imaginative, if moody leader — yielded. 'Because this spirit of contradiction may no more trouble us, I beseech you let the Bill of Ordnance be read; and that's the House's desire.' It was read; and then Sir Robert Wroth lent impetus to urgency by informing them 'that a ship is now upon the river, ready to go away, laden with thirty-six pieces of ordnance'.[1]

That afternoon, they read the bill a second time and committed it. Two days later, Mr. Browne, one of the committee-members, sponsoring the bill, won another struggle for priority, rising and saying: 'And, Mr. Speaker, I humbly present unto this House the natural-born child of us all, I mean the bill against transportation of ordnance', now amended. The bill was duly sent to ingrossing. Speaker and Councillors were evidently determined to let this favourite of the House perish of neglect, if they could, for on December 15th — with the end of the session only four days off — it needed further clamour to have it read. This time, Sir Edward Hoby put up a new obstacle. He told the House that the Lords had a bill on the same subject, far larger in matter and stricter in punishment than theirs. He was right. On December 12th the Lords had given a first reading to a bill against the transportation of money, coin, bullion and ordnance, and this very day it was read a second time and committed. Like

[1] TOWNSHEND, pp. 291-5, 306-7.

the Commons' bill, it must have come from an independent, not a government source. Hoby wanted the House to wait for its arrival. Parliament was near its end, and to proceed with both bills might lead to confusion, and 'just nothing done'.

Understandably, the House refused to be deflected from their purpose. They passed their own bill and sent it to the Lords that afternoon. There it was received with the same sense of urgency and at once given a first reading. Next day it was read again and committed. In committee, however, both bills — Lords' and Commons' — fell, as was later said, 'into an everlasting sleep'. We need not hesitate to conclude that the Queen instructed the Lords to proceed no further.[1]

On December 18th, the day before the dissolution of the Parliament, William Hakewill, having learnt the fate that had befallen their bill, moved that the Speaker should say something in his closing oration to the Queen about the transportation of ordnance. No reply was vouchsafed. Next morning another Member renewed the motion, and this time the Speaker answered that he intended to mention the subject, 'both for your satisfaction and performance of my duty'. He added that her Majesty had taken special heed to their grievance and excepted such offences from her Act of General Pardon: which was true.[2]

The afternoon came. Notes Townshend: 'The Speaker said not one word in his speech to her Majesty'. It 'was greatly murmured at . . . that the House should be so abused. But nothing was done therein'. What, we ask, could have been done? The Parliament stood dissolved. Either the Speaker had deliberately misled the House — which seems unlikely; or he had been warned at the last minute to omit any mention of the subject. Dudley Carleton wrote: 'It was much marvelled and grutched at that the bills touching the abuses in the Exchequer and the transportation of ordnance were put by'.[3]

---

[1] D'Ewes, pp. 678, 681-2, 686; Townshend, pp. 317, 326-7; *L.J.* ii. 248, 252-4.
[2] Townshend, pp. 333-4; Stowe MS. 359, fol. 301; *Statutes of the Realm*, IV, ii. 1013.
[3] Townshend, p. 334; S.P. Dom. Eliz. 283/48.

CHAPTER V

END OF THE SESSION

On December 10th the Queen had sent a warning to both Houses to speed up business as she intended shortly to end the Parliament; at the same time commanding the Lower House to sit also in the afternoons. A week later, in the afternoon of the 17th, the Lords asked the Commons to sit late, in order to receive some bills from them, since the Queen hoped to dissolve Parliament the next day.[1]

That same morning, towards the end of the sitting, the Commons had found themselves at leisure, and Sir Francis Hastings had taken advantage of this to remind them, as he put it, of 'some matters passed this Parliament', and deliver his opinion, with desire of reformation. 'I mean not', he added, 'to tax any man.'

He began by recalling the 'slanderous and defamatory' speeches that had been made concerning Justices of the Peace, and prayed the Honourable Privy Councillors of the House to countenance those Justices who served religiously, dutifully and carefully. 'The Church and Commonwealth', he went on, 'are two twins, which laugh and live together. Long have we joyed in her Majesty's happy government, and long may we.' Then he reminded them that they had two strong enemies, Rome and Spain, from whom all rebellions had proceeded and treasons had been hatched against the life of 'our sweet Sovereign'. The boldness of the Jesuits and Seminarists had greatly increased. 'We had need to have special care of them, for themselves do brag they have forty thousand true-hearted Catholics (for so they call them) in England, besides their retinue, poor Catholics and neuters, and I know not what. It is therefore fit we look to this dangerous case and not to think ourselves secure.' 'For my part, I am, and will be, ready to lay my life at her [Majesty's] feet to do her service.' It was the voice of the 1580s, crying in a new, unfanatical age.[2]

The Queen postponed the close of Parliament a further day, and therefore the Commons found themselves with very little to do on the mornings of Friday, December 18th, and Saturday,

---

[1] TOWNSHEND, *Historical Collections*, p. 309; D'EWES, pp. 676-7, 687.
[2] TOWNSHEND, pp. 330-1.

the 19th. On one morning there was a diversion when a Member 'swooned upon a sudden', and they speculated as to whether it was a bad or a good omen. On the other, they passed the time discussing a 'moot' question.[1]

Between two and three o'clock on the 19th a much-diminished company made their way to the Upper House, where their Speaker, Recorder Croke, delivered his ornate oration, with a proem on law and society. Theme and sentiment echoed the past, to which generation he indeed belonged. 'If', said he, 'a question should be asked, What is the first and chief thing in a Commonwealth to be regarded? I should say, religion. If, What the second? I should say, religion. If, What the third? I should still say, religion. Religion is all in all, the sure and firm band binding us in devotion and piety to God, by whom, only, all states and kingdoms are preserved.' His avowed Anglicanism surely pleased the Queen; though to Sir Francis Hastings and others like him it must have added a wry flavour to a speech otherwise heartening.

Once more we are reminded of what seems to us paradoxical, that, in the midst of war, Elizabethans counted peace among their blessings: meaning, of course, the immunity of their own land from actual fighting. Croke told the Queen of their thankfulness for 'the happy and quiet and most sweet and comfortable peace, which, under your most happy and blessed government, we have long enjoyed, and, blessed be God and your Majesty, do still enjoy'. 'Peace', he added, 'cannot be maintained without arms, nor armies continued without contributions.' Recalling Sir Robert Cecil's speech for supply, made early in the session, he turned his words against the enemies, Spain and Rome, who called 'their rapines and murders the war of God', and against the blasphemous design of the high priest of Rome to release the Queen's subjects from their oath of fidelity. 'Were not their eyes more than blind, they might see the hand of God against them, and His protecting arm toward you . . . even His angel to stand in the way against them, and God Himself to withstand them . . . They have tossed and turned themselves into all colours, only white excepted . . . These dish-traitors and bosom-snakes, most dear and dread Sovereign, are most dangerous: no religion, no fidelity, faithless unto God, ever false to man. And, howsoever the sly, Simon-like priests and hot-headed Jebusites make show of

[1] TOWNSHEND, pp. 332-4.

contentions amongst themselves, and thereby the priests would insinuate themselves into us' — an allusion to the quarrel of secular priests and Jesuits, current at this time — 'they all conspire ... to hold Antichrist for their God, and are all devoted Romanists, to lie in wait for blood, to overthrow religion, to subdue the State, to bring all under their subjection.'

'God is not changed. He hath said He will defend Queen Elizabeth, His anointed servant that trusteth in Him, and He hath done it. He hath spoken it and will still perform it. He hath seen none iniquity in His servant. Your blessed heart hath not departed from Him; always constant, always one. And therefore the Lord your God is with you.'

Grateful words tumbled like a cascade from his simple heart as he presented the subsidy bill. 'And we, your most bounden and devoted subjects and servants, with the bended knees of our heart, do offer all thanks to God and your Majesty for our conservation in true religion, in peace, and in all happiness, for our preservation from tyranny, from thraldom, from dishonour, from oppression, from being a prey and spoil to our malicious and cruel enemies, from which God and your Majesty have delivered us; and for your most gracious readiness to remove all grievances from us, at no time occasioned by any thing from your Majesty, though sometimes happening by abusers of your goodness.'[1]

To the aged Queen, who had little left to stir her heart save memories; conscious that this might be her last Parliament, and aware of the future — which was not to be hers — pressing hard upon the present, in many ways alien to her; what poignant satisfaction this old-fashioned speech must have given! As oratory it merited no garland, but it showed that there was still a little faith left in Israel. No wonder that in her 'coming down', at the end of the ceremonies, she gave — as Dudley Carleton reported — 'many particular thanks to the Speaker'.[2]

Lord-Keeper Egerton replied to the oration. We possess the preliminary notes he made for his speech, based, it seems, on the Queen's instructions. They contain a command to Members to return to their homes, among other reasons to prepare for the defence of the Realm. 'Mistake not this commandment, as

---

[1] Croke's own text (two slightly differing versions) is in All Souls Coll. Oxf. MS. 180, fols. 100-2, and Huntington Library U.S.A. Ellesmere MS. 2569. My excerpts are mainly from the former.

[2] S.P. Dom. Eliz. 283/48.

though it were of fear: a passion most far from her Majesty. It is to prepare, and not to fear.' After the notes on this theme, comes an authentic Elizabethan passage: 'A more wise [Prince] they may have, but a more careful and loving they shall never have. For she esteemeth the safety and happiness of her good subjects more dear and precious unto her than anything under heaven, etc.' A later passage gives the Queen's reaction to an anticipated plea from the Speaker for 'the errors and oversights of the Commons . . . to be pardoned and remitted'. Here Egerton's instructions were as follows: 'For the general [body of the Commons] her Majesty most graciously accepteth their dutiful travails and endeavours, and their loyal and faithful love and affection. For some few in particular, she wisheth their fervent zeal in considering and debating of important and weighty causes (specially concerning the Prince and State) were seasoned and tempered with more discretion and judgment, and their levity counterposed with the gravity and wisdom of those of riper knowledge and experience, whom, when they are better weighed,[1] they will learn to follow.'[2]

Such were his notes; but, judging from reports, he departed from them when speaking. Perhaps, in the verbal consultation with the Queen that always preceded these speeches, he received fresh instructions, and was told both to be brief and to omit any strictures on the levity of younger Members. 'I will deliver her Majesty's commandment', said Egerton, 'with what brevity I may, that I be not tedious to my most gracious Sovereign.' True, he reproached Members for spending too much time over private bills, contrary to the charge given them at the beginning of the Parliament: the Queen noted that 'private respects are carried in public affairs, which ought not to be'. But this was no more than a mild addendum to praise: 'She saith, touching your proceedings in the matter of her prerogative, that she is persuaded subjects did never more dutifully; and that she understood you did but *obiter* touch her prerogative, and no otherwise but by humble petition; and therefore that thanks that a Prince may give to her subjects, she willingly yieldeth.' A charitable view of the Commons' proceedings, no doubt; nevertheless, it is clear that Queen Elizabeth was very far from considering the Parliament of 1601 the most intransigent of her reign.

---

[1] i.e. of better judgment.   [2] Huntington Lib. Ellesmere MSS. 488, 489.

Turning to the grant of four subsidies, Egerton said that her Majesty acknowledged 'the loving bounty of her subjects to be extraordinary', praising both the spirit and the speed with which it was given. 'Though she accept it as a gift to herself, yet she requireth you and all her subjects to know that she hath never been [a] greedy griper nor covetous keeper, contemning ever mere wealth without honour. This bounty of her subjects is not to spare or supply her royal expenses, but in part of the charges bestowed for their defence, whereof her Majesty is so dearly affectionate that she hath sold and doth still sell of her ancient inheritance for the defence of her so liberal and loving subjects.' 'She commanded me to say that you have done (and so she taketh it) dutifully, plentifully and thankfully.'

For Speaker Croke she had words as comfortable as those he had addressed to her: 'You have proceeded with such wisdom and discretion that it is much to your commendation'. None before him had deserved more, she said. We are told that the two orations — of Speaker and Lord Keeper — lasted 'about one hour and no more': merciful temperance.[1]

The ceremony of the royal assent followed. Nineteen public and ten private Acts were passed: eight bills were vetoed.[2] The Lord Keeper then dissolved the Parliament, giving Members licence to depart at their pleasure. He ended with the words, 'God save the Queen!' to which all the Commons replied, 'Amen'.

Hayward Townshend, our diarist, must have seized this moment to slip away, without waiting for the Queen to make her exit through the crowd of Members at the bar. In so doing, he missed the climax of Elizabethan parliamentary history, for unexpectedly, with the inspired prompting of an artist, the Queen rose to make her last public speech to the Realm.

She seems to have written out the speech beforehand, as she probably did her Golden Speech of November 30th; and just as she lent the draft of that speech to the Provost of Eton to copy, so,

---

[1] TOWNSHEND, pp. 335-6; Wilbraham's Journal, *Camden Miscellany* x. 43-4.
[2] The vetoed bills were: for confirmation of Letters Patent by Ed. VI to Sir Ed. Seymour; to avoid double payment of debts; for reformation of abuses in selling and buying spices; for amending a statute of 8 Eliz. concerning the true making of hats; for reformation of abuses in sheriffs not executing proclamations upon exigents, according to 31 Eliz.; for making a harbour on the north parts of Devon; for better observation of orders in the Exchequer, by virtue of her Majesty's privy seal; for strengthening of grants for maintenance of St. Bartholomew's hospital. For all these, see *Lords Journals*.

we may conjecture, she lent the draft of this to Lord Henry
Howard. At any rate, the unique copy survives in Howard's
hand. It is the text now quoted:

'Before your going down at the end of the Parliament, I thought
good to deliver unto you certain notes for your observation, that
serve aptly for the present time, to be imparted afterward where
you shall come abroad — to this end, that you by me, and other
by you, may understand to what prince, and how affected to the
good of this estate, you have declared yourselves so loving subjects,
and so fully and effectually devoted your unchangeable affection.
For, by looking into the course which I have ever holden, since I
began to reign, in governing, both concerning civil and foreign
causes, you may more easily discern in what kind of sympathy my
care to benefit hath corresponded with your inclination to obey,
and my caution with your merit.

'First, civilly: yourselves can witness that I never entered into
the examination of any cause without advisement, carrying ever a
single eye to justice and truth; for, though I were content to hear
matters argued and debated pro and contra, as all princes must that
will understand what is right, yet I look ever as it were upon a
plain table wherein is written neither partiality nor prejudice.
My care was ever by proceeding justly and uprightly to conserve
my people's love, which I account a gift of God, not to be marshalled in the lowest part of my mind, but written in the deepest of my
heart, by cause without that alone all other favours were of little
price with me, though they were infinite.

'Beside your dutiful supplies for defence of the public — which,
as the philosopher affirmed of rivers, coming from the ocean
return to the ocean again — I have diminished my own revenue
that I might add to your security, and been content to be a taper
of true virgin wax, to waste myself and spend my life that I might
give light and comfort to those that live under me. The strange
devices, practices, and stratagems, never heard nor written of
before — that have been attempted, not only against my own
person (in which so many as acknowledge themselves beholding
to my care, and happy in my government, have an interest) but
by invasion of the State itself, by those that did not only threaten
to come, but came at the last in very deed, with their whole fleet —
have been in number many, and by preparation dangerous;
though it hath pleased God (to whose honour it is spoken, without

arrogation of any praise or merit to myself) by many hard escapes and hazards, both of diverse and strange natures, to make me an instrument of His holy will in delivering the State from danger and myself from dishonour. All that I challenge to myself is that I have been studious and industrious, in confidence of His grace and goodness, as a careful head to defend the body: which I would have you to receive from my own mouth, for the better acknowledging and recognizing of so great a benefit.

'Now, touching foreign courses, which do chiefly consist in the maintenance of war: I take God to witness that I never gave just cause of war to any prince — which the subjects of other States can testify — nor had any greater ambition than to maintain my own State in security and peace, without being guilty to my own self of offering or intending injury to any man: though no prince have been more unthankfully requited, whose intention hath been so harmless and whose actions so moderate. For, to let you know — what is not perhaps understood by any other than were or are conversant in state matters and keep true records of dealings past — even that potent prince, the King of Spain (whose soul, I trust, be now in heaven), that hath so many ways assailed both my realm and me, had as many provocations of kindness by my just proceedings, as by hard measure he hath returned effects of ingratitude. It is neither my manner nor my nature to speak ill of those that are dead, but that in this case it is not possible, without some touch to the author, to tax the injury. For when the colour of dissension began first to kindle between his subjects of the Netherlands and him — I mean not Holland and Zeeland only, but of Brabant and the other provinces which are now in the Archduke's possession — about the bringing in of the Inquisition (a burden untolerable), increase of impositions, planting foreigners in the chiefest offices and places of government, then I gave them counsel to contain their passions and rather by humble petition, than by violence or arms, to seek ease of their aggrievances: nay, which is more, I disbursed great sums of money out of my own purse to stay them from revolt till a softer hand might reduce these discords to harmony.

'After this, again, at such time as these malcontents — finding very small compassion of their complaints, much less abatement of the burdens which they purposed no longer to endure — made an offer of their state and service to myself, upon a condition that

I would secure their conscience and protect their liberties, I was so far from forgetting that old league that had lasted long between the race of Burgundy and my progenitors, and the danger that might grow to many states by giving countenance or encouragement to opposition against the prince in one, as I dissuaded them; and, though they sought to clear this scandal by vouching books and records of an oath taken to their states by Charles the Emperor for maintenance of their liberties, with this condition, that it should be for them to revolt from obedience whensoever he should anyway suppress, infringe or impugn their liberties — a very strange oath, I confess, but such a one as they produced for their warrant of their opposition — yet I advertised the King of Spain at sundry times and by some, his messengers, of this intent, advising him to be warned, lest his grieved subjects, being brought to despair, did not closely put their state into the protection of some other prince, that might turn the advantage to his prejudice in another sort than one of conscience and care to conserve the league, [as] I meant to do. If my endeavour only tended to this scope — that the prince's indignation and the subjects' opposition might be kept by mild and gentle lenitives from festering any deeper, till time might cure the corrosive of either part — I doubt not but you will imagine that it was an office of a true friend and a kind ally, considering in what sort the King of Spain had dealt with me. I know that some other prince — that had been wise according to the manner of the world, of high conceit, and apt to fish in waters troubled — would have cast this matter in another mould; but I proceeded thus out of simplicity, remembering who it was that said, "The wisdom of the world was folly unto God"; and hope in that respect that I shall not suffer the worse for it.

'But, to go on with the matter once again: after the coming of the Duke of Alva, when there was less hope of moderation than before, I still persisted in my preposition, advising them [i.e. the Netherlanders] to hold so good a temper in their motion as might not altogether quench that life-spark of expectation that the King, by looking better unto the true state of the cause, might in time grow more compassionate of their calamity.

'In recompence of this kind care and faithful dealing on my part, he first begins to stir rebellion within the body of my realm, by encouraging the Earls of Northumberland and Westmorland to take arms against myself, though by the providence of God I cut off the best means of their maintenance and, by the victory which I had over my own rebels, made him see how hard a matter it was to prevail against a prince, confident in the protection of God and constant to the grounds of honour. Not content with this bad motion, he sent his whole fleet afterward, with a proud conceit that nothing could withstand his attempt, and a purpose to invade this kingdom that had holden others from invading her. But it pleased God again to make him more unfortunate by this second enterprise, as the carcasses both of his subjects and his ships, floating upon all the seas between this and Spain, could testify.

'Now that the father is at rest, the son, whom I did never in my life offend, assails me in another parallel, seeking to take away one of two crowns [i.e. Ireland]: but very simply induced and as simply persuaded by his Council, the grounds considered whereon they build. And, therefore, take this with you for an encouragement, and assure all those [with] whom you deal: that such a quarrel, thus unworthily begun and unjustly prosecuted, without provocation by the least offence, since the death of his father from hence, can never prosper in this world, since both his conscience must acknowledge it and God will punish it.

'At this time it will be sufficient to let you know the grounds and nurtures of the war to which you contribute, the merit of the princess for whose sake you contribute; that my care is neither to continue war nor conclude a peace, but for your good; and that you may perceive how free your Queen is from any cause of these attempts that have been made on her, unless to save her people or defend her state be to be censured This testimony I would have you carry hence for the world to know: that your Sovereign is more careful of your conservation than of herself, and will daily crave of God that they that wish you best may never wish in vain.'[1]

In addition to this text of the speech, we possess reports by two gentlemen who were present: the Attorney General, and the diarist, Roger Wilbraham.[2] If we are correct in our surmise about the nature of the Howard text, then the two reports show

---

[1] B.M. Cotton MS. Titus C. VI, fols. 410-11.
[2] All Souls Coll. Oxf. MS. 155, fols. 2b-3; *Camden Miscellany*, x. 44-7. I quoted from the latter in my *Elizabethan House of Commons*, p. 431.

that — as with her 'Golden Speech', and on earlier occasions also — the Queen did not read her speech, but spoke extempore, guided by what she had previously written, yet freely responsive to the mood of the occasion, as any sensitive orator might be. She was evidently moved by Speaker Croke's simple fervour and his emphasis on divine protection, so that she changed the opening of her speech to recall 'the mercies and omnipotency of the eternal God, by whose providence' she had escaped all the malicious practices against her. On foreign affairs, she spoke in more detail than intended, revealing incidents in her relations with Spain and the Low Countries, known only to her Councillors. In her final declaration of affection, freed from the economy of the written word and warmed by the emotion of those about her, she rose to sublime heights of dedicated devotion, retaining — how sure the instinct — that perfect ending, written in the calm of her study, the last public words of England's Eliza: 'Our people, to whom I wish that they that wish them best may never wish in vain'.

The Bishop of Durham, Toby Matthew — an excellent judge of oratory — told Dudley Carleton that he had never heard the Queen 'in better vein'. It is not surprising. Only three weeks before, she had made her 'Golden Speech': which lends weight to the belief that now she was consciously rendering a solemn, final account of her stewardship. In the course of the reign, she had come to regard these parliamentary occasions — great actress that she was — as the supreme opportunity of projecting upon the nation, through its assembled deputies, her personality and affection, her discipline, her will and unrivalled gifts of leadership. This time she was taking her last curtain. The long line of her speeches — written and rewritten, as if for immortality, and quite inimitable in their diction — stood complete. The best of them, and perhaps something from most of them, will continue to be quoted so long as English history lives.

CONCLUSION

THIS volume opened in crisis: the threat from the Catholic Counter Reformation more acute than ever; Jesuits and seminary priests undermining the religious solidarity of the country and wittingly or unwittingly recruiting a Fifth Column on which, when the day of invasion arrived, the Enterprise of England would count; Mary Queen of Scots, focus of plot upon plot, prospective Queen of that other England of which *émigrés* and their supporters dreamt; Queen Elizabeth, now past remedy 'a barren stock', her life precious beyond price as the only sure guarantee of Protestantism; Spain and England drifting closer to war, on the issue of which this profound conflict of faith and politics depended. Is it any wonder that the revolutionary excitement of 1558, fanned by domestic and external happenings throughout the first twenty-five years of the reign, persisted; that the cult of the Queen, evolved during these years, absorbed the spirit of the nation; or that so many Englishmen saw in her fortunate escape from all perils the purposeful intervention of Providence? To men of burning zeal God and His servant, Elizabeth, were both 'mere English'.

Here was the dynamic of Elizabethan England. These enthusiasts lived in the present. The past had nothing to equal it, and caused no nostalgic yearnings. The future might cloud, it certainly could not surpass the present. Job Throckmorton's prayer in his parliamentary speech of 1587 was the quintessence of their *mystique*: that, if it so pleased God, the last day of Queen Elizabeth's life might be the last day of this earth, and 'that when she fleeteth hence . . . we may then behold . . . Jesus sitting in His throne of judgment, to our endless and everlasting comfort'.

While this exalted mood lasted, the House of Commons, not unnaturally, accepted the leadership of its radicals: men wanting to complete the religious revolution, marred by compromise in 1559, and to ensure its permanence by annihilating Catholicism throughout the land and by settling the succession to the throne beyond any peradventure. Fanatics were heard with respect, Puritan enthusiasts figured as choice patriots. In contrast, the Queen, in 1584 as in the preceding decades, still stood in the way of their desires. She remained immovably attached to the Religious Settlement of 1559. She continued moderate in her opposition to Catholics, too merciful to endorse the more ruthless policies of her Councillors and Parliament. In defence of the royal prerogative she was unwavering.

This divergence, both of temperament and policy, involved repeated collisions between Crown and Parliament. To find such conflict in a setting of personal monarchy is surprising; the strange, fundamental harmony underlying it is cause for wonder. The Commons did not think of themselves as opposed to the regime, but rather as its most sincere supporters, inspired by duty to God and the Queen. Our diarist, Fitzwilliam, gave striking expression to the sentiment when explaining the dilemma of Members in 1585, after receiving a prohibitory message from Elizabeth: 'Either they must offend their gracious Sovereign, towards whom ... they dared not so much as to lift up one evil thought or imagination; or else to suffer the liberties of their House to be infringed'. On Elizabeth's side there was the desire to convert her reign into a kind of romance: the feminine ingredient of her cult. Both parties were kept faithful by their common peril. Their differences seemed trivial while the storm of the Counter Reformation raged: lovers' quarrels, to which temperamental partners are prone.

A complex situation! at once so paradoxical and so rare that we might be tempted to imitate our Elizabethans and regard it as providential. To it we must attribute the phenomenal development of the House of Commons in the course of a single reign. Between 1523, when Sir Thomas More made his claim for freedom of speech, and November 1558, when Elizabeth came to the throne, the Commons had done no more — no more, but also no less, for it was a substantial advance — than exploit More's conception of the privilege as licence to oppose any bill or motion. In the next thirty-five years radical leaders taught successive assemblies to construe freedom of speech as a right to initiate policy, whether by bill or motion; and two definitions emerged — the defensive one framed by the Crown, conceding all that Sir Thomas More had claimed; the other by the Commons' leaders, reaching so far that personal monarchy was threatened and the constitutional revolution of Stuart times prepared. It is not only in the fervent extravagances of Peter Wentworth that we perceive this, but in the comments of Fitzwilliam, in the significant paper prepared by

Thomas Cromwell in 1587, in Robert Beale's line of thought, in the deliberate or casual statements of many others, and in the support, so often and so readily accorded them by a majority of the House.

From the constitutional point of view, the most important theme in our story is the relationship of the Puritan Movement to parliamentary development. In our earlier volume we were conscious of left-wing clergy stimulating and planning the religious agitations in the House of Commons. By 1584, with the formation of their Classical organization, we are presented with a case-study in revolution. Though we now know that the Puritan Presbyterian party was by no means so restricted or unrepresentative as was once thought and that these clergymen enjoyed considerable support among the gentry, nevertheless they were a minority group. But present-day experience has taught us that it is not numbers — it is organization and a fanatical purpose that count in subversive conspiracies. Expert as our own age is in the technique of revolution, we cannot but marvel at the precocious efficiency of the Elizabethan Classical Movement. Thanks to the inflexible determination of the Queen and the rigid character of Whitgift, their projects failed; but by skilful exploitation of propitious circumstances they were able to shake Crown, Church, Council and Parliament. In pursuit of their aims, they taught the House of Commons methods of concerted action and propaganda. Indeed, the art of opposition, which might be considered the outstanding contribution of the Elizabethan period to parliamentary history, was largely learnt from them or inspired by them. Take Peter Wentworth, their instrument and pupil for most of his parliamentary career: when in 1593 he finally acted on his own, over the succession question — an episode about which we are fortunately well informed — we watch him applying the lessons learnt from his earlier connection with Puritan campaigns.

So rapid a building up of parliamentary experience required hot-house conditions, supplied by the background of ideological warfare. In their nature, they did not last. Not the least interesting feature of our story is the change in temper and character of the last Parliaments of the reign. Here traditional history has been led astray by the chance availability of Hayward Townshend's diary of the Parliament of 1601, with its vivid account of the monopolies dispute; and it has seemed as if the Elizabethan House of Commons only then, on the eve of the Stuart period, awoke to its latent power. The monopolies campaign was undoubtedly important; but it pales in comparison with opposition activities in earlier Parliaments — pales, one might even be inclined to think, in comparison with so early a Parliament as that of 1566. The royal prerogative, though criticized and threatened, was not in real danger in 1601. The Crown could and did redress the grievances complained of, without surrendering its rights. Moreover, the mere discussion of them belonged to what Elizabeth termed 'commonwealth matters', and came within her definition of parliamentary privilege. Only the proposal to legislate infringed the prerogative; and that provoked doubts and opposition. For all its excitement and even its parliamentary maturity, the narrative lacks the heroic quality of the past. True, Robert Cecil spoke as if this Parliament were the most troublesome of those he had known. But the best judge was the Queen herself; and most emphatically she was not of that opinion. We may accept her verdict. After all, there was no longer a Puritan organization in the background, and the fanatical mentality of bygone assemblies was in disrepute. How and why the old intransigence reappeared under James I must be the concern of another narrator.

At journey's end it is good to recall those whose company we have kept. The age of Hawkins, Drake and Raleigh, of Sidney, Bacon and Shakespeare, has a reputation in our annals that yields to no superior and scarcely acknowledges a peer. But the memorials of its Parliaments were scattered by time, lost or forgotten, so that few could have imagined that the golden hue might extend within those portals. It is one of the happiest results of our new wealth of evidence that men have emerged worthy of inclusion among the celebrities of England's Parliament. Pym and Eliot would surely admit to their rank two at least of our Elizabethans: Thomas Norton and Peter Wentworth. Recorder Fleetwood, *sui generis* in his day, challenges place among the significant 'characters' who have done so much to mould the traditions of the House of Commons. Thomas Cromwell, one of the most surprising of our discoveries, stands out as the model type of parliamentarian: deeply versed in the history and procedure of the institution, though like all his generation — except that reprobate, Arthur Hall — hopelessly, yet profitably lacking in historical perspective; eminently responsible, but fearless in defence of liberty; liberal, not to say radical, by instinct. Sir Francis Hastings was rather like him, though more of the religious *dévot*. Then there were Robert Beale and James Morice, who, though misguided interpreters of the constitution, rested the cause of liberty firmly on the English Common Law and were among the founderfathers of a school of parliamentary thought to which our country and the world at large owe an incalculable debt. Lesser stars scintillate in this firmament: to name but two — Robin Snagge in earlier Parliaments, Job Throckmorton in the Parliament of 1586-87. The latter is as happy a discovery as Thomas Cromwell. We know him by three speeches only; but they rank with the prose of Martin Marprelate — if, indeed, the two were not one and the same person.

On the Front Bench were leaders worthy of seats that time and a succession of famous occupants have made venerable. Chief among them were Mildmay and Hatton. Hatton is yet another discovery. That a man so long, and apparently so firmly, installed in legend as a Queen's plaything should emerge with the stature he displayed in handling Parliament, is quite unexpected. To these two, to the honourable but slightly pathetic Sir Francis Knollys, to Burghley — the pervading, if dimly perceived spirit of ministerial authority — and to one or two more, we owe the happy adolescence of our English Parliament. They functioned as enlightened parents, guiding, restraining, reproving, yet tolerating the wayward instincts of youth. Robert Cecil was also a front-bencher of outstanding ability; but he belonged to a less admirable generation of Councillors, and was as yet not sufficiently sure of himself, not mellow enough, to reach his later heights of statesmanship. On the official fringe were two immortals, Bacon and Raleigh. As in the House of Commons of our own days, so then: character, no less — perhaps even more — than ability was required to command respect; and defects of this nature no doubt explain the rather ineffective role, verging on that of a busybody, that Bacon seems to have played. Raleigh was wayward and arrogant, but had plenty of character. He was apparently more successful: at any rate, he figures more attractively in our diaries.

One of our company remains: the Queen. She dominates the scene. Here, indeed, was character and personality. She has been thought, if not irreligious, to have had no deep convictions. Neither her speeches nor actions in Parliament support that judgment. Tradition has portrayed her as an opportunist, guided by expediency, a *politique*. But in the continuous trouble over Church and prerogative she showed unswerving purpose, holding firmly to principle, sometimes when principle alone remained the obstacle. No ruler, guided by mere expediency, would have pressed her compunctions, as she did in the Parliament of 1584-85, when the Act for her safety was under discussion; and in the final, agonizing episode of Mary Queen of Scots, though her role was not, and could not be, heroic, it was neither insensitive nor devoid of humanity. Tradition has also pronounced her parsimonious and ungenerous. But she repeatedly and genuinely asserted her reluctance to tax the people, and did not spare her own resources. Some of her parliamentary actions, wrenched from their time and setting, may seem harsh and despotic. Yet to understand is not merely to pardon; it is to respect. Even when most truculent or admonitory, her messages and speeches were suffused with queenly and motherly affection.

Now that we have all her speeches, their inclusion in the full severity of complete texts is surely justified. Unless a princely artificiality of style, or maybe our own cynicism, makes disbelievers of us, here will be found the truest display of the Gloriana her subjects adored: moving in their introspective moments, inspired in their courage and confidence, transcendent in their utter dedication of self to country and people.

If a memorial of this remarkable Queen be looked for, it may be seen in this: the parliamentary history of her reign imposes its own title — *Elizabeth I and her Parliaments*.

INDEX